★ THE ULTIMATE STALLONE READER ★

THE ULTIMATE STALLONE READER

Sylvester Stallone as Star, Icon, Auteur

EDITED BY CHRIS HOLMLUND

WALLFLOWER PRESS
LONDON & NEW YORK

For Steve, my loyal, smart and funny brother,
and for Diane, my long-time hiking and film friend extraordinaire,
with love and profound thanks.

A Wallflower Press Book
Published by
Columbia University Press
Publishers Since 1893
New York • Chichester, West Sussex
cup.columbia.edu

A complete CIP record is available from the Library of Congress

ISBN 978-0-231-16980-6 (cloth : alk. paper)
ISBN 978-0-231-16981-3 (pbk. : alk. paper)
ISBN 978-0-231-85064-3 (e-book)

Book design by Elsa Mathern

Columbia University Press books are printed on permanent
and durable acid-free paper.
This book is printed on paper with recycled content.
Printed in the United States of America

c 10 9 8 7 6 5 4 3 2 1
p 10 9 8 7 6 5 4 3 2 1

CONTENTS

Acknowledgements ix
Notes on Contributors xii

Introduction: Presenting Stallone/Stallone Presents 1
Chris Holmlund

Staying Alive: Stallone, Authorship and Contemporary Hollywood Aesthetics 27
Paul Ramaeker

Logic is the Cure, Meet the Disease: The Melos of *Cobra* 53
Scott Higgins

I, of the Tiger: Self and Self-Obsession in the *Rocky* Series 75
Eric Lichtenfeld

Stallone and Hollywood in Transition 97
Mark Gallagher

Adventures in Acting: Stallone the Performer 121
Chris Holmlund

Stallone's Stomach: *Cop Land* and the Weight of Actorly Legitimisation 147
Paul McDonald

The Rocky Effect: Sylvester Stallone as Sport Hero 171
Alexandra Keller & Frazer Ward

'Who wouldn't want a body like that?': Masculinity, Muscularity and Male
Audiences for the Films of Sylvester Stallone 197
Ian Huffer

Sylvester Stallone and John Rambo's Trek across Asia: Politics, Performance
and American Empire 217
Gina Marchetti

Stallone, Ageing and Action Authenticity 241
Yvonne Tasker

Filmography 263
Index 277

ACKNOWLEDGEMENTS

The Ultimate Stallone Reader has been a long time in the making. My curiosity about 'big men, pix and pecs' dates back to graduate school at the University of Wisconsin-Madison. Sly, Clint and Arnold offered such welcome cathartic distractions then from my dissertation on the obscure but intriguing films of French experimental novelist and film-maker Marguerite Duras!

Shockingly, until this volume, there has been no academic book devoted solely to Sylvester Stallone or to any of his films, despite his enormous box office success – especially in the 1980s – and despite the current revalorisation of the *Rocky* and *Rambo* franchises. (Numerous essays, articles and book chapters did appear, primarily in the late 1980s and 1990s.) When the Society for Cinema and Media Studies announced that it would hold its 2008 annual conference in Philadelphia, there-fore – and *Rambo* (directed by, written by and again starring Stallone) loomed on that summer's release horizon – the time seemed right to resume 'Stallone study'. Several of those who presented on the two SCMS 'Philly's Favorite Son' panels have authored essays here. Others joined the team afterwards. Many you will recognise from their previ-ous work on action adventure film and on Stallone.

Today action stars and films are scrutinised using new filters. The scholarly interest in their relation to ideology, masculinity, stardom and the body typical of earlier studies continues as well. In consequence, this anthology offers a cornucopia of perspectives on Stallone as star, icon and auteur. We scrutinise his work as director; we analyse his screenwriting; we examine his acting; we assess popular and critical response in the US, UK and around the world; we discuss his place in sport and film history.

Sincere thanks to my collaborators – Paul Ramaeker, Scott Higgins, Eric Lichtenfeld, Mark Gallagher, Paul McDonald, Alexandra Keller and Frazer Ward, Ian Huffer, Gina Marchetti and Yvonne Tasker – for scintillating exchanges of ideas, attitudes and approaches and for compelling essays. I appreciate more than I can say your enthusiasm, patience and team-spirit. Thanks, too, to Rebecca Bell-Metereau, Rikke Schubart, Andy Willis and Tim Corrigan for your presentations on and response to the SCMS Stallone panels. Your observations have influenced this anthology.

Super thanks to Eric Lichtenfeld, my partner-in-excited-planning for *The Ultimate Stallone Reader*. Eric has been a consistent source of knowledge and support. A consummate writer and editor, at several stages he functioned as a kind of co-editor. Two thumbs way up for you, Eric!

As is the case with any anthology, the number of people to acknowledge zooms upwards, though in this case it probably cannot quite compare with the (still)-rising kill counts in Stallone's *Rambo* films. Yoram Allon at Wallflower Press has been an enthusiastic editor from the start. Thanks also to Rebecca Barden for always encouraging all things 'action'. My gratitude to the fabulous librarians at the University of Tennessee-Knoxville, in particular Marie Garrett, Steve Milewski, Allison Roberts, Alan Wallace and Greg Womac, for their help with DVD-acquisition and citation-chasing. Warm hugs to Michelle Brannen for her assistance with frame grabs for the introduction and my chapter. I have always found the collections housed in the Academy of Arts and Sciences Margaret Herrick Library to be a source of information and inspiration; thanks to the staff for expert help and encouraging smiles, too.

The University of Tennessee-Knoxville has often funded my research. Without institutional support for archival investigations and conference participation, humanities scholarship like mine would be more difficult, less fruitful and less visible. Thanks to Alex (Alexandra) Keller for the invitation to present my performance-of-Stallone-the-performer at Smith College in 2009. I was pleased to be asked to give a revised, longer version of it as a keynote address at the 2010 Screen conference. The feedback I received from colleagues and students at each venue was invaluable. Thanks especially to Cynthia Baron and Tamar Jeffers-McDonald for their comments, and to Eric Lichtenfeld and Paul McDonald for their advice on the near final draft of the essay included here.

Over the years my students in courses on American independent film, genre film, action film and gender and sexuality in film at the University of Tennessee-Knoxville have provided insightful observations about Stallone and his films, among them *Tango & Cash*, *Rhinestone*, *Lock Up*, *Rocky*, *Rocky II*, *Rocky IV*, *Rocky Balboa*, *Cliffhanger*, *First Blood* and *Rambo: First Blood Part II*. (For students who are, like Dolly Parton, born and raised in East Tennessee, *Rhinestone* offers special pleasures...) Thanks also to the great students I taught for one year at the University of Western Ontario for their commentaries on action films.

Words cannot express my deep appreciation for all the colleagues, friends, chosen family and family in the US, Sweden, the UK, Spain, France, Canada, New Zealand, Hong Kong and Australia who have cheered me on since 2008. The time has been tumultuous: I lost my dear Dad, finished an anthology (on 1990s American films), taught in Canada, served as President of SCMS and underwent two surgeries. Listing everyone who makes my life a joy would take pages and pages. I do want to recognise here, however, those fellow travelers and core helpers who got me through the surgeries and onto the road to recovery. Sisterhood, solidarity and hugs to Eric Arnould, Karin Bark, Amy Bertram, Stephanie Brinson, Diane Carson, Linda Dittmar, Linda Ehrlich, Camilla Fojas, Steve and Daniela Holmlund, Anne Kern, David and Judy Lee, Karen Levy, Chuck Maland, Kathleen McHugh, Matthew Ownby, Maria Stehle, Bob Simpson and Diane Waldman. (Knowing that Sly, like other physical performers working in action film, has also surmounted injury and undergone life-saving surgery, I confess, provided additional motivation to finish this anthology. His character, Rocky, was a model of sorts for me as for many others: 'No pain, no pain!' 'All I wanna do is to go the distance...')

Eternal gratitude to my mother, Kerstin and my father, Chet 'the Jet'. I miss you both more than I can say. I think of you every day, and I sense you every time I hike in the mountains. From mountains to movies, with old and new friends, and music, books and wildflowers – it just doesn't get any better than that. I wish similar happiness to all of you reading these acknowledgements, and I hope that you will value – and enjoy – this book.

NOTES ON CONTRIBUTORS

MARK GALLAGHER is Lecturer in Film and Television Studies at the University of Nottingham. He is the author of *Action Figures: Men, Action Films and Contemporary Adventure Narratives* (Palgrave Macmillan, 2006) and *Another Steven Soderbergh Experience: Authorship and Contemporary Hollywood* (University of Texas Press, 2013), and co-editor of *East Asian Film Noir* (IB Tauris, 2014). He is working on a book on the actor Tony-Leung Chiu-Wai and other projects on male global stars.

SCOTT HIGGINS is Associate Professor of Film Studies at Wesleyan University. He is the author of *Harnessing the Technicolor Rainbow* (University of Texas Press, 2007) and the editor of *Arnheim for Film and Media Studies* (Routledge, 2011). He is working on a manuscript about sound serials of the 1930s-1950s.

CHRIS HOLMLUND is Arts and Sciences Excellence Professor of Cinema Studies and French at the University of Tennessee. She is the author of *Impossible Bodies* (Routledge, 2002), editor of *American Cinema of the 1990s* (Rutgers University Press, 2008), co-editor (with Cynthia Fuchs) of *Between the Sheets, In the Streets: Queer, Lesbian, Gay Documentary* (Minnesota University Press, 1997) and (with Justin Wyatt) of *Contemporary American Independent Film* (Routledge, 2005). Current book projects include those titled *Being John Malkovich* and *Female Trouble*.

IAN HUFFER is Lecturer in Media Studies at Massey University, NZ. His publications include '"New Man', Old Worlds: Re-articulating Masculinity in the Star Persona of Orlando Bloom' (*Scope: An Online Journal of Film Studies*, 2007), '"A zillion different cultural shards?": Online DVD Rental and Home Film Cultures in New Zealand' (*Studies in Australasian Cinema*, 2012) and '"A Popcorn-free zone": Distinctions in Independent Film Exhibition in Wellington, New Zealand' (*Watching Films*, Albert Moran and Karina Aveyard, eds, Intellect, 2013).

ALEXANDRA KELLER is Associate Professor of Film Studies and Director of the Film Studies Program at Smith College. She is the author of *James Cameron* (Routledge, 2006). She specialises in the American western, avant-garde and experimental film, and the relationship between cinema and other forms of artistic and cultural production. Her next book is entitled *The Endless Frontier: Westerns and American Identity from Reagan to the Digital Age*.

ERIC LICHTENFELD is an independent scholar and a film industry professional. He has taught cinema at Loyola Marymount University, and been a guest speaker at the Academy of Motion Picture Arts and Sciences (AMPAS), the American Cinematheque, Harvard Law School, and others. He is the author of *Action Speaks Louder: Violence, Spectacle, and the American Action Movie* (Wesleyan University Press, 2007). In addition to his scholarly work, he has written for AMPAS, several major motion picture studios, and numerous motion picture advertising campaigns.

GINA MARCHETTI is Professor of Comparative Literature at the University of Hong Kong. She is the author of, amongst other works, *Romance and the 'Yellow Peril': Race, Sex and Discursive Strategies in Hollywood Fiction* (University of California Press, 1993) and *The Chinese Diaspora on American Screens: Race, Sex, and Cinema* (Temple University Press, 2012). She has co-edited several anthologies, including (with Tan See-Kam) *Hong Kong Film, Hollywood and the New Global Cinema* (Routledge, 2007) and (with Esther M. K. Cheung and Tan See-Kam) *Hong Kong Screenscapes: From the New Wave to the Digital Frontier* (Hong Kong University Press, 2011).

PAUL MCDONALD is Professor of Cinema and Media Industries at the University of Nottingham. He is the author of *The Star System: Hollywood's Production of Popular Identities* (Wallflower Press, 2000), *Video and DVD Industries* (British Film Institute, 2007) and *Hollywood Stardom* (Wiley-Blackwell, 2013), and is co-editor of *The Contemporary Hollywood Film Industry* (Blackwell, 2008). For the British Film Institute he jointly edits the *International Screen Industries* book series. Currently he is co-editing an anthology entitled *Hollywood and the Law*.

PAUL RAMAEKER is Lecturer in Media, Film and Communication at the University of Otago, Dunedin, NZ. He is the author of '"You Think They Call Us Plastic Now...": The Monkees and *Head*' (*Soundtrack Available: Essays on Film and Popular Music*, Pamela Robertson-Wojcik and Arthur Knight, eds, Duke University Press, 2001), 'Notes on the Split-Field Diopter' (*Film History*, 2007) and 'Realism, Revisionism and Visual Style' (*New Review of Film and Television Studies*, 2010). His essay on cinematography in the New Hollywood will appear in *Behind the Silver Screen: Cinematography* (Patrick Keating, ed., Rutgers University Press).

FRAZER WARD is Associate Professor in the Department of Art at Smith College. He is the author of *No Innocent Bystanders: Performance Art and Audience* (Dartmouth College Press/University Press of New England, 2012). In 1987 he was the Australian Universities heavyweight boxing champion.

YVONNE TASKER is Professor of Film Studies and Dean of Humanities at the University of East Anglia, UK. She is the author or editor of numerous books exploring popular cinema and culture, including *Spectacular Bodies* (Routledge, 1993), *Working Girls* (Routledge, 1998) and *Soldiers' Stories* (Duke University Press, 2011), and is the author of *Hollywood Action and Adventure Cinema* (Wiley Blackwell, 2014). She is also the co-editor (with Diane Negra) of *Interrogating Postfeminism* (Duke University Press, 2007) and *Gendering the Recession* (Duke University Press, 2014).

INTRODUCTION
PRESENTING STALLONE/
STALLONE PRESENTS

CHRIS HOLMLUND

A Somali pirate ship, shrouded in darkness. Elite mercenaries slip aboard
to rescue a group of hostages. Flashes of red, purple and blue shine on
weapons and illuminate muscles. Intent on the task at hand, these men
nonetheless find time to joke. 'A little low', says one, as a pirate is literally blown in half by fire from another's massive gun. In the flickering
light, some of the biggest names in action materialise: Sylvester Stallone,
Dolph Lundgren, Jet Li, Jason Statham. Ultimate fighter Randy Couture
and former NFL star Terry Crews are also part of the titular team of *The
Expendables* (2010). Later, Bruce Willis, Arnold Schwarzenegger and
Mickey Rourke appear. Together these men offer the ultimate in macho
fantasy: big muscles, big guns, extreme bonding.

In 2012, the bruisers are back, in *The Expendables 2*. Willis and
Schwarzenegger now have major roles, and they are assisted by Chuck
Norris in a reprise of his character, Booker, from *Good Guys Wear Black*
(1978). Jet Li bails out from a plane over China. A woman (Nan Yu) joins
the team in his place. Everywhere the Expendables fight – Nepal, China,
Eastern Europe – the odds are stacked against them. The chief villain
(Jean-Claude Van Damme), self-consciously named Vilain, is ultra-bad:
he kills the youngest team member (Liam Hemsworth), plots to control the
world, imprisons the men of an Eastern European village and threatens
nuclear holocaust. To thwart him the team uses hands, fists, feet, bullets,
brass knuckles, bombs. Ultimately they save the day.

These two *Expendables* films resemble many of the films Sylvester
Stallone has made. Nostalgia fuels the new franchise's success: people
the world over have grown up with Stallone, watching his films in cinemas, on TV, video, DVD and online. Brought to international attention

1

Figure 1 - Rambo's revenge - and Sylvester Stallone's amazing torso. *Rambo: First Blood Part Two.* Producer Buzz Feitshans; director George P. Cosmatos; DVD distributed by Artisan Home Entertainment.

in 1976 with *Rocky*, Stallone became a top star in the 1980s thanks to *Rocky III* (1982), *Rocky IV* (1985) and *Rambo: First Blood Part II* (1985). During that decade, as screenwriter and performer, he helped launch a new kind of 'hard body' action hero and re-established traditional values, promoting a rugged, macho individualism that was nevertheless in tune with the times' emphasis on fitness and vigilante defence. Famously - or infamously, depending on your point of view - President Ronald Reagan proclaimed 'Rambo is a Republican'.

This introduction begins by exploring how the *Expendables* films are representative of Stallone's work as writer, director and actor. The second section samples the principal ways audiences have received his blockbusters, misfires and infrequent bombs, as all of his films contribute to his brand. The third section catalogues his global impact and iconicity. The conclusion describes the state of 'Stallone studies', briefly introduces the nine essays to come, and situates Stallone in film history.

SUBSTANCE AND STYLE À LA STALLONE

The two *Expendables* films illuminate how Stallone functions as an auteur - as an actor, writer and celebrity, and in the case of the first film, a director. As is typical of the other films he has written or co-written, fairy tale and cliché dominate. Stallone is best known for scripting and appearing in 'male' genres: war films, cop/crime thrillers, sports dramas. His scripts and films are rooted in melodrama: characters are good or bad; plots are episodic; visual effects are spectacular; sound is loud, threatening, wrenching and inspiring, by turn. Most of the heroes he pens and plays – Rocky, Rambo, Lincoln Hawk, Gabe Walker, John Spartan, Frank Leone, and others – are underdogs. When, as in the *Expendables* films, they fight as part of a team, that team is handicapped by age, imprisonment and/or smaller numbers. Good-hearted but flawed, the Stallone hero is redeemed by suffering and violence. As Stallone sees it, contests take place between 'right' and 'might'. Endings are happy because, he feels, audiences want hopefulness and uplift (Wright 1991: 65). His men are men, his women women, though this does not mean that his macho heroes are afraid to show their feelings. On the contrary, they often cry or cry out: Barney Ross sheds tears in *The Expendables 2*; Rambo breaks down in *First Blood* (1982); Rocky weeps for Adrian in *Rocky II* (1979) and mourns her in *Rocky Balboa* (2006).

Still, as written and performed, Stallone's dialogue is weighted more towards monosyllables and grunts than monologues or exposition – even though in interviews Stallone is nearly as talkative as Quentin Tarantino. Also, while his films often feature a female love interest for Stallone and/or his male pals, they include frequent 'wink wink' homoerotic exchanges. In *Tango & Cash* (1989) the sexually-charged buddy banter between Tango (Stallone) and his younger partner Cash (Kurt Russell) is constant; it helps that at one point Cash dons a dress and pretends he's a 'dyke on a bike' (see Holmlund 1993). The *Expendables* films are less overt in their homoeroticism than *Tango & Cash*, but undertones lurk here, too. In *The Expendables 2*, at film's end Hale Caesar (Terry Crews) rubs his muscular neck with a beefy hand, looks at Toll Road (Randy Couture), and says, 'I need a massage'. 'Don't look at me', Road quickly replies, his face averted.[1]

These themes and motifs have been seen before. The *Expendables* films are dedicated to 1980s hard body action ethics, but on a scale consistent with the genre's evolution. Violence has 'accelerated': today editing is faster, sound louder, kill counts higher.[2] *First Blood* had one death, *Rambo: First Blood Part II* had 69, *Rambo III* (1988) 132, *Rambo* (2008) 236, *The Expendables* 221, *The Expendables 2* 489 (Franklin 2008; Anon. 2013a and 2013b). Stallone and his team know weapons are important, and provide specifics in marketing materials,[3] although hand-to-hand combat receives more screen time than do explosions. The 1980s and 1990s films featured the testing and torture of Stallone's beautiful hard body in between *mano a mano* matches and gunfights (in this one respect, the *Expendables* films are somewhat atypical: they include little male persecution[4]).

Always, Stallone the writer-director-performer pays attention to rhythm. Tempo governs plot and delimits characterisation. 'It's like diced salad. Chop chop chop chop chop chop chop. You've got to keep it going', he once said (Pfeil 1997: 3). *The Village Voice*'s critic aptly describes the editing in *The Expendables* as 'julienned' (Pinkerton 2010: n.p.). Stallone-the-director and -star is intensely engaged with editing and lighting choices: with an eye to contrast he employs slow-motion, colour filters and tints. His goals as director and writer are to foreground 'emotional interest over technical perfection' and to keep 'the action personal' (Stallone 2010: DVD Audio Commentary).

Stallone-the-actor performs the bulk of his stunts himself and insists his co-stars do the same. Promotional materials and interviews detail the injuries he incurs, listing the difficulties of filming in high heat and humidity, damp and cold, downpours and snow; the injuries he endures during training and on set become part of his star myth. On *First Blood*, he cracked four ribs; on *Rocky IV*, he required heart surgery (see Wright 1991: 100, 137). Making *The Expendables* he suffered from bronchitis, thrush and shingles; incurred injuries to both shoulders; ruptured an ankle; broke a tooth; required two stitches in one ear. Worst of all, a hairline neck fracture necessitated fusion and a plate (see Strauss 2010: C2).

The biggest difference between the *Expendables* films and their predecessors is that Stallone and his co-stars are so visibly ageing. Stallone is thin and fit, but plastic surgery and Botox have restricted his facial movements: these days he can only suggest broad emotions. His voice is deeper and more gravelly. Among the older actors, only Dolph Lundgren and Jean-Claude Van Damme – both a few years younger – seem not yet frozen by surgical interventions: Lundgren's maniacal grins and lecherous leers from under his shock of blond hair provide crazed energy; Van Damme clearly relishes the chance to deliver punishing round-house kicks.[5]

A second difference between the two *Expendables* films and most other Stallone movies is, of course, that this latest franchise showcases a team. *The Expendables 2* is full of teasingly referential comments to its top actors' 1980s films. 'I'll be back', says Schwarzenegger. 'I'll go. You've been back enough', responds Willis. As he leaves to get more ammunition, Schwarzenegger mutters, 'Yippee kay yay', then, 'Who's next? Rambo?'[6]

The retro scripts and all-star casts of the *Expendables* films intrigued

Figure 2 - Big guys, big guns, big star power: nostalgic thrills with Arnold Schwarzenegger, Sylvester Stallone and Bruce Willis in *The Expendables 2*. Producers Avi Lerner, Danny Lerner, Kevin King Templeton, John Thompson and Les Welcon; director Simon West; DVD distributed by Lionsgate Home Entertainment.

financiers. Independent producer Avi Lerner put up nearly $10 million of his own money and secured more than $50 million in foreign pre-sales to help pay for the first (see Eller and Fritz 2010: B3). Helped by savvy casting – Jet Li is a major draw in Asia; Statham is popular in Europe – worldwide box-office returns were good: the first grossed nearly $275 million; the second over $312 million.[7] As has happened with so many Stallone movies, however, critics were contemptuous. The titles of their reviews say it all: 'The AARP Team' (Rainer 2010: 86), 'Twilight of the Bods' (Pinkerton 2010: n.p.), 'Take Two Explosions and Call Me in the Morning' (Genzlinger 2012), 'Schlock and Awe' (Debruge 2010: 16). Some critics nonetheless suggested that both movies border on being 'cult' films. Writing in *The Improper Bostonian*, Sean Burns maintained that *The Expendables* was 'cinematic junk food of the highest order ... a relic before irony seeped into popular entertainment and ruined everything' (2010: 56). A. O. Scott commented in *The New York Times*: 'As a whole, the movie ... might more aptly be described as Bad Kurosawa, Bad Peckinpah or Bad Leone. Which might be a way of saying that it's better-than-average Stallone. I can't quite say that it's not bad: it is bad! But not entirely in a bad way' (2010).

BLOCKBUSTERS, MISFIRES AND BOMBS

The themes, characters, rhythms and performance styles described above earmark any Stallone movie as 'A Stallone Movie'. He is most appreciated for – and has made most money thanks to – his two Roman numeral franchises: *Rocky* and *Rambo*.[8] He has also done well with his Arabic numeral *Expendables* franchise. By 1987 his movies had generated more than $1 billion in global box-office receipts. To date they have earned a total of $1.8 billion. The first statistic is especially impressive: ticket prices have risen dramatically in the last two decades and, translating for inflation, today $1 billion would be closer to $2 billion.

That Stallone's films have taken in less as ticket prices have risen locates his greatest box-office success in the first half of the 1980s. From 1986 on, his films have often misfired; he has, however, made few outright bombs.[9] Most (though perhaps not all) of his films, not just the *Rocky*s and the *Rambo*s, have provided comfort, cult and/or camp pleasures to audiences in theatres and – alternatively and/or additionally – on TV, VHS and DVD and online, in good part thanks to Stallone-the-star's iconic appeal. Some of the films have been inspirational. Most of the films rehearse his signature style. Whether fondly remembered, disregarded or laughed at, then, all contribute to making his a distinctive body of work.

Stallone's films are typically not among the most expensive of Hollywood productions. Many have mid-range budgets of $40–60 million.[10] Several of the *Rocky* and *Rambo* films, and *Cliffhanger* (1993), are appropriately termed blockbusters, however, if less because their production budgets are high (rarely $100 million, even adjusted for inflation) than because they showcase spectacle in formulaic narratives, have made lots of money everywhere, have been seen by millions and showcase A-list star Stallone.[11]

As Valerie Walkerdine's (1986), Martin Barker and Kate Brooks' (1998) and Ian Huffer's (2003, 2007) audience studies demonstrate, because Stallone is a top star, because several of his films are legendary, and because all the films can be easily found across multiple media, many people watch his movies repeatedly, and not only the 'great' ones. Repeat viewings on DVD and cable television bring a sense of control, combining 'mastery and solace' (Klinger 2006: 155) without necessarily precluding suspense and excitement (see Bordwell and Thompson 2011: 16, 97). Somewhat analogously, so do sequels and sequelisation in that they, too, enable audiences 'to continue, interact with and re-experience a film' (Jess-Cooke 2009: 72). That roughly a quarter of Stallone's films belong

Figure 3 - After running the steps, the author jubilates by the Rocky statue.

to a franchise, and that others share core traits, co-stars and supporting players, is reassuring. Savouring variation can, moreover, be both fun and rousing. A cartoon about *Rocky IV* gets at some of the pleasures on offer: two tubby guys exchange confidences, one saying, 'I like the *Rocky* movies – you don't have to learn a new plot every time' (see Thaves 1986: n.p.).

Phenomenally popular, Stallone's *Rocky* franchise has become a cultural phenomenon. Much like *Casablanca* (1942) and *The Rocky Horror Picture Show* (1975), the six *Rocky* films together promote identification around 'specific lines of dialogue, a gesture, a piece of clothing' (Corrigan 1991: 89). Viewers of all ages are familiar with 'Yo, Adrian', the *Rocky* statue, the Philadelphia Museum of Art steps. Stallone explains the appeal: 'There are very few things, iconic situations, that are accessible. You ... can't borrow Superman's cape. You can't use the Jedi laser sword. But the steps are there. The steps are accessible. And standing up there, you kind of have a piece of the *Rocky* pie. You are part of what the whole myth is' (in Vitez 2006: ix).[12] Every day of the year, come rain, come shine, in heat or snow, people visiting the Philadelphia Museum of Art pose next to the Rocky statue and run up the museum steps, emulating the working-class character who just would not quit and thereby became an international idol. Those who are more out of shape walk up or, wheelchair-bound, have themselves carried up. The last *Rocky* film, *Rocky Balboa*, showcases some of these people thanks to a hidden camera. As Stallone describes the end credits, 'These people, there were hundreds of them, and they were ... everyone. From Korea, from Europe, from America. Some of them were tall, and some were thin, and some were fat. But they all did their thing, running up and doing their little dance when they thought no one was looking' (in Corsello 2006).

Certain other Stallone films have gained more of a cult status, in part thanks to Stallone's star image. Made on a shoe-string budget before he became a star, grossing $300,000, *Death Race 2000* (1975) is one example. It could initially only be seen on film. It emerged as a cult favourite thanks to 1970s campus film societies and specialty theatres. After Stallone's breakthrough with *Rocky*, *Death Race 2000* was released theatrically in Europe, Japan and Colombia.[13] Designed to be 'bad' by low-budget producer Roger Corman and director Paul Bartel, the film has corny dialogue, inexpensive costumes, bargain-basement sets, cheesy special effects and acting that is at turns deadpan or hyper-exaggerated.[14] At one point or another all the leading players appear mostly or fully nude. The plot is bare bones: four race-car drivers cross the country, scoring points by killing pedestrians in a dystopian futuristic USA. Sub-plots feature revolutionaries and a love story. As villain Machine Gun Joe Viterbo (to Keith Carradine's hero, Frankenstein), Stallone makes Joe a nasty, competitive monster. Introduced by an obnoxious reporter as 'Machine Gun Joe! Loved by thousands, hated by millions!', the gum-

Figure 4 - Machine Gun Joe (Sylvester Stallone) makes his point: fans must cheer him or die. *Death Race 2000.* Producer Roger Corman; director Paul Bartel; DVD distributed by Buena Vista Home Entertainment.

chewing Joe snarls, then mows down the assembled Frankenstein fans with his submachine gun.

As Danny Peary underlines, cult movies 'elicit a fiery passion' which may have 'absolutely nothing to do with admiration for the filmmakers' skills – it's often to the contrary' (1981: xiii). Cult audiences relish excess; they're fond of films that ham it up, are '"over the top" … repetitive, un-nuanced, and one-dimensional' (Mathijs 2012: 136–7). *Judge Dredd* (1995) has also become a Stallone cult classic. At $85 million it was conceived as a blockbuster event film but only took in $114 million at the box office. As a production based on a long-running British comics sensation that 'openly ripped off a host of story-ideas from other media' including *Death Race 2000* and *Dirty Harry* (1971) (see Barker and Brooks 1998: 199), comic fans were eager to see what Dredd's 2039 world of Mega-Cities and the Cursed Earth would look like on the big screen. They also took 'Sylvester's measure', comparing his performance here with previous ones, at the same time as they experienced the delights of being 'done to' by a film and appreciated the scale and spectacle that belong to 'the magic of cinema' (Barker and Brooks 1998: 146, 147). The violence Stallone is famous for is both immediately at home and urgently in need.[15] With roughly two hundred special effects shots engineered by a 46-person crew (see Calhoun 1995: 45), there is plenty of spectacle on offer. The camera is rarely still. Sometimes it soars next to the flying motorcycles operated by the hero judge characters over the Mega-City. What Jennifer Barker (2009) terms the muscular and visceral apparatus of action film thus collaborates with the performers, foremost Stallone: through the film medium we, too, experience sensation, texture and time around and through his, and the camera's, nimble physicality.[16]

Figure 5 - Judge Dredd (Sylvester Stallone) lectures cadets on delivering justice and rendering punishment – even when your technological support malfunctions. *Judge Dredd*. Producers Charles Lippincott and Beau Marks; director Danny Cannon; DVD distributed by Buena Vista Home Entertainment.

Differently dependent on Stallone's hero persona and built body, another set of Stallone's films are at times regarded as 'camp' because of the ways that they 'insist on cliché, surface, image' (Flynn 1999: 61). Twentieth Century Fox's *Rhinestone* (1984) is an example. Bringing together two stars, Stallone and Dolly Parton, known for their 'state-of-the-art chassis' (Chute 1984: B1) the production cost $28 million.[17] When world box-office take netted only $21 million, studio heads rolled (see Litwak 1986: 29–31).[18] A reverse Pygmalion story, production materials billed

Rhinestone as 'a new twist on the battle of the sexes' (Twentieth Century Fox 1984: 1). Parton must teach Stallone to be a country singer. She brings him to East Tennessee to teach him country ways. There she bursts out of gingham and rick rack dresses, and overalls; everyone 'down home' plays guitar/banjo/drums/spoons or sings/clogs/drinks/dances.[19] Stallone wears form-fitting, cringe-inducing clothing and is extremely awkward: he is intent on sending up his tongue-tied, macho, Rocky/Rambo image. At film's end, back in New York, he does a muscle-bound impression of Elvis-cum-Mick Jagger, sashaying side to side on the club stage in a rhinestone-studded fringed jacket and trousers, belting out a country rock rendition of 'Stay Out of My Bedroom (If You Can't Take the Heat)' first to boos, but ultimately to tumultuous applause.

Notwithstanding *Rhinestone*'s nosedive, global audiences quickly forgave Stallone's misstep: 1985's *Rambo: First Blood Part II* and *Rocky IV* both grossed over $300 million. Also intended to be a blockbuster, follow-up *Rambo III* nevertheless misfired. At a price-tag of $58 million or $63 million – depending on who you consult – it went $25 million over budget yet recouped costs abroad and through pre-sold video rights (see McCarthy 1988: 56; Wyatt 2000: 44–5).[20] Shot in Israel with the Dead Sea region doubling for Afghanistan, Stallone's 180-pound body is impossibly ripped and cut. Down to 2.8% body fat for *Rocky III* (normal body fat for adult males is 18–20%), for *Rambo III* he gained 19 pounds of muscle; 'I almost had veins in my hair', he admitted (Stallone with Hochman 2005: 37). 'The quintessence of half-conscious camp', Rambo here outruns a bullet-spitting helicopter and cauterises a stomach wound with gunpowder 'while bathed in a fiery light that makes him look like St. Sebastian or Prometheus' (Wilmington 1988: 6).[21]

Figure 6 - Nude bodies beautiful: Sylvester Stallone and Sharon Stone make steamy love in *The Specialist*. Producer Jerry Weintraub; director Luis Llosa; DVD distributed by Warner Home Video.

Later, greater, misfire *The Specialist* (1994; budget $45 million; box-office take only $57 million) similarly capitalises on Stallone's built body. The climactic love sequence, with Stallone and slinky co-star Sharon Stone tumbling about naked in a shower, puts his body in front of hers and lights him more brightly as well.

Indeed, such are the multiple pleasures of 'A Stallone Film' that despite misfires only one film has ever gone straight to DVD in the US: the action romance *Avenging Angelo*

(2002). Stallone's latest cop/crime film, *Bullet to the Head* (2013), was a domestic box-office bust, with less likelihood of finding a lucrative foreign pick-up because so many other high-profile, mid-range action films have also recently failed in the US (see Shaw 2013). Watched on TV, on DVD or online, however, it may well afford audiences the 'adrenalised thrill' (Stadler 2010: 686) that accompanies violent action films. Directed by Walter Hill (*The Warriors* [1979], *48 Hours* [1982]), the film largely zooms along stylistically. Editing is rapid; shots are short; images 'pop' via canted angles, dissolves, lightning cuts, rack-focus shots, whip pans, red-tinted frames and red flares between frames. The sound-scape blends blues music with amped-up squeals, screeches, shots, blasts, grunts and thuds. *Bullet to the Head* is also, however, laden with hackneyed characters, stock locations and routine set pieces. Plot points are delivered in static bursts by all the characters except Stallone. At one point he appears tattooed and impressively topless in the public baths, but his movements are hampered by his many surgeries: he can only turn his torso, never just his head. The film exhorts us to recall his past successes by introducing his tough-guy criminal hero through supposed mug shots of Rocky and Rambo. Manohla Dargis describes the *schadenfreude* she experienced: Stallone 'seems more totem than man these days ... To look at the cubistic arrangement that constitutes [his] face and to witness his fairly restricted physical performance ... is to gaze upon a god at twilight' (2013).

Attentive to his fans, sensitive to his box office, Stallone has voiced dislike of his misfires. He called *Stop! Or My Mom Will Shoot* (1992) 'the most unhappy experience I ever had on a film'; he said of *Assassins* (1995), 'they should have assassinated more'; he lamented about *Daylight* (1996), 'I now understand how Poe felt every day. This was a premature burial' (Anon. 1997: 5-X).

In all of his films, however – whether blockbusters, misfires or bombs – one cannot help but see Stallone-the-star: behind characters he plays shimmers the everyman/übermensch celebrity he has oxymoronically come to embody. Even when his characters deviate from the generic moulds he is best known for, the Stallone stamp remains: for good reason Christine Geraghty refers to him as 'a professional star' (2000: 190).

ICONICITY AND IMPACT

Surprisingly, for a star with such a monolithic presence, Stallone has served the industry in a diverse range of capacities. He has acted in well over fifty movies. He has written or co-written 25 scripts and screen-plays. He has directed eight films. He is a credited producer on eight titles. He has made innumerable television appearances, and written and produced television shows. The majority of his films have been made for big studios (Warner Bros., Universal, Buena Vista, Twentieth Century Fox, DreamWorks, Paramount), but in the 1980s he worked with influential independents Carolco and Cannon, and in the 1970s and 2000s made films for smaller independents as well.

Thirty-five years after his start in film, Stallone's influence remains so great that whether onscreen or behind the scenes, as director, writer, actor or producer, he functions as an 'auteur' even when not techni-cally in the director's chair. His keynote characters, Rocky and Rambo, continue to inspire people around the world. Bootleg copies of the latest *Rambo* (2008) popped up all over Myanmar, despite efforts by authorities to prevent the film from being circulated. The rebels even appropriated the film's signature one-liner: 'live for nothing, die for something' (see Winfrey 2008). Recently Taliban militants carrying out high-profile kid-nappings in Pakistan watched carefully chosen excerpts of Hollywood titles on their laptops at night. Among these was Stallone battling Soviet soldiers in Afghanistan in *Rambo III* (see Walsh 2012).

Still, online and in interviews, Stallone insists that he is nothing like his more Rambo-esque characters: 'In my mind, I'm a very pleas-ant "Ferdinand the Bull" kind of guy, smelling the flowers, sensitive' (in Gaydos 2010: A4); 'I'm a tiny fairy' (in BANG Showbiz 2008). He has a substantial online following, including readers of such leading film web-sites as *Ain't It Cool News*. There he responds to questions from fans, the majority coming from abroad. He has also has been interviewed and had his films reviewed on JoBlo.com. He tweets with some regularity, updat-ing fans on his health and films or offering words of wisdom that build on his Rocky persona, for example 'When you can spit in REJECTIONS [sic] eye you will win' (Stallone 2013). Yet Stallone is perfectly aware that for many people he *is* Rocky: 'I am this conduit of the myth. It's not about performance. It's far and away beyond me' (in Christon 1990: 9). Asked what he thinks his legacy will be, he responds readily, 'The character of Rocky ... his 'never-give-up-ness' ... I'll always have this blue-collar con-nection. ... We can't all be the star of the team, but we *can* be a star in our life. That's where you set your goal. And that is attainable, because if *I* did it, it's feasible' (in Hainey 2010: 286).

Repeatedly, other films, television shows and online shorts reference Rocky and Rambo, if not his other characters. Franco-Iranian graphic novelist and director Marjane Satrapi has her lead character, a feisty feminist Iranian girl, sing *Rocky III*'s theme song, 'Eye of the Tiger', as she pulls herself out of depression and back into action in the acclaimed animated film *Persepolis* (2007). *Son of Rambow* (2007) tells the story of a group of movie-mad British lads who set out to recreate *Rambo: First Blood Part II*. Toni Collette's character, Rose, runs up the Philadelphia Art Museum steps in *In Her Shoes* (2005). Eddie Murphy's remake of *The Nutty Professor* (1996) also includes a 'Rocky Steps' scene, as do episodes of the US TV series *The Simpsons* and *Fresh Prince of Bel Air*. French TV has for years parodied Rambo through sketches presented by 'Les Guignols de l'info' ('the news puppets'), 'Les Inconnus' ('the unknowns') and 'Les Nuls' ('the dummies').[22] In the US 2008 presidential election campaign an anonymously authored cartoon featuring Barack Obama as Rocky went viral; other e-cinema parodies come and go all the time. Even experimental theatre has recognised Stallone: in 2009 Zacharay Oberzan presented a one-man show titled 'Rambo Solo' at the Soho Repertory Theatre. In it a crazed solo character narrated what was playing inside his head as home movie enactments were projected onto sheets behind him (see Isherwood 2009).

A plethora of secondary texts designed to inform, shock and intrigue those interested in following the 'daily life' of Stallone-the-star circulate. As told to us, his biography has a familiar rags-to-riches ring. In hindsight, there are three acts. Act One recounts his rise to fame from obscurity: forceps injury at birth, in a public clinic; early childhood in Hell's Kitchen, New York, without much money; parents' divorce; futile attempts to please his father; other kids make fun of his name, Sylvester; to escape he watches movies.[23] He is rebellious, sensitive and scrawny. At the peak of his fame, in 1987, the *National Enquirer* reports him as saying: 'My body was nothing like a man's – it was comprised of pipe cleaners. I didn't have a shadow. But I was fascinated by the character of Superman. So I dyed my tee shirt and socks blue, dyed my underwear red, took my father's barber cape and put an S on it with crayon, then put it all on under my clothes' (Anon. 1987: n.p.).[24] A self-described 'straight-D student', kicked out of high school for bad behaviour, his mother nevertheless manages to enrol him in a private college in Switzerland. There he blossoms into an entrepreneur, inventing his own version of a McDonald's burger, the *vacheburger* – part lamb, part beef, part sawdust. He sells the delicacy with the help of a mountain-climbing Swiss friend who scales the girls' dorm at night to deliver orders (see Linderman 1978: 86–8). He studies theatre at the University of Florida, but quits to try his luck at acting in New York.

This tale of failure and comeback, heartbreak and drive, neatly fuses with the plot line and character arc of *Rocky*. Act One of Stallone's biography culminates, in fact, with his refusal to sell the script for *Rocky* unless he himself plays the part.[25] The film earns him Academy Award nominations for Best Actor and Best Screenplay – an honour before accorded only Charlie Chaplin and Orson Welles. Though Stallone wins in neither category, *Rocky* does earn three Academy Award (for Best Editing, Best Director and Best Picture), beating out *Network*, *All the President's Men* and *Taxi Driver*. Frank Capra hails Stallone's accomplishments, writing to him that 'it befits the character you created that he should win Oscars for others but not for himself. But remember, the angels take notice of these little things' (in Lieberman 2000: 36). Muhammad Ali wires a congratulatory poem: 'You fought and you worked, / You're a determined guy. / Rocky is great, / And we all love you Sly. / And if you get an Oscar, / Remember, please do, / The greatest will also get one, / 'Cause I'm prettier than you' (Ali 1977: 18).

Act Two encompasses Stallone's early 1980s to mid-1990s mega-stardom. At first, Stallone is unsure of how to handle his fame. He develops a reputation for being an arrogant know-it-all on set and off. He gives colourful interviews, saying, for example, that he is certain he has lived before, roaming the earth as a wolf, losing his head in the French Revolution, dying in a boxing ring (see Wright 1991: 86). His first marriage fails, thanks in good measure to what his mother calls 'zipperitis' and he terms 'male pattern badness' (in Lieberman 2000: 36). What better front-page fodder could there be for gossip rags like the *National Enquirer* and *Star*? Throughout the 1980s, both eagerly chronicle his affairs with models and other stars, among them Janice Dickinson, Angie Everhart, Joyce Ingalls, Susan Anton, Cornelia Guest and Vanna White. Details of his short-lived, tempestuous marriage to the ambitious Brigitte Nielsen also sell papers.

Act Three features a settled, mature Stallone. In 1997 he marries on-again, off-again girlfriend and model Jennifer Flavin. Together they now have three daughters; earlier, with first wife Sasha Czach, he had two sons (Sage died in 2012). Recent newspaper coverage takes him more seriously. His art collection, we learn, is impressive.[26] He himself paints and has done so for years. His paintings now show and sell for a good deal of money: in Zurich in 2008 and at one of the four biggest art fairs in the world, Art Basel Miami Beach, in 2009, for example (see Anon. 2009a: n.p.; Rosenberg 2009). The British *Sunday Times Magazine* describes his artwork as 'aggressively expressionist' (Haden-Guest 2010: 15). 'High-brow' business ventures are also reported, among them a fashion line 'for the rebel and the gentleman' that features sunglasses, grooming products, footwear and fragrances' (Anon. 2011: n.p.) and a $6,000 line of specialty pens (see Susman 2011: n.p.).

His tough guy reputation nevertheless persists, delimiting his creative options. The script that he has written and rewritten about Edgar Allen Poe may never be made, even though a film was rumoured to be in pre-production back in 2007, with Viggo Mortensen attached as Poe (Robert Downey Jr. has also been interested in the role). Stallone doubts that he himself is right for the part: audiences, he feels, would expect him to say 'Yo, Poe' (see Staff 2005; Tyler 2007; also Stauth 1990: 26–7). Audiences remain riveted by the sight of his bulky body; a *Movieline* photo montage titled 'Behold, the Shirtless Evolution of Sylvester Stallone' provides titillating proof of his continuing mastery of 'the art of gratuitous torso' (Miller 2011).

STALLONE STUDIES

Stallone has often garnered institutional and international acclaim, if again especially for Rocky and Rambo. In 1998, *Rocky* ranked 78th on the American Film Institute's top 100 best films list; by 2007 the film had climbed to 57th place. Yet another indicator of the character's mythic status is the fact that Rocky's blood-soaked boxing shorts (from *Rocky IV*) and an autographed pair of his boxing gloves (from *Rocky II*) have been on display at the Smithsonian Museum since 2006. Foreign recognition has come from as unlikely a place as a sleepy farming village in Serbia, where a statue of Rocky graces the village square (see Bilefsky 2007). In 2009, the Venice International Film Festival awarded Stallone the Jaeger-LeCoultre Glory to the Filmmaker Award. The judges wrote: 'His is a cinema as tender and solicitous as it is ferocious and unyielding. Through the now legendary figures of Rocky and Rambo – all of whose adventures were written by Stallone – he explored both the light and the darkness of the American dream' (in Anon. 2009b).

Academic recognition has been spotty since the heyday of 'Stallone studies' in the late 1980s to mid-1990s. Key appraisals of masculinity, stardom, ideology and action then scrutinised his pumped-up physique and bloodthirsty heroes. Chief examples include Valerie Walkerdine's 1986 essay, Yvonne Tasker's *Spectacular Bodies: Gender, Genre, and the Action*

Cinema and chapter in *Screening the Male: Exploring Masculinities in Hollywood Cinema* (both 1993), my own and Cynthia Fuchs's essays in that same volume, Susan Jeffords's *Hard Bodies: Hollywood Masculinity in the Reagan Era* (1994) and Barker and Brooks's *Knowing Audiences: 'Judge Dredd'* (1998). More recent academic investigations of Stallone and his films have consisted of essays, never books. Chapter-length discussions include Eric Lichtenfeld on *Cobra* (1986) and the *Rambo* series in *Action Speaks Louder: Violence, Spectacle, and the American Action Movie* (originally 2004), Mark Gallagher on *Rambo* in *Action Figures: Men, Action Films, and Contemporary Adventure Narratives* (2006), Rikke Schubart on *Rambo: First Blood Part II* in *Violence and American Cinema* (2001) and on *Rocky* in *Stars in Our Eyes: The Star Phenomenon in the Contemporary Era* (2002), and Ian Huffer in *Contemporary Hollywood Stardom* (2003) and the online journal *Participations* (2007).

Our contributions here evaluate previously un- or understudied aspects of Stallone's output and celebrity, drawing on contemporary approaches in film and media studies. Readers will find our essays in dialogue. We comment from locations around the world: New Zealand, Hong Kong, the UK, the US. The ordering of our essays highlights the multiple ways in which Stallone figures as auteur, star and icon. A first set of essays highlights Stallone's importance as a commercial auteur. Paul Ramaeker examines the ways that as director – of *Paradise Alley* (1978), all but the first and fifth of the *Rocky* films, *Staying Alive* (1983), *The Expendables* – Stallone has not merely followed Hollywood trends, but helped to inaugurate them, pointing the way towards what David Bordwell has dubbed 'intensified continuity' (2002) and impacting not only action films but also MTV and musicals.[27] Scott Higgins puts Stallone's screenwriting under the microscope. He finds *Cobra* to be a quintessential 1980s action film, thanks to its action set pieces, bare bones melodramatic plot and relentlessly spectacular effects sequences. That it also includes horror elements is evil icing on the cake. Eric Lichtenfeld takes a holistic approach to Stallone's various contributions to the *Rocky* franchise by underlining how all six films are underpinned by the quest for validation. He looks at how writing, performance and visual iconography operate within the films and how marketing and publicity materials reinforce these functions. Mark Gallagher discusses 1981's *Nighthawks* and *Victory* in light of early 1980s industrial standards. Released by studios at a point when Stallone was a rising star, *Nighthawks* looks forward to new promotional, casting and narrative patterns, he argues, while *Victory* harks back to Hollywood productions of the late classical era.

A second group of essays studies Stallone's acting in light of his stardom, utilising perspectives drawn from recent approaches to performance. My essay analyses core sequences in nine Stallone films that span his career and showcase his range (*The Lord's of Flatbush* [1974], *Rocky*, *Victory*, *First Blood*, *Oscar* [1991], *Cliffhanger*, *Cop Land* [1997], *Antz* [1998], *Rocky Balboa*). I survey his preparation through diet, exercise and rehearsal, and trace his gestural and vocal work in drama, action, comedy and animation. For his performance in *Cop Land*, Stallone subjected himself to massive weight gain and self-consciously modified his mode or manner of acting. Paul McDonald uses the film to contemplate how Stallone's body and performance have positioned him in the arena of cultural production. He examines physical and performative transformations in *Cop Land* as strategic gestures aimed at accumulating artistic legitimacy. This perspective is used to consider how the performing body has defined Stallone's status within the power relationships that characterise hierarchies of cultural and commercial value. Alexandra Keller and Frazer Ward weigh the sports films – the six *Rocky*s, *Over the Top* (1987), as well as *Paradise Alley*, *Driven* (2001) and, briefly, *Cliffhanger*. After reading their essay (now an art historian, Ward is a former boxer; Keller is a film scholar), it will be clear why, in 2011, boxers and boxing critics cheered when Stallone, with Mike Tyson, was inducted into the Boxing Hall of Fame: Stallone excels at translating sports drama for the screen.

A third cluster of essays engages with Stallone's international iconicity. Ian Huffer's qualitative survey of gay and straight British male audience members finds differing responses to Stallone's buff physique, macho masculinity and sensitivity. Participants mention the *Rocky* films, *Rhinestone*, *Demolition Man* (1993) and *Judge Dredd*. Gina Marchetti evaluates the impact of what she calls the 'Rambo Act' – that is, the character's sexual mystique and largely conservative posturing – within the US on Asia. In conclusion she appraises Jet Li's character in *The Expendables*. Last, Yvonne Tasker asks what drug use, plastic surgeries and ageing portend for Stallone's action authenticity. Viewing his impressive muscularity in the latest *Rocky* and *Rambo* films against a backdrop of the other franchise films, *Cobra*, *Demolition Man*, *Judge Dredd* and *Lock Up* (1989), she wonders if changing attitudes in Western celebrity culture and Hollywood action film will affect perceptions of Stallone as an action star as he grows older.

Should audiences no longer find Stallone's brand of action performance authentic and should backers allow, Stallone will surely continue his work behind the camera. He will write. He will paint. As he told

Figure 7 - Rocky (Sylvester Stallone) celebrates. *Rocky.* Producers Robert Chartoff and Irwin Winkler; director John G. Avildsen; DVD distributed by 20th Century Fox Home Entertainment.

Playboy as far back as 1978, he has 'never functioned 100 percent as an actor. You see, I think the day of the single-talented performer is drawing to an end. Today, actors have to be involved in the politics of film making and in producing, writing and directing' (in Linderman 1978: 82). More philosophically, he stressed to *American Film* that 'Artists die twice. First creatively. Then physically. The second one is the easiest' (in Stauth 1990: 57).[28] Asked what he would like on his tombstone on the occasion of that second, actual death, he paraphrases his scripts: 'It's not how hard you hit, it's how hard you can *get* hit that makes all the difference in your life'. 'It's how much you can take, and how much you can give' (in Hainey 2010: 287).

Thanks to his many contributions as star, writer and director, Sylvester Stallone holds an important place in film history. It is astounding that no book-length academic analysis of his work has yet been published: this anthology is the first. Among top action stars, only Clint Eastwood has had a bigger creative impact. Harrison Ford has never served as writer, director or producer; Schwarzenegger has seldom directed or produced and has never written for the screen; Bruce Willis has rarely produced and never written or directed.

So, one might sum up Stallone's impact on action film as follows:

There's Chaplin and Keaton.
There's Clint.
And there's Sly.

NOTES

1   As writer, Stallone aimed for a 'commando comedy', but realised this is harder than it sounds (Boucher 2010: D10).

2   See Schubart (2001) and Bordwell (2002), as well as Paul Ramaeker's essay in this volume.

3   See, for example, Lichtenfeld's discussion of *Cobra* (2007: 71–2).

4   In the first, the chief female character (played by Gisele Itié) is bound, beaten and water-boarded. The second finds Trench (Schwarzenegger) hooded and tied to a chair, but probably not (yet) being tortured.

5   Van Damme was born in 1960, Lundgren in 1957, Willis in 1955, Schwarzenegger in 1947, Stallone in 1946 and Norris in 1940.

6   Stallone wrote a tall tale for Norris modelled on online fan entries such as 'There is no chin under Chuck Norris' beard, just another fist'. Stallone's contribution? Booker (Norris) is bitten by a cobra and 'after five agonizing days, the cobra died'.

7   Box Office Mojo says the second film made $300 million worldwide, but agrees with the figures for the first (2013). The *Expendables* films cost $80 million and $92 million, respectively (Anon. 2013c). The first film was heavily marketed overseas, with ads featured during the 2010 World Cup and placed on pornographic websites (see Eller and Fritz 2010: B3). Unless otherwise indicated, production costs and box-office figures subsequently come from Anon. 2013c.

8   A musical version of *Rocky* was a hit in Hamburg in 2012. It is scheduled to open in New York in 2014. Rocky's big Act I number, 'Fight from the Heart', has him trying to imagine advice from his hero, Rocky Marciano. The Bill Conti movie theme and *Rocky III*'s 'Eye of the Tiger' are also included. Stallone has, of course, been involved with both productions (see Healy 2012; Piepenburg 2013).

9   *Victory* (1981), *Rhinestone* (1984), *Over the Top* (1987), *Oscar* (1991), *Get Carter* (2000), *Driven* (2001), *Eye See You* (2002) and *Shade* (2004) all lost money at the box office. *Tango & Cash*, *The Specialist* (1994) and *Assassins* (1995) did lacklustre theatrical business. Only *Rhinestone* and *Eye See You* really bombed, the latter because as an incoherent retread of *Scream* (1996) and *Ten Little Indians* (1965), it was 'greeted like anthrax by test audiences'. Universal shot a new ending, but the film nonetheless tanked (see Goldstein 2002: n.p.). See also Byron (1981) and Box Office Mojo (2013). Box-office grosses are not available for *Death Race 2000* (1975); *Avenging Angelo* (2002) went straight to DVD in the US. Production costs are not available for *Paradise Alley* (1978), *Lock Up* (1989) or *Stop! Or My Mom Will Shoot* (1992).

10 Production costs and box-office statistics are incomplete and unreliable. Marketing and distribution expenses are not factored in; foreign statistics are especially flawed; downstream venues such as VHS, DVD, television and the internet, which also earn money and net viewers, are not included.

11 'The meaning of the term "blockbuster" is ... far from self-evident ... [it is] something of a moving target' (Stringer 2003: 2). Most critics would, however, concur that pre-sold elements, stars, large budgets, spectacle and strong profits help make a 'blockbuster' a success. See, for example, Allen (2003: 101) and Buckland (2003: 88).

12 The city of Philadelphia sponsors a yearly outdoor film screening of the first *Rocky*. Annually also, before the Army–Navy football game, the two teams compete in a footrace up the steps.

13 Today *Death Race 2000* is likely to be best known thanks to three Roger Corman executive-produced sequels. The first (from 2008) stars Jason Statham. Featuring none of the

original characters, *Death Race 2* (2010) and *Death Race 3: Inferno* (2012) went straight to DVD.

14 There is only one matte shot: a photograph of the New York City skyline is placed behind the grandstand of an Los Angeles racetrack. The race cars are modified Volkswagen Beetles (see Peary 1984: 154).

15 In publicity materials Stallone said he tried to distance *his* Judge Dredd from the 'authoritarian fascist bastard' enforcer of the comics (see Barber 1995: 23). He made his Dredd more like Rambo, a character who is struggling for redemption, not 'just a machine blowing away bad guys. He's moral enough to die for the principle' (Buena Vista 1995: 21-2).

16 Barker (2009: 69–119) argues that the 'musculature' of action films – tracking and circular shots, focal lengths, hand-held or Steadicam shots, editing patterns, aspect ratios – seductively resembles our own movements, engaging us in what is shown and heard.

17 Stallone was paid $5 million, Parton $4 million (see Wright 1991: 117).

18 Many had suspected the film was going to be a fiasco, among them writer Phil Alden Robinson, who tried to jump ship but was convinced to leave his name on the credits (see London 1984: 12).

19 Four of Parton's uncles and two of her younger brothers are part of the cast. Dolly wrote all the songs.

20 Stallone's $20 million salary was not part of the budget. It was advanced against a percentage of the box office (Rich 1988: 27). McCarthy (1988) reported 100+ firings and 'waste on every conceivable level'. Worldwide box-office take nevertheless approached $189 million.

21 For gay appreciations of Stallone's camp style in *Rhinestone* and *Demolition Man* see Ian Huffer's essay in this volume.

22 Many of these sketches can be found on YouTube. For sketches by 'Les Guignols de l'Info' see for example 'Rambo VS. sa voiture' ('Rambo against his car'), 'Le vrai Stallone face au faux' ('The real Stallone confronts the fake one'), 'La World Compagnie 2' and 'Sylvestre decripte un message de ben laden' ('Sylvester deciphers a message from Ben Laden'). For 'Les Inconnus' send-ups see, for example, 'Rambo-Jesus'. For 'Les Nuls' parodies see '*Rambo III*'. YouTube boasts numerous English-language parodies, too.

23 Stallone's eccentric mother told Steven Zebello 'how delighted she was when she realized that her son was reading porn, her reasoning being that *at least* he was reading' (1995: 40).

24 See also Faludi (1999: 398) and Stallone with Hochman (2005: 14–15).

25 United Artists had Paul Newman, Robert Redford, Gene Hackman, Al Pacino and Ryan O'Neal in mind instead (see Linderman 1978: 80).

26 Already in 1988 Stallone owned artwork by Francis Bacon, Paul Delvaux, Auguste Rodin, Andy Warhol (including a portrait of Stallone titled 'Two Sides of Sly'), William-Adolphe Bouguereau and Francis Botero (see Grant 1988: 104).

27 Compare *Slate* writer and executive editor Josh Levin, who claims that 'Sergei Eisenstein might have invented the montage … but Sylvester Stallone perfected it' (2006).

28 Paul Ramaeker (2014) cites Stallone as saying much the same thing about the difficulties he encountered getting *Rocky Balboa* off the ground. See Weiner (2006: online).

BIBLIOGRAPHY

Ali, Muhammed (1977) 'Ode to Sly from Ali', *Los Angeles Times*, 23 February, 18.
Allen, Michael (2003) 'Talking about a Revolution: The Blockbuster as Industrial Advertisement',

in Julian Stringer (ed.) *Movie Blockbusters*. London and New York: Routledge, 101–13.

Anon. (1987) 'Sly Stallone Booted Out of High School for Trying to Be Superman', *National Enquirer*, 6 January, n.p.

_____ (1997) 'Stop! Or My Career Will Tank', *Time*, 11 August, 5-X.

_____ (2009a) 'Tough Guy Sly's All Art in His Latest Role', *Hello!*, 14 December, n.p.

_____ (2009b) 'The Jaeger-LeCoultre Glory to the Filmmaker Award'. Online. Available HTTP: http://www.labieannale.org/en/cinema/news/stallone.html (16 August 2009).

_____ (2010) 'What Went Wrong – *The Expendables*', *People*, 23 August, n.p.

_____ (2011) 'Sylvester Stallone: *Rambo* Star Creates His Own Fashion Line', *Hello!*, 4 April, n.p.

_____ (2013a) 'Kill Count'. Online. Available HTTP: http://expendables.wikia.com/wiki/Kill_Count (12 April 2013).

_____ (2013b) 'Sylvester Stallone'. Online. Available HTTP: http://www.scms.ca/stal.html (12 April 2013).

_____ (2013c) 'The Numbers'. Online. Available HTTP: http://www.the-numbers.com/person/135950401-Sylvester-Stallone (12 April 2013).

BANG Showbiz (2008) '"Tiny Fairy" Sylvester Stallone', 23 January. Online. Available HTTP: http://ca.askmen.com/celebs/entertainment-news/sylvester-stallone/tiny-fairy-sylvester-stallone.html (3 February 2008).

Barber, Nicholas (1995) 'I Was a Teenage Dredd Head', *Independent*, 16 July, 23.

Barker, Jennifer (2009) *The Tactile Eye: Touch and the Cinematic Experience*. Berkeley, Los Angeles, and London: University of California Press.

Barker, Martin and Kate Brooks (1998) *Knowing Audiences: Judge Dredd, Its Friends, Fans, and Foes*. Luton: University of Luton Press.

Bilefsky, Dan (2007) 'Balkans' Idolatry Delights Movie Fans and Pigeons'. Online. Available HTTP: http://www.nytimes.com/2007/11/11/world/europe/11balkans.html? (8 November 2008).

Bordwell, David (2002) 'Intensified Continuity: Visual Style in Contemporary American Film', *Film Quarterly*, 60.3 (Spring), 16–28.

Bordwell, David and Kristin Thompson (2011) *Minding Movies: Observations on the Art, Craft, and Business of Filmmaking*. Chicago: University of Chicago Press.

Boucher, Geoff (2010) 'Stallone Reloads Old-Style Heroes', *Los Angeles Times*, 18 July, D1, D10.

Box Office Mojo (2013) Online. Available HTTP: http://www.boxofficemojo.com/people/chart/?id=sylvesterstallone.htm (12 April 2013).

Buena Vista (1995) *Judge Dredd* production materials.

Buckland, Warren (2003) 'The Role of the Auteur in the Age of the Blockbuster: Steven Spielberg and DreamWorks', in Julian Stringer (ed.) *Movie Blockbusters*. London and New York: Routledge, 84–98.

Burns, Sean (2010) 'Pumped Up', *Improper Bostonian*, 24 August–7 September, 56, 59.

Byron, Stuart (1981) '*Victory*', *Rolling Stone*, 8 December, 44.

Calhoun, John (1995) 'Dredd Details', *TCI*, August/September, 40–5.

Christon, Lawrence (1990) 'Can Sly Get Serious?', *Los Angeles Times*, Calendar, 28 October, 8–9, 90–1, 100.

Chute, David (1984) '*Rhinestone*: Glitter but Not Net Worth', *L.A. Herald-Examiner*, 21 June, B1, B6.

Corrigan, Timothy (1991) *A Cinema Without Walls: Movies and Culture after Vietnam*. New Brunswick, NJ: Rutgers University Press.

Corsello, Andrew (2006) 'Requiem for a Heavyweight', *Philadelphia*. Online. Available HTTP: http://www.phillymag.com/articles/requiem-for-a-heavyweight (4 September 2008).

Dargis, Manohla (2013) 'Bad, Badder, and Baddest', *New York Times*, 1 February. Online. Available HTTP: http://movies.nytimes.com/2013/02/01/movies/bullet-to-the-head-stars-sylvester-stallone.html (2 February 2013).

Day, Patrick Kevin (2011) 'Stallone behind *Rocky*'s Scenes', *Los Angeles Times*, 23 November, n.p.

Debruge, Peter (2010) 'Schlock and Awe', *Variety*, 9–15 August, 16, 19.

Eller, Claudia and Ben Fritz (2010) '*Expendables* May Be Vital for Studio', *Los Angeles Times*, 10 August, B1, B3.

Faludi, Susan (1999) *Stiffed: The Betrayal of the American Man*. New York: HarperCollins.

Flynn, Caryl (1999) 'The Deaths of Camp', in Fabio Cleto (ed.) *Camp: Queer Aesthetics and the Performing Subject – A Reader*. Ann Arbor: University of Michigan Press, 433–57.

Franklin, Garth (2008) 'New Rambo Has Biggest Body Count'. Online. Available HTTP: http://www.darkhorizons.com/news/9975/new-rambo-has-biggest-body-count (12 April 2013).

Fuchs, Cynthia (1993) 'The Buddy Politic', in Steven Cohan and Ina Rae Hark (eds) *Screening the Male: Exploring Masculinities in Hollywood Cinema*. London: Routledge, 194–210.

Gallagher, Mark (2006) '"I Married Rambo": Action, Spectacle, and Melodrama', in *Action Figures: Men, Action Films, and Contemporary Adventure Narratives*. New York: Palgrave Macmillan, 45–80.

Gaydos, Steven (2010) 'How Writing Saved Stallone from "Oblivion"', *Variety*, 9 August, A1, A4.

Genzlinger, Neil (2012) 'Take Two Explosions and Call Me in the Morning', *New York Times*, 17 August. Online. Available HTTP: http://www.nytimes.com/2012/08/17/movies/movie-review-expendables-2-brings-in-chuck-norris.html (19 August 2012).

Geraghty, Christine (2000) 'Re-examining Stardom: Questions of Texts, Bodies, and Performance', in Christine Gledhill and Linda Williams (eds) *Reinventing Film Studies*. London: Arnold, 183–201.

Goldstein, Patrick (2002) 'Hidden by Hollywood: All-star Cast of Bombs', *Los Angeles Times*, 15 October, D7.

Grant, James (1988) 'Stallone Alone', *Life*, July, 103–6.

Haden-Guest, Anthony (2010) 'Rocky Hits the Canvas', *Sunday Times Magazine*, 10 January, 13–17.

Hainey, Michael (2010) 'Yo', *GQ*, September, 282–8.

Healy, Patrick (2012) 'Yo, Adrian, I'm Singin'!' *New York Times* 9 December. Online. Available HTTP: http://www.nytimes.com/2012/12/09/theater/a-hit-in-germany-a-rocky-musical-aims-at-broadway.html (6 December 2012).

Heller, Zoë (1993) 'Sly's Body Electric', *Vanity Fair*, 56.11 (November), 144–49, 184–88.

Holmlund, Chris (1993) 'Masculinity as Multiple Masquerade: The "Mature" Stallone and the Stallone Clone', in Steven Cohan and Ina Rae Hark (eds) *Screening the Male: Exploring Masculinities in Hollywood Cinema*. London: Routledge, 213–29.

Huffer, Ian (2003) '"What interest does a fat Stallone have for an action fan?": Male Film Audiences and the Structuring of Stardom', in Thomas Austin and Martin Barker (eds) *Contemporary Hollywood Stardom*. London: Arnold, 155–66.

_____ (2007) '"I wanted to be Rocky, but I also wanted to be his wife!": Heterosexuality and the (Re)Construction of Gender in Female Film Audiences' Consumption of Sylvester Stallone', *Participations: Journal of Audience and Reception Studies*, 4.2. Online. Available HTTP: http://www.participations.org/Volume%204/Issue%202/4_02_huffer.htm (20 June 2010).

Isherwood, Charles (2009) '*First Blood* Obsession: No Man, No Law, No War Can Stop It'. Online. Available HTTP: http://theater.nytimes.com/2009/03/23/theater/reviews/23rambo.html (23 March 2009).

Jeffords, Susan (1994) *Hard Bodies: Hollywood Masculinities in the Reagan Era*. New Brunswick,

NJ: Rutgers UP.

Jess-Cooke, Carolyn (2009) *Film Sequels*. Edinburgh: Edinburgh University Press.

Klinger, Barbara (2006) *Beyond the Multiplex*. Berkeley and Los Angeles: University of California Press.

Les Guignols de l'Info (1993) (user-generated content 2010) 'La world company 2'. Online. Available HTTP: http://www.youtube.com/watch?v=KP-tMe5wlJs&playnext=1&list=PLM EVgaEd5shvQte3mk2m5tH-Z3gLXs6rP&feature=results_video (3 March 2013).

____ (user-generated content 2010) 'Rambo VS. sa voiture'. Online. Available HTTP: http://www.youtube.com/watch?v=KxFslq81KEc (3 March 2013).

____ (user-generated content 2010) 'Sylvestre decripte un message de ben laden'. Online. Available HTTP:http://www.youtube.com/watch?v=d6sjwR7HtNQ&list=PLMEVgaEd5shv Qte3mk2m5tH-Z3gLXs6rP (3 March 2013).

____ (user-generated content 2012) 'Le vrai Stallone face au faux'. Online. Available HTTP: http://www.youtube.com/watch?v=b44N26Ari2A (3 March 2013).

Les Inconnus (n. d.) 'Rambo-Jesus' (user-generated content). Online. Formerly available HTTP: http://www.youtube.com/watch?v=4DHzKO5ia8A (3 March 2013).

Les Nuls (n. d.) *'Rambo III'* (user-generated content). Online. Available HTTP: http://www.dailymotion.com/video/x3zq26_les-nuls-rambo-3_fun#.UOgOjawfg80 (3 March 2013).

Levin, Josh (2006) 'The Power and the Glory of the *Rocky* Montage', *Slate*. Online. Available HTTP: http://www.slate.com/id/2156024/slideshow/2155937/fs/0//entry/2155935 (8 May 2008).

Lichtenfeld, Eric (2007) *Action Speaks Louder: Violence, Spectacle, and the American Action Movie*. Revised and expanded edition. Middletown, CT: Wesleyan University Press.

Lieberman, Paul (2000) 'Still Trying to Get It Right', *Los Angeles Times Magazine*, 8 October, 13–15, 36–37. Online. Available HTTP: http://articles.latimes.com/2000/oct/08/magazine/ tm-33540 (12 March 2012).

Linderman, Lawrence (1978) '*Playboy* Interview: Sylvester Stallone', *Playboy*, September, 73–91.

Litwak, Mark (1986) *Reel Power*. New York: Morrow.

London, Michael (1984) 'The Rocky Road to a Hollywood Flop', *Los Angeles Times*, 20 July, 1, 12.

Mathijs, Ernest (2012) 'From Being to Acting', in Aaron Taylor (ed.) *Theorizing Film Acting*. New York and London: Routledge, 135–51.

McCarthy, Todd (1988) *'Rambo III:* Budget Run Amok', *Variety*, 25 October, 56, 62–3, 70.

Miller, Julie (2011) 'Behold, the Shirtless Evolution of Sylvester Stallone', *Movieline*. Online. Available HTTP: http://movieline.com/2011/12/29/behold-the-shirtless-evolution-of-sylvester-stallone/ (1 April 2013).

Peary, Danny (1981) *Cult Movies: The Classics, the Sleepers, the Weird, and the Wonderful*. New York: Dell Publishing.

____ (1984) *Omni's Screen Flights/Screen Fantasies*. Garden City, NY: Doubleday.

Piepenburg, Erik (2013) 'Rocky on Broadway Finds Its Apollo Creed', *New York Times*, 6 November. Online. Available HTTP: http://artsbeat.blogs.nytimes.com/2013/11/06/rocky-on-broadway-finds-its-apollo-creed/ (6 November 2013).

Pfeil, Fred (1997) *White Guys: Studies in Postmodern Domination and Difference*. London: Verso.

Pinkerton, Nick (2010) 'Twilight of the Bods', *Village Voice*, 11 August, n.p.

Rainer, Peter (2010) '*The Expendables*', *Rolling Stone*, 2 September, 86.

Rich [Richards, Dick] (1988) '*Rambo III*', *Variety*, 23 May, 3, 27.

Rosenberg, Karen (2009) 'Miami Fair: Big Pieces, Smaller Prices, and Relief', *New York Times*, 5 December. Online. Available HTTP: http://www.nytimes.com/2009/12/05/arts/design/05artbasel.html?pagewanted=all (5 December 2009).

Schubart, Rikke (2001) 'Passion and Acceleration: Generic Change in the Action Film', in J. David Slocum (ed.) *Violence and American Cinema*. New York: Routledge, 192–207.

____ (2002) 'Birth of a Hero: Rocky, Stallone, and Mythical Creation', in Angela Ndalianis and Charlotte Henry (eds) *Stars in Our Eyes: The Star Phenomenon in the Contemporary Era*. Westport, CT: Praeger, 149–64.

Scott, A. O. (2010) 'Manly Gore and Brawn, Not Tragedy or Poetry', *New York Times*. Online. Available HTTP: http://movies.nytimes.com/2010/08/13/movies/13expendables.html (12 April 2013).

Shaw, Lucas (2013) 'What Buyers Want at Cannes: More Jennifer Lawrence, Less Sylvester Stallone'. Online. Available HTTP: https://www.thewrap.com/movies/article/what-buyers-want-cannes-more-jennifer-lawrence-less-sylvestor-stallone-91056 (17 May 2013).

Stadler, Jane (2010) 'Cultural Value and Viscerality in *Sukyaki Western Django*: Towards a Phenomenology of Bad Film', *Continuum*, 24.5, 679–91.

Staff and agencies (2005) 'Stallone to Direct Poe Biopic', *The Guardian*, 24 May. Online. Available HTTP: http://www.guardian.co.uk/film/2005/may/24/edgarallanpoe (21 April 2013).

Stallone, Sylvester (2010) 'Audio Commentary'. *The Expendables*. Prod. Lionsgate.

____ (2013) 'Sylvester Stallone @TheSlyStallone'. Online. Available HTTP: https://twitter.com/TheSlyStallone (21 April 2013).

Stallone, Sylvester with David Hochman (2005) *Sly Moves*. New York: HarperResources.

Stark, Steven D. (1987) '10 Years into the Stallone Era: What It, Uh, All Means', *New York Times*, 22 February, 19, 21.

Stauth, Cameron (1990) 'Requiem for a Heavyweight', *American Film*, January, 22–7, 57.

Strauss, Bob (2010) 'Stallone Packs Some Punch with Ensemble of Action-Film Veterans for *The Expendables*', *(L.B.) Press-Telegram*, 13 August, C1–C2.

Stringer, Julian (2003) 'Introduction', in Julian Stringer (ed.) *Movie Blockbusters*. London and New York: Routledge, 1–14.

Susman, Tina (2011) 'Where the Pen Is Still Mighty', *Los Angeles Times*, 28 December, A1, A12.

Tasker, Yvonne (1993a) *Spectacular Bodies: Gender, Genre, and the Action Cinema*. London: Routledge.

____ (1993b) 'Dumb Movies for Dumb People', in Steven Cohan and Ina Rae Hark (eds) *Screening the Male: Exploring Masculinities in Hollywood Cinema*. London: Routledge, 230–44.

Thaves (1986) 'Frank and Ernest Cartoon: *Rocky IV*', *Daily News*, 13 January, n.p.

Twentieth Century Fox (1984) 'Announcement Story: *Rhinestone*'.

Tyler, Josh (2007) 'Scoop: Viggo Mortensen Is Edgar Allen Poe', 14 November. Online. Available HTTP: http://www.cinemablend.com/new/Scoop-Viggo-Mortensen-Is-Edgar-Allan-Poe-6925.html (21 April 2013).

Vitez, Michael (2006) *Rocky Stories: Tales of Love, Hope, and Happiness at America's Most Famous Steps*. Philadelphia: Paul Dry Books.

Walkerdine, Valerie (1986) 'Video Replay: Families, Films, and Fantasy', in Victor Burgin, James Donald, and Cora C. Kaplan (eds) *Formations of Fantasy*. London: Methuen, 167–99.

Walsh, Declan (2012) 'Taliban Gaining More Resources from Kidnapping', *New York Times*, 19 February. Online. Available HTTP: http://www.nytimes.com/2012/02/20/world/asia/pakistani-taliban-turn-to-kidnapping-to-finance-operations (20 February 2012).

Weiner, Allison Hope (2006) 'Yo Rocky, or Rambo, Gonna Fly Now at 60', *New York Times*, 21 November. Online. Available HTTP: http://www.nytimes.com/2006/11/21/movies/21sly.html (24 April 2013).

Welkos, Robert (2006) 'Down for the Count? Guess Again', *Los Angeles Times*, 17 December, E1, E16.

Wilmington, Michael (1988) 'Superhero Muscles', *Los Angeles Times*, 25 May, Part VI, 1, 6.

Winfrey, Michael (2008) 'Interview: Stallone Challenges Myanmar Junta, Eyes *Rambo 5*', Reuters, 2 February. Online. Available HTTP: http://www.reuters.com/assets/print?aid=USL02468068 (12 July 2008).

Wright, Adrian (1991) *Sylvester Stallone: A Life on Film*. London: Robert Hale.

Wyatt, Justin (2000) 'Independents, Packaging, and Inflationary Pressure in 1980s Hollywood', in Stephen Prince (ed.) *A New Pot of Gold: Hollywood under the Electronic Rainbow, 1980–1989*. New York: Scribner's, 142–59.

Zebello, Stephen (1995) 'On the Sly', *Movieline*, October, 38–42, 80, 82, 85, 95.

STAYING ALIVE:
STALLONE, AUTHORSHIP AND CONTEMPORARY HOLLYWOOD AESTHETICS

PAUL RAMAEKER

Sylvester Stallone's status as an icon of contemporary Hollywood cinema has long been secure thanks to the mythic stature of Rocky Balboa and John Rambo, but his iconicity is as a star rather than a filmmaker. His filmography lists over fifty acting credits, certainly, but also over twenty writing credits, a fact rarely acknowledged outside of apocryphal tales of *Rocky*'s creation. His directing has not been taken into account at all, though as of 2013 he had directed eight feature films over more than three decades, albeit with an unusual chronological distribution: a 21-year gap separates *Rocky IV*, in 1985, and *Rocky Balboa*, in 2006. Stallone wrote or co-wrote those eight films, and starred in seven of them, enjoying a degree of creative control best compared to Woody Allen and Clint Eastwood. He has proven himself to be a commercially astute filmmaker whose efforts have grossed more than $500 million at the US box office alone. Drawing on classical conventions of the melodrama and the backstage musical, he has in turn influenced both the contemporary sports film and musicals such as *Flashdance* and *Billy Elliot*.

Stallone's films see him returning again and again to stories of underdogs and outsiders; to themes of suffering, sacrifice, struggle for self-definition and triumph over adversity; and to a kinetic, largely editing-based aesthetic, as evidenced most clearly in the montage and fight sequences of the *Rocky* series. A close study of his first seven films as director – *Paradise Alley* (1978), *Rocky II* (1979), *Rocky III* (1982), *Staying Alive* (1983), *Rocky IV* (1985), *Rocky Balboa* (2006) and *Rambo*

(2008) – finds an arc from experimentation to maturity to creative and commercial rebirth (crucially predicated on his branding as an author). The films reveal a consistent approach to genre and narrative, and a clear progression in his approach to visual style in relation to shifting aesthetic norms in the last three decades of Hollywood cinema.

Stallone is not an *auteur* in the strictest, most traditional and critically charged sense because he has not created an idiosyncratic, immediately identifiable cinematic world or visual aesthetic in the manner of, say, the Coen Brothers, Michael Mann or Wes Anderson. Nonetheless, Stallone's films may be examined fruitfully using authorship as a heuristic in order to trace his contributions to the films as an historical agent working in a context that offers filmmakers a particular set of bounded alternatives. If not an *auteur*, then, Stallone can certainly be considered an author whose style is fluid and evolving in relation to contemporary trends. Sometimes Stallone's direction simply manifests the force of these trends; at other times he magnifies and even influences them. Distinctive patterns in his films include his use of melodramatic structures, debts to classical genre cinemas, innovative montage sequences, and variations on the hyperbolic climaxes prevalent across contemporary Hollywood cinema. In recent years, moreover, Stallone and his associates have been increasingly self-conscious in mobilising auteurist discourses to vouchsafe his continued relevance in the current cinematic landscape.[1]

In order to trace Stallone as a director working in contemporary Hollywood, I situate his work vis-à-vis genre and industry trends and prevailing aesthetic norms. I also discuss the ways authorship has functioned in marketing and reception. An examination of continuities and progressions in Hollywood practices from the 1970s to the 2000s helps to illuminate the influences on and options available to Stallone as a writer and director across this period, and form the background against which we can identify the authorial characteristics common to his films.

I begin by discussing *Paradise Alley* not only because it is Stallone's first film as a director, but also because it is an anomaly: a stand-alone, non-series film. In its mobilisation of classical Hollywood genre conventions and its systematic colour patterning, *Paradise Alley* is consistent with, yet offers a distinct variation on, Stallone's chief formal characteristics. *Rocky II–IV* and *Staying Alive* are examined in the next section of this essay. All are melodramas, and all in varying degrees are indebted to the classical-era backstage musical. In the series films, Stallone's directorial efforts are increasingly distinct in terms of framing and mise-en-scène, instead favouring editing as a stylistic tool, especially in the prominence and function of montage sequences. This progression is indicative at once of a developing authorial style and of larger trends across a period in which visual style in Hollywood moved away from the realism of 1970s art-genre cinema towards spectacle and a hyperbolised treatment of classical techniques. Discussions of melodrama as a narrative mode in Hollywood cinema further highlight Stallone's characteristic formal and stylistic features because melodrama is for him a generic touchstone. Finally, I turn to *Rocky Balboa* and *Rambo*, focusing on Stallone's adaptation to the context of Hollywood film aesthetics in the new millennium, and his attempts in the films and their marketing to establish his authorial credentials. If nostalgia is a factor in the commercial appeal of Rocky and Rambo in the contemporary marketplace, the films are determinedly contemporary both in style and in the role played by discourses of authorship in their production and reception. With them, Stallone stakes a claim both to artistic credibility and to commercial longevity.

THE EXPERIMENT: *PARADISE ALLEY*

While Stallone is often associated with 1980s blockbuster cinema and all that implies, *Paradise Alley* is steeped in the production trends and aesthetics of its day. The 1970s were marked by the prevalence of a genre revisionism that broke from or significantly reshaped conventions. In part this stemmed from the influence of the international art cinema on studio films aiming to appeal to the countercultural youth market in the late 1960s, which persisted in genre cinemas following the critical and commercial successes of *M*A*S*H* (1970), *The French Connection* (1971) and *The Godfather* (1972). Such films drew on techniques and strategies of European art film and direct cinema documentary to forge a realist aesthetic that incorporated digressions, downbeat endings and drifting, ineffectual or morally questionable protagonists; naturalistic mise-en-scène centred on location filming; and such cinematographic techniques as 'natural' lighting, desaturated colour, zoom lenses and handheld camerawork.

Another form of genre revisionism was more overtly self-conscious, highlighting artifice for the sake of homage or parody. If the most critical of the revisionist genre films sought to subvert Hollywood forms and the American myths which undergird them, another group sought to revivify those forms through the addition of a realist sheen, or a sense of playfulness and cinephilia. It is in this latter camp that we find *Paradise Alley*, Stallone's first film as director, his first attempt to reconfigure his star persona, and his most explicit homage to the 1930s Warner Bros. urban dramas that inform the *Rocky* series as well. Stallone here tells the story of three brothers in post-war New York City: an embittered veteran, Lenny (Armand Assante); the slow and hulking Victor (Lee Canalito); and the fast-talking hustler, Cosmo, played by Stallone in a strong break from the Rocky persona. To earn enough to escape the neighbourhood, Victor becomes a wrestler, and Lenny and Cosmo his managers, incurring the wrath of local hood Stitch (Kevin Conway). As with the Rocky films, *Paradise Alley* is riven with elements of the classical Hollywood melodrama; but here classical-era visual style is arguably the most salient touchstone.

Though set in 1946, *Paradise Alley* is more reminiscent of the portraits of down-at-heels city life in urban comedies, dramas and gangster pictures of the 1930s than *film noir*.[2] Stallone announces his debts to classical Hollywood from the very first image, using Universal's 1940s-era glass-globe studio logo. For his first film as director, Stallone worked with renowned cinematographer László Kóvacs, and consequently gave Kóvacs considerable room to play with 1940s styles, including low-key interiors and deep focus. Stallone's staging, however, rarely makes use of deep space, so that deep focus is used here mainly for momentary effects:[3] to provide texture to scenes in crowded spaces, and most notably to dramatise Victor's decision to abandon ice delivery to enter the ring, in a low-angle, slow-motion shot showing him throwing a block of ice down a set of stairs.

At the same time, a significant degree of image diffusion is used here, consistent with 1970s historical dramas generally. Classical-era historical pieces were more or less cinematographically indistinguishable from contemporaneous narratives, but in the 1970s, makers of period pieces across the whole spectrum of Hollywood genres resorted extensively to diffusion (besides filtration, pushing the film in development and/or 'flashing' it before shooting to supplement low levels of light in production, and create significant image diffusion). They also frequently used colour desaturation to signify past-ness and to refer to the look of period photographs. Hand-held camerawork and telephoto lenses invoke documentary realism. At the same time, diffusion here looks forward to cinematographic trends in the 1980s that saw filmmakers, including Stallone, exaggerating classical-era approaches to colour and lighting in a pictorialist fashion, with little regard for realism.[4]

If the use of diffusion in *Paradise Alley* marks it with a period film aesthetic then on the wane, Kóvacs's use of colour looks forward to the neo-classical, hyperbolic style of the 1980s. In *Paradise Alley*, Stallone has Kóvacs work with saturated colour combined with low-key lighting self-consciously borrowed from *film noir* to suit the film's setting. Key here is the use of reds, the colour functioning as a motif associated with relief or escape from the poverty and drudgery of the brothers' lives. Red is introduced with the opening titles, but Stallone and Kóvacs initially use a muted, desaturated palette. Red returns and begins to accrue significance when we are introduced to Annie (Anne Archer), a dancer loved by both Lenny and (initially) Cosmo, whose bright red hair and lipstick contrast dramatically with her surroundings outside the club where she works; the club's interior is suffused with an intense, saturated red. Red is less crucial but again notable in the lighting of Stitch's bar, with only intermittent practical motivation, and Stitch's wardrobe picks up the red theme: his tie, his armband, his handkerchief.

Both the bar and the club are settings associated with characters attempting to escape their lives through drinking, gambling or dancing. Against the muted tones of other settings, spots of red make frequent appearances: red shutters as Cosmo attempts to woo Annie; the red costume of the monkey Cosmo wins in a bet; red lights when Cosmo visits Bunch (Joyce Ingalls), his prostitute girlfriend; red jars in Lenny's morgue. Red becomes increasingly prevalent as the film continues. Late in the narrative, Cosmo and Bunch celebrate Christmas: Cosmo wears a red Santa costume, Bunch has a red ribbon on her neck and a red flower in her hair, the wrapping paper is red, and the room is partly lit with a red light. By this point, it should be noted, Cosmo and Bunch enjoy the film's only stable romantic union.

If red is most strikingly employed for Annie and the dance club, the crux of the colour patterning is Paradise Alley itself, where the brothers – Victor in the ring, Cosmo and Lenny in his corner – fight their key battles, struggling for a way out of their dead-end world. The set features bright neon blues and reds, echoed in the red poles surrounding the ring, the stripes on the ropes, the devil mural above the mat,[5] and the clown's costume. Between rounds, red is omnipresent. Yet during each round of the final match, bar the last, red is de-emphasised: the most dramatic effects are blue flashes signifying lightning. Finally, in the last round, the red of the combatants' blood carries the pattern to the film's end. Though it would be an exaggeration to argue that this is the culmination of the film's deployment of colour, Victor's red blood is suggestive: it marks his physical expenditure, and as always in Stallone, physical expenditure is the avenue for his protagonists' material, psychological and spiritual transcendence.

In most respects, *Paradise Alley* must be counted as a trial run at writing, directing and starring. It is a film of its era, partaking of the conventions of the 1970s period piece, and self-consciously paying homage to classical Hollywood in its look and narrative. At the same time, the kind of stylistic patterning seen in *Paradise Alley* would recur in Stallone's films right through to *Rocky Balboa*, reaching an apotheosis in the meticulously designed montages of *Rocky IV*. From *Rocky II* to *Rocky IV*, Stallone would develop a recognisable, even influential, approach to blockbuster form and style, foregrounding melodramatic constructions and montage sequences. If his films bear a signature, it is to be found in these areas.

THE SERIES: *ROCKY II–IV* AND *STAYING ALIVE*

Though *Staying Alive* has been largely forgotten, the other films Stallone directed in this period, *Rocky II, III* and *IV*, are the most central to his legacy as a filmmaker. To approach these films in terms of Stallone's contributions, we must begin with the context of that much-debated period in which American cinema turned from the realist, revisionist art-genre cinema of the 1970s to the more narratively and generically conservative, even neo-classical, blockbusters of the 1980s. Though shorn of art-cinematic formal experimentation, these blockbusters cannot be mistaken for products of the studio era; rather, their narrative and generic conservatism was accompanied by a kinetic, emphatic 'intensified continuity' style (see Bordwell 2006: 121–38). This frequently erupted into a hyperbolic stylisation that could function as product differentiation. It could even become a vehicle for authorial expression accompanying conventional narrative forms and structures.

This visual and aural hyperbole is most clearly manifest in moments of spectacle, and the issue of how narrative relates to spectacle in this context[6] has promoted a reconsideration of this balance in Hollywood cinema generally.[7] In turn this re-evaluation has encouraged a closer examination of melodrama as a mode characterised by sensational situations existing alongside or within the 'classical' mode of Hollywood storytelling that stresses unity, coherence, motivation and linear causality. The *Rocky* films are interesting cases of the narrative/spectacle dynamic as they are generically positioned somewhere between the action film (itself a subset of melodrama, driven by sensation and situational narration [see Higgins 2008]) and the melodrama proper. Their chief claim to consideration as action cinema is that they are punctuated with, and climax in, fight scenes, albeit in a sporting context. Yet they are primarily male melodramas revolving around Rocky's personal emotional struggles: to escape his lot in life as an uneducated working-class Italian-American; to form and maintain an harmonious domestic life; to resist the temptations of material success and hang on to his identity; to overcome the losses of Mickey (Burgess Meredith) and Apollo (Carl Weathers); ultimately, to be recognised as a man of value despite his background and limitations. Rocky's trials revolve not around his athletic prowess, but rather around his emotional and psychological commitment to battle. Likewise, in *Staying Alive*, the sequel to *Saturday Night Fever* (1977) directed and co-written by Stallone, Tony Manero (John Travolta) must overcome his fear of commitment in order to find the emotional grounding he needs to excel as a professional dancer.

Consideration of the formal properties of melodrama can give us a more nuanced sense of Stallone's approach. For Linda Williams, melodrama is *the* fundamental mode of popular cinema, centring as it does on action and pathos, lashing 'narrativity and visual spectacle ... together to produce affective response' (1998: 56). 'What counts in melodrama', she writes, 'is the feeling of righteousness, achieved through the sufferings of the innocent' (1998: 62). If in the family melodrama it is emotional suffering that performs this ideological and dramatic function, in the action film it is physical suffering. If Rocky is beset with emotional or psychological obstacles, the vehicle for his victories, his personal apotheoses, is the physical suffering he undergoes in training and fighting.

Williams identifies five key characteristics of melodrama: beginning and ending in a 'space of innocence'; a focus on the virtue of victim-heroes; the presence of realism only to serve 'melodramatic passion and action'; 'a dialectic of pathos and action – a give and take of "too late" and "in the nick of time"'; and 'Manichean conflicts between good and evil' (1998: 65–77). Stallone insists on Rocky's status as a victim-hero, even after he becomes heavyweight champion at the end of *II*; the narrative contortions that result fuel the dramas of the films (debilitating injuries, deaths of those close to him, etc). His challenge is to prove that he is not only a better fighter than his opponents, but a better person: less cynical, more humble, more humane. The final bouts are riven with variations on melodramatic 'in the nick of time' suspense: can Rocky last to the end of the fight, can he take enough pain to triumph? Rocky's fights become, as Mark Gallagher writes, 'emotional situations [transformed] into episodes of public violence', 'performative exhibitions' (2006: 48, 68) of his masculinity, morality and sense of self-worth. In this sense, the *Rocky* films can be located in proximity to the action film as a variant of melodrama, though unlike the *Rambo* series, they cannot be considered core cases.

The melodramatic qualities of the Rocky films extend from narration to visual style via Stallone's use of 'rhythmic montage' sequences which bring to bear melodrama's characteristic 'highlighted parallelism' (Williams 1998: 57–8). Visual style is central to melodrama and Stallone's in particular, just as it is to the increasingly hyperbolic stylisation of those 1980s films exemplified by *Rocky II–IV* and *Staying Alive*. By *Rocky IV*, Stallone has dispensed with the last vestiges of the earlier films' realism, rendering the films both quintessentially melodramatic and, like the 1980s blockbuster generally, increasingly classical in their 'high concept' simplicity and narrative conventionality. But this is a streamlined neo-classicism that readily accommodates, in fact foregrounds, visual spectacle.

The *Rocky* series' debt to classical norms is complicated by the difficulty of finding precedents for its narrative tropes within the sports film as a genre;[8] by contrast, its influence is readily apparent, even pervasive, from *Chariots of Fire* (1981), *Personal Best* (1982) and John G. Avildsen's own *The Karate Kid* (1984), to *Bend It Like Beckham* (2002), *The Rookie* (2002) and *Invincible* (2006). In fact, the classical Hollywood backstage musical provides at least as salient a model for the architecture of the *Rocky* films as the sports film does. *Rocky*'s influence, especially via the Stallone-ian narrative of overcoming personal obstacles to achieve recognition and self-worth through excellence as a performer, is at least as marked on contemporary musicals as on the sports film. Particularly important here are *Flashdance* (1983), *Billy Elliot* (2000) and *Save the Last Dance* (2001), which in turn have influenced a spate of films featuring such themes, including *Honey* (2003), *You Got Served* (2004), *Step Up* (2006), *Step Up 2: The Streets* (2008), *Step Up 3D* (2010), *Center Stage* (2000) and *Center Stage: Turn It Up* (2008). In positioning the series generically, therefore, the structural similarities between the musical, the melodrama and the action film should be noted.

For Marsha Kinder, action sequences work as 'performative "numbers"' which interrupt the linear drive of the plot with audio-visual spectacle, yet 'simultaneously serve as dramatic climaxes that advance the story toward closure' (2001: 68). Both the fight and the training sequences function as 'numbers' in the *Rocky* films in ways that invoke the backstage musical. They focus on the gradual improvement in the physical performance of an individual protagonist (including overcoming performance anxieties). In the *Rocky* films, this is conveyed via telescoped montages, leading up to a climax that is as much a 'show' as a 'big game'. The same basic strategies are integral to *Staying Alive*, unequivocally a backstage musical. These montage sequences become increasingly central to the *Rocky* films, demonstrating Stallone's awareness of their place in the series' spectacular appeal. The *Rocky* montages have proven hugely influential on individual-character-focused montages in subsequent action films, sports films and musicals.

Though *Rocky II*'s first use of montage is relatively subdued, showing the grinding, repetitive routines of Rocky's short-lived job at the meat-packing plant, the training montages are highlights as they were in two sequences in the original film, penned by Stallone and directed by Avildsen. Rocky's training is at first half-hearted, and montages are reserved for its resumption once Adrian (Talia Shire) emerges from her coma and gives Rocky her blessing to return to the ring. In *Rocky II*'s first training montage, each shot (bar a sequence of Rocky speed training by attempting to catch a chicken) highlights a separate action, all strung together with rapid editing and musical accompaniment. At its conclusion, we get one shot of Rocky cradling his newborn child before a montage of Rocky running begins, set to an updated disco version of Bill Conti's 'Gonna Fly Now'. This repeats many of the set-ups from the first film's iconic training run, but with Rocky now accompanied by scores of children through the city and up the Philadelphia Museum of Art steps. A short sequence paralleling Adrian and Rocky preparing leads directly into the final fight.

If Rocky's bout and rematch with Apollo is spread across two films, in *Rocky III* the rivalry of Rocky and Clubber Lang (Mr. T) develops from Clubber heckling Rocky at the statue dedication, to Rocky's loss to Clubber in the first act, to Rocky's triumph at the climax. This increases the opportunities for montages two-fold. The first, very early in the film and set to Survivor's iconic 'Eye of the Tiger' (it would be used again in *Rocky IV*), parallels Rocky's reign as champ with Clubber's inexorable rise. The second cuts between each of them training, contrasting their situations just as the earlier films had contrasted Apollo and Rocky. Whereas the first two films showed the state-of-the-art facilities enjoyed by Apollo as the heavyweight champion versus Rocky training at Mickey's, here this contrast is reversed. Clubber is granted some moral credit because he trains in

Figure 1 - Rocky (Sylvester Stallone) surrounded by fans while Clubber (Mr. T.) trains. *Rocky III*. Producers Robert Chartoff and Irwin Winkler; director Sylvester Stallone; DVD distributed by MGM Home Entertainment.

squalor. In contrast, Rocky's half-hearted regime becomes a noisy spectacle in a hotel ballroom. In Stallone's moral calculus, Rocky's loss is thus assured, notwithstanding Mickey's heart attack. Again Rocky's training for the rematch is half-hearted, and separate scenes focus on separate exercises; again Adrian must urge him on before he commits to the process; again training is represented in montage form from this point. And again we then see Rocky performing at peak condition, accompanied by another variation on 'Gonna Fly Now'.

Rocky IV is the culmination of Stallone's play with montage. There is a flashback montage in the wake of Apollo's death, incorporating images of Apollo, Drago (Dolph Lundgren), their fight, and Rocky's battles across the series. Accompanied by Robert Tepper's 'No Easy Way Out', this is a classic instance of the music-video-style montage widely noted in 1980s film style. It culminates in a series of shots paralleling Apollo falling at Drago's hands and Rocky falling in the ring. Training montages remain vital to the escalation of drama and spectacle, and they are by far the longest and most elaborate of the series. The first training montage occurs at 52:51, and is built around intricately designed parallels of Drago and Rocky. Crosscutting between each fighter readying for the upcoming bout had become a standard feature of the series, constructed so as to highlight differences in mise-en-scène, particularly colour, and functioning as intellectual montages highlighting the relative odds, and therefore moral strengths and weaknesses, of the combatants. This is far more developed and explicit here, contrasting Rocky's primitive training in the Russian countryside with Drago's precise, scientific, electronically monitored regime. Stallone cuts between Rocky exercising in exteriors and Drago in interiors, from barns and open countryside to gyms and laboratories; when Rocky runs up a mountain, Drago runs on an inclined treadmill. The screen direction of the two fighters is either opposed or matched in each cut of the segment, which runs to 56:20. The montage ends with Adrian's belated arrival at the rural outpost, but at 57:30 a second training montage begins. This proceeds until the 61-minute mark, at which point Stallone takes us directly to the fight. Not only are the montage

Figure 2 - Drago (Dolph Lundgren)'s high-tech training... *Rocky IV*. Producers Robert Chartoff and Irwin Winkler; director Sylvester Stallone; DVD distributed by MGM Home Entertainment.

Figure 3 - ...and Rocky (Sylvester Stallone)'s low-tech training. *Rocky IV*. Producers Robert Chartoff and Irwin Winkler; director Sylvester Stallone; DVD distributed by MGM Home Entertainment.

sequences here longer and more elaborate, but the dramatic sequences that have in the past bracketed the montages are minimised, such that the montages carry far more dramatic weight than in any other film in the series.

In the midst of these *Rocky* films, Stallone directed his only non-starring film, the only film he has made with no connection to the action film, and the only sequel where he was not involved in the original. *Staying Alive* is both backstage musical and melodrama, and its parallels to *Rocky* are pervasive. Picking up Tony Manero's story years after the conclusion of *Saturday Night Fever*, *Staying Alive* finds the former disco-dancer now attempting to forge a career as a professional on the New York stage. When he accompanies Jackie (Cynthia Rhodes), his friend and sometime lover, to an audition, he strikes up a brief affair with the mercurial Laura (Finola Hughes), the star of the show. Tony is hired as a dancer for the chorus, reunites with Jackie (the Adrian of the film), and with encouragement from her and a berating from the director, steps forward when the male lead proves inadequate. Where Rocky must overcome his insecurities to perform in the ring, Tony must overcome his vacillating personal and professional commitments to make himself a star through his opening night performance.

Once again, Stallone conveys much of this drama through montages, beginning with a credit sequence montage set to Frank Stallone's 'Far From Over' showing Tony auditioning as a dancer. Another, at ten minutes in, shows him giving his head-shot to agents, but repeatedly failing to get hired as an actor or as a dancer. Montages regularly recur for the balance of the film, including a romance montage of Tony and Laura, a rehearsal with Jackie that parallels it, and a rehearsal montage for the big show with Tony as the new male lead (again accompanied by 'Far From Over'). Anticipating what he would do in *Rocky IV*, the second of these proceeds directly to the beginning of the climactic performance. As with the climactic boxing matches of the *Rocky* films, this performance constitutes the film's central spectacle, in part because stylistically it stands apart from the body of the film.

But to understand how visual stylisation becomes spectacular here, and in Stallone's films from 1979 to 1985 generally – particularly the kinds of stylistic choices that prevail in the montages and fights – it helps to note developments in style and its functions from the late 1970s into the 1980s. *Staying Alive* and the *Rocky* films exemplify a general trend towards intensified, hyperbolic stylisation as much as they do Stallone's neo-classical use of genre, melodramatic forms and narration. Indeed, the latter very much favours the former, as this stylisation was grounded in an amplification of classical-era techniques in a move away from the documentary techniques which informed the realist, revisionist genre films of the mid-1970s: saturated colour and low-key lighting replaced desaturated colour and flat, naturalistic lighting; sharpness replaced diffusion; and dollies and Steadicams largely replaced the hand-held camera. Tracking visual style in the *Rocky* films from *I* to *IV*, all these shifts are evident. Shorn of realism, contemporary style uses accelerated editing, extremes of lens length, closer framing and more pervasive camera movement, an emphatic aesthetic as per Bordwell's 'intensified continuity' against which particularly hyperbolised moments function for kinetic effect, dramatic emphasis and stylisation for its own sake. Such hyperbolically styled passages function as spectacles in themselves and as expressions of authorship which distinguish filmmakers as stylists. In Stallone's films, such hyperbole principally occurs in montage sequences, fight scenes in the *Rocky* films, and dance numbers in *Staying Alive*.

For *Rocky II*, Stallone builds on the montage and fight sequences of the first film, but extends and varies them too (for example, the disco version of 'Gonna Fly Now' and the star-struck children following Rocky in the second training montage). Working with Bill Butler as cinematographer, Stallone's directorial tendencies begin to emerge. He emphasises character over setting: depth staging is simplified or minimised, focus is shallower, framing is closer, and travelling shots following character movements (rather than distanced observation) are more prevalent. This reframing imparts dynamism to sequences such as Rocky's proposal to Adrian as they walk through the zoo. Elsewhere, the camera arcs around the couple kissing in his apartment, and tracks to follow Rocky on the set of his aborted commercial; hand-held shots are employed as he works in the packing plant or chases the chicken.

All these characteristic strategies are still more evident in Stallone's later *Rocky* films as well as *Staying Alive*, as is a willingness to use more strongly marked stylistic effects not only in the fights but across the films. *Rocky III* incorporates slow-motion and zooms, as when Paulie smashes the Rocky pinball machine. In *Staying Alive*, Stallone uses camera movement only for reframing, apart from the montages and dance numbers. But *Rocky IV* reaches a high-point of stylisation, making extensive use of zoom shots, as well as hand-held camerawork when Rocky is surrounded by paparazzi. Stallone and Butler play with lens flare, diopter shots to achieve exaggerated depth of field,[9] helicopter shots of Rocky running up a mountain, and strobe lighting for the flashback montage.

Moreover, in a period when average shot lengths in mainstream films steadily shrank (see Bordwell 2006: 122), Stallone's films, *Rocky IV* in particular, are among the very fastest, and indicate his development and refinement of an editing-based aesthetic with a marked use of stylistic hyperbole in the fastest-cut sequences: the montages and the fights in the *Rocky* films, and the montages and the dance performance in *Staying Alive*. *Rocky IV* features notably faster cutting, not only in the montage sequences, but throughout. Because of faster cutting across the films, in the fights, and in the montages that take up more and more screen time, the average shot length of the *Rocky* films grows shorter and shorter. Avildsen's *Rocky* clocked in with an 8.25 second ASL. *Rocky II* jumps to a 5.6 ASL, while *Rocky III* comes in at 3.7 seconds and *Rocky IV* at a remarkable 2.16 seconds. It remains the fastest-cut film in the series.

In *Rocky II*, the training montages are highlighted as spectacles by cinematographic choices that set them apart from the body of the film, including dramatic, backlit silhouettes; magic-hour lighting; and freeze-frames. This logic extends to the fight, staged as in the first film. For the bulk of the action, Butler's camera is outside the ring, restricted to long and medium shots, only moving inside the ring for close-ups between rounds. But a sense of impact is achieved through a pattern whereby as the cutting and musical accompaniment gradually accelerate, Stallone and Butler steadily incorporate more hand-held shots, slow-motion, extremes of lens length and high/low angles, and perceptual subjectivity, with diffusion and a fish-eye lens as Rocky reacts to a particularly punishing blow. Stallone initiates a pattern here that will hold for the fights in each of his subsequent *Rocky* films: stylisation is more pronounced in the middle of the fights, thus emphasising the brute struggle (and fitting with Stallone's conception of the centrality of suffering to the melodrama of the series), rather than the climaxes, where Rocky triumphs. Keeping the stylisation apart from the crucial plot point (who wins the fight) is also very classical. *Rocky III*'s montages incorporate split-screen to contrast Rocky's life as the champ with Clubber's rise, as well as slow-motion, zooms, extreme close-ups and freeze-frames. For the fight sequences, Stallone and Butler follow *Rocky II*'s pattern, starting with long shots outside the ring, utilising zooms and slow-motion, moving into closer shots towards their middle sections. The final fight features the fastest cutting in the series to that point, and a great deal more camera movement around the combatants, and in particular more slow-motion shots.

None of the series' montages are as rigorously patterned as the training sequences in *Rocky IV*. Canny use is made of graphic matches and paralleled screen direction even as colours and settings stand in stark contrast. *Rocky IV* also adds superimposition to the arsenal. The first fight is overtly spectacular: a stage show featuring James Brown, an elaborately designed set, and dancers, only then culminating in the Apollo/Drago match. Too, throughout the fight sequences, shots are closer and isolated singles take us inside the ring sooner than previously. For the first time, we see a whole series of slow-motion shots emphasising punches connecting and sweat flying off faces clearly recalling *Raging Bull* (1980).

Staying Alive takes the aesthetic of the hyperbolically styled, spectacular performative climax to what is, even for Stallone in the 1980s, an extreme. The montages become increasingly stylised as the film progresses. While early rehearsal montages are principally filmed in long shot, once Tony becomes the male lead, Stallone uses medium shots leading into close-ups, strikingly deep-focus wide-angle shots, bravura Steadicam movements to heighten the kinetic impact of the dancing, and even hand-held shots. The climactic number of the opening night performance plays out a mini-drama of spiritual temptation and functions as the culmination of Tony's tense relationship with Laura. It is also the most spectacular sequence in Stallone's films of the period, incorporating slow-motion, saturated colour, highly expressive theatrical lighting and a rapidity of cutting that suggests it is a montage sequence, though it is not. Characteristically, Stallone emphasises the athletic, sweaty, muscular physicality of Tony and Laura's movements. The performance is a triumph

Figure 4 - The spectacular performance climax emphasises Tony (John Travolta)'s physicality and Sylvester Stallone's stylisation. *Staying Alive*. Producers Sylvester Stallone and Robert Stigwood; director Sylvester Stallone; DVD distributed by Paramount Home Video.

for Tony, proof of his moral superiority through his physical exertion.

Stallone's own stylistic exertion is proof of his command of the chief formal features of the 1980s neo-classical blockbuster: *Staying Alive* is a backstage musical that is fully a melodrama, culminating in a hyperbolically styled spectacle. Working within the aesthetic palette normative to Hollywood filmmakers of the late 1970s and 1980s, then, Stallone pursued a consistent, specific approach to form and style. Yet focus was on his stardom; his craft as a filmmaker got little attention. This was not the case when he returned to directing over two decades later. With this 'comeback' his authorship became as much an issue of extra-cinematic discourses as of signature techniques. He now would tout himself as both director and *auteur*.

THE COMEBACK: STALLONE-AS-AUTEUR, *ROCKY BALBOA* AND *RAMBO*

Stallone's return saw him reviving his two most iconic roles, Rocky Balboa and John Rambo.[10] If *Rocky Balboa* and *Rambo* constitute an attempt to resuscitate his career as a star, Stallone also used these films to explicitly position himself as an *auteur*. For the first time, he uses 'A Film by Sylvester Stallone' for the opening credits, and interviews see him assert that directing would be his future (see Schwartz 2006). Publicity surrounding these films also shows a Stallone self-consciously crafting an authorial persona that would lend him a new legitimacy and relevance. *Variety*'s review of *Rambo* further demonstrates Stallone's uphill battle: 'The Sylvester Stallone nostalgia tour that began with another *Rocky* continues with this fourth *Rambo*. Although Stallone plays it completely straight, the mere idea of the ageing action star strapping on the bandana again is risible enough to let the movie play like a comedy too, albeit one with an unusually high body count' (Lowry 2008: 44).

This was the sort of reaction that Stallone and associates sought to forestall in publicity for *Rocky Balboa* in particular, with much of his commentary on its production focusing on the obstacles he faced: 'People were saying the parade had gone by, and who was I to try to bring it back again? ... An artist dies twice, and the second death is the easiest one. The artistic death, the fact that you are no longer pertinent – or that you're deemed someone whose message or talent has run its course – is a very, very tough piece of information to swallow' (in Weiner 2006). Stallone took part in career-retrospective interviews with the likes of

Entertainment Weekly, justifying the continuing relevance of *Rocky* in specifically auteurist, autobiographical terms: "'I thought the character had something to say,' explains Stallone, who wrote, directed, produced and stars in the movie. "Which I guess means that I had something to say." If the Rocky of *Rocky Balboa* is a has-been, then this too reflects Stallone himself: "When you get older, you get less of a forum to speak. It's like, 'Oh, you had your moment, time to move on.' ... I am a has-been, no question. But that doesn't mean you can't still contribute". Joe Roth, president of Revolution Studios, one of *Rocky Balboa*'s financers, is even more explicit: "The script was a perfect metaphor for Stallone's life – at 60, he becomes an underdog again. ... The character is an expression of his own heart. Rather than fight it, he's using it to tell us how he feels"' (Schwartz 2006). Authorship here, then, is first a question of discourse, serving to render Stallone's authorship as a marketing commodity by insisting on the personal nature of the film.

The narratives of both *Rocky Balboa* and *Rambo* are nonetheless the discursive crux of Stallone's attempt to engineer his comeback as a star and as a filmmaker. *Rocky Balboa* sees the fighter now retired from the ring and a widower, mourning Adrian's death while managing her restaurant, one section of which is devoted to Rocky's past glories; indeed, his main job is going from table to table telling tales of his glory days. When a computerised simulation of a hypothetical bout between Rocky and the heavyweight champion, Mason Dixon (former light heavyweight champion Antonio Tarver), suggests Balboa (in his prime) would have won, he petitions to regain his licence, and is soon approached by Dixon's management for an exhibition bout. The question is, does an over-the-hill former champ stand a chance in the ring against an opponent still in his youthful prime? The issue is not whether he will win; rather, it is whether this old man can go the distance.

The parallels between Balboa and Stallone are unmistakable: the former is a man who was a former star in his chosen profession, now seeking to regain if not his title then at least his vocation and his self-respect; the latter is doing exactly the same by making the film. To do so, both must rely on skill, experience and sheer will, 'the stuff in the basement', to prove their worth despite their advancing years. Consistent with the series, Rocky's triumph not only is emblematic of his demonstrable worth as a fighter, but enables a personal renewal (allowing him to move beyond his mourning for Adrian).

Likewise, Rambo's predicament parallels both Balboa's and Stallone's, but imprecisely. As *Rambo* opens, the former warrior is making a living captaining a boat and catching snakes for a tourist attraction near the Myanmar border. Like Balboa, time has passed him by, until he must fight to save a group of missionaries he had ferried into the civil war zone. Like Rocky, like Stallone, Rambo's fight, finally, is to recapture some meaning in his moribund existence.

In renewing his career by both reviving his signature characters and establishing his status as a writer-director, Stallone must establish links to the preceding series films, yet demonstrate his awareness of current norms. *Rambo* includes flashbacks to earlier films, while *Rocky Balboa*, dealing with ageing and nostalgia, is suffused with an awareness of the arc of the series. The opening credits of *Rocky Balboa*, with Conti's fanfare, mimic earlier entries in the series. They are followed by a montage of Philadelphia locales accompanied by Frank Stallone's 'Take You Back' (making its fourth appearance in the series). This ends on a bedside photo of Adrian, and Rocky rising to feed his turtles (a call-back to the first film). Of all Stallone's films, *Rocky Balboa* is most marked by subjective narration, laced with a series of flashback montages of characters and incidents from the previous *Rocky*s that positions it as the culmination of the narrative arc of the series. When the anticipated training montage comes, a re-recorded version of Conti's 'Gonna Fly Now' is heard, but one that closely follows the arrangement heard in the first film.

Throughout, Stallone engages with the contemporary cinematic context, which has again intensified continuity and hyperbolised stylisation. As the demand for stylistic novelty has escalated, the range of techniques has broadened. In part this means that the realist techniques of the 1970s, rendered passé in the 1980s, are once more common components of filmmakers' arsenals. In the 2000s, desaturated colour sits alongside saturated colour, and hand-held cameras alongside Steadicams and dollies, forming a stylistic palette that is as open-ended technically as it is dominated by intensified or hyperbolic effects functionally. Formerly realist techniques are not always used in conjunction with a sustained realist aesthetic, but rather are used to impart a heightened kinetic effect to scenes of physical action and violence. This is what Geoff King calls the 'impact aesthetic' of the contemporary blockbuster, stemming from an imperative to find a form of spectacle that is easily translated to television; key to this impact aesthetic is 'rapid editing or rapid and/or unstable movement of the camera' to 'create an impression of subjective immersion in the action' (2003: 116–17). As Eric Lichtenfeld puts it, 'filmmakers try to approximate physical sensation with technique that in the digital age, has become increasingly expressionistic' (2007: 277).

On the *Rocky Balboa* DVD, 'Skill v. Will' draws attention to Stallone's use of realist techniques, always careful to make the case for their compositional motivation. If locations were chosen to make the film 'as real as possible', the 'jerky' hand-held camera indicates Rocky is feeling 'unsettled' ('Skill vs. Will' 2007). The imperative to be 'realistic' motivates the film's most stylised visual effects: mimicry of HBO fight coverage, including graphics and camera set-ups at each corner of the ring, with 'soft cuts' utilised, to 'blur the lines between reality and ... just a cinematic fight' (Stallone 2007).

Cinematographer Clark Mathis writes in *American Cinematographer* of the varied imperatives of the film's visual style, particularly the need to update its look for the current cinematic climate. Mathis speaks of 'aspects of past and present' within the film's characters as motivating a range of techniques. But it is their stylisation that aligns the film with the contemporary Hollywood hyperbolism: 'I've always had the desire to create multiple styles within a single film without leaning on the more traditional motivations: flashbacks, altered states, or uncertain points of view. Rocky Balboa was the perfect vehicle for this approach. I realised I could do my part to bridge the Rocky generation gap by creating a visual syntax that firmly led viewers out of the old and into the new' (Mathis 2006: 128).

The film establishes this stylisation early, with the monochromatic colour and slow-motion of Mason's opening fight; monochrome will be used later for Rocky's flashbacks. As in earlier films, one stylistic principle is to establish contrasts between the combatants. Stallone and Mathis contrast the warmer colours and organic textures of Rocky's world with the cooler colours and sterility of Mason's; in training footage, Rocky's gym is shot with low-key lighting while Mason's is high-key. At the same time, winter in Philadelphia allows the filmmakers to recall the desaturation of *Rocky*, while the Las Vegas setting of the fight allows for colour saturation more reminiscent of *Rocky IV*. The training montage evidences a balance between stylistic continuity with the larger series and the incorporation of contemporary visual stylisation; here, 'Gonna Fly Now' accompanies hand-held camerawork, closer shots and fast shutter speeds. Editing throughout is quicker than in any other film in the series bar *Rocky IV*. Again, Stallone relies on close framings with little camera movement or depth staging. Yet while for most of the film Stallone uses longer takes than in *IV*, this is balanced by the speed of the cutting in the final fight, such that while the film as a whole has a 2.9 second ASL, that scene has a 1.3 second ASL.

Figure 5 - Incorporation of HBO pay-per-view graphics as both realism and spectacle. *Rocky Balboa.*
Producers William Chartoff, Kevin King Templeton, Charles Winkler and David Winkler; director Sylvester
Stallone; DVD distributed by Sony Pictures Home Entertainment.

Throughout, Stallone and Mathis use very sharp images, never more
so than in the final fight, shot in HD to mimic HBO. The incorporation
of televisual graphics here is referential, yet becomes part of the film's
spectacular appeal, much like the light show that precedes the fight. This
duality of realism and spectacle defines the aesthetics of the fight itself,
and helps Stallone situate himself in a contemporary context where such
a duality is normative. Though the opening moments of the fight are
extreme long shots (consistent with the pattern established in *Rocky II, III*
and *IV*), otherwise very close framings are used throughout, much more
so than in previous *Rocky*s. Use of hand-held cameras is more extensive,
too, with wide-angle lenses that both recall television fights and enhance
movement and kinetic effect. With no motivation apart from decorative
effect and hyperbolic impact, Stallone oscillates between black-and-white
and colour footage during the fight, with monochrome flashbacks between
rounds, and colour digitally added to monochrome shots, particularly the
red of the fighters' blood. At the fight's conclusion, though, Rocky shakes
a fan's hand, punctuated with a freeze-frame, a recurring series device.

    Rambo ventures even further into the waters of contemporary (action
film) style. Instead, publicity for *Rambo* seeks to root the film's realist
style in Stallone's conception of the character as he has written him. He
asserts that the guiding idea of the film is: What if Rambo himself was
directing this film? 'What if the film has his personality? His jittery, very
suspicious, alert kind of movements. In other words, the camera is never
steady, but it's not overly active either. It's just – it's alive, it's prowling'

(Stallone 2008). Because Rambo's life is unsettled, and because he lives in jungle terrain, the camera must remain unsteady, and Stallone therefore eschewed tracking shots (see 'The Long Road' 2008). Stallone describes the shooting as quasi-documentary-like:[11] when the villagers are massacred, five cameras were used simultaneously, each operator given their own 'zone' of the action and told to 'just go at it', to 'shoot people from obscure angles as though you're eavesdropping and there's never a sense that anyone is playing to the camera' (Stallone 2008).

In contrast, *Rambo: First Blood Part II*, directed by Ted Kotcheff, is relatively conventional, though featuring considerable focal depth. Action scenes tend to be in long shot, with isolated close-ups, slow-motion and low angles for specific effects. Directed by George P. Costmatos, *First Blood* uses telephoto lenses for a shallow depth of field, and only isolated bits of deep staging and long shots to establish the space, especially in action scenes. Like the first film, the camerawork is steady throughout, with sharp and saturated images. Peter MacDonald's *Rambo III* uses only isolated wide-angle shots, for a generally shallow effect (often using silhouette lighting), with occasional rack-focus shots; again, the camerawork is quite steady, with not a single hand-held shot in the entire film.

Motivated in part by Stallone's sense of his character's perceptual subjectivity, *Rambo* instead makes considerable, if not constant, use of hand-held cameras, with tripods rarely evident outside of dialogue scenes. Images are sharp throughout, and the hand-held realism is supported by telephoto and zoom lenses. In this respect, *Rambo* departs from

Figure 6 - Close framing enhances kinetic impact in the climactic fight. *Rocky Balboa*. Producers Charles Winkler, William Chartoff, Kevin King Templeton and David Winkler; director Sylvester Stallone; DVD distributed by Sony Pictures Home Entertainment.

Figure 7 - Low-key lighting in *Rambo.* Producers Avi Lerner, Kevin King Templeton and John Thompson; director Sylvester Stallone; DVD distributed by Lionsgate Home Entertainment.

the template of the 1980s action film that marked the earlier films in the series, Stallone instead staking his claim to aesthetic currency by offering a variation on the highly kinetic realism of the likes of the *Bourne* series. *Rambo* also features the most extensive use of low-key lighting in any Stallone film to date, consistent with its increased application across the full range of Hollywood output since the 1980s. Colour tends to be desaturated, most consistently in scenes of violence, while other scenes are highly saturated, especially when red and purple smoke emerges from the tent where the soldiers harass the female prisoners. Saturated colour is also used for isolated effects in violent moments, as when Rambo rips a guard's throat out as Sarah (Julie Benz), the missionary whose idealism spurs him to action, watches horrified. As in *Rocky Balboa,* dream-sequence flashbacks are in black and white, with isolated bursts of digital colour, and blurring to denote mental subjectivity.

When Stallone and cinematographer Glen MacPherson use backlighting or silhouetting, it is to create planimetric compositions for decorative effects (for example, Rambo in the boat at dusk). Dialogue scenes are shot conventionally in shallow focus; wide angles are used infrequently. Conventionally, action scenes in particular are dominated by hand-held camerawork, for both documentary and kinetic effect. This is rigorously observed: every appearance of violence is rendered through an abrupt shift to hand-held shots, the jaggedness of which mirrors the film's extraordinarily brutal and explicit violence. On the one hand, this can be described as realism;[12] on the other, in the action film, violence is key to spectacle. Likewise, the hand-held camera here implies a degree of realism yet also enhances the impact of the violent action.

This is exemplified by the function of the hand-held camera in relation to editing here. Earlier *Rambo* films maintained a tight narrative focus on the character while alternating between him and his antagonists for suspense, much as the *Rocky* films alternated between the contenders in the lead-up to the final fight. Now, though, Rambo is no longer the lone warrior, but one of a team of mercenaries. Consequently, at the climax the crosscutting is more dispersed, alternating between Rambo, alone and with Sarah and School Boy (Matthew Marsden), the latter two, the rest of the mercenaries and missionaries, and the army in pursuit. It is in part this alternation that enables Stallone to speed up the cutting, but as he does so, the camerawork becomes steadier. An exception is a series of hand-held shots following Sarah and School Boy running through the jungle, but even here, wide-angle lenses are used to enhance the movement and reduce shakiness; the speed of the movement partially negates the need for the added kinesis of unsteady framing. This suggests a functional equivalence between shaky, mobile cameras and rapid cutting that speaks not to documentary realism but to the impact aesthetic of action films. That Stallone has absorbed such contemporary norms is demonstrated by *Rambo*'s 2.12 second ASL, his fastest ever, even though the film ends on a five-minute take of our hero walking down a dirt road to his father's farm.[14]

CONCLUSION

Stallone's accomplishments with *Rocky Balboa* and *Rambo* are considerable. He has made significant progress in recovering his stardom via a resuscitation of his signature roles, but also in forging an authorial

Figure 8 - Wide angle lens use in an otherwise shallow focus film. *Rambo.* Producers Avi Lerner, Kevin King Templeton and John Thompson; director Sylvester Stallone; DVD distributed by Lionsgate Home Entertainment.

identity, in part extra-textually. Textually, he has demonstrated a mastery of contemporary Hollywood aesthetics, while extending the strategies of his earlier films, particularly with regard to editing. In this, he continues to offer a distinct variation on prevailing trends. In *Paradise Alley*, this meant overt colour symbolism alongside a self-conscious mobilisation of classical Hollywood conventions in relation to 1970s genre revisionism. *Rocky II*, *III* and *IV* saw him develop a form of melodramatic storytelling that is nonetheless classicist, inflected with elements of the backstage musical seen most explicitly in *Staying Alive*.

In the process, Stallone substantially reshaped the sports film, and the backstage musical as well. The intensified and often hyperbolic stylisation of those films, in their use of montage sequences and their spectacular performative climaxes, is representative of the neo-classical blockbusters of their day, but Stallone's editing, shot through with parallelism, is idiosyncratic as well. Such characteristics remain apparent in *Rocky Balboa* and *Rambo*, even as Stallone mobilises realist techniques to suit the impact aesthetic of current Hollywood cinema.

My aim here has been to show Sylvester Stallone's contributions as a director whose films are at once exemplary of contemporary Hollywood aesthetics and yet very much his own. Not an *auteur* in the classical sense, he is nevertheless an author with an identifiable approach to narrative and form, and with his comeback, increasingly a branded commodity, a commercial *auteur* whose cultural capital is, for now, once again on the rise.

NOTES

1   Note here that *The Expendables* (2010) is his first ensemble film as a writer-director, its commercial pull not solely dependent on Stallone himself.
2   The casting of Tom Waits as 'Mumbles', a barroom pianist, functions as an oblique kind of allusion, via Waits's own romantic invocation of mid-century urban lowlife in his series of 1973–78 albums.
3   By contrast, Norman Jewison's *F.I.S.T.*, released the same year, starring Stallone and shot by Kóvacs, uses deep focus much more consistently in relation to depth staging.
4   For Kóvacs, *Paradise Alley* represented the end of his use of diffusion in the context of the historical film. Discussing *F.I.S.T.*, he defended the lack of diffusion in that film, claiming that for a period look it 'is beginning to get a little cliché by now' (Kóvacs 1978: 152).
5   This is a knowing contrast to the painting of Jesus above the ring in *Rocky*'s first fight scene.
6   The argument that spectacle overwhelms narrative in the contemporary blockbuster is exemplified in Corrigan (1992), Schatz (1993) and Bukatman (1998). The response that narrative in such films often proceeds *through* spectacle can be seen in Tasker (1993),

Thompson (1999), King (2000) and Bordwell (2006).

7 For Leo Charney, 'the coexistence of narrative and sensation is neither simply a new phenomenon nor simply the reiteration of an old phenomenon; the balance between the
two elements has been in negotiation throughout the history of cinema', such that the
contemporary rise of action films, rather than constituting a post-classical rupture in
Hollywood storytelling, in fact represents 'but one ceaselessly evolving stage in a relationship between sensation and storytelling that at most has defined the unfolding nature
of American filmmaking from its first years and at least has run coterminous with that
history' (2001: 54).

8 Most boxing plots had been fuelled by more complicated melodrama plots (*The Champ*,
1931; *Champion*, 1949), the fighter's involvement with criminal elements (*Body and Soul*,
1947), or the more inclusive narrative fetch of the biopic (*Gentleman Jim*, 1942; *The Joe
Louis Story*, 1953; *Somebody Up There Likes Me*, 1956).

9 'Lens flare' refers to visual artefacts caused by the reflection of light off the camera lens as
recorded by the film. A split-field diopter is a supplementary lens (a secondary lens placed
on top of the primary lens) that has two separate focal planes, comparable to bifocal glasses; this allows for focusing on near and far planes simultaneously so as to approximate
the effects of deep-focus cinematography. See Ramaeker (2007).

10 It is fitting that the former in particular would be the focus of his initial re-emergence,
as the *Rocky* films have long been identified as foundational to Stallone's star persona,
not least by the man himself: 'Everything I am and everything I have boils down to Rocky
Balboa. I didn't create Rocky. He created me' (cited in Schubart 2002: 149).

11 Consider here, too, the use of stock news footage at the opening of the film to provide an
historical context for the narrative.

12 Stallone proudly declares in the DVD commentary that he has been told that he has achieved a remarkably realistic depiction of the effects of bodies hit with a 50-calibre gun.

13 Excluding this shot, the film's ASL is 2 seconds.

BIBLIOGRAPHY

Bordwell, David (2006) *The Way Hollywood Tells It: Story and Style in Modern Movies*. Berkeley:
University of California Press.

Bukatman, Scott (1998) 'Zoning Out: The End of Offscreen Space', in Jon Lewis (ed.) *The New
American Cinema*. Durham: Duke University Press, 248–72.

Charney, Leo (2001) 'The Violence of a Perfect Moment', in J. David Slocum (ed.) *Violence and
American Cinema*. New York: Routledge, 47–62.

Corrigan, Timothy (1992) *A Cinema Without Walls: Movies and Culture After Vietnam*. London:
Routledge.

Gallagher, Mark (2006) *Action Figures: Men, Action Films, and Contemporary Adventure
Narratives*. New York: Palgrave Macmillan.

Higgins, Scott (2008) 'Suspenseful Situations: Melodramatic Narrative and the Contemporary
Action Film', *Cinema Journal*, 47.2, 74–96.

Kinder, Marsha (2001) 'Violence American Style: The Narrative Orchestration of Violent
Attractions', in J. David Slocum (ed.) *Violence and American Cinema*. New York: Routledge,
63–100.

King, Geoff (2000) *Spectacular Narratives: Hollywood in the Age of the Blockbuster*. London:
I.B. Tauris.

_____ (2003) 'Spectacle, Narrative, and the Blockbuster', in Julian Stringer (ed.) *Movie Blockbusters*. London: Routledge, 114–27.

Kóvacs, László (1978) 'The Photography of the Film Called *F.I.S.T*', *American Cinematographer*, February, 142–5, 184–5, 204–5.

Lichtenfeld, Eric (2007 [2004]) *Action Speaks Louder: Violence, Spectacle, and the American Action Movie*. Revised and expanded edition. Middletown, CT: Wesleyan University Press.

'The Long Road' (2008) *Rambo* DVD extra, Lionsgate Home Entertainment.

Lowry, Brian (2008) '*Rambo* Rumble Ready', *Variety*, 28 January–3 February, 44.

Mathis, Clark (2006) 'Filmmaker's Forum', *American Cinematographer*, December, 128, 130–31.

Ramaeker, Paul (2007) 'Notes on the Split-Field Diopter', *Film History*, 19.2, 179–98.

Schatz, Thomas (1993) 'The New Hollywood', in Jim Collins, Hilary Radner and Ava Preacher (eds) *Film Theory Goes to the Movies*. New York: Routledge, 8–36.

Schubart, Rikke (2001) 'Passion and Acceleration: Generic Change in the Action Film', in J. David Slocum (ed.) *Violence and American Cinema*. New York: Routledge, 192–207.

_____ (2002) 'Birth of a Hero: Rocky, Stallone, and Mythical Creation', in Angela Ndalianis and Charlotte Henry (eds) *Stars in Our Eyes: The Star Phenomenon in the Contemporary Era*. Westport, CT: Praeger, 149–64.

Schwartz, Missy (2006) 'Sylvester Stallone: *EW* Catches Up with the Star as He Prepares to Film Rocky's Final Round', *Entertainment Weekly*, 14 December. Online. Available HTTP: http:www.ew.com/ew/article/0,,1569864,00.html (10 September 2009).

'Skill vs. Will' (2007) *Rocky Balboa* DVD extra, MGM Home Entertainment.

Stallone, Sylvester (2007) Director's Commentary, *Rocky Balboa* DVD, MGM Home Entertainment.

_____ (2008) Director's Commentary, Rambo DVD, Lionsgate Home Entertainment.

Steele, Gregg (1971) 'On Location with *The Godfather*', *American Cinematographer*, June, 568–71.

Tasker, Yvonne (1993) *Spectacular Bodies: Gender, Genre, and the Action Cinema*. London: Routledge.

Thompson, Kristin (1999) *Storytelling in the New Hollywood*. Cambridge, MA: Harvard University Press.

Weiner, Allison Hope (2006) 'Yo Rocky, or Rambo, Gonna Fly Now at 60', *New York Times*, 21 November. Online. Available HTTP: http://www.nytimes.com/2006/11/21/movies/21sly.html (10 September 2009).

Williams, Linda (1998) 'Melodrama Revised', in Nick Browne (ed.) *Refiguring American Film Genres: Theory and History*. Berkeley: University of California Press, 42–88.

LOGIC IS THE CURE, MEET THE DISEASE: THE MELOS OF *COBRA*

SCOTT HIGGINS

Cobra (1986) refines and concentrates the early 1980s action film, boiling the genre down to its melodramatic essence. As scripted by Sylvester Stallone and directed by George Cosmatos, few films better exemplify the genre which, according to Eric Lichtenfeld, repurposed the police procedural by emphasising punishment over investigation (2007: 4). From its eponymous title to its casting, *Cobra* celebrates its debt to *Dirty Harry*, which helped launch the genre in 1971. Stallone invoked Clint Eastwood's aura to gain credibility in the action-cop subgenre, hoping to launch a popular franchise. Stallone muscles conventions put into play fifteen years earlier to shoulder the weight of a major summer release. Far more than Eastwood's series, however, *Cobra* distils the genre to its rudiments, stripping its generic situations of motivation and psychological complexity and barrelling across its brief 87-minute stretch propelled by imagery, action set pieces and montage editing. Analysis of its plot structure and pictorial strategies reveals *Cobra* to be the work of a filmmaker who embraces the genre's roots in blood-and-thunder melodrama.

Popular Hollywood cinema's indebtedness to melodrama is often noted, and scholars including Yvonne Tasker (1993), Steve Neale (2000), Linda Williams (2001) and Jennifer Bean (2004) have helped to broaden our sense of the tradition's influence beyond women's pictures, weepies and family melodramas. Action films, which Tasker notes are 'typically melodramatic', are perhaps the most powerful contemporary avatars of what was born as a nineteenth-century theatrical form (2004: 5).[1] Ben Singer, in his history of silent serials, offers a functional definition of melodrama as a 'highly variable but not utterly amorphous genre' (2001: 7). Singer seeks an inclusive definition that will track industry use of the term and still hold explanatory power. He proposes that melodrama be considered a 'cluster concept' involving five basic features: pathos, emotional intensification, moral polarisation, sensationalism and what he calls 'nonclassical narrative structure' (2001: 44–50). Works of melodrama cluster together because they share some, but not necessarily all, of these constitutive elements. Singer's approach tracks colloquial use of the term, and it admits texts as diverse as *The Terminator* (1984) and *Terms of Endearment* (1983).

Elsewhere, I have argued that the contemporary action film can draw on all five elements, harkening back to the theatrical tradition (see Higgins 2008). By 1986, Stallone had built his career on variants of melodrama. The pathos, overwrought emotion, moral polarities and sensationalism of the *Rocky* and *Rambo* franchises are self-evident. In his screenplay of *Cobra*, Stallone avails himself of the recipe once again, but without the emotion and pathos that so strongly flavoured his earlier efforts. In their place, the film offers a remarkably arbitrary, 'nonclassical' plot structure and an arsenal of visually hyperbolic iconography.

ATTACK OF THE PSYCHOS: PLOTTING IN *COBRA*

In constructing his plot for *Cobra*, Stallone filtered out the complexities of Paula Gosling's 1974 novel and relied on basic tenets of melodrama. In this section I will briefly survey melodramatic plotting and take stock of how Stallone developed Gosling's source material. With these contexts in mind, my analysis of the film's narrative structure reveals how Stallone arrays generic conventions and basic situations with little regard to causal logic or psychological development. His choices yield a work that may be inadequate in classical terms, but is nonetheless powerful melodrama.

Cobra's melodramatic plotting contrasts with classical cinema's tight causality, as described by David Bordwell, Janet Staiger and Kristin Thompson in *The Classical Hollywood Cinema* (1985). Where the classical text imposes strict limits on coincidence and seeks to motivate action through character psychology and verisimilitude, melodrama thrives on juxtaposing thrilling situations, emotional reversals and dramatic happenstance. Ben Brewster and Lea Jacobs have convincingly demonstrated the importance of nineteenth-century stage melodrama's narrative structures to the early feature films of the teens. These would inform the action film. In *Theatre to Cinema* (1997) they argue that melodrama's 'aesthetics of spectacle' provided a popular, if critically disreputable, model for early multi-reel narratives. In particular, they note that rather than causal plotting, screenwriters employed 'situational dramaturgy' which conceptualised storytelling as the selection and arrangement of stock pictorial, sensational moments. Melodramatic plots thus tended towards loose plausibility and strong coincidence, but they also packed in crowd-pleasing episodes (1997: 19–29).

The American film industry's emphasis on character causality from around 1917 on led filmmakers to disclaim and discard situational plotting, though as Bordwell, Staiger and Thompson admit, classical cinema resulted from a 'mixed parentage in vaudeville, melodrama, and other spectacle-centered entertainments' (1985: 14). To be sure, we might see classical causality as a means of adapting and sustaining elements of melodrama, as Frank Borzage suggested in the early 1920s when he explained, 'today in pictures we have the old melodramatic situations fitted out decently with true characterisations' (Bordwell *et al.* 1985: 14). In an earlier essay, I have suggested that the contemporary action film presents a strong continuation of melodrama's legacy, building plots from a narrow set of pre-defined situations but tempering arbitrariness with character arcs and a strong, familiar three-act structure (see Higgins 2008).

With *Cobra*, Stallone amplifies the genre's situational character by joining together a few autonomous building blocks. A glance at Paula Gosling's novel, which Stallone's screenplay adapts, throws his choices into relief. The original novel, *Fair Game*, offers a conventional structure that would be well suited to action filmmaking formulas.[2] Malcheck, Gosling's Lieutenant Detective protagonist, is a standard-issue haunted hero. A Vietnam vet, emotionally crippled by his experience as a covert assassin during the war and by the death of his father, Malcheck faces his inner demons by vanquishing his archrival, Edison, the international hit man he has been tracking for years. Malcheck's psychic turmoil is physicalised by ill-timed bouts with malaria, which he contracted during his tour of Vietnam. Crippled by fever and hallucination, he must learn to trust and love Clare, the woman he is keeping under protective custody. The character arc is far from original, but it is perfectly serviceable for the action genre. In fact it follows exactly the model of inner conflict recommended by William C. Martell in his manual *The Secrets of Action Screenwriting*: 'he must become himself INSIDE before he becomes himself OUTSIDE' (2000: 36).

In his adaptation, Stallone erases the character motivations and embellishments with which Gosling filled out her thriller. Essentially, the skeleton of the plot remains: a tough-but-handsome city cop is assigned to protect a beautiful young woman from a killer; together they leave the city and drive north, tracked by the killer; on the road, the hero and heroine form a romantic bond; finally the cop and the killer do battle and the hero is victorious. The book interweaves three related plot lines: Malcheck investigates the identity of the killer and discovers that it is his old nemesis, Edison; Clare and Malcheck fall in love as he defends her from the hit man's attacks; and Edison becomes increasingly frustrated by his inability to eliminate Clare. Of these, Stallone focuses on the second line, largely reducing the investigation and the killer's story to montage sequences. Further, within the remaining line of action, Stallone devotes only three brief scenes to the romance: two sequences of humorous flirtation on the road, and one of seduction the night before the final attack. Where Gosling's version is a hybrid romance novel and thriller, Stallone's screenplay streamlines the property down to a pattern of attacks and defences, a structure most amenable to the action film.

His revision is actually more condensed than other similarly structured entries in the genre. *The Terminator*, for instance, also features a romance between hero and heroine as he protects her from a killer's near-constant assault. James Cameron's film, though, builds a much larger mythology around this conflict using a science-fiction back story and places more narrative weight on the relationship between Reese (Michael Biehn) and Sarah Connor (Linda Hamilton).[3] *The Terminator*'s success two years earlier likely impelled Stallone's foray into the 'couple on the run' action formula, though, of course, Stallone installed himself as the hero and accordingly reduced the part played by the killer, a part which had allowed Schwarzenegger to dominate his movie.

In minimising investigation and relationship building, Stallone's version foregrounds the bare-bones cycle of attack and defence. His story follows the exploits of Marion Cobretti (Stallone), an officer on the LAPD's 'zombie squad' who, with his partner Gonzales (Reni Santoni), confronts a murderous cult of axe-wielding killers led by a depraved murderer called the Night Slasher (Brian Thompson). When he is assigned to protect Ingrid (Brigitte Nielsen, who married Stallone in 1985), Cobretti takes her to San Remos, where he repels an axe-cult assault and defeats the Night Slasher. The film offers a conventional three-act structure.[4] The first act runs 29 minutes, beginning with the 'supermarket killer's' attack and climaxing with the axe cult's attack on Ingrid in a parking garage. Act two lasts roughly 35 minutes, during which Cobra fights off the cult and struggles to protect Ingrid through two more attacks and then formulates a plan of action. At the film's midpoint, a conventional place for the hero to stop reacting and become active, Cobra, Ingrid, Gonzales and officer Nancy Stalk (Lee Garlington), who is a secret axe-cult member, leave Los Angeles and drive north to escape the killers. The final act features 15 minutes of solid action, which begins as the axe cult attacks Cobra's and Ingrid's motel and climaxes in Cobra's hand-to-hand fight with the Night Slasher in a steel foundry. Stallone's quick two-minute epilogue reveals that the wounded Gonzales will survive, allows Cobra to have the last word with (and to deliver a left-hook to the face of) Detective Monte (Andrew Robinson), his strident critic throughout the film, and closes as Ingrid and Cobra ride a motorcycle into the sunset.

This structure is notable for compressing the second and third acts. Screenwriting convention suggests that the second act should run roughly 60 minutes and the third should last 30 minutes; Stallone boils them down to 35 and 15 minutes respectively. After setting up the characters and large-scale situations in the first act, Stallone's screenplay speeds through the second with little complication or development. Since the hero is largely reactive in the final act, Stallone saves time establishing, laying out and executing a goal-oriented plan. Instead of a full 30-minute act, we get a half-sized climax in which the hero, once again and with finality, fends off another attack.

There is little need for Cobra to investigate because the villains are constantly putting themselves in his way. Through the first half of the film, the axe cult is constantly on the offensive. Violent attacks at the supermarket, in the diner parking lot and on the highway are spaced between two and five minutes apart. The longest time between action sequences is a six-minute stretch at the end of the first act, during which the police captain assigns Cobra to the case and a music video-style montage depicts his search for the killer while Ingrid models for a photo-shoot. This ends in the elaborate parking-garage attack in which the axe cult kills three men but somehow manages to leave Ingrid alive. A mere two minutes elapse before the next action sequence, a double attack in which anonymous hit men assail Cobra at his apartment while, across town, the Night Slasher kills three people at the hospital in another failed attempt to reach Ingrid. Three minutes later the axe cult attacks again, this time resulting in a pyrotechnically ornate car chase as Cobra attempts to move Ingrid to a safe house. In the first fifty minutes of running time, Stallone packs in seven scenes of axe-cult belligerence, five of which develop into full-scale action sequences.

From the midpoint on, the attacks diminish and Cobra takes charge, but crosscutting immediately begins foreshadowing the final confrontation. As soon as the team takes to the road, the plot alternates between the heroes and scenes of the cult clanging axes, loading guns and mounting motorcycles. Rather than engage the hero in a game of problem solving or investigation, the second half of Stallone's screenplay essentially elongates the onset portion of another attack. The fifteen minutes between the film's midpoint and its climactic assault feel much more like an extended build-up to the fight than an elaboration on the protagonist's quest for a goal. The axe cult, not Cobra, drives the final half of the film.

In terms of melodramatic plotting, *Cobra* repeats and varies a single situation involving the violent threat to innocents by the villain. The structure encourages us to view the plot not in terms of an active hero overcoming obstacles to reach a goal, but as an assemblage of pre-existing parts that are glued together to form a serviceably unified work. In this case, the basic building block is the violent attack, which has two stages: onset, in which the villains make themselves known to the viewer, often stalking their prey, and confrontation, in which they are usually repelled by the hero, but only after taking a few lives. The manner in which the screenplay repeats and varies this pattern resembles horror film plotting as much as a conventional action film. Indeed, the horror film had entered an exceedingly repetitive and formulaic period by the mid-1980s, typified by the slasher cycle. *Cobra*'s indebtedness to this trend is evident in the Night Slasher's attack on Ingrid in the hospital bathroom, in which she barricades herself as he hacks at the door with his knife, a scene strongly reminiscent of sequences from *Halloween* (1978), *Halloween II* (1981) and *The Shining* (1980). Repeated reference to Cobra's position on the 'zombie squad' and the Night Slasher's very name further suggest an action/horror-film hybrid. In referencing this formula, Stallone calls up the slasher film's basic Manichaeism, which presents killers as wholly unknowable, virtually unstoppable others, or, as the screenplay refers to the cult members, as 'psychos'. The axe cult is a monster terrorising Los Angeles until it targets an adversary it cannot defeat.

In applying the attack-and-defence model to *Cobra*, though, Stallone uses it to generate sturdy action-film set pieces including a car chase, a hostage standoff (at the supermarket), a race to the rescue (in the hospital), a siege (in the motel) and a final confrontation (at the steel foundry). *Cobra*'s melodramatic arbitrariness owes much to the fact that the screenplay repeatedly mobilises the same narrative device (attack and defence) to launch its standard generic sequences. If the classical model seeks to temper situations, as Borzage noted, by 'fitting them out decently' with characterisation and causal logic, *Cobra* relishes repeating and varying bald-faced conventions (see Bordwell *et al.* 1985: 14). This is not to argue that causality is absent in the screenplay, but that the situational skeleton is laid bare by its own simplicity. For Stallone, Gosling's novel provided a railway track for delivering the requisite number of thrills, not an emotionally engaging story of characters achieving goals.

An informative foil to Stallone's work of adaptation is Charlie Fletcher's screenplay from Gosling's novel for the 1995 Billy Baldwin and Cindy Crawford vehicle *Fair Game*, directed by Andrew Sipes. Fletcher's adaptation manages to fulfil basic classical requirements in a rote manner; it is a standard compromise between the genre's melodramatic base and causal storytelling, resulting in an entirely undistinguished film. By contrast, Stallone's approach welcomes arbitrary incident with enthusiasm; it celebrates the action film's heritage of situational plotting, and this may be its strength.

Fletcher's adaptation, while completely generic, makes a fair effort to establish causal connections and character development; he casts the film's situations in classical terms. In this version, tough-but-handsome city cop Max Kirkpatrick (Baldwin) protects Kate McQuean (Crawford), a beautiful civil law attorney, from a team of former KGB agents turned super criminals. The former KGB agents are out to steal billions of dollars from offshore bank accounts. Sticking marginally closer to Gosling's novel, Fletcher maintains both the romance and the killer's line of action. Kirkpatrick and McQuean investigate their hunters, and learn their identities and motive, which revolves around evidence in a divorce case that McQuean is handling. The couple's investigative progress eventually leads to Kirkpatrick's final raid on the bad guys' stronghold, and his rescue of McQuean. Unlike in *Cobra*, the heroine has a tangible connection to the criminals, and both hero and villain have fairly well-defined plans that collide in the final standoff.

Kirkpatrick's character arc is far less internal than Malcheck's in the novel, but still more developed than Cobretti's. Instead of a dark past in the military, Fletcher gives the hero an ex-girlfriend who has kicked him out of the house and left him nearly penniless. He may not have Malcheck's inner demons, but Kirkpatrick must regain his trust in romance and take a chance with McQuean, which in *Fair Game* amounts to character development. The relationship receives a good deal of screen time, climaxing in an implausible coupling aboard a speeding boxcar, interrupted when the laser sight of a bad guy's assault rifle creeps up Kirkpatrick's naked backside. By contrast, *Cobra*'s seduction scene is far less elaborate and the romance is not tied to any meaningful character or plot development. Ingrid must talk Cobra away from cleaning his guns to receive a single kiss at her bedside, and the hero's feet remain firmly on the floor. It is as though Stallone has filtered the love story through *Dirty Harry*'s vision of detached and insulated masculinity. Romantic involvement could only weaken his warrior's armour.

Meanwhile, in *Fair Game* the killer's story is elaborated, if no less clichéd. The bad guys must eliminate McQuean before they make a big transfer of funds, and they are clever problem solvers, using computers to track their prey. Where *Cobra*'s villains clang axes and ride motorcycles, in *Fair Game* the villains pursue a specified goal under a deadline. When McQuean compromises them, we spend time with the bad guys as they struggle to eliminate her. Fletcher's storyline for the villains is less developed than Gosling's, in which the killer commits two international assassinations and plays a game of cat-and-mouse with his long-time rival Malcheck. Still, it is positively intricate compared to Stallone's. The axe cult is an unadorned force of evil, a melodramatic engine purer, more potent and simpler than Fletcher's criminal gang.

Stallone's action plot is an assembly of situations and genre conventions that he has stripped of complexity and amplified with moral polarisation. Viewing *Cobra* in this light helps illuminate its debt to the *Dirty Harry* franchise. Stallone drafted Reni Santoni, who played Harry's partner Chico Gonzalez, as Cobra's partner Tony Gonzales (both are incapacitated during violent confrontations with the villain). More bizarrely, Andrew Robinson, who played Scorpio, the serial killer in the original film, appears as Detective Monte, Cobra's maniacally shrill superior on the force. Eastwood's and Stallone's characters are, of course, cut from the same generic cloth. As Eric Lichtenfeld observes: 'both ... heroes are of the action film's urban vigilante tradition; but if Harry is its archetype, then Cobra is its apotheosis' (2007: 73).

Stallone's homage to Eastwood's franchise is not merely window dressing; it allows shortcuts in storytelling. The iconic scene in which the hero is called before his disapproving superiors is a vivid example.

Like Harry, Cobra is at odds with a legal bureaucracy designed to protect suspects, but while this dynamic is built up over the course of *Dirty Harry*, it is immediately assumed at the outset of *Cobra*. If Harry proclaims 'I'm all broken up over that man's rights!' after Scorpio is released from custody owing to the violation of his Fourth Amendment civil liberties, then Cobra can declare after the very first action sequence: 'As long as we have to play by these bullshit rules and the killer doesn't, we'll lose.' Cobra is twice brought into headquarters for reprimand after major action sequences, and each scene functions like a module, plugged in as a generic marker. The first of these scenes, which takes place immediately after the hospital attack, opens with Captain Sears (Art LaFleur) shouting 'you almost got everyone killed doing it your way, now maybe you'll do it the right way' over a close-up of Cobra, beaten and sheepish. The accusation is all bluster; in fact Cobra has not taken any action beyond being attacked by the axe cult. By the end of the scene, despite having been called on the carpet, nothing has changed for Cobra. The next sequence finds him escorting Ingrid to a safe location and being attacked once again. The dressing-down scene, a moment borrowed from *Dirty Harry* and innumerable other action procedurals, is so inconsequential that it could be moved elsewhere in the screenplay with little effect. It serves to reinforce Cobra's moral superiority, gives Stallone a fleeting opportunity to indulge his famed heroic masochism, and references the genre. It does not further the plot.

The second office reprimand scene is more central to the story because it introduces Cobra's plan to take Ingrid out of Los Angeles. It is also remarkably nonsensical. In one of the plot's more glaring conveniences, Cobra's superiors refuse to believe his theory that the Night Slasher is a collective of 'psychos' rather than a lone murderer. As Lichtenfeld has pointed out, by this point in the film Cobra has killed two hit men at his apartment and been chased by two cars simultaneously, yet Detective Monte still maintains, 'this army theory sounds weak' (2007: 75). Where *Dirty Harry*'s district attorney can at least offer a rational disagreement with the hero, in *Cobra*, Monte is simply wrong for the sake of being wrong.

The scene takes another remarkable leap when Cobra defends his rationale for leaving the city. Both the novel and the draft screenplay make clear that Cobra needs to break contact with the LAPD because he suspects a mole in the department. In the final film, though, the scene fails to make this point. When asked why he would take Ingrid away from the security of the police force, Cobra replies, 'because we're dealing with fanatics who will do anything to waste her, that's why'. The police commissioner ultimately assents to Cobra's plan, reasoning that at least it might get 'those psychos' out of the city. He has apparently forgotten the aims of protecting the witness and bringing the killer to justice. The very familiarity of generic convention helps the audience leap over such logical canyons; the scene feels right as a tonal beat after an exhilarating action sequence. Like a car chase or race to the rescue, the office reprimand amounts to another building block with which Stallone can assemble his plot: a free element to be deployed with little regard to causal or procedural logic.

AMERICAN FLAGS ON CHRISTMAS TREES: THE PICTORIALISM OF GOOD AND EVIL

But if *Cobra*'s melodramatic plotting threatens to fly apart, the twin forces of Manichaeism and pictorialism unify the film. Strong imagery and moral polarities, rather than dialogue or causal plotting, are *Cobra*'s backbone. Stallone reduces crime and investigation to images of threatened innocence and righteous vengeance. In this, *Cobra* engages in melodrama's tradition of elevating spectacular pictures over the dramatic text. Ben Brewster and Lea Jacobs invoke the term 'pictorialism' (1997: 9) to describe stage melodrama's visual spectacle, which theatrical impresarios would emphasise above and beyond the organisation of story. The act-ending situations would resolve themselves into striking tableaux and spectacular effects, aiming to astound the audience with the power of stagecraft and embody the dramatic stakes of the scene. Early feature films, in Brewster and Jacobs' account, rendered the pictorial impulse through 'a new panoply of cinematic techniques' (1997: 76) involving composition and editing, but maintained the primacy of the spectacular. An inheritor of melodrama's mantle, the contemporary action film trades in visual novelty and expressive technique: modern equivalents to the on-stage ice flows and locomotive crashes of the nineteenth-century stage. The remainder of this essay explores how *Cobra*'s visual style and iconography engulfs, and in some instances replaces, its plot.

Stallone opens his screenplay with a scene that is both visually excessive and narratively efficient. On the page, he crosscuts between an assembly of cultists clanging axes in an 'abandoned warehouse basement' lit by kerosene road lanterns and the 'supermarket killer', who walks into a grocery store with a pump shotgun and opens fire. The psycho and his brethren are unconditionally evil, personified by axes, flame and skull-and-crossed-axe icons painted in the warehouse and tattooed on the killers' flesh. Once Cobra arrives, he is held outside the supermarket by Monte, who pleads with the killer to 'please communicate with us'. In answer, the cultist shoots a 'bespectacled, harmless-looking young boy of twelve' in the back, blowing him out the market's doors to the feet of the stunned policemen. In melodramatic fashion, the villain's mortal violence against a child galvanises the viewer and spurs the hero's pursuit and punishment. Cobra's righteousness is defined by his ability to swiftly meet unambiguous evil.

The final film embellishes the draft screenplay with vigorously over-the-top imagery. After Stallone's credit in red over a black frame, the film cuts to a brief prologue, in which the star intones a series of crime statistics over a shot of Cobra's ivory-handled Colt .45 turning towards the camera and firing. As Lichtenfeld has noted, this scene invokes Eastwood's aura by replaying the opening of the first *Dirty Harry* sequel, *Magnum Force* (1973). It also previews the Manichean battle that the supermarket scene will literalise. As the camera zooms and dollies out from a close-up of the king cobra face that emblazons the pistol grip, Stallone's voiceover sternly lays out the evidence of evil: 'In America, there's a burglary every 11 seconds, an armed robbery every 65 seconds, a violent crime every 25 seconds, a murder every 24 minutes, and 250 rapes a day.' The list culminates in the statistic for rape, melodrama's archetypal violation of innocence. Surpassing murder, rape is the ultimate evil, and its mention is accompanied by a quick dolly in towards the barrel of the gun just as it fires, point-blank, at the camera. Violent justice counters the threat to innocence 'in America'. The prologue offers a strictly emotional and personal appeal, not an actual background for any of the action in the film: axe-wielding psychos were not a major source of crime in America. Indeed, the scene seems to emanate from a non-diegetic netherworld between star and character. This prologue is wedged between Stallone's credit and the film's title, and he seems to directly address (and fire upon) the viewer.[5] This is the voice of the showman, and from the outset, Stallone himself signals his allegiance to the highly charged expressive pictorialism and moral clarity of melodrama.

Graphically ornate pictorialism carries the film forward through the opening act, keying viewers to expect a strong dose of melos from the next eighty minutes. A shot of a bullet speeding towards the camera smash cuts to the film's title in black caps against a blood-red sky, nicely inverting the colour scheme of the previous credits. The silhouette of a lone motorcyclist rides into this shot, framed against the red clouds. Editors James Symons and John Zimmerman craft a propulsive montage from shots of the motorcycle and of the cult clanging axes in what appears to be an empty and decrepit swimming pool standing in for the script's 'warehouse basement'. Images of the cult are nearly monochrome greys and blacks, broken only by burning trash barrels that illuminate the proceedings, and this lends hard contrast to the red-drenched motorcycle shots. The black/red contrast creates a forceful graphic opposition, and cinematographer Ric Waite supports it by shooting through a red filter when depicting details of the motorcycle. Midway through the montage, the editors begin to add flash-frames of the cult's symbol, a red spray-painted skull in front of a pair of crossed axes. With a quick cut to the same symbol tattooed on the motorcyclist's inner forearm, the editors effectively complete the assailant's character profile. He is a force of malevolence from the grim depths charging our way out of a hell-fire red sky. Little more is ever explained about the axe cult and their motivations; they are monsters defined entirely by ritual, iconography and violence. Brutal imagery stands in for exposition.

In his performance as the supermarket killer, Marco Rodríguez seethes with hatred, fully embodying the one note he has been given to play. He walks haltingly through the aisles, barely containing the explosive anger that breaches each time he brushes past a customer. In his screenplay, Stallone writes that the character 'moves catatonically ahead', and Rodríguez plays him as a single-minded automaton. But it is not enough for the villain to be evil; he must invade the site of innocence, and art directors Adrian Gorton and William Skinner achieve precise shorthand by setting the film at Christmas. The holiday setting is entirely a matter of set decoration; the screenplay does not specify the season and in the film, aside from the toy commercial that plays in Cobra's apartment, it is never mentioned or made important to the plot. Instead, Christmas time generates instantly readable emotional discord with the violence that ensues. Before the mad man arrives, we are offered a series of detail shots that establish the grocery store exterior. The first is a medium shot of a coin-operated mechanical horse in front of a mural of a Christmas tree and snow-covered village lane painted on the market window. The low synth-rumble on the score makes the image palpably foreboding. Notes of childhood innocence and quaint holiday

Americana are hit again one shot later: a father talks to his daughter as she rides a mechanical frog in front of another Christmas tree on the same snowy mural. Meanwhile, the killer rolls into the parking lot. The juxtapositions come to a head with the shooting of an innocent. The bespectacled boy in the script has been replaced by a fairly anonymous twenty-something on screen, but holiday mise-en-scène amplifies the sense of violation, as if by compensation.

At the moment Captain Sears orders Monte to 'call the Cobra', the film cuts to the killer training his gun on the hostage fleeing down the aisle. The shooting is spread across a blistering 23 shots in as many seconds. The filmmakers mix slow-motion and normal-speed shots of the victim running down the aisle towards the camera with rapid, dynamically framed glimpses of the killer, the barrel of his gun, his point-of-view down that barrel, and the muzzle flash. Red and green Christmas decorations stand out amid this spate of images. In one image that condenses all the values that the axe cult and its members threaten, the victim crashes into a Christmas tree festooned not only with the traditional glass bulbs and ribbons, but also with small American flags. The supermarket gunman is not just killing a hostage; he is abasing Christmas and the United States.

This craven display is answered, and answered immediately, when Cobra's gunmetal-grey 1950 Mercury swerves around a corner in the very next shot. From here on, the scene replays the prologue's exercise in

Figure 1 – The Christmas tree with American flags – all the values that the axe cult threatens. *Cobra.* Producers Yoram Globus and Menahem Golan; director George P. Cosmatos; DVD distributed by Warner Home Video.

crime and retribution. After crossing paths with Monte, Cobra stealthily infiltrates the market, dodging between aisles and coolly sipping a beer before throwing the can to draw the killer's fire. The hero's command of the situation is summed up in a series of overwrought compositions of Cobra making his way through gathering mists in the freezer aisle past a mother and her young child and a man in a wheelchair. Cobra is more than a policeman; he is a saviour sent to deliver the meek innocents from the clutches of evil. Stallone's inflated mythos serves well the demands of blood-and-thunder melodrama; it creates a world perfectly suited to Cobra's succinct mantra which he rehearses before dispatching the supermarket killer: 'You're a disease, and I'm the cure.' In the screenplay, Stallone sets up this line with the ranting of the killer, who proclaims 'This place is diseased. ... It's a diseased world!' The filmed version is more definitive; Cobra does not engage with the madman's rhetoric but confidently brings his diagnosis already fully formed. Indeed, the imagery has made the argument for him.

The film's opening sets the standard of visual rhetoric for the entire movie, and *Cobra*'s elevation of imagery over character and plot complexity is not limited to direct engagements of hero and villain. Though largely structured around action set pieces, *Cobra* is also a police procedural. True to Stallone's screenplay, the film consolidates most of its depiction of investigation and procedure into a single three-minute montage sequence. Elsewhere in this volume, Paul Ramaeker discusses Stallone's proclivity for the montage sequence in the films he directs. Notably, as *Cobra*'s screenwriter, Stallone builds the montage into his script, giving his director an outline to follow in depicting the hero's police work. Precedents for this kind of montage sequence were readily available in Stallone's *Rocky* films and, equally important, in Michael Mann's television series *Miami Vice*, which aired between 1984 and 1989. The series updated the television police procedural to appeal to an MTV audience that, according to one of its directors, 'is more interested in images, emotions and energy than plot and character and words' (Zoglin 1985).[6] By 1986, *Miami Vice* had become a highly rated show with the first top-selling soundtrack for a television series. The theme song topped the Billboard charts in 1985 and Glen Frey's 'You Belong to the City', which originally backed a montage of *Miami Vice* star Don Johnson walking through the streets of Miami, lingered for sixteen weeks on the charts, peaking at number two. The series' music-video model (it was referred to as 'MTV cops' within NBC) set a trend for crime films including *Cobra*, William Friedkin's *To Live and Die in L.A.*

(1985) and Michael Mann's own *Manhunter* (1986). Stallone's montage, set to Robert Tepper's 'Angel of the City', is more than a little indebted to the ground-breaking television show. *Cobra* distinguishes itself by charging the montage with a narrative load while delivering some of the strangest juxtapositions of mid-1980s popular cinema. It epitomises the film's displacement of story by style.

The 'Angel of the City' montage begins with a mechanised rhythm and synthesised drum licks over a shot of Cobra and Gonzales peeling away from the parking garage roof where Captain Sears has commanded the hero to 'do what you do best'. On each strike of the drum, editors Symons and Zimmerman cut to close-ups of gleaming chrome robots framed against a bright white background.[7] The imagery is so wholly unexpected, and so far outside the film's generic grounding, that it comes as a shock. The sequence rockets to the heights of unintentional surrealism when the robot shots are followed by images of Los Angeles vagrants sleeping, wandering and urinating on the streets. Coupled with an a-linear sequencing of events and the brazenly overt cutting on the beat, the invasion of robot imagery into this police procedural ruptures the story, immediately marking the sequence as a stylised interlude between actions.

The imagery seems to have escaped the storyteller's control, taking on a life of its own. But this narrational freedom also helps consolidate disparate strands of the story. As the montage progresses, it is brought back to the story in phases. First, shots of the homeless are revealed to be from Cobra's point of view as he patrols the streets with a spotlight mounted on his car. Next we see Cobra and Gonzales walking past a pornographic theatre at night (intercut with detail shots of a neon sign reading 'SEX'). Thematic links between the lines of action come forward when the filmmakers flash two images of robots with exaggerated chrome breasts and then cut to Cobra and Gonzales interviewing several prostitutes in front of a triple-X 24-hour movie parlour.

The narrative situation pulls into focus as the song's regular beat kicks in and the editors provide a wider shot of the robots, revealing that they are the background to Ingrid's fashion shoot. Next, the montage brings in the villains. The Night Slasher wades through a grimy gutter, amid flash cuts of his absurdly aggressive knife and of the cult clanging axes. In just over a minute of screen time, *Cobra* disorients us from its story and then reorients us to a sort of free association among the three lines of action that will shortly collide.

The scene's visual hyperbole and strangeness help cover for Cobra's

Figure 2 - Brigitte Nielsen poses among robots in a montage of wholly unexpected imagery. *Cobra.* Producers Yoram Globus and Menahem Golan; director George P. Cosmatos; DVD distributed by Warner Home Video.

and Gonzales's otherwise complete lack of investigative progress in the film. When the policemen visit a tattoo parlour, the editors use the occasion to cut between illustrations posted on the wall and quick shots of the axe cult's skull symbol spray-painted in their lair and tattooed on the forearm of the supermarket killer. The flurry of graphics is intercut with a close-up of Cobra's eyes, creating a false point-of-view structure that suggests some narratively impossible deductive work (Cobra never actually sees the axe-cult symbol and the tattoo clue never pays off). The same apparent eye-line match connects shots of Cobra to Ingrid, and this is answered by an interchange of the Night Slasher looking, also cut with Ingrid. The corresponding lyric, 'Tell me where can you be? In time I'll find you, angel of the city', creates a quasi-narrative in which the Night Slasher and Cobra are racing one another in search of Ingrid. Cobra, of course, has yet to meet Ingrid, but the suggestion of a triangle boosts the *impression* of a story, and it prepares the way for the axe cult's simultaneous attacks on our protagonists. Meanwhile, excruciatingly literal connections between lyric and image bind the sequence into an autonomous music-video unit. The 'angel of the city' refrain is always coupled with Ingrid among the robots, while the phrase 'the air is thick with dreams on fire' corresponds to a shot of Cobra and Gonzales descending a smoke-filled stairway. Perhaps most on the nose, the phrase 'livin' on the edge of a knife' accompanies a cut to a close-up of the Night Slasher sharpening his blade. The tactic forcefully identifies the sequence with mid-1980s music-video conventions (such as cutting on the beat, matching lyric and image, and striking visual contrasts) and formally isolates it from the film as a whole. At the same time, the 'Angel of the City' montage bypasses causality and plot development. Stallone uses the tools of popular cinema and television to condense the police procedure, to plaster over gaps between the lines of action, and to essentially replace story with overwrought imagery. This is not categorically deficient storytelling; rather it exemplifies one way in which melodramatic pictorialism drives Stallone's vision of the 1980s action film.

BURNING PASSIONS: *COBRA*'S INFERNAL CLIMAX

From the film's midpoint onwards, imagery simply takes over. *Cobra*'s second half is structured by the crosscutting pattern of its montage sequences to prepare for the hero's inevitable clash with the source of all evil, the Night Slasher. Music-video editing re-emerges in modified form as Cobra, Ingrid, Gonzales and Stalk drive out of Los Angeles to the beat of Jean Beauvoir's 'Feel the Heat'. The song binds together shots of axe-cult members following the heroes on motorcycles, a cultist loading his shotgun in the shadows of the cult's lair, and Cobra explaining to Ingrid 'we put 'em away, they let 'em out ... like I say, you got to tell it to the judge'. These economical two minutes clarify the situation and give Cobra another chance to telegraph *Dirty Harry*'s vigilante politics, a point that takes somewhat more dialogue in the draft screenplay. In the next several scenes, the filmmakers keep the stakes clear and the morality black-and-white, by juxtaposing glimpses of Ingrid and Cobra's accelerated courtship on the road with the axe cult's preparations and fiery rituals in their abandoned swimming pool. When Ingrid asks Cobra 'what is this place?' and he replies 'it's a foundry town', the impending confrontation has been so effectively flagged that his choice of hideout needs no further explanation: the genre audience knows that a foundry will be an ideal industrial space for the hero to dispatch his adversary. Rather than motivate or nuance convention, Stallone's screenplay wallows in it.

The turning point to the third act follows briskly: as the axe cult, now a small army, 'saddle' their cycles toting shotguns and automatics, the film cuts to Cobra's motel courtyard, which prominently features a light-up nativity scene. Once more, the forces of depravity are set to descend on the site of innocence. Two brief expositional scenes break up the montage. Cobra intercepts Stalk as she returns from a suspicious call at the courtyard pay phone. If Cobra has realised that she is the mole, he does nothing about it: the narrative thread is cited and dropped. Instead the editors move quickly back to montage, crosscutting between Cobra methodically organising his hand grenades and snapping together the parts of his JATI 9mm submachine gun, the axe-cult motorbikes speeding over rain-soaked pavement, and Ingrid lying awake. The three terms of the situation – hero, victim and villain – visually coalesce in *Cobra*'s version of the battle-preparation montage, an action-film staple. Lichtenfeld observes that the scene 'makes the assembly process a ritual, the weapon is made to embody the warrior aspect of Cobra's character … as well as of Stallone's persona' (2007: 73). The sequence builds to a climax, over a drone of synthesisers broken up by exotic percussion, when Cobra, unlit match clenched between his teeth, flicks on the laser sight he has attached to his JATI. The red light reflects off a motel mirror and bounces back onto Cobra, introducing a visual motif that will culminate in the foundry scene.

The crosscutting pauses again as Cobra grudgingly assents to Ingrid's plea that he come to bed. Their embrace, so central to both the novel and its 1995 adaptation, is perfunctory. With a thunderclap, the drone returns and a montage of characters' eyes builds to the reveal of the motorcycles cresting a hill, an extreme close-up of Cobra blinking his eyes, paired with the screech of a red-tailed hawk on the soundtrack,[8] and details of his JATI. If the expositional moments seem clumsy, the film's heart and soul is in its montage aesthetic, which forecasts the final confrontation with mythic grandeur. Like all good melodrama, *Cobra* is unabashed: weather systems and wildlife join the hero in anticipating the onslaught.

The 15-minute action climax (nearly 20 per cent of the film's total running time) packs in stock generic building blocks. It begins as a siege of the motel as the axe cult's troops stage an all-out assault of bullets and motorbikes on Cobra and Ingrid in their room. Cosmatos is an adequate action director, and each phase of the climax hits its pyrotechnic marks. Amid the welter, the iconography of church and state returns. Families bearing Christmas gifts scramble in front of a church as the motorcycles roll into town; the sheriff's office is besieged by thugs in a series of shots that foreground the American flag; and a bad guy is sent crashing into the motel's crèche. Gonzales is winged and taken out of action; Reni Santoni completes his structural role from *Dirty Harry*. The scene becomes a chase as Cobra fires at cycles from the back of a pickup driven by Ingrid. The climax slides easily into a final confrontation in the steel foundry.

The imagery reaches apocalyptic heights once the action, rather arbitrarily, moves to the foundry. The final fight in an industrial setting had solidified into a generic convention since Dirty Harry first met Scorpio in a rock quarry, and *Cobra* clearly draws on *The Terminator*'s showdown in an automated production plant, and *Commando*'s (1985) in a boiler room. Production designer Bill Kenney embellishes the architecture with copious amounts of fire. Stallone's script specifies the infernal imagery, calling for gas jets, burning melting pots, a pit of molten steel and a conveyor of giant metal hooks that move through a glowing blast furnace.[9] The plumes of fire and showers of sparks create a rather loose geography for the action to develop without strict continuity from space to space.

Cobra dispatches henchmen with a mixture of sadism and creative desperation, turning fire into a weapon when he drops a burning match on a gunman doused with gasoline and intones 'you have the right to remain silent'. The flames help cinematographer Ric Waite motivate red modelling light on Cobra and the Night Slasher's faces, externalising their burning passions. When the Night Slasher finally explains his cult's founding ideology, his utter vacuity is masked by the raging imagery. The killer proclaims: 'We are the hunters. We kill the weak so the strong survive. You can't stop the new world. Your filthy society will never get rid of people like us. It's breeding them. We are the future!'

Figure 3 - Red modelling light on Sylvester Stallone externalizes his burning passion. *Cobra*. Producers Yoram Globus and Menahem Golan; director George P. Cosmatos; DVD distributed by Warner Home Video.

Figure 4 - Good annihilates evil as the Night Slasher (Brian Thompson) careens into a blast furnace. Writer Sylvester Stallone wields heavy-duty images. *Cobra*. Producers Yoram Globus and Menahem Golan; director George P. Cosmatos; DVD distributed by Warner Home Video.

The Night Slasher's empty and illogical sloganeering is buoyed up by the graphic inferno that surrounds him. When Cobra responds with the quip 'no, you're history', he steps into a deep scarlet side light, and, in a quick cut, trains his red laser sight on the camera. The burst of chroma punctuates his move and carries its emotion. Moments later Cobra fires back at the Night Slasher's taunts with the couplet 'this is where the law stops and I start, sucker' as the camera alternates between the opponents' faces covered in sweat and framed by fire. After a struggle at the edge of a lake of molten steel, the sequence's visual bombast crests when Cobra impales his nemesis on a giant hook and sends him careering into the blast furnace, his silhouette consumed by flame in slow-motion. Good has annihilated evil. As a popular auteur, Stallone wields heavy-duty images.

CONCLUSION

Pictorialism, Manichaeism and situational plot structures may well be the foundation of many early 1980s action films, but few are so fiercely excessive as *Cobra*. In some respects, Stallone's film finds its brethren not in Hollywood but among Hong Kong's flourishing genre cinema of the same decade. *Cobra* approaches what David Bordwell calls the 'audacious exhilaration' and unabashed conviction in cliché of John Woo's crime films of the 1980s, and may indeed have influenced them (2000: 106, 108).[10] In the heat of Hong Kong's copycat cinema, Chow Yun Fat's fondness for firearms, trench coats and chomping on unlit matchsticks in *A Better Tomorrow* (1986) seems scarcely removed from Stallone's imagery, which hit screens three months earlier. Unlike Woo, who filtered and intensified Hollywood conventions through an outsider's lens, Stallone sought differentiation from within the heart of the American industry. Yet his means of invention are very much the same: to simultaneously strip down and inflate the action genre through the resources of melodrama. *Cobra* may not be a great film, it may not even be a good film, but it remains a remarkable distillation of the action-cop movie. Ultimately in its conventionalism, and lack of character or plot complexity, the film was on its way to being outdated. It could not spawn a franchise as *Dirty Harry* did, or *Lethal Weapon* (1987) and *Die Hard* (1988) would. But it shows Stallone to be a canny producer and crafter of image, who could crystallise trends by dwelling within popular cinema's melodramatic fundament.

NOTES

1   Tasker's *Action and Adventure Cinema* (2004) collects essays on early film melodrama by Bean and Ben Singer. Neale (2000) provides a useful overview of the genre. None of this work dwells on connections between the contemporary genre and the nineteenth-century theatrical tradition, but all of it affirms the need for further investigation.

2   *Fair Game* was first published in the UK under the title *A Running Duck* in 1974, and retitled for release in the US in 1978. In this chapter I make reference to a 1996 paperback rerelease, which was a market tie-in with the film *Fair Game* (1995).

3   These two elements are, of course, largely responsible for the long-term success of Cameron's franchise, as each instalment in the *Terminator* series replays the central plotline of attack and defence, while also complicating the science fiction frame story and tracing the effects of Sarah and Reese's romantic coupling.

4   Throughout I make reference to the film's theatrical release and to a draft of the screenplay labelled 'Final Draft' and dated 17 October 1985.

5   The conflation of star and character was a point of the film's poster, which centred the words 'STALLONE COBRA' in the bottom third of the image as though it was the film's title.

6   Zoglin's comments on *Miami Vice*'s style and narrative could well apply to *Cobra*: 'With its rich, almost operatic texture and stripped-down story lines, *Miami Vice* has brought TV's cops-and-robbers genre back to its roots: the mythic battle between good and evil.'

7   The robots are found and reused object sculptures by American artist Clayton Bailey. Bailey explains that Stallone and Brigitte Nielsen discovered his robot sculptures at the Henry Gallery in Seattle and decided to give them a role in the film. See Clayton Bailey's website (www.claytonbailey.com) for more detail.

8   The screech of the red-tailed hawk is a standard effect used by sound designers in place

of an eagle cry, because it is louder and more elongated.

9   Lichtenfeld quotes production designer Jackson DeGovia's description of the conventional industrial space as 'Orpheus-into-the-underworld, where evil comes from' and concludes that the foundry in *Cobra* is 'what Hell would be like if Hell were a union shop' (2007: 76).

10 Stallone's film differs from the Hong Kong tradition in its lack of the sincere pathos with which Woo turns his acrobatic gunfights into full-fledged male weepies.

BIBLIOGRAPHY

Bailey, Clayton (2010) 'A Short Chronology of the Artist's Life'. Online. Available HTTP: http://www.claytonbailey.com/chronology.htm (2 June 2010).

Bean, Jennifer (2004) 'Trauma Thrills: Notes on Early Action Cinema', in Yvonne Tasker (ed.) *Action and Adventure Cinema*. New York: Routledge, 17–30.

Bordwell, David (2000) *Planet Hong Kong: Popular Cinema and the Art of Entertainment*. Cambridge, MA: Harvard University Press.

Bordwell, David, Janet Staiger, and Kristin Thompson (1985) *The Classical Hollywood Cinema: Film Style and Mode of Production to 1960*. New York: Columbia University Press.

Brewster, Ben and Lea Jacobs (1997) *Theatre to Cinema*. New York: Oxford University Press.

Gosling, Paula (1996 [1974]) *Fair Game*. New York: Little, Brown.

Higgins, Scott (2008) 'Suspenseful Situations: Melodramatic Narrative and the Contemporary Action Film', *Cinema Journal*, 47.2, 74–96.

Lichtenfeld, Eric (2007) *Action Speaks Louder: Violence, Spectacle, and the American Action Movie*. Revised and expanded edition. Middletown, CT: Wesleyan University Press.

Martell, William C. (2000) *The Secrets of Action Screenwriting*. Revised edition. Los Angeles: First Strike Productions.

Neale, Stephen (2000) *Genre and Hollywood*. New York: Routledge.

Singer, Ben (2001) *Melodrama and Modernity: Early Sensational Cinema and Its Contexts*. New York: Columbia University Press.

____ (2004) '"Child of Commerce! Bastard of Art!": Early Film Melodrama', in Yvonne Tasker (ed.) *Action and Adventure Cinema*. New York: Routledge, 52–70.

Stallone, Sylvester (1985) *Cobra*. Final Draft, 17 October.

Tasker, Yvonne (1993) *Spectacular Bodies: Gender, Genre, and the Action Cinema*. London: Routledge.

____ (2004) *Action and Adventure Cinema*. New York: Routledge.

Williams, Linda (2001) *Playing the Race Card*. Princeton: Princeton University Press.

Zoglin, Richard (1985) 'Cool Cops, Hot Show', *Time Magazine*, 16 September. Online. Available HTTP: http://www.time.com/time/magazine/article/0,9171,959822,00.html (10 August 2010).

I, OF THE TIGER:
SELF AND SELF-OBSESSION
IN THE ROCKY SERIES

ERIC LICHTENFELD

There is a tale Sylvester Stallone was fond of telling. It is 1975 and
Stallone, an aspiring writer and actor, is nearly broke. For his 29th
birthday, he gives himself permission to finally write what appeals to
him: stories of heroism and triumph – the kind of screenwriting that the
New Hollywood had largely displaced. With the last of his entertainment money, he watches a closed-circuit broadcast of ranked but little
regarded Chuck Wepner virtually going the distance with heavyweight
champion Muhammad Ali. Stallone sees how the unknown's resolve
invigorates the audience. And Rocky Balboa is conceived (see United
Artists 1976: 6).

In the story, Stallone writes the first draft of *Rocky* (1976) in three
days; producers offer to buy it; Stallone refuses to sell unless he can
play the title character; the amount of money offered climbs. Stallone
holds fast – even though he has only $106 in the bank, a pregnant wife
and an angry landlord. Ultimately, producers Robert Chartoff and Irwin
Winkler persuade United Artists to gamble a meagre budget ($1 million)
on the film with Stallone in the lead (see United Artists 1976: 1–4).[1]

The reality of *Rocky*'s creation is more nuanced. Stallone's legendary three-day writing fit followed a nearly year-long 'inspiration' and
'incubation' phase (Klemesrud 1976: 111). Stallone had already sold
a script about a loveable club fighter (*Hell's Kitchen*, later to become
Paradise Alley) and unveiled *Rocky* only after it became advantageous
to shoulder aside that script's original producers (see Suppa 1996: 6–9).
Finally, Stallone turned 29 on 6 July – months after Wepner fought
Ali (on 24 March). Still, the lore has endured. The tale is compelling –
even by Hollywood standards – and from it, two icons were born: the

character of Rocky Balboa and the personage of Sylvester Stallone. The fact that they emerged jointly adds resonance to how Stallone articulated *Rocky*'s dramatic stakes: 'The quest for recognition ... that's what "Rocky's" about' (Kilday 1977: F1).

This quest – for recognition, validation, *self* – is *Rocky*'s central concern and is the most holistic attribute of the entire franchise. The series (1976, 1979, 1982, 1985, 1990, 2006) is a rare one in that its star is also its creator, exclusive writer and frequent director. Thus, this essay considers the films' obsession with Rocky's *self* in the variety of modes Stallone uses to give it expression: visual, verbal, narrative, performative and iconographic (as well as its central place in the films' marketing and publicity). The essay also examines this preoccupation in the broader, more thematic contexts these modes serve, including patriotism, other-ness, martyrdom and the salvation Rocky offers the supporting characters.

Of course, I use terms such as 'self' and 'narcissism' not as they are used in psychoanalytic theory or practice, but as they are commonly understood. Still, it is worth pausing to note a serendipitous bit of etymology. The English word *ego* is derived from the German term Sigmund Freud coined as an umbrella for the various words he used to discuss both the self as it is experienced (in English, 'I', 'me') and its 'underlying psychic structures and functions' ('ego'). In German, this is *das Ich*. In French, *le moi*. In Spanish, it is, fittingly, *el yo* (see Spruiell 1995: 421).

'THAT UNKNOWN IS YOU'

In *Rocky*, the title character's 'quest for recognition' begins with the viewer's search for him within the frame. Director John G. Avildsen (who would win an Academy Award for his efforts) and cinematographer James Crabbe merge Rocky and his environment with the opening scene: a club fight in which Rocky crudely bests the washed-up Spider Rico. Photographed from outside the ring, Rocky appears in shadows, with his back to us. Even between rounds, when Rocky is seated in his corner, his face is partially concealed.

With Rocky established as an artless brawler, the opening credits begin, taking us through Rocky's walk home. With the images underexposed, it is difficult to see Rocky – or very much else. To whatever extent Rocky is defined, he is an extension (or manifestation) of his environment. Underscoring this link, one detail that does draw the eye is the garbage-strewn sidewalks. Soon, however, the balance between the fighter and his environment tips. As Rocky enters his apartment, the film stresses his surroundings, and the stress they exert on him. In a long shot, Rocky stands by his refrigerator. In the foreground, a lampshade augments the distance between the camera and Rocky, making him appear even smaller. Rocky approaches us to feed his turtles. Though he grows in stature, he is now pinned in a vertical composition, between the lampshade and the turtles' bowl.

The environment further suggests Rocky's insignificance when we see Rocky working at his actual vocation: muscle to loan shark Tony Gazzo (Joe Spinelli). After Rocky fails to collect on a debt, he walks off, towards a ship that visually dwarfs him. A match-cut then frames a diminished Rocky between a bridge and an elevated train, another industrial background. In this couplet of shots, the mise-en-scène makes more explicit that which Rocky's apartment implies: Rocky's marginalisation is rooted in the existential and also in the economics of the community (South Philadelphia, and by extension, mid-1970s America). At the conclusion of the scene, Rocky walks away as the camera zooms out, reducing Rocky in size against the environment around him. Again, Rocky is harder for the eye to track.

This visual motif dovetails with one of the film's verbal ones. When others ask about his fight with Spider Rico, Rocky answers: 'You should have seen me.' By saying this four times in less than six minutes, Rocky is saying more than 'You should have seen me fight'. He is also saying – insisting – 'I am *here*; someone should have *seen me*'. This corresponds to a quirk of Stallone's performance: often finishing his lines with a tossed-off 'you know?' or 'y'know what I mean?' More than a by-product of the performance's naturalism, this idiosyncrasy betrays Rocky's yearning to be heard. Notably, this trend wanes as Rocky becomes more grounded in his relationships with others, and in his sense of self.

In the screenplay (also nominated for an Academy Award), the concern with Rocky's self runs deeper than verbal affectation. It is structural. *Rocky*, like most mainstream American cinema, has three acts. Films conforming to this structure typically feature a break between Acts I and II around the half-hour mark, and a break between Acts II and III, between 70 and 90 minutes into the running time (see McKee 1997: 217–21). In *Rocky*, both act breaks are delineated not by major plot developments, but by acts of self-assessment. The second of these transitions is Rocky's soliloquy, on the sleepless night before the climactic fight. Here, he recognises that if he can go the distance with Apollo, then he will know he is more than 'just another bum from the neighbourhood'. The significance of the speech is underscored – and enhanced – by the camera's slow zoom-in on Rocky as he speaks. This realisation resonates with how the community has defined Rocky all along, established for us by a fight attendee's derision ('You're a bum! You're a bum, you know that? You're a bum!') not even four minutes into the film. More fundamentally, however, the speech represents a departure, as Rocky becomes the agent of his own definition.

By asserting this mastery, Rocky also answers the question that ends Act I. This earlier moment comes after Rocky tries to counsel 13-year-old Marie on the value of having self-respect, of making nice friends, of using nice language. When she rejects his help, Rocky turns away and repeats her slur. 'Who are you to give advice to anyone, creepo?' he asks himself, 'Who are you?'

Some might hesitate to identify this seemingly incidental beat as the film's first structural pillar. Yet the moment falls just over 28 minutes into the film's 119-minute running time. Also, the film then cuts to Apollo Creed (Carl Weathers) in a scene that establishes Apollo's need to find a new opponent. One could argue that Apollo's scene marks the act break, as it establishes the plotline that will change Rocky's life, but the seemingly innocuous 'Who are you?' remains the better candidate. Firstly, identity is more central to the film than is boxing. Secondly, the cutaway to Apollo marks the first time we leave Rocky. Thus, the audience experiences this moment as an actual break, a fundamental change.

Rocky will not receive Apollo's challenge for nearly 30 more minutes, or 56 minutes into the picture. Typically, the one-hour mark represents a film's midpoint, the point at which the hero stops being *re*active and becomes *pro*active. *Rocky* uses the time between the end of Act I and the midpoint to contrast the future opponents. Apollo's scenes indicate what is to come, and therefore drive the narrative's forward momentum. Rocky's scenes, on the other hand, are vignettes that simply reinforce the personal and societal lack that attend his everyday life. These scenes advance what might just appear to be the sub-plot: Rocky's courtship of Adrian (Talia Shire). This structuring reveals a deep irony: the first half of *Rocky* unspools more like a post-war neorealist film than the modern-day David-and-Goliath tale the movie has become in public memory. But while American cinema of the 1970s was strongly influenced by neorealism, *Rocky* subtly inverts one of the movement's core values.

Neorealists used the individual as a lens through which to focus the image of a time, a place, a people; ultimately, *Rocky* uses a time, place and people as a platform from which to elevate its title character.[2]

Once Rocky asks, 'Who are you?' the rest of the series agitates over this question. Writing and directing *Rocky II* (1979), Stallone furthers his use of supporting characters to define Rocky. The best example may be his trainer and manager Mickey Goldmill (Burgess Meredith), who addresses Rocky in two ways. One is admonishment: 'You got the heart but you ain't got the tools no more'; 'you're training like a damn bum! ... Go back to the docks, where you belong. You go back to being a two-bit nothing ... 'cause I'm too old to waste my time trying to train a no-good loser like you, you *bum!*' The other is with reverence: 'You got guts to go back in the ring with him, kid'; '[Apollo] said you're a one-time lucky *bum*. ... I think you're a *hell* of a lot more than that, kid. A *hell of a lot*.'

During the climactic rematch, Mickey's preoccupation with Rocky's essence emerges even more clearly. After round one, Stallone cuts between the opposing corners where Mickey and Apollo's manager, Duke (Tony Burton), each tries to rally his fighter. Duke's dialogue consists of, 'Did the switching bother you? ... You shoulda had him. ... [D]on't let up on this man; this man is dangerous.' Mickey, however, declares, 'You can't be hurt. ... You can't be hurt 'cause you are too tough. ... You can beat him 'cause you're a champion. You're a greasy, fast, 200-pound Italian tank.' The contrast between Duke's dialogue and Mickey's may be subtle, but Stallone's intercutting brings it into raised relief: whereas Duke's dialogue is more grounded in strategy, Mickey's stresses who and what Rocky *is*.

Apollo also expresses the films' fixation on Rocky's identity. In fact, Apollo makes Rocky's name – the cornerstone of identity – central to challenging him: 'I know a lot of people out there wanna see me in a rematch with a timid fellow who *calls himself* the Italian Stallion. But this man does not have the honour to meet me in the [ring.] Or is it "scallion"? What's his name? What *is* your name?' (emphasis in original).

But as Rocky and Apollo's relationship evolves over the series, so does Apollo's function in defining Rocky. In *Rocky III* (1982), Apollo becomes Rocky's trainer following Mickey's death and Rocky's defeat at the fists of Clubber Lang (Mr. T). 'You lost that fight for all the wrong reasons', Apollo admonishes. 'You lost your edge.' During this exchange, held in the haunted space of Mickey's gym, director Stallone frames Apollo in close-ups, his head seeming to float out of the darkness. Rocky appears in better-lit medium shots. Compositionally, Stallone privileges Apollo. Dramatically, however, the effect of Apollo's greater stature is to put more pressure on Rocky, and increase the viewer's identification with him.

Apollo steers Rocky to a comeback that is all the more triumphant because it requires Rocky to conquer both another fighter and his own trauma. 'I'm proud of you', Apollo says before the final fight. 'It takes a hell of a man to change.' Strangely, however, Apollo takes the opposite position while defining Rocky in the next film. Early in *Rocky IV* (1985), Apollo accepts a challenge to face Soviet champion Ivan Drago (Dolph Lundgren) in what will be a fatal exhibition bout. As Rocky and Apollo watch their own fight footage, Rocky tries to dissuade his friend with his own assessment of what they are: 'That's not us no more. We're changing. We're like turning into regular people.' Apollo then counters:

> Maybe you **think** you're changing, but you can't change what you really are. ... [W]e're born with a killer instinct that you can't just turn off and on like some radio. We have to be right in the middle of the action 'cause we're the warriors. And without ... some damn war to fight, then the warrior may as well be dead...

Apollo's contradictory stands represent more than a breakdown of continuity. One of the functions Apollo serves in *Rocky IV* is to argue what Rocky alone can disprove, to be wrong so Rocky can be right. Adrian also serves this function, as she has before. Her opposition to the rematch in *Rocky II* ('The doctor said you shouldn't fight anymore') is amplified in *IV* ('*You can't win!*'). These oppositions exist as a crucible for the forging of Rocky. Notably, *Rocky III* finds Adrian *encouraging* Rocky's rematch with Lang – but only when Rocky has given up on himself. While this may seem to invert their dynamic in *II* and *IV*, it actually maintains her role as the flint *against which* Rocky's self is sharpened.

AN EYE FOR AN I

As a complement to how the supporting characters tell Rocky who he is, Rocky also keeps counsel with his own likeness. This is embodied in Rocky's engagement with mirrors and other forms of his image. The series introduces this motif early in the first film. After Rocky feeds his turtles, he stares at a photograph of himself (an actual picture of

Figure 1 - Portrait of the pugilist as a young man: the Italian Stallion (Sylvester Stallone) contemplates himself in an early scene from *Rocky*. Producers Robert Chartoff and Irwin Winkler; director John G. Avildsen; DVD distributed by 20th Century Fox Home Entertainment.

Stallone) wedged into the frame of his mirror. The camera zooms in, creating a sense of the psychological pressure building within Rocky as he considers himself.

Rocky's image, as seen through his own eyes, has the power to shame or motivate, depending on the narrative's needs in a given scene. While still trying to court Adrian, Rocky offers to walk her home from her job at the neighbourhood pet store. 'There's a lot of creeps around here. Every other block has a creep. You can always tell a creep', he insists. During the speech, much of which Stallone delivers with his face hidden from view, the camera pans to find Rocky's reflection in a distant mirror. The smallness of Rocky's reflection in this unusually awkward composition, along with his insistent repetition of the epithet, suggests that Rocky's disgust with the neighbourhood 'creeps' is compounded by his fear that he is one.

The series uses mirrors more overtly in *Rocky III* and *IV*. The latter recalls the original film's moment in which Rocky considered his photograph alongside his reflection. Inside his Russian farmhouse training camp, Rocky places two pictures in his bedroom mirror: a photograph of his son and a newspaper clipping of Drago. The scene concludes with a zoom-in on Drago's likeness, from which Stallone launches the first of two almost adjoining training montages. During the second montage, Rocky's hand crumples Drago's picture, revealing his own reflection. Before the montages, however, Stallone uses shots of the mirror to bracket Duke's motivational speech: 'You're the one. You're the one that's gonna keep [Apollo's] spirit alive. You're the one that's gonna make sure that he didn't die for nothing. ... [I]n the end, I know you'll be the one standing.' Here, Stallone's quest to define Rocky is manifested not only in Duke's dialogue, but also in Burton's performance. His slight emphasis on, and pauses after, each 'you're the one' vaults the phrase from mere repetition to rhetorical device.

In *Rocky III*, Apollo's attempt to motivate Rocky is also linked to mirror imagery. His admonishment 'There *is no* tomorrow!' echoes three times over a triptych of images: Apollo, Adrian and, finally, Rocky looking in the mirror. Stallone then cuts to a tighter, over-the-formidable-shoulder close-up of Rocky's reflection. Later, as Rocky becomes physically and psychologically stronger, he and Apollo practice footwork before a full-length mirror. The sequence's final composition consists mainly (from right to left) of Apollo, Rocky and Rocky's reflection.

Rocky IV recycles these images (along with that of Rocky considering his childhood picture in the first film) in an angst-driven music-video montage of Rocky's memories. While the sequence is propelled by the matching of action shots, the repurposed mirror imagery stands out. Projecting his reflection onto the screen of his memory, Rocky visualises himself *looking at* himself – a Russian doll of self-regard.

The series surrounds Rocky with other, more symbolic representations, often as shaming devices. In *Rocky*, the triumphant training sequence is quickly followed by his soulful, even mournful, assessment of his chances and of his station. Stallone bridges these otherwise incongruent scenes with Rocky's visit to the ring where he and Apollo will fight. Two angles show Rocky dwarfed by his surroundings – including the huge portraits of Rocky and Apollo hanging overhead. Rocky-the-man is outmatched by Rocky-the-image. Moreover, when he tells the promoter that in his portrait, the shorts are painted the wrong colour, the promoter answers, 'that really doesn't matter, does it?' Through Stallone's performance, we see that Rocky now understands he is only a commodity.

Stallone similarly exploits the disconnect between Rocky and his image in *Rocky II*. Before accepting Apollo's challenge, Rocky lowers himself to cleaning Mickey's gym, which is adorned with promotional images from the fight with Apollo. When Gazzo appears and Rocky rejects his invitation to reclaim his old job, the loan shark glances at Rocky's portrait. 'Remember that guy, Rock?' he asks. This marks an inversion: whereas *Rocky* uses the likeness to represent the hero Rocky is not, this moment uses his likeness to represent the hero he is no longer. As screenwriter, Stallone's motivations are naked: Gazzo's offer justifies the scene, but is a pretence. The scene's true purpose is its shaming climax.

Rocky II ends with Rocky's victory. *Rocky III* begins with a montage establishing his growing fame and wealth. The film goes on to depict the corrosive effect celebrity can have on one's character – a theme also touched upon in the previous instalments. But whereas *Rocky* and *Rocky II* distinguish mainly between Rocky and more literal renderings of his likeness, *Rocky III* is studded with representations that are more abstract, symbolic or commercialised. One example is a pinball machine. The backglass artwork features Rocky with his arms upraised, and duplicates the pose in the 'Y' of Rocky's name. Significantly, this is the pose known to audiences from the first film's famous training sequence. Thus, the image is iconic both in the films' fictive universe and on the audience's side of the screen.

Rocky III makes pointed use of Rocky's commercialisation with its first training sequence, which all but doubles as a fan convention. In a rented hotel ballroom, admirers meet Rocky and buy buttons, balloons and other merchandise under a neon 'ROCKY' sign. Prominently featured in the mise-en-scène is an enormous, semi-expressionistic portrait of a bare-chested Rocky wearing his championship belt. This depiction of Rocky – cobbled together from splashes of muted colour – is further exaggerated by the severe low angle in which Stallone frames it.

Stallone takes the quest for Rocky's recognition into still other media when the city unveils a statue of Rocky atop the steps of the Philadelphia Museum of Art, a setting made famous by *Rocky*'s training montage. Before the unveiling, the mayor makes a reverential speech:

Every once in a while, a person comes along who defies the odds, who defies logic, and fulfils an incredible dream. On behalf of all the citizens of Philadelphia, and the many who have been touched by your accomplishments and your untiring participation in this city's many charity functions, it is with tremendous honour that we present this memorial, which will stand always as a celebration to the indomitable spirit of man. Philadelphia salutes its favourite son: Rocky Balboa!

Though the speech speaks for itself, we may pause to note that it is written by Stallone and about his own alter ego. More interesting still are Rocky's reactions and the statue's design. Throughout the speech, Rocky appears uncomfortable, and when the statue is revealed, he is surprised.

Figure 2 - Positive self-image: a half-ton bronze statue of the champion is dedicated in *Rocky III*. Producers Robert Chartoff and Irwin Winkler; director Sylvester Stallone; DVD distributed by 20th Century Fox Home Entertainment.

This stretches credulity (after all, what did Rocky think the ceremony was for?) while also suggesting Stallone's shrewdness. The character's humility is his writer-actor-director's *false* humility, undoubtedly designed to endear Rocky to viewers. In contrast with Rocky's unease is the statue, arms flung upward in the pose from the museum steps. As with the pinball machine, Stallone is placing the status he and Rocky share into a feedback loop: an image from the first film becomes so iconic, it becomes part of the franchise's diegesis, which cements its stature in viewers' eyes.[3]

'HE LOOKS LIKE A BIG FLAG'

Though the series is deeply vested in representations of Rocky, each film proves the man is bigger than his own iconography. He must therefore be represented by still greater symbols. Chief among them is the American flag. More than merely signifying patriotism, this underpins the series' conflation of the Italian Stallion with the United States. *Rocky* establishes this motif by couching Rocky's once-in-a-lifetime chance in a sentimentalising (and exploitation) of America as the land of opportunity. Visually, the motif finds expression in the American flag shorts Apollo wears and that later become Rocky's. In *Rocky III* (a film trumpeted by its trailer as 'an American tradition'), Rocky wears the shorts for his rematch against Clubber Lang. They are used more pointedly in *IV*, when Rocky faces the Russian fighter and, by extension, the Soviet empire.

In *Rocky III* and *IV*, the shorts signal the American-ness of Rocky, and, by contrast, the other-ness of his opponent. Compared to the fourth instalment, *Rocky III* defines Rocky, in part, through a subtler, but more insidious xenophobia. Whereas Drago is a bona fide *other* (at least in terms of nationality), Lang is an American – although 'native' might be a more apt label. Lang, an African American, sports Native American iconography – specifically, a Mohawk and Indian feathers. This, combined with Lang's wild-man violence and his sexual aggression towards Adrian, puts him in league with frontier-era fears of Native Americans that would later be applied to African Americans. Thus, when Rocky wears the American flag shorts in their rematch, the imagery suggests a contest not between two Americans, but rather between an American and a savage.

This other-ness is more explicit in *IV*. From Drago's introduction, underscored by an ominous, synthesised drone, Stallone renders him as a mindless automaton. For instance, while fighting Apollo, Drago strikes only when triggered by a cutaway to his trainer shouting. The abruptness of the cut and the power of the ensuing onslaught – along with later images of Drago being technologically and chemically enhanced – depict Drago as a dangerous instrument being controlled and manipulated: the Manchurian Heavyweight. Rocky, by contrast, is a rugged individual and frontiersman, an American ideal.

Of course, *Rocky IV* represents the peak of the franchise's patriotic zeal, but the seeds were always germinating. In fact, reviewing *Rocky II*, Frank Rich sarcastically – but no less prophetically – suggests that 'one almost expects [Rocky] to wrap himself in the flag: perhaps he is saving that *pièce de résistance* for *Rocky III*' (1979: n.p.). The critic would be off by one Roman numeral, but in fairness to Rich, *Rocky III* was conceived to pit Rocky against a Russian boxer in the Coliseum. As the project developed, Stallone chose instead to explore his ambivalence towards his post-*Rocky* success. 'I used those emotions to get back to the person I was before all the glamour and notoriety', he would tell *Time* magazine. 'Rocky is a once-in-a-lifetime coming together of self and character' (in Reed 1982: 60).

Rocky IV was so nationalistic, a United Artists marketing memo suggested theatres distribute American flags to moviegoers before each performance (1985: 30). The value the film places on patriotism is established with the main title as Stallone cuts between two boxing gloves revolving towards each other. On their reverse sides, one is adorned with the Stars and Stripes; the other with a hammer and sickle. This imagery is notable for its place in the evolution of the franchise's title sequences. *Rocky*'s main title is simple: the word 'Rocky', in white, scrolling over blackness. The main title of *Rocky II* utilises yellow lettering on black, establishing the colour palette that will characterise much of the film and dominate its final sequence. *Rocky III* opens with the title scrolling over a championship belt, uniting language and iconography. With the opening of *Rocky IV*, however, this balance is upended. Iconography trumps language – much as the film privileges montages and music videos over narrative and character development.

Indeed, several of the film's music videos embody its nationalism. When Rocky arrives in Russia to begin training, the song 'Burning Heart' (written and performed by Survivor, the band famous for *Rocky III*'s 'Eye of the Tiger') drives the soundtrack. An early verse conflates the personal with the national: 'Does the crowd understand? / Is it East versus West / Or man against man? / Can any nation stand alone?'

More overtly patriotic is the song 'Living in America'. Performed by James Brown, the song includes a celebratory roll call of American cities and the promise that 'somewhere on the way / you might find out who you are'. In the film, Brown's performance is an opening act for Apollo's fight with Drago. With Apollo dressed in the Uncle Sam regalia from *Rocky*, the scene recalls Apollo's patriotic display in the original film. Moreover, 'Living in America' was a pillar of *Rocky IV*'s marketing and ancillary revenue. Of all the potential hit singles featured on the soundtrack album, this song (originally titled 'Only in America') was the second track released, timed to coincide with the film's Thanksgiving opening (see United Artists 1985: 18).

Ultimately, Rocky proves that patriotism is not something one performs, but something one embodies. Having won the hearts and minds of the Russian crowd, Rocky is lifted and wrapped in the American flag. This marks the film's most iconic image. Indeed, it is the sole image on *Rocky IV*'s theatrical poster (and by extension, the front covers of the soundtrack, the novelisation and, later, the home video packaging). Notably, this poster is the only one in the series that has no tagline. In this advertising material, as in the film, the action speaks for itself.

Perhaps even more noteworthy is the film's final image: Rocky's face framed by the flag, held in a freeze-frame for twelve seconds as the end credits roll. Just as important as the image's duration is its composition. On one side of Rocky's head appear the stars; on the other, the stripes.

Figure 3 - The draped white hope: the American flag frames an American champion (Sylvester Sylvester Stallone) in the final image of *Rocky IV*. Producers Robert Chartoff and Irwin Winkler; director Sylvester Stallone; DVD distributed by 20th Century Fox Home Entertainment.

Thus, Rocky is not merely backed by the flag (as he is during the fight in *Rocky II*); he becomes one of its compositional elements. The flag becomes a triptych – with Rocky occupying the centre position, no less. The image may seem to balance narcissism and nationalism, but the balance is tipped when one considers that by wrapping himself in the flag, Stallone violates three provisions of the United States Flag Code, which articulates how the flag should – and should not – be handled, and which Congress adopted as federal law in 1942.[4]

YOU CAN'T SPELL *MESSIANIC* WITHOUT *ME*

The exultation of this finale comprises twin facets: pain and glory. Thus *Rocky IV* concludes by embodying martyrdom and the messianic – two of the franchise's other thematic mainstays, and lenses through which Stallone continually views and magnifies Rocky's self. On the most immediate level, we witness the extreme suffering Rocky withstands. In *Rocky III*, for instance, Rocky is not merely defeated; he is literally toppled. In the rematch, Lang's hooks are augmented by plainly artificial *whooshes* meant to impress upon us their lethality. Rocky's suffering is further stylised in *Rocky Balboa* (2006), when Rocky faces champion Mason 'The Line' Dixon (then light heavyweight champion Antonio Tarver), whose very name suggests a gauntlet that Rocky must cross. During the fight, Stallone utilises spot-colourised black-and-white footage. In one instance, Rocky's corner contains just a dash of yellow, and, more prominently, the red of Rocky's blood. Of course, the prototype for the series' contests is the first film's bout. While Avildsen relies less on such overtly cinematic devices, Rocky's goal of going the distance means, by definition, that he must suffer for all fifteen rounds, the maximum time possible.[5]

Throughout the series, Stallone martyrs Rocky not only in battle, but also in his preparations for it. Images of training satisfy the expository need to show Rocky building his muscles, but moreover, they suggest he is preparing his heart, purifying himself through pain. Analysing action cinema's tendency to martyr and marginalise its heroes, Rikke Schubart gathers these conventions and others under what she calls the genre's 'passion plot', both implicitly and overtly acknowledging the sacrifice of Jesus as the archetype (2001: 192).[6]

A particularly Christological image of martyrdom is seen in *Rocky II*, as Rocky performs lunges with a massive log laid across his shoulders. Its effect is bolstered by how the sequence follows another form of sacrifice: the vigil Rocky keeps over a comatose Adrian. His refusal to train, to see their newborn son or to leave the hospital is rendered even more pointed when Paulie (Burt Young), who 'can't do any more of this watching stuff', leaves his sister's bedside. Even in keeping vigil, Rocky is the one who goes the distance. This is echoed in *Rocky Balboa* when Paulie decides he can no longer join Rocky on his annual tour of landmarks from Rocky and the now-deceased Adrian's relationship. Here, however, Stallone implies that Paulie is correct, thereby inverting and critiquing the corresponding scene in *Rocky II*.

The suffering Rocky withstands on-screen is mirrored by what Stallone would endure off-camera – and mine for publicity grist. The films would often be trumpeted by press accounts detailing the extreme training and dieting (that is, exertion and deprivation) Stallone had suffered. Stallone's comments in one such piece (see Smith 1979: n.p.), promoting *Rocky II*, is illustrative:

> I was working with Franco Columbo. ... Mr. Olympics, I think he is called. ... At the end of a workout he said, 'Let's see you bench-press 200 pounds'. I said, 'I'm kind of tired and I hate to press', but he said, 'Just once', so I laid back and pressed 200. 'Try 210', he said. I didn't want to, but he insisted, so I did. 'Now 220', and I said, 'Franco, knock it off'. 'Just once', he said, so I tried 220 pounds and the weight fell on me and I heard a pop. The pain was something awful and pretty soon the arm turned black. I had to go to the doctor. 'Look',

Figure 4 - Let us worship: Rocky (Sylvester Stallone) martyrs himself during a training sequence from *Rocky II*. Producers Robert Chartoff and Irwin Winkler; director Sylvester Stallone; DVD distributed by 20th Century Fox Home Entertainment.

he said, 'I'm writing this medical book. Let me take a picture of that arm.'

Stallone's tale is remarkable for how archetypically it is constructed. The increasing burden not only gives the drama its necessary escalation, but also is composed as a triplet – a structure fundamental to jokes, fairy tales, speeches, advertising copy and other forms. This structuring, along with the strangely self-glorifying coda, suggests how naturally Stallone positions both Rocky and himself as archetypes.[7] It is little wonder, then, that Frank Rich considers *Rocky II* to be 'the most solemn example of self-deification by a movie star since Barbra Streisand in *A Star Is Born*' (1979: n.p.).

Throughout the series, as Rocky endures the effects of his profession, we witness the inspirational effect he has on others. Of the series' myriad images of Rocky in training, one is particularly notable for how it merges his roles of martyr and messiah: during one of *Rocky IV*'s montages, Rocky lifts an ox-cart carrying Adrian, Paulie and Duke. As part of an extended montage, the image's effect may be sublimated to that of the larger sequence; nevertheless, the image is a perfect emblem for this dual facet of Rocky's self. Rocky's literal exertion is matched by his power to metaphorically lift those who share his journey.

The series is replete with more overt instances in which Stallone defines Rocky through his ability to inspire. *Rocky II* features the most literal example, when throngs of children follow Rocky as he runs to the Art Museum steps. As he ascends, they follow, chanting his name. On

Figure 5 - No child left behind: in *Rocky II*, the contender (Sylvester Stallone) trains while children flock behind. Producers Robert Chartoff and Irwin Winkler; director Sylvester Stallone; DVD distributed by 20th Century Fox Home Entertainment.

the soundtrack, Bill Conti's 'Gonna Fly Now' is reprised, with an angelic children's choir singing the chorus. In *Rocky Balboa*, former opponent Spider Rico (Pedro Lovell) provides an example more grounded in a realist aesthetic, and also in language. Just before Rocky enters the arena, Spider reads from Zachariah 4:6 – 'It is not by strength, not by might, but by his spirit we have already claimed a victory in our lord Jesus Christ.' This may rank among the series' most literal equations of the champion with his saviour, but it is not its most explicit. In fact, the first image of *Rocky* is of a frame-filling, stained-glass rendering of Jesus, from which the camera withdraws to reveal a boxing ring in which Rocky and Spider brawl. With this opening, *Rocky* establishes the trope that Stallone will mine in this film and in each of its sequels.

Mickey well represents those Rocky saves. Although he has long disregarded Rocky, once Rocky accepts Apollo's challenge, managing Rocky becomes Mickey's last hope at having a purpose. Indeed, arriving at Rocky's apartment to press his case, Mickey must complete a long climb up Rocky's steps, making his errand all the more quest-like. Rocky's role as Mickey's redeemer is more explicit in *Rocky V* (1990), as Rocky remembers a display of affection from his deceased trainer/manager:

> If you wasn't here, I probably wouldn't be alive today. The fact that you're here and doing as well as you're doing gives me, what do you call it, the motivisation to stay alive. 'Cause I think people die sometimes when they don't want to be alive. ... With you, kid, I got a reason to stay alive.

In this memory, Mickey shows more tenderness than the audience ever saw him display in life. Moreover, director Avildsen and writer Stallone make explicit what they implied in the original film: that Rocky is, quite literally, Mickey's reason to live.

Likewise, it is through Rocky that Adrian comes to life. Initially meek, hidden by jackets, sweaters, glasses and a hat, Adrian flourishes once she begins to reciprocate Rocky's romantic feelings. The relationship lends her the strength to beat back her domineering brother when she exclaims 'I'm not a loser!' in a moment that marks the climax of her emotional journey in *Rocky*. As with Mickey, Rocky's redemption of Adrian is even more explicit in the sequels. On the beach in *Rocky III*, Adrian delivers a volcanic speech to rally a self-doubting Rocky. When she is finished, Stallone cuts to a two-shot of Rocky and Adrian that suggests their renewed unity. 'How'd you get so tough?' Rocky asks. Stallone cuts back to a dramatic low angle, enhancing Adrian's formidability as she answers: 'I live with a fighter.'

The speech itself is also worth consideration. 'You were a champion', Adrian insists,

> ... But it doesn't matter what I believe, because you're the one that's gotta carry that fear around inside you, afraid that everybody's gonna take things away, afraid you're gonna be remembered as a coward, that you're not a man anymore. ... But it doesn't matter if I tell you ... because you're the one that's gotta settle it, get rid of it! Because when all the smoke is cleared, and everyone is through chanting your name, it's just gonna be us. ... Apollo thinks you can do it. So do I. But you, you've got to wanna do it for the right reasons. Not for the guilt over Mickey, not for the people, not for the title, not for money or me. But for you. Just you. Just you alone.

The passion in Talia Shire's performance almost hides the fact that for all of Adrian's strength and self-possession, Rocky is their focus and frame of reference. In light of this, Shire's identification with her character should come as no surprise: 'There's something about her that is me – which is, she can partner a man to his destiny' (Broeske 1985: AB34). Nor should we be surprised that *Rocky IV* further illustrates how supporting characters complete their journeys only as a by-product of helping Rocky complete his. Thus, Rocky's battle with Drago is pregnant with Apollo's redemption and Duke's recovery from grief. This motif also informs more incidental moments, as when Rocky presents Adrian with a cake to celebrate their anniversary. Decorated with bride and groom figurines opposing each other in a boxing ring, the cake situates their marriage within his world.

To Stallone's credit, *Rocky V* interrogates the notion of Rocky-as-saviour, while citing the original. The Jesus imagery that opens *Rocky* is reprised in *Rocky V*, for which Avildsen returned to the series. Here, a retired Rocky mentors an aspiring fighter, Tommy 'The Machine' Gunn (Tommy Morrison, then an actual heavyweight boxer). Avildsen establishes the space of Tommy's first fight (which occurs at the film's midpoint) by pulling the camera back from a stained-glass Jesus to reveal Tommy in the ring. The suggestion that the torch is being passed is enhanced moments later, in Tommy's corner. As Rocky assures his charge: 'I'm like this angel sitting on your shoulder.' Avildsen frames Rocky in a dramatic low angle such that the stained-glass Jesus seems to be sitting on Rocky's. Thus, the composition forms a diagonal line from Jesus to Rocky to Tommy.

As *Rocky V* progresses, Tommy becomes an errant ward, betraying – and in an early version of the script, even killing – his benefactor (Anon. 1990a: 37). Even so, when Tommy gets the title fight he has long desired, Rocky lives vicariously through him. This is embodied in the editing of the sequence: cuts between Tommy fighting and Rocky replicating the fight at home match such that one seems to begin an action that the other completes. However, while Rocky exults in Tommy's achievement, the editing layers another perspective into the scene. Cutaways to Adrian, Paulie and Rocky Jr. (Sage Stallone), who are all clearly uncomfortable, combine to create a critical view of Rocky.

Rocky V's interrogation of this trope may be a consequence of the film's status as a late-stage entry in the series. But sixteen years later, Stallone reinvigorates it with *Rocky Balboa*. With Adrian deceased, Rocky carries two families on his shoulders: his own, and that of Little Marie (Geraldine Hughes), now grown up and living the hardscrabble life of a single mother in a bad neighbourhood. Rocky promotes Marie socioeconomically by giving her a hostess position in his restaurant, and befriends her teenage son, Steps (James Francis Kelly III).

Rocky and Steps share one substantive scene as Rocky mentors the teen in adopting a dog. Under Rocky's gentle but insistent influence, Steps marks a trajectory from disaffected to engaged. Steps completes his arc in the beginning of the following scene as he surveys Rocky's memorabilia, starting with the painting of Rocky and Apollo clashing seen under the end credits of *Rocky III*. By dissolving between Steps and the mementos, and foregrounding opera on the soundtrack, Stallone dramatises Steps's awe. Significantly, Steps then virtually disappears from the film, only 35 minutes into its 102-minute running time. Thus, Stallone equates the completion of Steps's journey with his discovery of Rocky's greatness.

Stallone similarly resolves the troubled relationship between Rocky and his son, Robert (Milo Ventimiglia), who blames his father's shadow for his own professional frustrations. Their conflict becomes most pitched after Rocky accepts the offer to fight Dixon. They exchange impassioned speeches, with Rocky admonishing Robert that he must fight to make his own way. The next scene ends with their reunification, as Robert tells Rocky that he has quit his job to join Rocky's crusade. Robert has found peace and Rocky can begin training, but Stallone has violated his screenplay's logic. Robert has not fought to make his way. He has forsaken his own fight to aid Rocky in his. This negation of Rocky's speech to his son suggests that the theme of Rocky's grace is so powerful, not even Stallone can escape it.

Stallone uses Marie as another supporting character who finds fulfilment through defining and supporting Rocky. Near the film's midpoint, Marie offers a motivational speech that resolves the last of Rocky's self-doubt. 'Look, I know I usually don't say a lot. I'm always listenin' and lookin'', she says.

> ... [T]hat part of you that's so full of life ... This is who you are. This is who you'll always be. ... And it doesn't matter how this looks to other people. All that matters is how it looks to you. Rocky – Rocky, look at me. How. It looks. To you. And if this is something that you wanna do, and if this is something that you gotta do, then you do it. Fighters fight.

Though the difference may appear subtle, what distinguishes this speech from those of the other *Rocky* films is Marie's preamble. Her acknowledgment that she is primarily an observer makes explicit that to deliver this message requires her to make a special effort. For Rocky, this is a pep talk, but for Marie, it is a crossing. And it is Rocky's friendship that has enabled her to make it.

TITLE SHOTS AND THE FINAL BELL

Marie's speech does more than distil the symbiosis shared by Rocky and the supporting characters. It provides what may be the series' most sweeping – and also succinct – summary of who Rocky is. It is fitting that this summary should appear in the final film, as the whole film is rich with the sense of summation. This is manifested in the very title, *Rocky Balboa*. In all probability, this was designed to mitigate the public's sense of *Rocky* as a franchise from a bygone era, now being taken out of moth balls – a sense that would have been stronger had the word *Rocky* been followed by a Roman numeral *VI*. More substantively, however, utilising the character's full name suggests *this* is the film that gives expression to who Rocky is in his totality.

This sensibility dovetails with the film's preoccupation with Rocky's (and the franchise's) past. Indeed, critic Kenneth Turan notes how the film 'is a kind of Museum of Stallonic Technology, the equivalent of having a tour around the greatest hits of Rockydom personally guided by the man himself' (2006: E1). Turan is being quite literal. In addition to Rocky memorabilia, the film features Paulie and Rocky's annual tour of old Philadelphia haunts: the pet store where Adrian worked, the ice skating rink of Rocky and Adrian's first date, Mickey's gym.

Of all the *Rocky* films' locations, the most iconic is the Art Museum steps. It is here that Stallone concludes the series. As the credits roll, the steps appear inside a frame within the frame. They are scaled by a succession of real-life Americans, male and female, varying in age, race and physique. While this represents a departure for the franchise's end credit sequences, it is worth noting that the end titles of the last three films all utilise montages. In *Rocky IV*, the montage consists of still images from the film. *Rocky V* elaborates on this, with a montage of stills from the entire series. Not incidentally, underscoring that presumed end of the franchise, is a ballad, 'The Measure of a Man', commissioned by Stallone to 'summarize what the *Rocky* character is' (Archerd 1990: n.p.).[8]

Rocky Balboa's end title sequence bears two distinctions: it is the last montage in a franchise well known for its montages, and it is also the first in which Rocky is not present. But, of course, he is. Clearly, it is meant to visualise what Stallone, as writer, director, performer and spokesman, has always both implied and stated outright: in each of us, there is a Rocky Balboa. Thus, taken together, the film's title and its end title sequence render *Rocky Balboa* a summation in several senses of the word. They offer an overview of the series as well as a closing argument. The former makes a full-throated declaration of Stallone's ongoing preoccupation with Rocky's self. The latter stands as justification for that interest. Rocky, Stallone seems to be saying, is everybody.

He is us.

We are him.

The Alpha-male and the Omega.

NOTES

1 This aspect of the story is repeated almost verbatim in the studio's press materials for *Rocky II* (1979) and *Rocky III* (1982), all but enshrining it in pop-culture mythology.

2 Also of note is the fact that while *Rocky* was made in the context of the New Hollywood of the 1970s, Stallone would become a cultural figure much more closely associated with the blockbuster, Reaganite 1980s.

3 The statue was no mere prop, but an actual bronze sculpture. Stallone and Chartoff-Winkler Productions offered the statue to the city to be put on permanent display. The gift was declined after a 'rancorous meeting' of three city commissions, but later was permitted to be placed at the museum for the duration of filming (see Beale 1981: 3). Stallone then took possession of the statue and claims it spent five months in his backyard, tied to a tree. The statue was returned to the museum, where it was installed as a temporary attraction (see Robbins 1982: A16). The dedication ceremony, held on 24 May 1982, coincided with *Rocky III*'s premiere and a celebration of Philadelphia's tri-centennial (see United Artists 1982). The new arrangement dictated the statue's relocation to a permanent site outside the Spectrum, the city's indoor arena and the setting of Rocky and Apollo's two bouts (see Robbins 1982: A16). This move proved problematic when it was discovered that for this temporary placement, United Artists had installed the statue in cement. Amusingly, the studio's pressbook for *Rocky III* refers to the statue as 'already widely reported in the press' (MGM/United Artists 1982: 2). In March 1990, after the filming of *Rocky V*, Philadelphia's University of the Arts revisited the issue with a symposium titled 'Perspectives on the Rocky Controversy' (Anon. 1990b: n.p.).

4 The United States Code, Title 4, Section 8 ('Respect for the Flag') specifies that, among other prohibitions: '(d) The flag should never be used as wearing apparel, bedding, or drapery; (e) The flag should never be fastened, displayed, used, or stored in such a manner as to permit it to be easily torn, soiled, or damaged in any way; ... (i) The flag should never be used for advertising purposes in any manner whatsoever. It should not be ... printed or otherwise impressed on paper napkins or boxes or anything that is designed for temporary use and discarded' (see Luckey 2008).

5 To reinforce the significance of this punishment – and therefore, of Rocky's courage – Stallone utilises boxing commentators at each fight. A few examples: 'Balboa's taking a tremendous beating here. ... What's keeping him up?' (*Rocky*); 'Balboa's got to be in great shape to withstand that butchering, and I'll tell ya, that's just what it is: it's plain, old butchering' (*Rocky II*); 'How can he come back from a beating like that?' (*Rocky III*).

6 While Rocky all but tortures himself in the franchise's training sequences, Stallone's other iconic character, John Rambo, like other action heroes, withstands literal torture administered by others. Among other functions, such sequences prove, and even enhance, the hero's moral superiority. See Lichtenfeld (2007), particularly chapters 1 and 2.

7 Note how the story that begins this essay is also anchored by a triplet: Stallone's depleted bank account, pregnant wife and angry landlord.

8 The song's performer, Elton John, originally declined Stallone's offer to sing on the soundtrack. When Stallone received a demo of the song, he renewed his petition by playing John

the track over the phone. 'I got him out of bed ... and I told him if I didn't feel 1000% about it, I wouldn't ask him to do it.' John agreed, and less than a week later, Alan Menken had recorded the song with a 70-piece orchestra, flown the tracks to London, recorded John's vocals, and returned to the United States for the final mix (Archerd 1990: n.p.). What is notable about Archerd's piece is how Stallone describes his recruitment of the singer. While the story has a touch of self-deprecation, Sir Elton John emerges as yet another character who Stallone – or Rocky – brings along on a journey.

BIBLIOGRAPHY

Anon. (1990a) 'Relax, Rocky Lives', *People*, 20 August, 37.
____ (1990b) 'Perspectives on the Rocky Controversy', *Philadelphia Inquirer*, 3 March, n.p.
Archerd, Army (1990) 'Just for Variety', *Daily Variety*, 29 October, n.p.
Beale, Lewis (1981) 'Reaction to *Rocky* Not Brotherly', *Los Angeles Times Calendar*, 22 March, 3.
Broeske, Pat. H. (1985) 'Outtakes', *Los Angeles Times*, 27 October, AB34.
Kilday, Gregg (1977) 'Stallone Eager for Round 2 in Hollywood', *Los Angeles Times*, 5 January, F1.
Klemesrud, Judy (1976) '"Rocky isn't based on me", says Stallone, "but we both went the distance"', *New York Times*, 28 November, 111.
Lichtenfeld, Eric (2007) *Action Speaks Louder: Violence, Spectacle, and the American Action Movie*. Revised and expanded edition. Middletown, CT: Wesleyan University Press.
Luckey, John (2008) *CRS Report for Congress: The United States Flag: Federal Law Relating to Display and Associated Questions*. Washington, DC: Congressional Research Service. Online. Available HTTP: http://www.senate.gov/reference/resources/pdf/RL30243.pdf (15 January 2009).
McKee, Robert (1997) *Story*. New York: HarperCollins.
MGM/United Artists (1982) *Rocky III* pressbook.
Reed, J. D. (1982) 'Winner and Still Champion', *Time*, 14 June, 58–64.
Rich, Frank (1979) 'Plastic Jesus', *Time*, 25 June, 52.
Robbins, William (1982) 'Rocky's Homecoming Hailed; Statue Fights End in a Draw', *New York Times*, 25 May, A16.
Schubart, Rikke (2001) 'Passion and Acceleration: Generic Change in the Action Film', in J. David Slocum (ed.) *Violence and American Cinema*. New York: Routledge, 192–207.
Smith, Red (1979) 'Rocky Fights It Over', *Los Angeles Times*, 13 June, n.p.
Spruiell, Vann (1995) 'Self', in Burness E. Moore, MD, and Bernard D. Fine, MD (eds) *Psychoanalysis: The Major Concepts*. New Haven: Yale University Press, 421–32.
Suppa, Ron (1996) 'Taking Rocky to the Mat after 20 Years', *Creative Screenwriting*, winter, 6–9.
Turan, Kenneth (2006) 'Punch Drunk and Down for the Count', *Los Angeles Times*, 20 December, E1.
United Artists (1976) *Rocky* publicity and promotion.
____ (1982) 'News from United Artists'. *Rocky III* production file.
____ (1985) *Rocky IV* marketing guide.

STALLONE AND HOLLYWOOD IN TRANSITION

MARK GALLAGHER

Sylvester Stallone has been widely understood as the embodiment of 1980s Hollywood action cinema and of Reagan-era heroic masculinity. Perhaps surprisingly, though, few scholars have devoted attention to the films in which he appeared at the outset of the decade. This essay concentrates on two films in which he starred in the spring and summer of 1981: *Nighthawks*, released in the US in early April, and *Victory*, with wide release in the US in late July.

Stallone has received much attention as a solitary 'tentpole star'. However, his film roles have repeatedly depended on his affiliation with or differentiation from his co-stars. The cop thriller *Nighthawks* pits him against Dutch actor Rutger Hauer, partners him with blaxploitation star Billy Dee Williams, and casts television's onetime bionic woman, Lindsay Wagner, as his estranged wife. The sports film *Victory* finds him in another ensemble, granting him top billing over renowned British actor Michael Caine and Swedish stalwart Max von Sydow. Both *Nighthawks* and *Victory* surround Stallone with co-stars and supporting performers who animate and magnify his star persona and character construction. These co-stars expand the scope of the films' address to multiple film-going demographics. The two films' releases contributed to Stallone's recovering marketability as well.

Because his previous starring role had been nearly two years earlier, in the June 1979 release *Rocky II*, we might in hindsight regard *Nighthawks* and *Victory* as place-holder efforts keeping his star image in circulation before the next heavily promoted *Rocky* film and the franchise-launching *First Blood*.[1] At the time, however, they undoubtedly seemed legitimate ways to expand his stardom and earn commercial success. This retrospective view of star-image circulation might additionally suggest a consistent promotional or industrial strategy, with a studio keeping a valuable star in the public eye in the interval between instalments of a successful franchise. Unsurprisingly for post-classical Hollywood, though, each of Stallone's 1981 and 1982 films was released by a different distributor: the *Rocky* films by United Artists, *Victory* by Paramount, *Nighthawks* by Universal, and *First Blood* by Orion. In the context of what Paul McDonald terms the 'post-studio star system' (2008: 167), we can therefore more precisely regard Stallone's choice of roles as the work of the performer himself and his management, particularly agents Stan Kamen of William Morris and Ron Meyer of Creative Artists Agency (CAA).[2]

Though not yet a global superstar and creative force, by 1981 Stallone had four screenplay and two directing credits to his name in addition to many performances. He did not play multiple creative roles on *Nighthawks* and *Victory*, but remains nonetheless the key figure in their production and reception. Because he was the best-known actor and star in *Nighthawks*, Universal promoted him above all other elements. His star image dominates the film's publicity campaign. For example, a glossy, oversized portfolio distributed with the film's US press kit displays a large photograph of Stallone in his costume for the film. The text begins, '*Night Hawks*, a dynamic film for the 1980s, brings to the screen Sylvester Stallone and an impressive international cast in a contemporary suspense thriller' (Universal City Studios 1980). The most frequently used poster graphic features an extreme close-up of Stallone's face alongside that of the antagonist played by Hauer, then mostly unknown to US audiences.

With *Victory*, Stallone receives top billing, but the principal US poster image shows him alongside co-stars Caine and Brazilian soccer star Pelé, each with an arm raised; the graphic thus arranges the men in a 'V' shape. The image, a photorealist drawing not reproducing an exact image from the film, positions Pelé behind the others, but Caine appears virtually equal to Stallone. Alternative graphics on the British quad and one-sheet posters include a similar central 'V' graphic along with smaller images of Allied POWs and Nazis, including the third-billed von Sydow.[3] Though Stallone was arguably the film's most recognisable star worldwide, virtually all posters for the film mark him as part of an ensemble, joined to established global star Caine and the internationally famed (though retired since 1971) Pelé.

The two 1981 releases demonstrate how a rising star was positioned in the emerging 'Conglomerate Hollywood' era.[4] Stallone would go on to command record salaries in the mid-1980s (and well beyond), in the

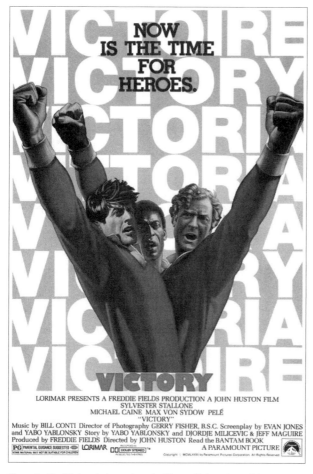

NOW
IS THE TIME
FOR
HEROES.
"VICTORY"

VICTORY

LORIMAR PRESENTS A FREDDIE FIELDS PRODUCTION A JOHN HUSTON FILM
SYLVESTER STALLONE
MICHAEL CAINE MAX VON SYDOW PELÉ
"VICTORY"
Music by BILL CONTI Director of Photography GERRY FISHER, B.S.C. Screenplay by EVAN JONES
and YABO YABLONSKY Story by YABO YABLONSKY and DJORDJE MILICEVIC & JEFF MAGUIRE
Produced by FREDDIE FIELDS Directed by JOHN HUSTON Read the BANTAM BOOK
A PARAMOUNT PICTURE
PG PARENTAL GUIDANCE SUGGESTED   LORIMAR DD DOLBY STEREO ™
Copyright © MCMLXXXI by Paramount Pictures Corporation. All Rights Reserved

Figure 1 - The US theatrical one-sheet for *Victory* displays three of the four leads
but puts Sylvester Stallone in the foreground. Producer Freddie Fields; director
John Huston; DVD distributed by Warner Home Video.

wake of the success of the *Rocky* and *First Blood* sequels. *Nighthawks'*
accompanying promotional materials indicate ways the studio situated
the film in consumption contexts including but not limited to television, newspaper and magazine reviews. In turn, professional discussions
largely deferred to Stallone's pre-existing image and its renewed promotion. As will be discussed in depth, *Nighthawks* locates Stallone
amid presumably complementary textual elements such as setting,
genre signifiers and other story-world attributes that suit his talents
and existing persona. *Victory* provides a different fit for Stallone: its
World War II, European – and particularly European-sports – contexts
do not mesh obviously with his strongly American-affiliated persona

(notably, *Victory* focuses on the European experience of World War II, and Stallone is the film's only American character and actor). Building on the star template established through the *Rocky* films, though, *Victory*'s promotion and publicity emphasise Stallone's physicality, and the film narrates his character's assimilation into European cultures, settings and sports.

Nighthawks provides a snapshot of Hollywood on the brink of a new global expansion. In contrast, *Victory* showcases the kinds of locations, casts and storylines long associated with Hollywood internationalism during the late classical era. In both films, though, casting choices, generic appeals and narrative elements all indicate the industry's specific attempts to attract diverse viewerships locally and internationally. With *Nighthawks* in particular, Stallone's domestic and international star power – based partly on national and ethnic affiliation – provides the foundation for the creative and marketing choices. Analysis of *Nighthawks* in terms of industrial contexts and gender and ethnic representation sheds light on the interdependent relationship between a transforming industry and a rising international star. In comparison, *Victory* embodies an older model of Hollywood's global perspective. It offers a combination of the historical film and inspirational sports drama. Its ensemble cast is international but mostly white. Its European location shooting recalls 1950s and 1960s production strategies and content. Its director, John Huston, brought prestige from work on paradigmatic classical-Hollywood films such as *The Maltese Falcon* (1941) and *The African Queen* (1951) and the influential New Hollywood effort *Chinatown* (1974). Victory thus has its roots in past Hollywood practice, while *Nighthawks* anticipates Hollywood's future, but both make Stallone the locus of market interest and viewer attention. In what follows I investigate the articulation of Stallone's star persona in *Nighthawks* and *Victory* to understand how his image circulated to global audiences during a period when Hollywood itself was in transition.

A NEW(ER) HOLLYWOOD FOR THE 1980S: *NIGHTHAWKS'* CASTING, CREATIVE PERSONNEL AND GENERIC HYBRIDITY

Andy Willis argues that stars 'cannot be separated from the industrial contexts of their production and their films' distribution and exhibition' (2004: 3). Correspondingly, attention to a film's overall production profile can illuminate many facets of industry transformations that involve and impact stars and other creative personnel. *Nighthawks'* story combines international thriller and urban cop-film templates: a German terrorist called Wulfgar (Hauer) bombs a London department store, then travels to New York, where he faces off against off-white, working-class policeman Deke DaSilva (Stallone) and his black partner (Williams).[5] DaSilva has an estranged wife (Wagner); Wulfgar has a Moroccan-born female accomplice (Persis Khambatta). Narratively, then, *Nighthawks* operates in familiar territory laid out in films such as *The Day of the Jackal* (1973), *Three Days of the Condor* (1975) and myriad other globe-trotting thrillers that arose in the wake of the James Bond successes from the early 1960s on.

In the contexts this chapter emphasises, *Nighthawks'* significance is threefold. First, its cast and crew highlight the early 1980s as a gestation period for current industry practice. Second, the film is a generically hybrid effort, and we can see many earlier and later films built from similar components. Third, neither the makeup of the film's creative team nor its generic mix resulted in commercial success. The case thus alerts us to the significance of shifting industrial strategies. Just as aesthetic norms and regimes of representation change according to historical circumstances, so do industrial preferences and formulae. Attention to *Nighthawks'* profile can help us identify precedents for now-dominant configurations of creative resources, and explain the ways those configurations have or have not historically contributed to individual films' circulation and popular success.

Nighthawks' casting seeks to exploit potential US niche audiences as well as overseas markets, a profile now commonplace among highly market-sensitive studio releases. To distinguish its merger of conventional spy-thriller and police film plotlines, the film gathers creative workers from US film and television industries and casts several foreign actors. Billy Dee Williams, leading man of black-themed films such as *Lady Sings the Blues* (1972), *Mahogany* (1975) and numerous blaxploitation films, here makes a second inroad into the Hollywood mainstream, following his own high-profile role as Lando Calrissian in the *Star Wars* sequel *The Empire Strikes Back* (1980). For Lindsay Wagner, star of the US's successful *Bionic Woman* television series of 1976–78, *Nighthawks* marks the first of her few roles in studio film productions.[6]

Most notably, *Nighthawks* represents the Hollywood debut of Dutch film and television star Rutger Hauer. Prior to *Nighthawks*, Hauer had already appeared in fifteen films, mostly Dutch productions but also

two West German films, two Belgian/French co-productions and one British production. In particular, attentive filmgoers might have recognised Hauer as a lead or featured player in four films from international auteur director Paul Verhoeven, including the graphic World War II drama *Soldier of Orange* (1977). Hauer thus brings to *Nighthawks* an established persona as a dramatic actor of international art cinema. Broadening its appeal to international audiences, the film additionally features British film, television and stage veteran Nigel Davenport as Stallone's mentor; and as a villainess, the Indian-born Khambatta, who had appeared in Hindi, British and German productions prior to her own ingénue turn in 1979's *Star Trek: The Motion Picture*. The film's multiracial and transnational casting is commercially strategic: virtually all of *Nighthawks'* key acting roles go to performers who are already recognised, respected or cult figures and who had appeared in previous regional or transnational successes.

As with its casting, *Nighthawks'* creative personnel brought diverse experience, suggesting the changing talent pools from which film-industry production draws in the 1980s as a by-product of industry decentralisation.[7] Screenwriter David Shaber had few prior production credits but was known for adapting the 1979 exploitation hit *The Warriors. Nighthawks'* original director, Gary Nelson, worked throughout the 1960s and 1970s in television, directing dozens of series.[8] The choice of a small-screen veteran indicates the rising commonality of film and television industry cross-pollination.[9] Crossover with the advertising industry was soon to follow, as Nelson left early in the production and was replaced by Bruce Malmuth, then best known as director of a series of 'Excedrin Headache' commercials.[10] Other directors at the time, including Ridley Scott and Adrian Lyne, had also moved from working on television ads to directing features (Scott debuted as a feature director in 1977; Lyne in 1980). While not the most common career trajectory for filmmakers, numerous contemporary directors – in the late 1990s and 2000s, for example, Spike Jonze, Michel Gondry and Charles Stone III – have followed the same path. The selection of directors from outside the film industry shows one facet of Hollywood's evolving production profiles, with extensive feature expertise no longer seen as requisite for direction of a film showcasing international stars.

In its other technician credits and in its aesthetics as well, *Nighthawks* resembles Hollywood output at the end of the 1970s. Continuing Stallone's pattern of maintaining working relationships with crew members, the film's two credited editors, Stanford Allen and Christopher Holmes, had both worked on Stallone's previous film, *Rocky II*. In its visual style and editing, *Nighthawks* does not substantively innovate. Cinematographer James Contner came to the production with arguably the most conventional profile, having worked as camera operator on numerous 1970s productions, though none featuring Stallone. In the manner of many 1970s films, *Nighthawks* relies on an overall high-key lighting scheme, with hard, bright light particularly in indoor scenes. The editing is primarily linear, although it includes repeated cross-cuts between scenes of its protagonists' and antagonists' activity. The film displays little rapid cutting. Its repeated use of handheld camera shots follows 1970s practice, too, though this aesthetic would eventually become one of contemporary action cinema's stylistic hallmarks.[11]

Overall, however, *Nighthawks*' production points forward rather than back. Its roster of cast and crew shows the early 1980s as a gestation period for contemporary Hollywood practice – with personnel from television, advertising and music-video production moving into feature films, where they work alongside casts drawn from English-language performers from Western Europe as well as the global south. *Nighthawks*, moreover, supplies an exploitable narrative element in a bid for topicality: the film's international-terrorist plot links it to scores of terrorist bombings and assassinations that occurred at the outset of the 1980s.[12] The so-called 'Iranian hostage crisis' had begun in late 1979 with the capture of dozens of US Embassy personnel and ended with their release in January 1981. While a degree of topicality is de rigueur for Hollywood thrillers, this level of cultural verisimilitude may indeed have hurt the film commercially. The hit films of the period largely eschewed strong topicality, with terrorists in particular becoming a high-concept staple only in the wake of the success of *Die Hard* (1988). Elements that might today be seen as essential for star-driven, genre-modelled studio productions were thus of little benefit in 1981, at least in the particular case of *Nighthawks*.

A first-act emphasis on New York City subways, tenements and fire escapes, along with DaSilva's long hair, beard and glasses, promise *Nighthawks* will deploy 1970s-era cop-film thematics à la *Serpico* (1973).[13] The film's limited characterisations (nearly all characters, Stallone's included, are typologically rather than psychologically defined), its incident-driven plot and abundant action and thriller set pieces, and its proliferation of genre elements all showcase narrative and genre appeals associated with later 1980s high-concept cinema. The film's premise and chief character conflicts anticipate the hugely successful *Die Hard*. In both, a sneering Euro-terrorist plays cat-and-mouse games with a no-nonsense New York City policeman, our protagonist's closest friend is a black fellow cop, and the hero's back story includes a failing marriage. Otherwise, however, in terms of narrative and genre, *Nighthawks* replicates the combination of gritty undercover policing and international intrigue from the much earlier *The French Connection* (1971).[14] Also like *The French Connection* and countless earlier spy/caper films, *Nighthawks* features multiple high-profile settings – New York, London and Paris (and location shooting in each city) – to construct cosmopolitan appeals. Here, the international-terrorist plot motivates the inclusion of these locations. Unusually for the time, it also includes scenes with subtitled German and French dialogue. Thus, the film grants domestic US audiences a fleeting view of recognisable foreign locations and languages, while offering a measure of cultural-linguistic specificity for European markets.

Generically, *Nighthawks* is thus a bridge film in that it contributes to templates for the mixed-race buddy-cop action film (the *Lethal Weapon* series [1987, 1989, 1992, 1998] in particular), the internationally situated terrorist thriller and the working-class drama. Given Stallone's appearance in other films with similar profiles, these genres and modes show the centrality of flexible stars such as Stallone to 1970s and 1980s Hollywood institutional logic. While often critically derided as a performer with little range, Stallone's roles through *Nighthawks* and *Victory* show reasonable versatility, and arguably it is this diversity of

Figure 3 - Terrorist Wulfgar (Rutger Hauer) at the United Nations building as he plots his New York City escapades. *Nighthawks*. Producers Herb Nanas and Martin Poll; director Bruce Malmuth; DVD (UK) distributed by Universal Home Entertainment.

roles that catalyses reviewers' scorn (after all, stars can only be derided for branching out beyond expected roles after they do so). Beginning with the *Rocky* sequels, his roles suit the industry's marketing of stars through ancillary channels such as celebrity magazines, and its growing attention to pre-sold properties through sequelisation and promotion of tentpole stars and star-driven franchises. *Nighthawks* demonstrates that Stallone's rising popularity did not guarantee domestic or global success. Nonetheless, the film's generic hybridity and its diverse casting show attempts to fortify the release with appeals distinct from those of its lead actor.

REVIVING (THE OLD) GLOBAL HOLLYWOOD: *VICTORY*'S CREATIVE TEAM AND MARKET POSITION

Victory also attempts to endow Stallone with attributes recognisable to international audiences. Set during World War II, the film follows a group of Allied prisoners of war who accept an offer to play an exhibition football match against the German national team, with the POWs using the event to engineer their escape. *Victory*'s script, casting and locations situate Stallone *within* rather than wholly at a remove from European cultures. Like *Nighthawks*, *Victory* includes some foreign-language dialogue – subtitled German spoken by the Nazi characters, as well as some unsubtitled German and French. Like *Nighthawks*, too,

Victory showcases European settings and locations, with Budapest-area locations standing in for the story's German and Parisian settings.[15] Stallone plays an American serving in the Canadian army, with this national affiliation stated in passing in early exposition, presumably to explain his presence in a POW camp among British rather than American soldiers. The film thus explicitly avoids framing Stallone as an icon of American values. One British character refers to him as a 'Yank', but the film does not markedly thematise American nationalism. Instead, the split affiliation makes Stallone's character, Robert Hatch, doubly an outsider: the narrative grants him no strong connection to the army whose uniform he wears, and his individualistic attitude is at odds with the outlook of the tight-knit British POW group. Like *Nighthawks*, *Victory* defines Stallone's character in relation to a range of characters of other nationalities. These include a French woman (played by French-Canadian actress Carole Laure) who acts as an almost-love interest and a virtual United Nations of POWs – Caine and others representing the UK and Ireland, Afro-Brazilian soccer star Pelé playing a character from Trinidad, and numerous other international football stars from Poland, Denmark, Norway, Holland, Belgium and Argentina named in the final credit sequence (if not all in the central narrative). The film is also generically hybrid, combining elements of the war film (specifically the World War II POW drama, in the mode of *Stalag 17* [1953], *The Great Escape* [1963] and US television's *Hogan's Heroes* [1965–71]), the sports film and – according with a key strand of director John Huston's work – the historical drama.

Behind the camera, *Victory* assembles an experienced and in some cases venerable production team. At the time of its release, Huston was approaching his 75th birthday, producer Freddie Fields was approaching his 59th, cinematographer Gerry Fisher was nearly 55, and co-screenwriters Yabo Yablonsky and Evan Jones were aged 50 and 54, respectively (in contrast, *Nighthawks*' credited director Malmuth was 47 at the time of that film's release). Fields had turned to occasional producing in the mid-1970s but was best known as a major talent agent and co-founder in 1960 of Creative Management Associates, which evolved into industry powerhouse International Creative Management.[16] Veteran cinematographer Fisher had worked occasionally in Hollywood (including on Huston's previous work, 1979's *Wise Blood*) but more extensively in British and French productions since the late 1940s. Editor Roberto Silva would become a more frequent Huston collaborator, working on four of Huston's late efforts, beginning with *Wise Blood*.

Other key crew members had no affiliation with Huston but had worked instead on numerous Stallone films. Many, such as co-producers Mario Kassar and Andrew Vajna, were at fairly early stages in their careers and would work extensively in Hollywood later.[17] Composer Bill Conti (a bit younger, aged 39 at the time of *Victory*'s release) had scored four of Stallone's previous starring efforts, beginning with *Rocky*. He would continue in that role for much of the 1970s and 1980s. Makeup artist Michael Westmore also began a collaboration with Stallone on *Rocky* that would continue intermittently through the 1990s. Another key collaborator for the actor, costume designer Tom Bronson, first worked with Stallone on *Rocky II*, continued on both *Nighthawks* and *Victory*, and would earn credits on a total of eleven Stallone films. Both *Nighthawks* and *Victory*, then, show Stallone working with frequent collaborators, who help manage the look and surround of his performances even as he ranges into different character types and production settings.

Certain aspects of the film, particularly its locations and casting, clearly mark it as a production in tune more with the industry's past than with its future, however. *Victory*'s European shooting (some in Paris but mostly around Budapest) would not represent standard 1980s practice. In its casting, the film, released internationally as *Escape to Victory*, gives weightier dramatic roles to European actors Caine and von Sydow than to Stallone. Both enjoyed more established international reputations than did Stallone. Caine's Captain John Colby leads the POW football team, while von Sydow takes third billing as the central German character, the sympathetic Nazi officer Major Von Steiner. Lightly echoing the thematics of *The Grand Illusion* (1939), the screenplay showcases the psychological duel between Colby and Von Steiner, linking the men through their shared back stories as professional football players.

While they would continue to play lead and supporting roles in Hollywood films in the 1980s and beyond, Caine and von Sydow had both enjoyed long careers before *Victory*, and their most iconic roles were behind them. Both had played roles in many US films and alongside American actors. British star Caine had already appeared in over fifty films, including major UK hits and numerous US releases. In the year preceding *Victory*'s release, he played the lead in two Hollywood films, *The Island* (1980) and *The Hand* (1981), and co-starred as a cross-dressing killer in a third, *Dressed to Kill* (1980). Swedish actor von Sydow earned his substantial art-cinema reputation as a major figure in Ingmar Bergman's, Jan Troell's and other Swedish films from the 1950s to the 1970s. Troell's *The Emigrants* (1971) and its follow-up *The New Land* (1972), both with von Sydow in the lead as a nineteenth-century Swedish farmer who emigrates to the US, earned successive Academy Award nominations for Best Foreign Language Film. These roles aided von Sydow's global visibility and helped position him alongside American performers. He had begun appearing in Hollywood productions in the mid-1960s, rising to supporting roles in *The Exorcist* (1973) and its 1977 sequel. His performance in *Victory* was sandwiched between two roles in campy fantasy films, as the diabolical Ming the Merciless of 1980's *Flash Gordon* and then as the grave King Osric of 1982's *Conan the Barbarian*.

The narrative of Hatch's efforts to prove his worth to his fellow POWs and to the French Resistance members he encounters parallels Stallone's own efforts to be valued beyond American-cinema contexts. Notably, Stallone's character interacts with von Sydow's only once, in a passing exchange near the beginning of the film. In comparison, the story affords Colby and Hatch numerous scenes together, first as adversaries – with the upcoming football match repeatedly complicating Hatch's solo escape plans – and eventually as friends and teammates. And while Hatch appears in numerous dialogue scenes with the British-officer characters, the film uses Colby to link Hatch to the other football players. Hatch has virtually no one-on-one dialogues with the other players, aside from a brief exchange with Pelé's character, Fernandez, who compliments Hatch's goalkeeping ability. Particularly when viewed retrospectively as a stepping stone in Stallone's long career, *Victory* uses its cast to accentuate Stallone's construction as a cosmopolitan figure who ultimately belongs among international stars and sports figures. Stallone's name appears first on promotional posters for *Victory*'s international as well as US releases, likely owing to the visibility of the first two *Rocky* films and *Victory*'s related status as in large part a sports film. Nevertheless Hatch is essential to the overall narrative, particularly through a sub-plot in which he escapes the prison camp alone to meet with the French Resistance fighters coordinating the larger POW escape that occurs at the film's climax. In the parallel sports narrative, he becomes the POW team's goalkeeper for the climactic match against the German team, where he makes a dramatic save.

Beyond its derivative plot, stylistically *Victory* utilises a conventional look and a pacing typical on the one hand of the prestige historical drama, on the other of the sports film, with episodes of period flavour and military-personnel interactions alternating with sports-training scenes and eventually the centrepiece match. Filmed in Panavision's 2.35:1 anamorphic widescreen format (as compared to *Nighthawks'* less wide, 1:85 spherical-lens format), *Victory* uses its wide frame for many of the scenes where POWs train or plot, as well as long shots of sports action in the climactic match, which takes up the last third of the film. Stars Stallone and Caine in particular appear alone in many medium shots from the chest up. In another sign of stylistic conservatism, the vast majority of the film's scenes take place in daylight. The film reserves its handful of night-time scenes for depictions of escape attempts and for Hatch's brief mission to Paris to deliver information to French Resistance fighters. *Victory* relies on an overall high-key lighting aesthetic, particularly for its many outdoor scenes, though interiors such as the Allied camp bunker and tunnels that feature in escapes appear in sculpted, low-key light. The film ends with a characteristic 1970s effect: a shot of football fans rushing out of the stadium turns into a blue-tinted, solarised frame (used also for the final shot of 1971's *The Omega Man*, for example, as well as in psychedelic sequences of such films as *2001: A Space Odyssey* [1968]). The subsequent credit sequence, with freeze frames of stars and professional football players, reiterates the film's prestige style and mainstream address.

The climactic football match includes much footage shot in extreme long shots that capture most of the field, with extensive panning and some zooms to follow the action. The match sequence does intersperse closer views, though, and shallow-focus photography helps draw players and lead actors out from colourful background space. Stallone receives considerable visual attention. His blue goalkeeper's jersey distinguishes him from the mostly white outfits of his teammates, and the film repeatedly frames him in isolation, in wide shots of the goal area. Aside from Colby/Caine, the other players remain largely anonymous, recognisable to football aficionados but mostly not named as characters in the film itself.[18] Most significantly, placement of Stallone in the goalkeeper role makes effective use of his physicality. Whether static or in motion, Stallone registers as a far more athletically capable performer than his fellow professional actors.[19] Still, *Victory*'s casting of numerous real-life sports stars – in particular Pelé, who receives fourth billing and choreographs the film's sports sequences – underscores Stallone's lack of a European-football background.

Victory primarily uses Stallone/Hatch's ineptitude at European football as an occasion for comedy. This character trait also provides some

Figure 4 - During a football practice in *Victory*, Stallone's character receives advice from more experienced sportsmen played by Pelé and Michael Caine. *Victory*. Producer Freddie Fields; director John Huston; DVD distributed by Warner Home Video.

dramatic tension. Another sub-plot, for example, concerns the strategy used to get Hatch on the POW football team given his lack of skill. Over Colby's objections, Hatch designates himself the team's ostensible trainer. 'I just wanna be around the guys', Hatch asserts, articulating the film's assimilation of him into both an international-ensemble film and a sports narrative showcasing a sport without a long US tradition. Indeed, Hatch aggressively pursues this integration, using his wits and will first to gain the British officers' assistance for his escape, then to engage with French Resistance members, and finally as a member of the POW football team, which he rejoins on the field despite an opportunity for the team to escape at halftime of the climactic game. Through events, sub-plots and tonal variations, the film thereby traverses wide generic terrain.

Yet while Stallone's sometimes comic predicaments additionally broaden *Victory*'s address, the film withholds elements such as a romance plot that might hybridise it further. Stallone does play a scene with the lone credited female character, Carole Laure's Resistance operative, and their encounter concludes with an embrace and kiss. The scene mostly shows that Hatch and Stallone belong in the world of European intrigue. Afterwards the film forecloses further romantic possibilities by putting Hatch on a truck back to join his fellow POWs. Once again, this time by sacrificing even token opportunities to involve women characters and broaden generic appeals, *Victory* recalls the overwhelmingly male world of war melodramas such as *The Guns of Navarone* (1961) and *Where Eagles Dare* (1968). Once again, too, it references past rather than contemporary films.

EARLY 1980S STALLONE: COSMOPOLITANISM, NATIONAL IDENTITY AND GLOBAL STARDOM

The characters Stallone plays in *Victory* and *Nighthawks* stand out as North American but pursue cosmopolitanism out of necessity – in *Victory*, for Hatch's temporary escape into occupied Paris and for numerous displays of European rather than American football; in *Nighthawks*, as part of DaSilva's attempt to adopt the mindset of Hauer's Euro-terrorist. Contrastingly, Stallone's key roles – as Rocky and Rambo – succeed by presenting him as the exaggerated, spectacular incarnation of an irrefu-table ethnic Americanness. Rambo, notes Yvonne Tasker, 'function[s] for various cultural commentators as the literal embodiment of American interventionism' (1993: 92). As Tasker and others have convincingly argued, this strategy proves successful too for other 1980s male stars such as Arnold Schwarzenegger – a performer stripped of Teutonic origins in key 1980s and 1990s roles, and eventually Americanised both on-screen and off. Notably, however, whether embodying insular Americanness or engaged with the larger world, Stallone's characters are typically either explicitly working class or tied to working-class origins, attitudes and environments. *Nighthawks* manages the steady drift of Stallone's character from streetwise to cosmopolitan. This construction looks ahead to populist hits in which down-to-earth urban cops best pretentious Europeans, with instinct and heart trumping craftiness. In *Victory* too, Hatch's enlisted man status connotes a working-class background, manifest in his easy engagement with the rumpled proletarians who comprise the French Resistance in the film. Here, though, Hatch's assimilation into a European-inflected morality – he gives up his stereotypically American efforts at solo escape and embraces the British sense of fair play that pervades the film – ties *Victory* to a value system not in vogue in later 1980s Hollywood.

Nighthawks' and *Victory*'s attempts to internationalise Stallone represent different versions of transitional industry practice. These efforts largely failed during the early Reagan era, in which Hollywood films such as the hits *Raiders of the Lost Ark* (1981) and *E.T.* (1982) were perhaps received less as global commodities than as characteristically American exports. Subsequent appraisals of 1980s Hollywood – both as industry and as site of representation – also repeatedly emphasise blockbuster hits composed of predominantly American flavours. True, *Raiders of the Lost Ark*, the most successful US film of 1981, offers a globe-trotting American protagonist and a range of international actors and settings, as does the year's number-three film, *Superman II*. Most of the 1980s' later domestic hits, though, feature not only US characters but also US settings, and were received abroad as such.[20]

Nighthawks' iconic New York settings can be seen as anticipating the many subsequent hits in which urban cops fend off villains who target American cities (usually New York or Los Angeles) that serve as proxies for the world at large. *Nighthawks* is mixed in this regard: it gives viewers a globe-trotting villain, but makes New York the site for most of his activity and for his battle with the city-bound DaSilva. *Victory*, on the other hand, brings Stallone to Europe and limits his Americanness, most prominently by making him a member of the Canadian rather than US military. Notwithstanding its director's and lead star's American origins, the film has an explicitly European focus that makes it comparable to glossy co-productions of earlier vintage. In their relative geographic and cultural emphases, then – *Nighthawks* showing Europeans drawn to the US, *Victory* showing Europeans in their own element and resisting the American outsider – the two films again look respectively forward and back. Hollywood's global success in the 1980s arguably depended not on the provision of international-themed content inherently resonant with viewers' geographic and cultural situations, but on overseas audiences' willingness to align more or less 'foreign' texts to their specific experiences. With locally specific content already available in national cinemas and on television in many countries in 1981, Hollywood films carried distinctively American narrative appeals, along with high production values made possible by economies of scale.

STAR POSITIONING, DISPLAY AND INDUSTRIAL LOGIC

Nighthawks' and *Victory*'s positionings of Stallone's character alongside darker- and lighter-skinned co-stars are consistent with the cast profiles of his subsequent 1980s efforts (while *Victory* puts Stallone mostly in the company of white Europeans, he does share the screen repeatedly with Pelé). Both films thus contribute to a longstanding pattern of casting Stallone alongside ethnic-minority characters – such as Carl Weathers in *Rocky III*, Singapore-born Eurasian Julia Nickson in *Rambo: First Blood Part II* (1985) and Reni Santoni in *Cobra* (1986) – and against Soviet or other white Euro-villains such as Dolph Lundgren and

Brigitte Nielsen in *Rocky IV* (1985).

Amid the lukewarm response to *Nighthawks*, the interplay of Stallone and Hauer is one of the few features repeatedly celebrated. Demonstrating the film's transitional status for its star and for the industry, some reviews explicitly or implicitly praise Stallone's performance in the film, while hinting at the critical punching bag he will later become. *The New York Times*' Janet Maslin, for example, observes that *Nighthawks* 'is particularly helped by the performances of Rutger Hauer, a Dutch actor who makes a startling impression as a cold-blooded fiend, and Sylvester Stallone, from whom less is definitely more'; she later remarks that 'Mr. Hauer is so sleekly diabolical, Mr. Stallone so bearish and enraged, that their antagonism works in physical terms even if it hasn't been keenly established in dramatic ones' (1981: C6). Considering Stallone in isolation from his co-stars, in *Nighthawks* in particular we see one of the numerous reinventions of his star persona. Although retaining a back story of working-class ethnicity from the actor's 1970s films, *Nighthawks* promises a more cerebral Stallone, his Deke DaSilva character often costumed in sport coats and adorned with a beard and glasses.[21] DaSilva's facial hair helps contrast him with Hauer's Wulfgar, who also appears bearded in the first act but is clean-shaven following plastic surgery and for the rest of the film. DaSilva's beard contributes to his apparently natural style, set against Wulfgar's diabolical artifice. Remarkably, Stallone is also in drag twice in the film, disguised as a woman in its opening sequence as a lure to would-be muggers, and donning a wig and dress for its climax to foil a murder attempt on his wife. Still, the sub-plot of DaSilva's faltering marriage (a union jeopardised by his conventionally masculine obsession with work) and his many scenes with Hauer, Davenport and Williams in work and action contexts help consolidate his securely heterosexual, professional, aggressive masculinity. Offering another variation on Stallone's existing persona, *Victory* defines him not only in the sports and POW milieus but as a kind of undercover agent, donning disguises and learning French for a trip to occupied Paris to meet with the Resistance. Overall, Stallone's early to mid-1980s efforts demonstrate a consistent strategy on his and his management's part to foreground the singularity of his persona through distinctive co-casting.

Starting with *Rocky* and throughout the 1980s, Stallone's starring roles present his sculpted body as an object for display and a site of narrative conflict, arguably serving as his chief marketable asset. In *Victory*, though, Stallone carries less muscle than in the surrounding

Rocky films, having slimmed down to play a credibly underfed POW. With its many scenes of soccer practice and play, *Victory* puts Stallone on display, though not markedly so in the spectacular fashion of many of his other films. He appears in a tank top in one scene and shirtless for the brief scene of his night-time escape from the camp, for which he climbs into the roofing of a shower area. For the rest of the film, he is fully clothed – even the football-training sequences keep him in a shirt and trousers, with the team members wearing shorts only in the third-act match against the Germans. *Nighthawks* also withholds displays of Stallone's muscled body, perhaps in so doing limiting its commercial appeal. Stallone's previous and subsequent roles as Rocky and Rambo include abundant display, and Stallone's training regimen circulates throughout body-building discourses in the 1980s. In *Victory*, Stallone's body matters less to the film's narrative and thematics than does his ability to be European: to eschew American individualism for English reserve and team spirit, to speak French and wear a black turtleneck convincingly enough to walk unimpeded around Paris, and most significantly, to learn to play the sport at which nearly all the other POWs excel. For its part, *Nighthawks* tests the professionalism of Stallone's character more than his purely physical attributes, again likely in efforts to broaden his star persona, though without success at this time.

Since *Nighthawks* and *Victory* frame Stallone not so much in terms of his muscled body as through his engagements and conflicts with other characters – Hauer in *Nighthawks* and Caine in *Victory* – these and other co-stars become instrumental to the films' circulation. As mentioned, at the level of industrial strategy, *Nighthawks'* mixed-gender, multi-ethnic and transnational casting appears as a precursor to the calculated rainbow coalitions of such films as *Lethal Weapon 4* (1998), the *Rush Hour* series (1998, 2001, 2007) and the *Pirates of the Caribbean* sequels (2006, 2007, 2011), which deploy white, black and East Asian faces from among a pool of regional and global talent to maximise local and cosmopolitan appeals. *Victory's* ensemble aims at some level for similar appeals, though the film's long-term reputation indicates its principal appeals to older men and fans of European football rather than to the young audiences that Hollywood would reliably court across the 1980s.

Neither of Stallone's 1981 releases has earned a prominent place in film culture. *Victory* enjoys a modest cult reputation largely as a result of its supporting cast of professional football players but makes its way into few academic studies or histories. *Nighthawks*, despite being representative of many industry trends, also has largely escaped critical and historical attention.[22] When invoked in contemporary fan discourse, *Nighthawks* often appears with qualifiers such as 'overlooked' or 'underrated'.[23] Such responses define the film not by ideological weight and blockbuster status as with the *Rocky* and *Rambo* films, nor by the supposed personal and industrial miscalculations that govern discourse on films such as *Rhinestone* (1984), nor by the regenerative reading of the star that *Cop Land* (1997) singularly engenders. *Victory*'s reception moves in a different direction, with IMDb and other forums' commentary heavily emphasising its generic status as a sports film. Accordingly, fan response judges the film strongly in terms of its stars' contributions to the perceived inspirational appeals of sports films. Often taking a stand against the film's poor critical reputation, fans discuss *Victory* as a feel-good male-bonding showcase and particularly as a document of well-known professional players circa 1980.

In both cases, receivers make cases for the films as suitable genre works, one aesthetically satisfying, the other as a confection for fans of the genre and the sport. More prominent (or notorious) Stallone vehicles map tidily onto prevailing, retrospective discourses about the film industry and US culture. *Rocky* and its sequels exemplify the post-classical blockbuster; *Rambo* offers a proxy for the Reagan era; *Rhinestone* offers the kind of stunt casting that Hollywood studios would later use successfully (e.g. with the Arnold Schwarzenegger/Danny DeVito pairing in *Twins* [1988]); and *Cop Land* hints at the mutual attractions of avowedly independent cinema for performers and studio interests (with the Disney-owned Miramax benefitting from Stallone's name recognition). The key significance of *Victory* and *Nighthawks*, then, may be that neither can be recuperated by any of these (more or less credible) accounts. Instead, in their international and multi-ethnic casting and their untimely deployment of other textual and transtextual attributes, both films illustrate how casting, genre, narrative and setting figure in the industry's long transition from an artisanal and entrepreneurial network comprising craftsmen and idiosyncratic moguls to a component of global mega-corporations.

Both films highlight the roles of creative individuals, particularly stars, in organising understandings of textual production. While critics and some fans approach *Victory* in terms of director John Huston, most receivers frame the film in terms of its most visible stars, Stallone and Caine. For *Nighthawks*, with a not well-known director and a supporting cast lacking high-profile careers in Hollywood film, Stallone provides the dominant lens through which both critics and popular audiences judge the film. The two films together help us recognise the creative choices stars make across their careers and amid ongoing industry changes. Star studies historically have focused on the narrow category of representation across a discrete filmography of individual performances. Locating these performances in wider industrial contexts can produce rich insights about the place of creative labour in Hollywood's commercial-industrial system. Stallone's managed self-construction works alongside industrial shifts occurring over the course of his career. His versions of masculinity, muscularity, ethnic whiteness and more depend on his evolving status as a rising A-list star in what would become an increasingly blockbuster-driven industrial ecology.

Nighthawks and *Victory* are key to Stallone's move from supporting and finally showcase performer in 1970s realist dramas to iconic embodiment of spectacular masculinity in stylised 1980s action-fantasies. In the wake of these 1981 films, *Rocky III* and *First Blood* contribute further to Stallone's outsized hero persona. Just as other contributors to this collection study Stallone's creative work outside film acting, we should consider how he functions as an industrial commodity and agent. Awareness of industrial developments illuminates Stallone's manoeuvres within a changing industrial climate and his role as a commercial asset linked to but also distinct from his well-examined function as repository for ideological sentiments.

NOTES

1   *Nighthawks* opened on 4 April 1981 in the US, where it grossed just under $15 million and ranked 49th at the box office for the year; it earned another $5 million overseas (Box Office Mojo 2012a). *Victory* opened wide on 30 July in the US, where it grossed just under $11 million and ranked 64th at the box office for the year (Box Office Mojo 2012b). *Nighthawks*, with a $5 million budget (IMDb 2012a), was not an outright failure, but it achieved nowhere near the box-office impact of the surrounding Rocky films. Compare *Rocky II* and *III*. In 1979, *Rocky II* grossed over $85 million domestically (Box Office Mojo 2012c); and in 1982, *Rocky III* grossed nearly $12.5 million in its opening weekend alone in the US, en route to a $125 million domestic total (Box Office Mojo 2012d).

2   During production of *Nighthawks* and *Victory*, William Morris's Stan Kamen represented Stallone. In addition to attracting other major stars at the turn of the decade, Michael Ovitz poached Stallone for CAA in July 1981 (see Prince 2000: 163–6). CAA's Ron Meyer (himself a former William Morris agent) represented Stallone into the mid-1990s.

3   For international poster images for *Victory/Escape to Victory*, see Harris (2012). Another alternative poster, for the film's Australian release, does showcase Stallone, showing him

alone in a central three-quarter body shot as well as in two of six other photographic images on the poster.

4 Regarding 'Conglomerate Hollywood', see for example Schatz (2008).

5 On 'off-white' ethnicity, see Negra (2001).

6 In a 2006 interview, Stallone claims that Universal cut additional *Nighthawks* scenes featuring Wagner, whose role in the film is somewhat smaller than her third billing might suggest; see Anon. (2006).

7 Stephen Prince credits the rising power of talent agencies such as the venerable William Morris and the newer CAA and ICM, noting in his industrial history of 1980s Hollywood that 'as deal making became essential to film production and the number of people with whom deals had to be struck increased, the industry grew more decentralized' (2000: 160).

8 Nelson's television credits include nearly two dozen episodes of *Get Smart* (from 1966 to 1969) as well as series such as *Gilligan's Island* (1965–67), *The Courtship of Eddie's Father* (1970–72) and *Love, American Style* (1969–72). He had directed features as well, including the successful Disney comedy *Freaky Friday* (1976) and the expensive science-fiction flop *The Black Hole* (1979), also for Disney.

9 The credited production company for *Nighthawks*, the independent entity 'The Production Company', had only two previous credits, both television movies, airing on ABC and NBC (see IMDb 2012b).

10 Numerous capsule biographies of Malmuth cite his advertising work; see also Archerd (1980; cited in Lichtenfeld 2007: 349). Assessing directing credits for *Nighthawks* is somewhat complicated. Malmuth is the credited director, but many sources repeat the anecdote that Stallone himself directed a day of shooting between Nelson's exit and Malmuth's arrival. Some sources, including *Variety*'s online profile of the film (Anon. 2008) credit William J. Cassidy (aka Bill Cassidy) as director alongside Malmuth. The film's opening credits show Cassidy as second-unit director (as does the film's IMDb credits listing; see IMDb 2012c). One of numerous people with whom Stallone worked repeatedly, Cassidy also served as the production designer on *Rocky* (1976), *Rocky III* and *Rocky V* (1990) (IMDb 2012d).

11 For a comprehensive account of 1970s tendencies in cinematography, see Cook (2000: 355–83). On cinematographic style in the 1980s, see Prince (2000: 190–3). For a cross-historical view of film technology as stylistic determinant, see Salt (2009).

12 In fact, *Nighthawks* was almost unwittingly topical, though not to its advantage. The assassination attempt on Ronald Reagan occurred on 30 March, just five days before the film's release, and the shooting of Pope John Paul II took place on 13 May, about five weeks after the release. Also in May, Libya entered the limelight as a potential terrorist state, with leader Muammar el-Qaddafi threatening to assassinate US diplomats in Europe.

13 In his 1981 *Washington Post review*, Gary Arnold explicitly makes the *Serpico* connection.

14 *Nighthawks* updates *The French Connection*'s opening scene as well. Both begin with a pair of police protagonists working undercover, one in comic disguise – Gene Hackman in a Santa Claus outfit in the 1971 film, Stallone in drag as a middle-aged woman a decade later. Likewise, both start with a foot chase that evolves into a fistfight.

15 This production decision represents part of a move towards overseas production made by Hollywood studios since the 1950s. Settings outside the US supplied a degree of visual realism as well as lower-cost, below-the-line labour.

16 On Fields's career, see Natale (2007).

17 Earning executive-producer credits, Kassar and Vajna (the latter a Budapest native) first

worked with Stallone on *Victory*. They were aged 29 and 25, respectively, during the summer-1980 production. The pair subsequently used Stallone's casting to secure production financing for *First Blood*. This was the first release of the company that would become Carolco, one of the principal major independents of the 1980s; see Prince (2000: 144).

18 See Ramsden (2006) for a thorough evaluation of the film's combined nationalist and football appeals.

19 Given Caine's stocky physique, viewers must suspend much disbelief to imagine his character as a professional-calibre sportsman, and in the third-act football match, a much thinner stunt double replaces him for nearly all play action not filmed in close-up or medium shot.

20 The top domestic earners of 1982 – *E.T.*, *Tootsie* and *An Officer and a Gentleman* – all showcase American characters, stories and settings. The number-six film of 1982, *Star Trek II: The Wrath of Khan*, is the only film in the year's domestic top ten to include non-US actors and settings (for 1981 and 1982 box-office listings, see Box Office Mojo 2012e and 2012f). Similarly, in 1983's top ten, only the top performer, *Return of the Jedi*, and the Bond instalment *Octopussy* (number six at the US box office) include non-US characters and settings (for 1983 listings, see Box Office Mojo 2012g).

21 See also Lichtenfeld (2007: 61).

22 Ramsden (2006) and Lichtenfeld (2007) offer the only detailed studies of *Victory* and *Nighthawks*, respectively, I have encountered in academic work.

23 Each adjective appears in hundreds of online postings about *Nighthawks* on IMDb, YouTube, Amazon's various national sites, and other entertainment discussion forums.

BIBLIOGRAPHY

Anon. (2006) 'Round One with Sylvester Stallone Q&A', *Ain't It Cool News*, 1 December. Online. Available HTTP: http://www.aintitcool.com/node/30861 (20 April 2012).

_____ (2008) *'Nighthawks'*. Online. Available HTTP: http://www.variety.com/profiles/Film/crew/29394/Nighthawks.html (1 March 2008).

Archerd, Army (1980) 'Just for *Variety*', *Daily Variety*, 1 February, 3.

Arnold, Gary (1981) '*Nighthawks* Nosedives' (film review), *Washington Post*, 13 April, C3.

Box Office Mojo (2012a) *'Nighthawks'*. Online. Available HTTP: http://www.boxofficemojo.com/movies/?id=nighthawks.htm (6 February 2012).

_____ (2012b) *'Victory'*. Online. Available HTTP: http://www.boxofficemojo.com/movies/?id=victory.htm (6 February 2012).

_____ (2012c) *'Rocky II'*. Online. Available HTTP: http://www.boxofficemojo.com/movies/?id=rocky2.htm (6 February 2012).

_____ (2012d) *'Rocky III'*. Online. Available HTTP: http://www.boxofficemojo.com/movies/?id=rocky3.htm (6 February 2012).

_____ (2012e) '1981 Yearly Box Office Results'. Online. Available HTTP: http://www.boxofficemojo.com/yearly/chart/?yr=1981&p=.htm (6 February 2012).

_____ (2012f) '1982 Yearly Box Office Results'. Online. Available HTTP: http://www.boxofficemojo.com/yearly/chart/?yr=1982&p=.htm (6 February 2012).

_____ (2012g) '1983 Yearly Box Office Results'. Online. Available HTTP: http://www.boxofficemojo.com/yearly/chart/?yr=1983&p=.htm (6 February 2012).

Cook, David A. (2000) *Lost Illusions: American Cinema in the Shadow of Watergate and Vietnam, 1970-1979*. Berkeley: University of California Press.

Harris, Roger (2012) *'Escape to Victory'*. Online. Available HTTP: http://www.michaelcaine.

org/03CainePosters/1981%20Escape%20to%20Victory/ (19 February 2012).

Internet Movie Database (IMDb) (2012a) 'Box Office/Business for *Nighthawks*'. Online. Available HTTP: http://www.imdb.com/title/tt0082817/business (6 February 2012).

____ (2012b) 'The Production Company'. Online. Available HTTP: http://www.imdb.com/company/co0032939/ (6 February 2012).

____ (2012c) 'Full Cast and Crew for *Nighthawks*'. Online. Available HTTP: http://www.imdb.com/title/tt0082817/fullcredits (6 February 2012).

____ (2012d) 'William J. Cassidy'. Online. Available HTTP: http://www.imdb.com/name/nm0144256/ (6 February 2012).

Lichtenfeld, Eric (2007) *Action Speaks Louder: Violence, Spectacle, and the American Action Movie*. Revised and expanded edition. Middletown, CT: Wesleyan University Press.

Maslin, Janet (1981) '*Nighthawks* with Sylvester Stallone' (film review), *New York Times*, 10 April, C6.

McDonald, Paul (2008) 'The Star System: The Production of Hollywood Stardom in the Post-Studio Era', in Paul McDonald and Janet Wasko (eds) *The Contemporary Hollywood Film Industry*. Malden: Blackwell, 167–81.

Natale, Richard (2007) 'Agent Freddie Fields Dies at 84', *Variety*, 12 December. Online. Available HTTP: http://www.variety.com/article/VR1117977570 (20 April 2012).

Negra, Diane (2001) *Off-White Hollywood: American Culture and Ethnic Female Stardom*. London: Routledge.

Prince, Stephen (2000) *A New Pot of Gold: Hollywood Under the Electronic Rainbow, 1980–1989*. Berkeley: University of California Press.

Ramsden, John (2006) 'England Versus Germany, Soccer, and War Memory: John Huston's Escape to Victory (1981)', *Historical Journal of Film, Radio, and Television*, 26.4 (October), 579–90.

Salt, Barry (2009) *Film Style and Technology: History and Analysis*. Third edition. London: Starword Press.

Schatz, Tom (2008) 'The Studio System and Conglomerate Hollywood', in Paul McDonald and Janet Wasko (eds) *The Contemporary Hollywood Film Industry*. Malden: Blackwell, 13–42.

Tasker, Yvonne (1993) *Spectacular Bodies: Gender, Genre, and the Action Cinema*. London: Routledge.

Universal City Studios (1980) *Nighthawks* production edition.

Willis, Andy (2004) 'Introduction', in Andy Willis (ed.) *Film Stars: Hollywood and Beyond*. Manchester: Manchester University Press, 1–7.

ADVENTURES IN ACTING: STALLONE THE PERFORMER

CHRIS HOLMLUND

ADVENTURES IN ACTING: YOU ARE WHAT YOU EAT?

What to make of Stallone's adventures in acting? What to make of how they are *valued*, when action films are often dismissed by critics even though – indeed, because – they are popular with audiences and beloved by fans. Is this why most of Stallone's *performances* have not yet been studied? To date only his work in *Cop Land* (1997), playing opposite revered Method actors Robert De Niro, Harvey Keitel and Ray Liotta, has received sustained academic attention, by Rachel Adams (1999) and, in this anthology, also by Paul McDonald.

And/or is the lack of attention attributable to the fact that 'you are what you eat' has often seemed to be Sylvester Stallone's approach to preparation for his roles? Anyone watching the films witnesses the results. In interviews, moreover, Stallone often details the ways he has used diet and exercise to create his characters. With *Rocky* (1976), for example, a strict shrimp-and-shellfish diet meant 'my intelligence level dropped to the point where I'd want to listen to country-and-western music, which is really bizarre for me' (in Linderman 1978: 79). For *F.I.S.T.* (1978) he gained 35 pounds by switching to bananas and water. With other films, he has eaten junk food to lard on the pounds or engaged in a high-protein, low-fat diet to get 'tight, tight, tight' (Savello 1998: 69–70, 88).[1] More recently, he bulked up for *The Expendables* (2010), then lost the extra weight after shooting ended because he needed, he said, 'to let my body relax. You learn that your body's got to take a vacation, just deflate down' (in Strauss 2010: C2). Add to these dietary regimens: exercise or lack thereof, steroids, Botox, surgery and human growth hormones.[2]

With nearly four years of acting training at the University of Miami, Stallone at first maintained that he was 'an instinctual actor'. Doubtless referring to Konstantin Stanislavski's idea that the body is the actor's instrument and that training benefits acting, he told the *New York Times* in 1976: 'I don't understand terms like "tuning your instrument". I'm not an oboe or a bass fiddle' (in Klemesrud 1976: 48). Such statements make him sound like a naïf, but his tastes in theatre have often been highbrow.[3]

Perceptions of his acting ineptitude abound. Mimicking the tag line of *Cobra* (1986) – 'Stallone is a disease. Acting lessons are the cure' – talk show host David Letterman's snipe is typical of popular critical response in the US. Academic appraisals in the 1990s fixated primarily on Stallone's body and muscles, assessing them in relation to ideology, without analysing his performances per se.[4] Is this because the training that Stallone relies on to shape his body – body-building and weight-lifting – is associated with working-class taste? As Pierre Bourdieu argues, 'a strong body, bearing the outward signs of strength – this is the working-class demand, which is satisfied by body-building'; he continues: 'nor is it an accident that the Olympic authorities took so long to grant official recognition to weight-lifting, which, in the eyes of the aristocratic founders of modern sport, symbolized mere strength, brutality and intellectual poverty, in short the working classes' (1978: 835–36).

Bourdieu maintains, further, that film, like jazz and photography, is a 'middle art', reliant for cultural capital on its 'fixed relationship' to 'the legitimate arts'. 'High-minded film criticism' thus valorises certain forms of acting and certain kinds of films (for example, prestige and art films), disdaining 'Hollywood's usual product' (Cagle 2007: 301).[5] Simply put, Stallone's is not the kind of acting that is favoured or even noticed.

This essay showcases how Stallone alters not only his body but also, and more importantly, his movements, stance and delivery, studying Stallone's vocal and gestural performances in key scenes taken from nine films released from 1974 to 2006.[6] Some are action extravaganzas, others low-budget dramas, others comedies. In some, he stars; in others, he co-stars; in others he is an ensemble player.

My first section examines three films made between 1974 and 1981, when Stallone first came to national and international attention. At this point (and often later as well), Stallone's performances can best be described as naturalist or Method-influenced: he conveys psychological depth through words, stance and gestures. In two of these films he also shows off his physical talent. Critics on the whole approved.

The second section concentrates on Stallone mid-career, from 1982 to 1996. Now Stallone crafts his second trademark character, Rambo, more skilfully than is typically recognised. He branches out to comedy but is known primarily for physical roles. Critics on the whole disapproved, for reasons mostly unhooked to the calibre of Stallone's performances, dismissing him largely because he had become an action star.

The third section examines the latest phase of Stallone's career, when, wanting to continue working, Stallone has confronted what it means to be an ageing actor. Intentionally, at times he risked his star status to explore acting and to gain greater critical legitimacy. In certain films he mocks his star persona – something he tried already to do with *Rhinestone* (1984). Frequently he brands his performances with reference to his trademark characters. Anglophone critics praised certain films and hated others, but most continued to ignore him as a performer.

The time has come for a reassessment. In conclusion I reconsider Stallone's performance legacy, commenting on the evaluations of his work by film professionals and comparing critical reception in English-speaking countries with European reception.

YOUNG TURKS, ITALIAN STALLIONS

Many of Stallone's early screen appearances reveal acting promise. He adjusts his shape, voice and movements to portray a sensitive thug (*The Lord's of Flatbush* [1974]), a lovable underdog (*Rocky*), a fearless labour leader turned ruthless union boss (*F.I.S.T.*), a New York undercover cop (*Nighthawks* [1981]) and an imprisoned World War II resistance fighter (*Victory* [1981]).

His first role of note was as Stanley Rosiello in the low-budget ($160,000) *The Lord's of Flatbush*.[7] Directed by Martin Davidson and Stephen Verona, and written by Verona and Gayle Gleckler, Stallone receives credit for 'additional dialogue'. The film's coming-of-age narrative centres on four high school pals: Stanley, Chico (Perry King), Butchey (Henry Winkler) and Wimpy (Paul Mace). Stanley is the gang's resident tough guy, a macho man who is both defensive and sensitive. He protects Wimpy and, like Marlon Brando in *On the Waterfront* (1954), tends pigeons on a roof. In his longest monologue, he even imagines he is a pigeon flying above Tokyo.

To play the beefy bruiser, Stallone gained 40 pounds, 'gorg[ing] on whatever was cheap and fattening' (Stallone with Hochman 2005: 19). At 210 pounds, wearing a black T-shirt, studded leather belt, black leather jacket, black trousers and heavy boots, the extra weight shows on his arms. His face is baby-fleshy. Because he is young he moves fluidly, bouncing as he walks, lounging casually outside school, hands hooked onto his trouser pockets. Under pressure from his girlfriend, Frannie (Maria Smith), Stanley's immaturity and insecurity emerge. Stallone fusses with his hair and rubs at his eyes as if fighting back tears, using surface mannerisms to indicate what his character is feeling.

His delivery shifts noticeably when Frannie tells him she is pregnant. Stallone's first response is belligerent denial: 'Tell me who the guy is and I'll kill him, Fran!' Then, more softly, he tries avoidance: 'You're the one is pregnant, not me.' His last answer to her shrill barrage of questions – what should she say to her mother, the priest, her friends? – is mumbled and punctuated by pauses: 'I ... don't ... know ... Fran.'

As most actors do, Stallone uses objects – the pool ball, cue chalk, table, jacket – so that his exchanges do not become ping pong games. When Frannie enters, he backs against the pool table as if for support. When she insists it is his baby, he squats, grins foolishly, and agrees. When she threatens to tell his friends that he cries when he comes, he drops the pool ball he has been fiddling with and, fingers of his left hand out-splayed, protests, 'That's enough!' Finally he drums his knuckles on the table, stands slowly, back to the camera, and implies he can help her obtain an abortion. Kneeling in front of the pool table he hits his head with the pool ball and toys with the cue chalk, then shuffles over for a cigarette to the comparative safety of his jacket, all spring gone from his gait. Throughout the sequence Maria Smith stands back. Our focus, aided by cinematographers Ed Lachman and Joseph Mangine's framing, is on Stallone even when his back is turned. As a performer, he slips into the role: we see the character and forget the actor.

Critics liked Stallone, singling him out in reviews. *New York*'s Judith Crist's response was typical. She argued that Stallone makes Stanley both believable and likeable: he 'invests the hulking Stanley with a punky dignity. ... As the pressure mounts, [his] face goes through a generation of changes. In these few desperate moments, the viewer can see everything slipping away ... watch him feel a loss that has not quite happened' (1974: n.p.).

Stallone's fondness for playing 'good guys' like Stanley with whom everyone can identify has become legendary. Written by Stallone, and

Figure 1 - Downcast eyes and nervous fingers translate Stanley (Sylvester Stallone)'s dashed hopes. *The Lord's of Flatbush*. Producer Stephen Verona; directors Stephen Verona and Martin Davidson; DVD distributed by Columbia Tristar Home Video.

produced independently for $1 million, *Rocky* is the most famous example: it grossed $225 million worldwide. As an actor Stallone sought to morph into the character. Then-wife Sasha said she

> *'went through horrors'. He trained for five months as if he really were preparing for a championship. ... For* Rocky, *it had to be the real thing – getting up at dawn to run for five miles. Driving to a gym ... to work with a trainer. And, of course, the punching bag in the living room. He used to shadowbox around the apartment grunting and breathing heavily. The only way Sasha could bring him back to reality was to ring the bell on the kitchen oven and yell, 'Time ... time!'* (Farr 1976: 73)

Where *The Lord's of Flatbush* invoked *On the Waterfront*, *Rocky* harks back to another award-winning picture, *Marty* (1955). The sequence in which Rocky brings Adrian (Talia Shire) to his studio apartment is one of many that paint Rocky as a creature of his surroundings: he judges and acts based on what he has been exposed to and knows. Rocky's actions here respond to his working-class 'habitus', for Bourdieu the web of class-linked social arrangements and categories of understanding that shape actions, values and tastes.[8] To play Rocky 'realistically', Stallone the actor again employs naturalist, Method-inspired techniques. He talks and moves constantly: Rocky is nervous but eager to seduce Adrian. His gestures and hand movements express awkwardness yet at the same time signal interest. Where, as Stanley, Stallone's body language closes inwards and he moves away from Frannie, as Rocky he opens up and edges closer to Adrian. When the two enter, Stallone sniffs, casually takes off his black leather jacket and porkpie hat, drapes both on a hook, then whips off his wool sweater and long-sleeved shirt. Underneath he wears a muscle T-shirt; it has a sizeable hole on one side. He puts mood music on the record player, picks up his pet turtles, reminisces about buying them, carefully sets them back, wipes one hand on his trousers, then both hands together. Rocky is inexperienced and jumpy. He wants to make a good impression but needs to do something with his hands.

Moving to a hideous green couch littered with newspapers, he sits, pats the sofa, and softly urges Adrian to sit down. Head back, arms outstretched, hands crumpled non-threateningly, he teases, his rumbling bass voice pitched lower than usual: 'There's big bugs in there, you know.' Every movement he makes is small: he gestures with one finger, half circles with the other hand. The shy Adrian continues to stand near the door. When Stallone finally stands and advances he does so with his hands held behind him, hooked on his trouser pockets. Propping his muscular arms onto his chin-up bar he looms above Adrian but does not touch her. Instead, plaintively yet seductively he asks, 'What's the problem? You don't like me? You don't like the turtles?' Shot from below, his white muscle T-shirt brightly lit, he is the centre of Adrian's – and our – attention. He coaxes her into taking off her glasses and letting down her hair. The scene ends, famously, in their kiss.

With only a few exceptions, critics were enthusiastic, heralding Stallone as a talent to watch. Frank Capra loved the film's nostalgic, fairy tale quality. Muhammad Ali wired a congratulatory poem. Elvis invited Stallone to Tennessee. Chaplin invited him to Switzerland (see Stallone with Hochman 2005: 19). Pauline Kael wrote: 'In his deep, caveman's voice he gives the most surprising, sharp, fresh shadings to his lines. He's at his funniest trying to explain to his boss why he didn't break somebody's thumbs, as he'd been told to; he's even funny talking to his turtles. ... We're constantly charmed. ... He's like a child who never ceases to amaze us. ... Stallone's the picture. Yet she was also presciently critical of what she called Stallone's 'hamminess': 'He may not know how good he could be if he'd stop snuggling into your heart.' The same reserve marks her evaluation of his writing: '*Rocky* is shameless, and that's why on a certain level it works. What holds it together is innocence' (1976: 157).

Rocky won Academy Awards for Best Picture, Best Editing and Best Director. Like only Chaplin and Welles before him, Stallone was nominated for Best Actor and Best Original Screenplay. He won neither award but nevertheless bragged: 'I am at the beginning of a new cycle of actors. ... Again we are going to see the communicative actor, the actor who will be a hero, the actor who will inspire confidence and, ah, imitativeness in his viewers. Positiveness!' (in Kasindorf 1977: 72).

Released in 1981 by Paramount, *Victory* follows *Rocky* in combining drama with action, but places less emphasis on romance. Again, Stallone draws primarily on Method techniques to play characters caught up in personal melodrama. Here, as in *Rocky*, Stallone moves between what Richard Maltby calls 'autonomous' and 'integrated' performance. For Maltby, 'autonomous' performance is associated with ac*tion*, spectacle and technical display; 'integrated' performance is associated with acting, narrative and character psychology. The latter is accorded higher status, although, Maltby underlines, 'few Hollywood performances are so schematic as to fall entirely into one category' (2003: 388–9).

The casting of renowned co-stars Michael Caine and Max von Sydow, both known primarily for 'integrated' acting, was clearly intended to boost *Victory*'s critical cachet and expand the film's international appeal. The presence of professional football stars in the cast, among them Brazil's Pelé, promised 'autonomous' display. Stallone plays a World War II American POW, Captain Hatch, who escapes with his teammates after winning an exhibition soccer match in Paris. He lost weight for the part, plunging from 200 to 159 pounds in less than five months on a rigid high-protein subsistence diet (see Anon. 1981: B5). He also learned to be a goalie, breaking his right little finger, re-fracturing two ribs, and suffering a shoulder separation as he trained (see Archerd 1980: n.p.).[9]

From the start, Stallone's defiant stance and forthright delivery transmit Hatch's rebelliousness. Chasing a ball that the camp commander (von Sydow) has stopped with his foot, Stallone pitches his voice higher than usual to communicate energy and insolence. In each of his 'integrated' acting scenes he conveys psychological complexity through rapidly shifting facial expressions and fluid movements. A good example is the sequence in which Hatch sits for a forged passport photograph. Wearing a sleeveless T-shirt and high-waisted trousers that accentuate how slim he is, Stallone pauses outside the barracks to glance at his watch. He grins boyishly. Once inside, he quickly changes into a blue jacket, tie and dress shirt. Facing forward, he ruffles up his hair, furrows his brow, and frowns, eyes burning. The photo taken, he is asked what name he wants on the passport. He changes demeanour as he rapidly strips off jacket, tie and shirt, licking his lips and blinking eagerly. Within the space of a few moments, Stallone-the-performer moves from depressed solemnity to nervous excitement to steadfast resolve, creating a carefully delineated character. Elsewhere, however, as in the final thrilling football match, we are reminded of Rocky, and of Stallone-the-newly-minted-star. In knee socks, relatively tight white shorts and blue jersey open at the neck, his skill as a physical actor is what counts. When Hatch's team wins thanks to a brilliant goal by Pelé and a save by Stallone, the crowd surges forward chanting 'Victoire! Victoire!' as if *Victory* were *Rocky*.

Reviewers ignored all the actors' performances in *Victory*, fixating instead on the derivative *Great Escape*-like narrative and John Houston's uninspired direction. Only *Film Journal*'s and *Variety*'s reviewers mentioned that they enjoyed seeing Stallone in an ensemble piece reminiscent of *The Lord's of Flatbush* (Shifren 1981; Step 1981). With *First Blood* (1982) and, especially, with *Rambo: First Blood Part II* (1985) and *Rocky IV* (1985), Stallone became a mega-action star. He would not return to ensemble acting until *Cop Land*.

MID-LIFE CLIFFHANGERS AND CRISES

Stallone enjoyed peak popularity between 1982 and 1985. His box-office returns languished from 1986 to 1992, but because he did not want to be locked into action stardom, he periodically switched genres, moving to comedy with *Rhinestone*, *Oscar* (1991) and *Stop! Or My Mom Will Shoot* (1992). He even directed a musical starring John Travolta, *Staying Alive* (1983). Frequently he wrote his own scripts. Sometimes he adapted pre-existing material. In films authored by others he contributed additional dialogue.

With few exceptions, however, 'middle-brow' critics in the US and UK despised all the films he made during this period. Pat Broeske summed up her colleagues' response: 'What Stallone does to the bad guys, critics usually do to Stallone movies' (1986: 20). Had these critics seen and appreciated Stallone as an actor and erstwhile 'auteur' rather than simply as a stellar body, they might have understood what provoked him to make both hard-core action films and comedies: physicality is key, after all, to both action/adventure and slapstick.

To craft the character who would become the 1980s super hero bar none, Rambo, Stallone, Michael Kozoll and William Sackheim rewrote David Morrell's 1970 novel *First Blood* to make Rambo more attractive and less violent. Released in 1982 by independent studio Orion, the film portrays Rambo as an outcast and a victim who is always in retreat. As usual Stallone-the-writer added healthy dollops of melodrama and redemption. Noteworthy is the fact that this Rambo wounds rather than kills his opponents.[10]

Stallone prepared himself for this part through purging. On set, he isolated himself. He wanted to feel lean and lonely. 'I think I function best with this character when I'm not at peace with myself', he said. 'When I'm playing Rambo, I look in the mirror, and I see that my eyes have lost a certain zest for life. ... Rambo doesn't revel in his adventures. And, even when he wins, he doesn't win' (in Broeske 1987: 46). His muscles are nicely shaped but not grotesque. Held prisoner inside Sheriff Teasle's (Brian Donnehy) police station, Rambo escapes using punches, kicks and a spin over a desk top. Outside, clothed in army trousers and tank top, tarp tied at the waist, he leaps and dives like a latter-day Douglas Fairbanks, Sr. Roger Ebert recognised his talent in terms that recall Maltby's descriptions of 'autonomous' performance: 'Stallone is one of the great physical actors in the movies, with a gift

Figure 2 - Rambo (Sylvester Stallone), the hunted, in breakneck flight. *First Blood.* Producer Budd Feitshans; director Ted Koetcheff; DVD distributed by Artisan Home Entertainment.

for throwing himself so fearlessly into an action scene that we can't understand why somebody doesn't really get hurt. ... [A]lthough almost all of *First Blood* is implausible, because it's Stallone on the screen, we'll buy it' (1982).

Stallone's performance is haunted, silent, but also occasionally comic. When Teasle's deputies try to fingerprint Rambo, Stallone mutely registers stubborn opposition through jabbing gestures. He avoids eye contact. 'Just roll it across!' admonishes the younger of two officers. Rambo/Stallone pulls back against him, away from the ink pad, jaw set, eyes averted. A second try is equally unsuccessful. Sheriff Teasle enters and takes charge. Stallone adds subtle slapstick touches. Grimacing, he studies his finger, picks up a paper towel, and starts to wipe away the ink smear. 'Leave the ink on the hand!' shouts the deputy. Teasle menaces: 'Just what is your problem? Now listen hard ass!' Stallone glances sideways, picks up another paper towel, shakes it open, and pointedly wipes his finger off once more. His sullenly repetitive resistance is humorous.

Stallone is also quite funny in Disney-affiliate Touchstone's *Oscar*. Now verbal braggadocio is also involved, because the film is based on a 1958 French farce (a 1967 French film version starred renowned comedian Louis de Funès). The French film and play revolve around mistaken identities, bombast and bluster. The American version rewrites the lead character to recall Stallone's ethnic star persona: he plays Snaps Provolone, a Depression-era crime boss.

Snaps wants to become respectable. 'Readin''s my passion!' he declares proudly to his thug companions. Stallone's line readings exaggerate his trademark bass and Italian working-class accent. His talent for carefully calibrated physical reaction and well-timed verbal repartee is especially apparent when, wearing the new pin-stripe suit the foppish Fanucci Brothers (Harry Shearer and Martin Ferrero) have designed to make him look 'like a banker', he tries to pressure his accountant Anthony (Vincent Spano) into marrying his daughter Lisa (Marisa Tomei). Both his delivery and his gestures acknowledge queer as well as heterosexual audiences. As Anthony grabs for a satchel full of jewels, Snaps/Stallone intercepts him: 'I wouldn't do that if I were you.' 'You forget, Mr. Provolone, you're going straight today', reminds Anthony. Stallone archly raises his eyebrows: 'That's right, I am...' Leaning in unison with Anthony around the doorframe, he points at the Fanuccis and gleefully threatens, '...but they're not!' Right legs identically crossed, clad in matching suits and spats, the Fanuccis sit prissily

Figure 3 - Carefully calibrated comedy: control, calculation, manipulation and bemusement expressed through stance, gesture, wide eyes and raised eyebrows. *Oscar.* Producer Leslie Belzberg; director John Landis; DVD distributed by Touchstone Home Entertainment.

on a settee playing cards, muttering in Italian. 'You mustn't let that fool you', says Stallone, then, one finger at his throat, mimes throat-slitting: 'One word from me and it's ... cccrrrrrrraaaackkk!'

Stallone's body language is menacing one moment, cajoling the next. His facial expressions range from a pout to a snarl, with eyebrows, eyes and mouth all in play. His expressions contrast with yet accompany Shearer and Ferrero's fey moves: where they are sissies, he plays 'butch'. When Anthony refuses to marry Lisa – Snaps thinks she is pregnant – Stallone shakes his head and coos, 'We are talking about my baby's ... baby', then, with a jerk of his head, bellows, 'Fine! Fanuccis!' In perfect synchronicity the Fanuccis jump up, clicking their heels. Cowed, Anthony acquiesces. Snaps/Stallone grins mischievously at the success of his ruse.

Certain critics applauded Stallone's performance. 'One of the biggest surprises in *Oscar* is the performance of Sylvester Stallone, who is genuinely funny as the beleaguered Spats [sic]. ... Stallone is up to the slow burns, double takes, and other attitudinal conventions of the genre', wrote Abbie Bernstein in *Hollywood Dramalogue* (1991: 22). The *New York Times*'s Janet Maslin applauded his 'gameness, even ... flair, for the kind of broadly durable comedy that is the television sitcom's specialty' (1991: C10). Most critics, however, were not eager to accept Stallone in comedy, something *Stop! Or My Mom Will Shoot* proved again the following year. Stallone agreed *that* film was dreadful: 'If it was a question of having my spleen removed with a tractor or watching it again, I'd say, "Start up the engine"' (in Turan 1997: F4). His career in danger, he returned to what audiences liked most: rough, tough physical performance. 'Once you make your reputation as a so-called he-man or physical fella', he admitted, 'it's *rill* hard for people to accept you with your clothes on' (in Case 1993: 20).

Rewriting *Cliffhanger*'s script, Stallone softened the bellicose image he had earned in the *Rambo* sequels, *Cobra* and other 1980s action films. Shades of *Rocky*, he made sure that mountain-climbing hero Gabe Walker would be redeemed, the ending happy. Stallone's preparation for the role emphasised physical training over diet. He learned to climb, adjusting his work-outs accordingly. 'You have to literally build up a whole different set of body muscles and redefine your anatomy because everything is holding, clenching, pulling, and you're not using your legs as much as the back and tendons. I ... used very, very heavy poundage and did lots of pulling versus tremendous resistance' (in TriStar 1993: 6). He even overcame his fear of heights to perform half of his own stunts (Savello 1998: 168): he prides himself on doing his own stunts.

In the scenes where he plays opposite Method-trained Janine Turner ('Jessie') and Shakespearean-professional John Lithgow ('Qualen'),[11] Stallone's performance style shifts to complement theirs.[12] When Gabe pleads with former girlfriend Jessie (Turner) to leave the mountains to live in the city with him, for example, Stallone expresses caring and regret, hope and shame, through small eye movements, unobtrusive head gestures and subtle shifts in posture. He also conveys his character's anguish and desire through intonation and expression. His control is greater than it was in *Rocky*.

Such scenes are, admittedly, in the minority: an expensive film ($70 million), *Cliffhanger* needed spectacular action to attract wide audiences. Stallone delivers. Arm muscles bulging, hanging upside down from a harness, Gabe/Stallone valiantly tries to save a woman friend (Michelle Joyner) whose safety harness is breaking in the harrowing 11-minute opening sequence. The two inch across an abyss on a cable stretched between a 13,000-foot mountain top and a waiting rescue helicopter. Gabe's grip slips; screaming, the woman falls to her death. When Gabe first climbs again after her death, Stallone's talent for 'autonomous' acting is showcased. Qualen orders the captured Gabe to 'fetch' a suitcase full of stolen money from a ledge high above. Stallone's response is a wordless snarl and a defiant stare worthy of Rambo. Qualen's gang

Figure 4 - Upper body strength and tactical hand holds: Sylvester Stallone the mountaineer. *Cliffhanger.*
Producers Renny Harlin and Alan Marshall; director Renny Harlin; DVD distributed by Columbia Tristar Home
Video.

strip him of his coat and attach a rope to his leg to prevent his escape.
Wearing only a T-shirt, fingerless gloves and trousers, Stallone looks
up, grabs a first outcrop, jumps, manages toe holds, looks up again,
pauses, propels himself upwards to a smaller ledge. Slowly he inches
upwards, grunting with effort. Finally he pulls himself over the cliff.
The suitcase is almost buried in snow. Stallone smashes it open with a
rock, mouth contorted with effort.

Rapid camera movements, shifting perspectives, blowing wind,
shrilling violins and frenetic horns up the action ante. Stallone's climbing skills are impressive. Both Janet Maslin and Todd McCarthy praised
his physical prowess. *Cliffhanger* 'treats Mr. Stallone as a smaller, more
mobile and no less impressive piece of scenery. His muscles bulging,
the veins of his neck etched in sharp relief, his jaw set determinedly,
[he] is every bit as physically impressive as the material requires him
to be', wrote Maslin (1993: C3). Todd McCarthy concurred: 'Looking
great, Stallone is clearly into this one, and it pays off in one of his most
rugged screen appearances' (1993: 44). Unlike the bundled up actors in
most mountain pictures, Stallone wore little as he climbed because he
wanted his body and movements to be visible. Shot in large part in the
storm-ridden Italian Dolomites (somewhat implausibly doubling for the
Colorado Rockies), the entire production was a test of endurance – for
Stallone especially.

On the verge of turning fifty, he started taking better care of himself,
using exercise as a 'way of gathering momentum rather than losing it'.
He practiced yoga and tai chi. He 'focused more on smoothing out than
on bulking up', working out three or four hours a week, not twenty-five

(Stallone with Hochman 2005: 42). As had been the case before, he teamed up with talented co-stars – among them Wesley Snipes, Sandra Bullock, Antonio Banderas, James Woods and Viggo Mortensen. His old fans were on the whole loyal, but he did not garner many new admirers. Nothing enhanced his cultural cachet with critics.

OLD MASTER OR *DEATH RACE 2015*?

After a string of misfires in the mid-1990s, Stallone again took a chance on ensemble work. He worried that he would never be taken seriously: 'I was just part of the production team. I was part of the equipment' (in Tunison 1997: 18). So eager was he to play broken-down sheriff Freddy Heflin in James Mangold's relatively low-budget ($28 million) independent *Cop Land* that he went to New York to see Mangold instead of summoning Mangold to his home in Miami. Producer Cary Woods commented, 'I think that's probably as close to an audition as he's had in maybe twenty years' (in Clark 1997: 60). Stallone contracted to waive his $20 million per-picture fee and to work for scale (roughly $50,000). The character appealed to him because Freddy 'was the antithesis of who I usually play, a character who creates no menace whatsoever, furniture with a heartbeat' (in Turan 1997: F4). He agreed with his detractors that contemporary action films – as opposed to *Bullitt* (1968) or *The French Connection* (1971) – are 'performance ... athletics ... sleight of hand ... illusion [but] not in-your-face, tear-out-your-heart, flesh-and-blood acting' (in Tunison 1997: 9).

Mangold's script, Lester Cohen's production design and Eric Alan Edward's cinematography incorporate western, crime film and noir elements.[13] Award-winning, critically acclaimed co-stars Robert De Niro, Harvey Keitel and Ray Liotta brought the kind of prestige Stallone himself desired. To prepare for what he anticipated would be a talent match up of 'genre number one, meet genre number two', Stallone followed De Niro's recipe for success à la *Raging Bull* (1980): he gained nearly forty pounds, gorging on pancakes 'topped ... with mountains of whipped cream and washed down with chocolate milk' (Stallone with Hochman 2005: 45), for breakfast alone consuming 'five pancakes smothered with peanut butter and whipped cream, a bowl of oatmeal, two bagels with more peanut butter, ten fried eggs, French fries and cheesecake' (Savello 1998: 175). His 31-inch waist swelled to 39³/₄ inches; he drew the line at 40 (see Turan 1997: F4). Mangold wanted to undermine his iconic star status: 'I was interested in making him human. Just pushing away the iconography of Stallone and seeing the man' (in Eimer 1997: 19).

Freddy is hearing-impaired, so Stallone went to specialists to learn how partially deaf people react. As he had done with *Rocky* and *First Blood*, he sought to stay in character offset. His pregnant girlfriend (now wife), Jennifer Flavin, commented approvingly that 'in his personal life he became much more docile, much more Freddy-like'. Onset he carried a small ivory turtle in his pocket to remind him that Freddy was slow-moving and non-threatening. Teasingly, Liotta called him 'fat man walking' (see Clark 1997: 60).

When early on we see Freddy in a bar, playing pinball and drinking beer, Stallone's stooped shoulders, shy smiles, ineffectual hand movements and heavy walk ensure that we 'read' Freddy as deferential, beaten down, insecure. He speaks indistinctly, in a low monotone. The camera insists on his paunchy stomach, then pans up to reveal his puffy face and greasy, dishevelled hair. The plaid, mis-buttoned shirt he wears over an untucked, bunched-up white T-shirt makes him look larger. Repeatedly Freddy/Stallone tilts his head as though favouring a good ear. He looks fleetingly at two NYPD cops, Gary Figgis (Liotta) and Berta (Edie Falco), then, chastised for staring by Berta, he quickly mumbles 'sorry'. In the next shot he contritely cradles his beer in one hand, making Freddy seem like a scolded child.

Hailed in the next shot by Figgis, Freddy/Stallone turns from the bar and moves closer to make out what Figgis is saying. He tells Figgis it is his birthday; he is spending it alone. Figgis gets a phone call and turns away, ignoring Freddy. Stallone's sad eyes betray rejection but also acceptance: Freddy is a human Eeyore. Out of quarters to play his video game, he raids an outside parking meter: his infractions of the law are petty ones. In close-up, wearing rolled-up baggy trousers and cheap flip-flops, Stallone's legs look pudgy, his feet pasty. For Rachel Adams this shot is 'the obverse of the glorifying "under-the-chin" shot of the action film' (1999: 9).

Not until the final showdown with the venal New York cops led by Ray Donlan (Keitel) does Stallone revert to an action performance, recasting his movements, however, to fit Freddy's persona. Shot in the ear by the policemen he thought were his friends, Freddy is rendered almost completely deaf. Mangold and Edwards track Stallone's flat-footed, staggering zigzag down the town's streets, shotgun in hands, in extreme long shot, then switch to slow-motion close-ups of his out-turned feet, swollen belly and hefty rear end. When, with Figgis's help,

Freddy kills Keitel and crew, Stallone's expressions register resolve and pain, but not triumph. Freddy is no Rambo.

Writing for *Slate*, David Edelstein said of Stallone's performance: 'He's never more winning than when he projects loserdom' (1997). Miramax promoted Stallone for Best Actor at the Academy Awards, including quotes from *Rolling Stone*, *Time Magazine* and the *Detroit News* in print ads that tout Stallone's 'subtly reactive performance', 'virtuoso acting' and 'spectacularly effective ... delicately shaded turn'. The Stockholm Film Festival named him 'Best Actor'. Others remained sceptical.[14]

The weight he gained introduced Stallone to the perils of ageing: he developed heart palpitations, high blood pressure, sciatica, back problems, digestive problems, acid reflux, headaches and flat feet. As soon as the production wrapped, he returned to a high-protein diet, got back into a cardiovascular routine and resumed weight training. He claims he lost the pounds in two months (see Stallone with Hochman 2005: 46). Savello maintains it took him six months (1998: 180).

Stallone's next role also played with his action hero image. Thanks to his friendship with producer Jeffrey Katzenberg, at last children would encounter Stallone – or at least his plummy voice – in a family-friendly context, performing together with highly regarded screen and stage co-stars such as Gene Hackman, Woody Allen, Danny Glover, Sharon Stone, Christopher Walken and Anne Bancroft. DreamWorks animators designed the bodies of *Antz*'s characters to fit the actors' personalities. Playing a soldier ant named Weaver, Stallone counsels the neurotic, lovelorn Z (Allen) and struts his stuff opposite sultry worker Azteca (Jennifer Lopez). New to vocal work – as was everyone in the cast – Stallone threw himself into the role. 'When you're doing the dialogue you tend to physically act it out', he explained. 'You're trying to convey everything through your voice, but your body begins to enact the part because you're just totally in the moment. After a few hours, I got as sweaty and worn out as I do working on a live-action film' (in DreamWorks Pictures 1998: 5).

In light-hearted tones Stallone sends up the heroism and masochism for which his franchise action characters are known. Nowhere is this more evident than when Weaver meets Azteca. Replacing Z on a worker ant brigade, Stallone grunts happily and energetically as, on-screen, Weaver hurls his pickaxe. Behind him Azteca pauses to admire his massive back, one 'hand' resting on her 'hip'. Aware of her interest, Weaver starts to show off. 'Love it!' Stallone says with gusto, as Weaver picks

Figure 5 - Weaver, the Sylvester Stallone ant, struts his well-developed thorax for the Jennifer Lopez ant. *Antz*. Producers Brad Lewis, Aron Warner and Patty Wooton; director Eric Darnell and Tim Johnson; DVD distributed by DreamWorks Home Entertainment.

up a second pickaxe, twirls both rapidly, then pounds both into the rocks. 'Hey, hey, hey!' Lopez yells, then seductively breathes, 'Take it easy, Muscles. You're making the rest of us look bad. ... What happened to Z?' Stallone replies in tongue-tied pauses, 'He's ... taking a personal day. ... So I'm filling in.' Lopez comments approvingly, 'You fill in any more and you'll explode.' Azteca is curvaceous and bronze-toned, Weaver red-toned with grey arms, huge muscles and a bulging thorax. Flattered, Weaver starts tossing boulders around. Stallone accentuates certain syllables and, as if straining, blurts out: 'Nobody told me digging was so much *fun*. You pick the dirt *up*. ... You move it. ... You pick it up *again*.' Weaver heaves two boulders at once. 'You move it *again*. ... Lots of reps.' Close-ups show Weaver's heaving chest. 'You exercise the arms ... *and* the thorax!' Weaver strikes a muscle-man pose. The line boss, a smaller worker ant, interrupts sarcastically: 'Fascinating!' Stallone reverts to a brusque military delivery as Weaver salutes. 'Sorry *sir!* I was just having a little chat with my friend, *sir!*'

Finally critics agreed that Stallone's performance merited applause. Duane Byrge wrote, '[His] clipped cadence and good-hearted tones infuse his soldier character with just the right amount of humanity' (1998: 8). Tom Shone lauded the film's adroit usage of its stars: 'Any film in which Woody Allen and Sylvester Stallone swap dating tips at a bar gets my vote' (1998: 7). At last Stallone succeeded in comedy.

His next studio ventures were, however, again unsuccessful. Critics hated *Get Carter* (2000), *Driven* (2001) and *Eye See You* (a.k.a. *D-Tox*, 2002), and all lost money. Stallone returned to 'prestige', low-budget ensemble work with *Shade* (2003), taking a small role as a card shark, but that film also did not do well.

With no hit in over ten years, no wonder it took a long time for *Rocky Balboa* to be green lit. Finally an independent production company, Revolution Studios, in partnership with MGM and Columbia, stepped in: the film cost under $25 million (see Arnold 2006: R2). Prior to *Rocky Balboa*'s 2006 release, Stallone was subjected to endless ridicule. Stallone remained resolute: 'I wanted to show I had balls at 60. ... People said my time had come and gone'; writing and rewriting the script, he designed the older Rocky as someone who 'deals with the frustrations of his youth ... without screaming, the only way he knows how. Through his body. Rocky has always been a guy who's about giving and receiving pain' (Jordan 2006: 114). Still a man of the people, this older Rocky is generous, gallant and guileless.[15]

Originally Stallone planned to play Rocky as someone who looks his age and is out of shape. Then he thought, 'Why am I listening to this? It's bad enough that he is going to get a beating, but one of the reasons he can survive is because he's in shape' (in Welkos 2006: E16). He upped his work-outs to five days a week in the gym. He boxed for three to four hours a day, six days a week. For the first time in years, he again relied on diet:

> I wanted to be a legitimate heavyweight, so I ate a lot of carbohydrates, knowing that I would burn them up. A lot of Italian foods; a lot of pasta. I didn't eat much cheese, but a lot of protein drinks, a lot of supplements. In four weeks I was able to burn off a lot and get into the shape I was in the film. But I don't recommend it. Do not try this at home or anywhere! (Ibid.)

Forty pounds heavier than in the original *Rocky*, Stallone's chest bulges underneath his T-shirts. His eyebrows look painted on. In the first half of the film, especially, he lumbers along, arms at his side, slowly shrugs his shoulders, shifts his weight heavily from foot to foot, eyes dead. This Rocky is angst-ridden, lost without Adrian. His more meditative moments are reminiscent of the existentialist and absurdist plays Stallone loved as an undergraduate: 'Am I just tryin' to replace old pain with new pain?' (ibid.) *Variety* picked up on the affiliation, describing Rocky and Paulie as 'sometimes resembling Beckett characters as if they were goombahs, endlessly mus[ing] about how "the whole world is fallin' apart" but without a deeper sense of loss and regret' (Koehler 2006: 50).

In sequences such as the one where Rocky surprises his son, Robert (Milo Ventimiglia), at his upscale workplace, Stallone again gives a naturalist performance, expressing Rocky's emotional reactions without words. As director he blocks the scene using 'temporal counterpoint' (Baron and Carnicke 2008: 197) to indicate the characters' respective power and class standing. As actor he calibrates his stance, gestures, facial expressions and delivery to show Rocky's struggle to connect with his son. The scene starts with Rocky looking through the building's glass doors at Robert being berated by his boss (Michael Kelly). It is obvious who is in control. Kelly stands erect, weight evenly distributed over both feet, arm crooked outwards. The slimmer Ventimiglia looks cowed. Stallone strides in. His faded jeans, sweat shirt and inexpensive jacket are out of place. Voice rumbling, Stallone throws one arm into the air as he calls out, 'Yo Robert! Yo! Hey! How ya doin'?' Rocky's trademark porkpie hat is tilted at a rakish angle. Rocky is eager, but he also looks like a clown.

For the rest of the sequence Stallone only moves sideways: Rocky does not want to seem threatening. When he invites Robert to come to his restaurant for dinner, Stallone uses broad hand movements, his fingers outstretched, to indicate how much Rocky wants to please. 'We could have something made *special* for you', he promises, accenting 'special'. Robert pretends he has prior plans. Rocky/Stallone squints but maintains eye contact. Pursing his mouth, giving a sideways move of his head, Stallone asks gently, 'Did I do somethin' wrong? ... All I know is when I come here, you don't feel so comfortable and I certainly don't want to do that.'

Robert's boss returns and interrupts the father/son exchange: 'I've told Robert twenty times I wanted to meet you.' Dutifully Stallone shakes the hand tendered him, blinks, and shrugs sideways with his whole body. He realises that Robert is embarrassed. Slinging his arm around Stallone's shoulders, the boss insists Robert take a picture of him with Rocky. When he finally leaves, satisfied, Robert at last agrees to come to dinner, gives his dad a sham punch to the chest, then a hug. Stallone says to the air, 'Ah – that'd be great!'

The movie met with mixed reviews,[16] but many critics were by now nostalgic for Rocky. Audiences welcomed the champ's return. The film was a modest box-office success.[17] Crucially, the character Rocky Balboa was once again a cultural icon.

FROM HUNK TO HULK – AND BEYOND?

Today Stallone has a greater command of acting technique. In the first *Rocky* he knew little about lighting or makeup and he had no idea what his best side was. In 1993 he nonetheless told *Vanity Fair* that he thought his early performances were best because they were 'the most visceral' (in Heller 1993: 188). Director/teacher Milton Katselas voiced similar sentiments:

> *There was an innocence to the early work which was his most inward and least contrived. Now he's developed formulas. It's very hard to become a millionaire and then run the risk of slipping on a banana peel. ... You stop working out of your own conception and begin acting towards what you think people expect of you. You stop baring your soul. [...] I believe he's a good actor. [His] major problem is that his sensitivity and delineation of character have been sacrificed to caricature. It'd help him to do theater, because there an actor has to hold an audience for an evening. That's why our best actors ... are stage-trained.* (In Christon 1990: 91, 100)

Katselas's preference for stage training is reminiscent of Bourdieu's contention that cinema is a middle-brow art, reliant for legitimisation on established arts. The privileging of stage over screen is a cultural judgement, based on the hierarchical status accorded different media and not on a solid evaluation of acting skills. Acting is, of course, necessarily different for the stage than for the screen. Acting for the stage is continuous, and audience members' perspectives on the performances do not change. Screen acting is, in contrast, often shot out of sequence, from differing distances and angles, by fixed and moving cameras; screen acting is also usually heavily edited.

Many of the cinematographers, producers and actors who work with Stallone do recognise his screen acting talent; many also acknowledge his general cinematic savvy. Cinematographer László Kóvacs, who worked with Stallone on *F.I.S.T.* and *Paradise Alley* (both 1978), was an early fan: 'Sly knows acting well, he's a very good writer, and I think he's one helluva [sic.] director' (in Stanley 1978: 29). *Cobra* (1986) producer and *Over the Top* (1987) director Menahim Golan raved, 'I've never seen an actor know the camera like that. He knows every lens, every angle. He knows how it will look on the screen. He's not just a man who stands in front of the camera and acts' (in Broeske 1986: 21). As collaborators, their comments should be taken with a grain of salt, but renowned cinematographer Vilmos Zsigmond has similarly praised him: '[he knows] exactly where the lights should be. In fact, he knows everything about movie-making' (in Zebello 1995: 40).

As an A-list celebrity Stallone has become what Christine Geraghty calls a 'professional star'; he enjoys a well-rehearsed, stable, action-based image (2000: 190). But even in action he delivers performances that not only showcase technical skill but also sketch character psychology. Knowing how frequently acting in action is denigrated, from the mid-1990s on Stallone has defended the genre:

> I take offense to people writing off action films as some occupational hazard that actors occasionally must do so that they can be in something financially profitable, then do something 'serious'. Action films are a physical challenge and, because you don't have a great deal of dialogue, you have to become a partial mime to get things across. People dismiss them with a stroke of the pen, but, if there were no action films, there would be no Warner Bros. (In Zebello 1995: 85)

His statements do not change reviewers' opinions, of course. Writing for *Newsweek* and *LA Weekly*, respectively, reviewers' assessments of *Rambo: First Blood Part II* and *Cliffhanger* were particularly pejorative. They vituperatively dismissed what they saw as these films' appeal to working-class taste. 'Nobody much likes Stallone or his works, that is to say, except the people' (Goldman 1985: 58); 'It's futile trying to critique Stallone's acting anymore, since he gave up on the craft years ago. He's merely a massive id performing on screen for the unwashed masses who delight in super hero worship' (Powers 1993: 31).

Bourdieu comes to *my* mind, because he insists that how class shapes 'distinction' and 'legitimacy' varies by location and over time, however. Noteworthy in Stallone's case is the fact that European critics have consistently been more appreciative than American reviewers. The French love physical performers such as Jerry Lewis, Harpo Marx, Jacques Tati – and Sylvester Stallone. At a black-tie *séance spéciale* at Cannes, they applauded *Cliffhanger* an unprecedented eight times (see Hunter 1993: 11). The Zurich Film Festival awarded Stallone the first Golden Icon Award for an actor's life work in 2008 (see Blaney 2009). The Venice Biennale chose him as the 2009 recipient of the Jaeger-LeCoultre Glory to the Filmmaker Award, a recognition given earlier to Takeshi Kitano, Agnès Varda and Abbas Kiarostami. The Venice judges praised Stallone's acting, moreover, not just his directing, writing: 'Even when he participates in films solely as an actor, Stallone shapes his characters with precision, creating a gallery of vivid portraits that also count among the most lucid icons of the contemporary American cinema' (Anon. 2009).

As this essay has detailed, time and again Stallone sought to expand his range and repertoire, moving from action to drama to comedy and back again. He skilfully partnered other performers in ensemble films such as *The Lord's of Flatbush* and *Cop Land*. He carefully modulated his starring performances to complement those of supporting players in movies such as *Cliffhanger* and *Rocky Balboa*. Periodically, as he does in *Antz*, he sends up his iconic action image.

As Cynthia Baron and Sharon Carnicke point out, 'questions about who performs and where actors perform are separate from questions about *what audiences watch when they encounter performances*' (2008: 78). The same can be said of reviewers. Hierarchies of taste are always involved: most critics promote middle-brow, middle-class values. As Bourdieu argues: 'most people' experience 'legitimisable' arts like cinema 'as simple consumers'; as such their aesthetic 'may be ... reduced, without being reductive, to the sociology of the groups that produce them, the function which they assign to them and the meanings which they confer upon them, both explicitly and, more particularly, implicitly' (1990: 96, 98).

After years of paying close attention to Stallone's acting I take away five principal, interlocking lessons: 1) consistently he is an effective, and often a riveting, action performer; 2) in many films he is a talented and generous team player; 3) his strengths in reaction have not to date been adequately appreciated; 4) more than most action stars, he excels at suggesting the gentler sides of macho characters; and 5) given the right script, he can be good at comedy.

A photo Annie Leibovitz took of Stallone for the November 1993 cover of *Vanity Fair* captures the diverse impulses that animate his performances. Seated naked on a slab of marble, looking directly at the camera, Stallone rehearses Rodin's statue *The Thinker*. The caption reads, 'Stallone's Body of Art'. Stallone wants to be seen as an art-loving intellectual, as 'legitimate'. At the same time, however, frozen as a statue in inaction, he and Leibovitz pay tribute to his sculpted body and ability to pose as prime sources of his success, in *action*.

NOTES

1   In another early interview, Stallone maintained that he also ate two pounds of beef a day to gain the required 'aggressiveness'. He consumed no juices, fruits, vegetables or bread. 'I became very, very strong but had no endurance and very, very little going on in the brain. Sometimes I would forget my lines. But what came across in close-ups was the stuttering, bumbling, lethargic look I wanted, and I could do it without pretending.' For *F.I.S.T.* he also consumed 'cheese and "fresh-squozen" [sic] juice' (Tavris 1976: 168). More recently he said that for *Rocky* he 'beefed up on fried chicken and potatoes, burgers and fries, spaghetti and baked ziti, whatever I thought would build muscle mass' (Stallone with Hochman 2005: 19). He consumed lots of ice cream and milkshakes, too.

2   In May 2007 Stallone was found guilty of bringing to Australia 48 vials of the muscle-building hormone Jintropin – in luggage belonging to his entourage. He was fined AUS$1,267 and ordered to pay AUS$4000 in court costs; see Anon. (2007) and AskMen. com Editors (2007).

3   He did 'pretend' versions of Ionesco, Beckett and Pinter monologues while waiting to shoot sequences in *Cliffhanger* (Case 1993: 20; see also Stauth 1990: 25).

4   See, for example, Holmlund (1993), Tasker (1993a, 1993b), Jeffords (1994), Dyer (1997) and Mizejewski (1999).

5   See also Bourdieu *et al.* (1990: 95–8).

6   What he wears is also important. As Eric Lichtenfeld argues, while action films 'seek to dazzle audiences with the exposed bodies of their heroes, how they *cover* these bodies also comes to be a potent, if more subtle, convention of the genre' (2007: 62).

7   Produced as a non-union independent, the film was picked up by Columbia and somewhat scandalously released under the International Alliance of Theatrical Stage Employees seal. The union forced removal of the union label: it was involved with post-production only (see Anon. 1974: n.p.).

8   A system of dispositions, habitus 'expresses first the *result of an organizing action*, with a meaning close to that of words such as structure; it also designates a way of being, a habitual state (especially of the body) and, in particular, a *predisposition, tendency, propensity* or *inclination*' (Bourdieu 1984: 562, note 2; emphasis in original).

9   Gradually Stallone got better at catching balls. Booed by a crowd of watching extras he protested: 'I'm *supposed* to be a lousy goalkeeper!' (Archerd 1980: n.p.).

10 There is one on-screen fatality, but it is an accident. Intent on killing the defenceless Rambo, a blood-thirsty cop plunges to his death when a rock Rambo has thrown hits the helicopter windshield. The cop is standing on the side of the helicopter, despite the pilot's warnings, trying to get a better shot. The helicopter is not seriously damaged; the pilot is unscathed. Rambo even rushes, though too late, to his pursuer's rescue.

11 Lithgow appeared with both the Royal Shakespeare Company and the Royal Court Theatre.

12 Maltby snidely says that Stallone's is a 'pantomimic version of the Method' (2003: 409).

13 Mangold, Cohen and Edwards took as references *3:10 to Yuma* (1957), *My Darling Clementine* (1946), *Once Upon a Time in the West* (1968), *Serpico* (1973), *Dog Day Afternoon* (1975), *Shadows* (1959), *Q and A* (1990) and *The Sweet Smell of Success* (1957) (see Pizzello 1997: 56).

14 The *Washington Post*'s Rita Kempley wrote, for example: 'while Stallone gives his most affable, least narcissistic performance since *Rocky*, he is no Gary Cooper. He's a pooped palooka, surrounded by actors of Cooper's caliber' (1997).

15 The cast features real people rather than award-winning actors: then-reigning light

heavyweight champion Antonio Tarver plays Rocky's opponent; an actual referee and professional sports commentators also participate. Stallone enlisted people with no idea who he was as well. 'This one girl I saw on the street in front of a drug rehab. I stopped the car and said, "You wanna be in a movie?" She said, "I don't know about no fuckin' movie". I said, "Perfect"' (in Jordan 2006: 114).

16 *The Village Voice* disparaged Stallone's acting: 'he tends to lead with his chin – and I don't mean that metaphorically' (Nelson 2006: 81). *Film Threat* and *L.A. Weekly*'s critics were impressed: 'The acting in the film is grade A, with Stallone bringing the more mumbled Rocky from the first film spliced with some rousing inspirational monologues when the moment is right (not forced, not preachy … just perfect)' (Bell 2006); 'What gives *Rocky Balboa* its unexpected pathos is the titanic humility of Stallone's performance, the earnestness with which he plays a man knocked down (but not out) by the ravages of time' (Foundas 2006).

17 *Rocky Balboa* grossed $70 million domestically, and $129 million worldwide.

BIBLIOGRAPHY

Adams, Rachel (1999) '"Fat Man Walking": Masculinity and Racial Geographies in James Mangold's *Cop Land*', *Camera Obscura*, 42 (September), 4–29.

Anon. (1974) 'Union Bug Off Col's *Flatbush*', *Variety*, 15 May, n.p.

_____ (1981) '*Victory* Highlighted by Sports Action and High Adventure', *Los Angeles Herald Examiner*, 31 July, B5.

_____ (2007) 'Quick Takes: Stallone Hits Rocky Patch in Australia', *Los Angeles Times*, 14 March. Online. Available HTTP: http://articles.latimes.com/2007/mar/14/entertainment/et-quick14 (18 March 2013).

_____ (2009) 'The Jaeger-LeCoultre Glory to the Filmmaker Award'. Online. Available HTTP: http://www.labiennale.org/en/cinema/news/stallone.html (16 August 2009).

Archerd, Army (1980) 'Just for *Variety*', *Variety*, 18 August, n.p.

Arnold, Thomas K. (2006) 'Lord of the Ring', *Hollywood Reporter*, 12–18 December, R1-8.

AskMen.com Editors (2007) 'Sylvester Stallone Fined', 21 May. Online. Available HTTP: http://www.askmen.com/celeb (21 January 2013).

Baron, Cynthia and Sharon Carnicke (2008) *Reframing Screen Performance*. Ann Arbor: University of Michigan Press.

Bell, Mark (2006) '*Rocky Balboa*', *Film Threat*, 20 December. Online. Available HTTP: http://www.filmthreat.com/reviews/9498/ (25 January 2013).

Bernstein, Abbie (1991) '*Oscar*', *Hollywood Dramalogue*, 22.18 (2–8 May), 22.

Blaney, Martin (2009) 'Zurich to Welcome Sly Stallone for First Golden Icon Award'. Online. Available HTTP: http://www.screendaily.com/zurich-to-welcome-sly-stallone-for-first-golden-icon-award (16 August 2009).

Bourdieu, Pierre (1978) 'Sport and Social Class', *Social Science Information*, 17, 819–41.

_____ (1984) *Distinction: A Social Critique of the Judgement of Taste*, trans. Richard Nice. Cambridge, MA: Harvard University Press.

Bourdieu, Pierre with Luc Boitanski, Robert Castel, Jean-Claude Chamboredon and Dominique Schnapper (1990) *Photography: A Middle-Brow Art*, trans. Shaun Whiteside. Stanford: Stanford University Press.

Broeske, Pat H. (1986) 'Coming to Grips with Sly', *Los Angeles Times*, Calendar, 14 September, 1, 20–22, 38–40.

_____ (1987) 'Third Blood', *Los Angeles Times*, Calendar, 11 October, 4–7, 44–47.

Byrge, Duane (1998) 'Antz', Hollywood Reporter, 21 September, 8.

Cagle, Chris (2007) 'Two Modes of Prestige Film', Screen, 48.3, 291–311.

Case, Brian (1993) 'Mountain Excitement', Time Out, 19–26 May, 18–21.

Christon, Lawrence (1990) 'Can Sly Get Serious?', Los Angeles Times, Calendar, 28 October, 8–9, 90–1, 100.

Clark, John (1997) 'Babes in Cop Land', Premiere, August, 59–61.

Crist, Judith (1974) 'Duck Tale', New York, 13 May, n.p.

DreamWorks Pictures (1998) 'Antz' press materials.

Dyer, Richard (1997) White. London and New York: Routledge.

Ebert, Roger (1982) 'First Blood', Chicago Sun-Times, 1 January. Online. Available HTTP: http://rogerebert.suntimes.com/apps/pbcs.dll/article?AID=/19820101/REVIEWS/201010324/1023 (3 February 2013).

Edelstein, David (1997) 'In the Company of Men: Sylvester Stallone Plays with the Big Boys', 16 August. Online. Available HTTP: http://www.slate.com/id/3228 (10 March 2003).

Eimer, David (2002) 'Body Language', Time Out, 29 July, 19–20.

Farr, Louise (1976) 'Rocky: It Could Be a Contender', New York, 18 October, 70–3.

Foundas, Scott (2006), 'Rocky Balboa', LA Weekly. Online. Available HTTP: http://www.metacritic.com/movie/rocky-balboa/critic-reviews (20 December 2006).

Geraghty, Christine (2000) 'Re-examining Stardom: Questions of Texts, Bodies and Performance', in Christine Gledhill and Linda Williams (eds) Reinventing Film Studies. London: Arnold, 183–201.

Goldman, Peter (1985) 'R&R', Newsweek, 23 December, 58–62.

Heller, Zoë (1993) 'Sly's Body Electric', Vanity Fair, 56.11 (March), 144–9, 184, 186–8.

Holmlund, Chris (1993) 'Masculinity as Multiple Masquerade: The "Mature" Stallone and the Stallone Clone', in Steven Cohan and Ina Rae Hark (eds) Screening the Male. London: Routledge, 213–29.

Hunter, David (1993) 'Cliff Notes', LA Village View, 4–11 June, 11.

Jeffords, Susan (1994) Hard Bodies: Hollywood Masculinity in the Reagan Era. New Brunswick, NJ: Rutgers University Press.

Jordan, Pat (2006) 'Arms and the Man', Premiere, December, 114–18, 144–5.

Kael, Pauline (1976) 'The Current Cinema: Stallone and Stalin', New Yorker, 20 November, 154, 157.

Kasindorf, Martin (1977) 'KO's Hollywood', Newsweek, 11 April, 71–72, 77–79.

Kempley, Rita (1997) 'Cop Land', Washington Post. Online. Available HTTP: http://www.washingtonpost.com/wp-srv/style/longterm/movies/review97/coplandkemp.htm (2 February 2013).

Klemesrud, Judy (1976) '"Rocky isn't based on me", Says Stallone, "but we both went the distance"', New York Times, 28 November, 17, 48.

Koehler, Robert (2006) 'Review: Rocky Balboa', Variety, 15 December. Online. Available HTTP: http://variety.com/2006/film/reviews/rocky-balboa-1117932317/ (20 December 2006).

Lichtenfeld, Eric (2007 [2004]) Action Speaks Louder: Violence, Spectacle, and the American Action Movie. Revised and expanded edition. Middletown, CT: Wesleyan University Press.

Linderman, Lawrence (1978) 'Playboy Interview: Sylvester Stallone', Playboy, September, 73–91.

Maltby, Richard (2003) Hollywood Cinema. Malden: Blackwell.

Maslin, Janet (1991) 'Stallone the Comedian is a Sport in Oscar', New York Times, 26 April, C10.

____ (1993) 'High Anxiety Amid the Vistas', New York Times, 28 May, C3, C10.

McCarthy, Todd (1993) 'Cliffhanger', Variety, 351.4 (24 May), 44.

Mizejewski, Linda (1999) 'Action Bodies in Futurist Spaces: Bodybuilder Stardom as Special Effect', in Annette Kuhn (ed.) *Alien Zone*. London and New York: Verso, 147–50.

Nelson, Rob (2006) *'Rocky* v. Ahmadinejad: Another Sequel, Another Chance for Rocky to Persevere in America', *Village Voice*, 51 (20 December), 80.

Pizzello, Chris (1997) *'High Noon* Hits the Jersey Turnpike', *American Cinematographer*, 78.9 (September), 54–64.

Powers, John (1993) 'Twin Peaks', *LA Weekly*, 28 May–3 June, 31.

Savello, Frank (1998) *Stallone: A Rocky Life*. Edinburgh and London: Mainstream.

Shifren, David (1981) *'Victory'*, *Film Journal*, 20 July, 16–17.

Shone, Tom (1998) 'A High Ant-Society Attack', *Sunday Times*, 8 November, 7.

Stallone, Sylvester with David Hochman (2005) *Sly Moves: My Proven Program to Lose Weight, Build Strength, Gain Will Power, and Live Your Dream*. New York: HarperCollins.

Stanley, J. (1978) 'The Art of the Cinematographer: László Kóvacs', *Filmmakers*, 11.9 (July), 28–32.

Stauth, Cameron (1990) 'Requiem for a Heavyweight', *American Film*, January, 22–7, 57.

Step (1981) *'Victory'*, *Variety*, 303 (21 July), 18.

Strauss, Bob (2010) 'Stallone Packs Some Punch with Ensemble of Action-Film Veterans for *The Expendables*', *(Long Beach) Press-Telegram*, 13 August, C1–C2.

Tasker, Yvonne (1993a) *Spectacular Bodies: Gender, Genre, and the Action Cinema*. London: Routledge.

____ (1993b) 'Dumb Movies for Dumb People', in Steven Cohan and Ina Rae Hark (eds) *Screening the Male*. London: Routledge, 230–45.

Tavris, Carol (1976) 'Down for the Count – Or Still a Winner?', *Redbook Magazine*, July, 35, 168–71.

TriStar Pictures (1993) *'Cliffhanger* Production Information', 1–30.

Tunison, Michael (1997) 'The Rocky Road Back', *Entertainment Today*, 15 August, 9, 13.

Turan, Kenneth (1997) 'The Ridiculous and the Sublime', *Los Angeles Times*, 12 May, F1, F4.

Welkos, Robert W. (2005) 'Forever the Underdog', *Los Angeles Times*, 26 November, E1, E22, E23.

____ (2006) 'Down for the Count? Guess Again', *Los Angeles Times*, 17 December, E1, E16.

Zebello, Stephen (1995) 'On the Sly', *Movieline*, October, 38–42, 80, 82, 85, 95.

STALLONE'S STOMACH: COP LAND AND THE WEIGHT OF ACTORLY LEGITIMISATION

PAUL McDONALD

Since 1981 the Golden Raspberry Awards or 'Razzies' have operated as an alternative index of cultural value. Unlike the Academy Awards, which celebrate the highest accomplishments in film over the previous year, the Razzies dishonour achievements in various categories including acting, directing and writing. For his performance in *Rhinestone* (1984), Stallone won the 1984 Razzie for Worst Actor. In the following year Stallone picked up the same award for his performances in *Rambo: First Blood Part II* (1985) and *Rocky IV* (1985). After further wins for *Rambo III* (1988) and *Stop! Or My Mom Will Shoot* (1992), and nine other nominations in the Worst Actor or Supporting Actor categories, in 1999 organisers of the Razzies gave Stallone special distinction by dishonouring him as Worst Actor of the Century 'for 99.5% of Everything He's Ever Done'.

Although engaging with the culture of popular film, the Razzies preserve rather than upturn cultural hierarchies. They do not celebrate popular film but rather assert its trashiness. As James F. English writes in *The Economy of Prestige*, 'on balance, you could say that the Razzies serve as a negative exercise of the cinematic taste whose positive expression is the Oscars. If you like the films and actors that win Academy Awards, you'll dislike the ones that win Razzies' (2005: 101). In Stallone's case, his Razzies are representative of the critical response which has greeted his acting. *Rocky* (1976) provided Stallone with his first commercially successful role, and his performance attracted a positive response amongst critics, but since his acting has consistently been dismissed and ridiculed by critics. It was against this background of criticism that Stallone's decision to take the role of Freddy Heflin in

	WORST ACTOR	WORST SUPPORTING ACTOR	WORST ACTOR OF THE CENTURY
2003		Spy Kids 3-D: Game Over	
2001		Driven	
2000	Get Carter		
1999			'for 99.5% of Everything He's Ever Done'
1998		An Alan Smithee Film: Burn Hollywood Burn	
1996	Daylight		
1995	Assassins / Judge Dredd		
1994	The Specialist		
1992	Stop! Or My Mom Will Shoot!		
1991	Oscar		
1990	Rocky V		
1989	Lock Up / Tango & Cash		
1988	Rambo III		
1987	Over the Top		
1986	Cobra		
1985	Rambo: First Blood Part II / Rocky IV		
1984	Rhinestone		

Table 1 - Stallone at the Golden Raspberry Awards: Nominations and Wins (wins highlighted).
Source: compiled from the Golden Raspberry Award Foundation (www.razzies.com).
Members of the Golden Raspberry Award Foundation are allowed to nominate and vote for the awards.
Membership is open to the public for payment of an annual subscription.

the 1997 police drama *Cop Land* (1997) was viewed by many commentators as a bid to gain critical respect and recognition as an actor. As the star himself openly acknowledged:

> When you're lumped into a group of three or four people that are basically known for their physical flexibility and musculature, and then there's another group of people like [Robert] De Niro, [Al] Pacino, [Harvey] Keitel, [Christopher] Walken, and that group is always mentioned as great actors ... you keep wondering, 'Are they ever gonna slip me in there?' ... You could see a line of demarcation. ... If you wanted a superficial film, call Sylvester. If you

wanted something that had artistic merit and could win awards, go to the other group. I had morphed into a completely physical character, someone totally nonverbal. I wasn't even aware of it. ... But when the time came for me to want to do something noteworthy, no one wanted me. No one wanted me. ... Cop Land was literally a last attempt to change that. ... Last year, it had all come together: Turning fifty, getting married, having my daughter, Rocky's twentieth anniversary ... it felt like a countdown situation. I was feeling the encroachment of time every morning. (In Rodriguez 1997: 11)

As Stallone observes, commercial success does not translate into artistic recognition. During the 1980s, Stallone scored hits at the box office yet his performances were regularly lambasted by critics. Meanwhile, the actors he identifies – De Niro, Pacino, Keitel and Walken – received praise for their acting in films without the same commercial popularity as those he made.

For Pierre Bourdieu, cultural production rests not only on the production of certain categories of objects or events as works of art but on the production of belief in, and recognition of, those artefacts as art; cultural production therefore involves not only the producers of the work but also those agents who have a hand in the production of belief in the work, for example critics (1993: 37). From Bourdieu's perspective, the production of belief in art is never under the control of a single practitioner but rather is something created collectively by multiple agents. It is these institutional conditions which Bourdieu describes as 'the field of cultural production'. As some works gain artistic legitimacy when others don't, then the field becomes an arena of struggle and power, with some practitioners granted artistic status when others aren't: 'the field of cultural production is the site of struggles in which what is at stake is the power to impose the dominant definition of the writer and therefore to delimit the population of those entitled to take part in the struggle to define the writer' (1993: 42). Consequently, power relationships in cultural production are witnessed in how certain creative producers are granted greater artistic status and credibility than others. In the case of film acting, this is visible whenever certain performers enjoy critical approval when others don't. In many respects, such evaluations merely function to distinguish the good from the bad in film acting, but at another level what is involved in such judgements is the definition of who, or rather what, is a legitimate film actor.

As Stallone's reference to 'a line of demarcation' implies, evaluations of good and bad acting are never simply aesthetic judgements about the accomplishments of individual performers but emerge from deeply instituted distinctions which patrol the artistic status of stars, regulating who will and who will not be recognised as legitimate screen performers. Although cultural production positions practitioners in hierarchies of artistic and cultural power, for Bourdieu the field operates as a dynamic set of relationships, meaning that possibilities exist for agents to negotiate their positions. My interest in exploring *Cop Land* is to identify what actions were taken by Stallone as ways of strategically negotiating his position to gain legitimacy as a credible film actor.

As a general description, acting can be understood as the representation of character through the media of the performer's voice and body. As film actors are differentially positioned across distinctions in cultural power, so their voices and bodies are framed by those hierarchies. Some voice and bodies will be recognised as good acting, others won't. Focusing on the significance of the body in modern visual culture, Chris Holmlund has suggested that 'the question for media analysts is to define *what* kind of body this is, or kind of bod*ies* are needed and/or tolerated by current societies, and to describe how the apparatus of body and power functions in popular culture today' (2002: 18; emphasis in original). Holmlund's concern is with how certain bodily types when featured in popular culture are tolerated as proper and appropriate, whereas others are rejected as abnormal or abhorrent. By the time of *Cop Land*, Stallone's body had made millions at the box office but was critically dismissed: there was no *belief* in his body as representative of legitimate screen acting. My interest in addressing this film, therefore, is not only to consider how the star attempted to gain greater artistic respectability to make himself a believable actor by negotiating a path through hierarchies which structure the field of cultural production, but to see how the process of negotiation was enacted precisely through the actor's body.

STALLONE CAN'T ACT

Rocky made Stallone's name as an actor, with the film and his performance receiving positive responses from many critics. Not all agreed, however. Vincent Canby of the *New York Times* dismissed Stallone's acting, commenting:

Mr. Stallone's Rocky is less a performance than an impersonation. It's all superficial mannerisms and movements, reminding me of Rodney Dangerfield doing a nightclub monologue. The speech patterns sound right, and what he says is occasionally lifelike, but it's a studied routine, not a character.

It's the sort of performance that could have been put together by watching other actors on television. Throughout the movie we are asked to believe ... Rocky is compassionate, interesting, even heroic, though the character we see is simply an unconvincing actor imitating a lug. (1976b: 19)

Canby may not have been representative of the wider positive appraisal which Stallone received as Rocky, but as chief film critic for a leading metropolitan newspaper with one of the largest daily readerships in the US, his opinion carried more influence and had greater reach than the judgements of other reviewers. Commenting on roles by David Carradine in *Bound for Glory* (1976) and Robert De Niro in *The Last Tycoon* (1976), Canby praised these actors for how their performances conveyed a quality of simply 'behaving', 'the simulation of being natural ... devoid of irrelevant mannerisms' (1976a: 1). In Canby's eyes, with Carradine and De Niro, 'each behaves with the kind of assurance that gives weight, urgency and conviction to their films'. This he contrasted with 'the flamboyant, flashy and, to me, skin-deep performance of Sylvester Stallone as the plug-ugly fighter in *Rocky*. ... The problem is that the characterization has such a busy surface one inevitably suspects there's nothing much below' (ibid.). These criticisms rest on the evaluative convention so frequently drawn on in evaluations of acting, according to which quality acting is judged to reveal the psychological depth of the character whereas poor acting only gives a shallow exterior. Compared to performances by Carradine, De Niro or other actors, Stallone's performance as Rocky was disparaged for being all surface. At the foundation of Canby's criticisms was an evaluation of Stallone's body, for his acting was dismissed for being made up of 'superficial mannerisms and movements', appearing only 'skin-deep'. If behaving is the measure of quality film acting for Canby, then overall Stallone failed because his body could only impersonate – that is, represent the externalities – of the character he played. Through Canby's eyes, Stallone was just something to be seen, a moving object rather than a character or performer. All actors must use their bodies to convey character, but for Canby, Stallone was presenting the wrong form of body to qualify him as a quality actor.

Canby is just one voice, however, amongst the critical orthodoxy which has endured across Stallone's career. When Stallone's prison feature *Lock Up* (1989) opened, one review concluded that the 'story is so stupid that you tend to overlook Stallone's acting and, at the very least, that's a mixed blessing. He never changes, nor do the characters he chooses to play' (Hagen 1989: C1). The comedy *Oscar* (1991) was a departure from the action features which had made Stallone's name in the 1980s, but most critics were equally unforgiving. 'Acting in farce is a tricky, specific skill, one of the essentials of which is playing the material straight and never letting on that it's supposed to be funny', wrote critic Edward Guthmann in the *San Francisco Chronicle*. 'Stallone, on the other hand, shows his hand in every scene. He's incredibly clumsy, an amateurish comedian who declaims his lines instead of tossing them off, a hack with all the grace of John Madden hawking cars in a TV commercial' (1991: E1). Over a decade later, the criticism persisted. It was the opinion of one reviewer of *Eye See You* (2002) that 'Stallone's acting consists mostly of grimacing and teeth-clenching. Meanwhile, his body is now a grotesquely veiny mass of too-much muscle. He has become downright unpleasant to look at' (Kelly 2002: 21).

While still agreeing that Stallone's acting is limited, other critics, albeit writing for less esteemed publications than the *New York Times*, have defended Stallone, arguing his performances deliver popular pleasures in ways that cannot be measured just by acting. When *Judge Dredd* (1995) was released, the reviewer for the *St. Louis Post-Dispatch* commented: 'Sure, Stallone's acting is as flat as the character he's supposed to bring to life and it's hard to find any relevant message in the work, but at least he's back in tight clothing, killing people left and right with high-tech weaponry, and that's the way his fans like him now' (Rinaldi 1995: D12). A similar assessment was made in the *Buffalo News*: 'Sure, Sly Stallone's acting in *Judge Dredd* is stiffer than a 2-by-4, but hey! He fights a giant robot that dispenses full automatic, armour-piercing death from its fists! That is what we pay to see' (Yungbluth 1995: 18G). In many respects, these reviews shared a similar logic to Canby, for in each case Stallone was regarded as a spectacular object who could not act.

Yet where these commentators differ from Canby and others is in their praise for Stallone's status as spectacle. While conceding Stallone's acting may have weaknesses, they want to assert and defend the pleasures which his performance brings. Stallone is valued for delivering a pleasurable performance which is not defined by acting but rather in terms of spectacle. What this seems to do is to open up a space between acting and performance. Acting is only a certain form of performance – the representation of dramatic character. But, Philip Drake argues, performance is a wider category: '"acting" [i]s a subset of "performance" … describing a dramatic mode of performance that highlights the presence of character. Other kinds of performance – song and dance routines, action and stunts, physical comedy – are often less committed to character and instead focus on the display of skills' (2006: 85). If acting is about representation, performance is about show and accomplishment. In Stallone's case, his critics disparage his ability to act (i.e. to represent characters), yet by praising his ability to accomplish certain types of action feats – fighting, killing and dangerous sports – his defenders are valuing his capacities as a performer. From one perspective, Stallone is dismissed for failing to comply with accepted standards of quality acting, but from the alternative view he is praised for his ability to carry out spectacular achievements and feats.

CROSSING OVER

In many respects, the narrative of *Cop Land* can be read as allegorical of Stallone's struggle for actorly legitimisation. Heflin, played by Stallone, is sheriff in the small town of Garrison, New Jersey. Keeping the peace in Garrison is easy because the town is largely populated by members of the NYPD and their families, who have set up home across the Hudson River, away from the pressures of fighting crime in Manhattan. In the city, the law is represented by the likes of officers Ray Donlan, Gary Figgis and Internal Affairs investigator Moe Tilden, played respectively by Harvey Keitel, Ray Liotta and Robert De Niro. These characters occupy a different world to Heflin. Law enforcement in Garrison is a sedentary occupation, largely confined to sitting behind desks or cruising in cars, and this has obviously shaped Heflin's body. With a big belly, he is a hollow, lumbering figure of the law. In the city, however, crime is hard and brutal. Although Donlan is the leader of a bunch of cops from the 37th precinct who are fundamentally corrupt, funding their lives in Garrison through payments from the mob, the world they inhabit requires real authentic crime fighting. Heflin envies the world which Donlan occupies and has an ambition to join the NYPD himself. Although Heflin knows Donlan and his associates do not follow the law, still he pines for the respect which comes with being a cop. Between Garrison and Manhattan, the Hudson stands as a line of demarcation, and repeatedly in the film Heflin/Stallone is shown looking longingly across the river towards the world occupied by Donlan/Keitel, Figgis/Liotta and Tilden/De Niro.

Metaphorically then, this narrative represents Stallone's status as an actor and his position in the field of cultural production. Separated from the world occupied by Keitel and De Niro, Stallone enviously looks on at a distance. Most significant, considering Stallone's standing as an actor, is how it is the body which prevents Heflin from achieving the status which he desires. Although Heflin has many credentials which would make him a good cop, a physical disability prevents him from joining the NYPD: years ago, when still a young man, he dived into the river to save Liz (Annabella Sciorra) from drowning, and damaged his right ear, making him partially deaf. The legacy of that day stays with him: because he acted like a hero in the past he can now never realise his dreams. Consequently, although at the end of the film Heflin acts heroically once more, finally rising up to fight and wipe out the corrupt presence of Donlan and his associates, afterwards he is still left in the same role, although now he seems resigned to his place.

Just as Stallone and Keitel may both be film actors but hold different degrees of artistic reputation, so Heflin and Donlan are both agents of the law, yet the former does not hold the respect granted to the NYPD officer. Heflin's work is light, insubstantial and superficial compared to the serious 'deep' crime fighting which Donlan and his colleagues must practice. Heflin and Donlan occupy a 'field' of hierarchically organised professional relations, spatially mapped onto the distinction between Garrison and Manhattan, with the Hudson marking both a physical and an institutional separation between what Heflin has and what he wants. Above all, it is the body which is the main hurdle preventing Heflin crossing over the river. Heflin can try his hardest, but no matter how much he endeavours, his physical disability, the result of past heroics, blocks him from renegotiating his position within his chosen profession. His body carries the legacy of those heroics, and in this manner the character's professional struggle is analogous to Stallone's artistic struggle. For both character and actor, the body was shaped and defined by previous actions which now present an obstacle to realising desired goals. *Cop Land* therefore not only represented Stallone self-consciously aiming to turn in a performance which would gain him the artistic recognition he longed for, but also through its narrative metaphorically enacted exactly the struggle for acceptance which Stallone was attempting to put to rest by reshaping his action hero past.

STRATEGIES OF DISAVOWAL

This narrative, however, operates as allegory only. Stallone's bid for actorly legitimisation saw him making actual creative choices to negotiate his artistic status, repositioning himself in the field. In one way or another, these choices involved him in attempting to shed the legacy of the commercial past in action cinema on which his stardom was built. I therefore suggest his bid for legitimisation can best be thought of in terms of what I will describe as three strategies of disavowal.

1) GENRE RE-ALIGNMENT

For Stallone, *Cop Land* came after the string of films in the 1980s and early 1990s which had established him as an action star. It was action which made and defined Stallone's star status. Although the original film in the *Rocky* series saw Stallone appearing in a character-focused drama, as the series progressed this focus was diminished because successive instalments simply provided ritualistic build-ups to the end fight. Likewise, while the first act of *First Blood* displayed an interest in exploring the anxieties which motivated John Rambo, by the time of *Rambo: First Blood Part II* and *Rambo III*, character psychology had been replaced by all-action shoot-'em-ups. With *Tango & Cash* (1989), Stallone's action image also became channelled towards comedy. Consequently, during the 1990s, in the years leading up to *Cop Land*, Stallone's career was divided between straight, serious action roles in *Cliffhanger* (1993), *The Specialist* (1994), *Assassins* (1995) and *Daylight* (1996), and comedy performances in *Oscar* and *Stop! Or My Mom Will Shoot*.

Taking the role of Heflin in *Cop Land* distanced Stallone from both of these trends. The film can claim various generic credentials. Critics referred to the film as a 'police-corruption drama' (McCarthy 1997: 56), as an 'anti-cop thriller' (Campbell 1997: 4), as 'a compelling Eastern that plays like a vintage Western about personal redemption' (Clark 1997: D1), as a 'suburban New Jersey *High Noon* ... a good, small-scale morality fable, a classic Western masquerading as an arty cop drama' (Carr 1997: D1), as 'aspir[ing] to a realist genre (the police expose)' (Taubin 1997: 81) and as an 'involving modern urban Western' (Erstein 1997: 3). Although the film ends with a shoot-out, it is not an action film. In fact, most of the film centres on the inability of Heflin to act. *Cop Land* is nearer to the elements of character-based drama seen in

Rocky and the early parts of *First Blood*. If the action films deal with conflicts which are largely externalised through fighting and combat, the conflicts in *Cop Land* are internalised through Heflin's dilemmas over professional duty and his unrequited love for Liz. With *Cop Land*, Stallone disavowed the physical universe inhabited by the action star in search of the artistic legitimisation afforded by moral drama.

2) ECONOMIC DISINTEREST

Stallone's career has traversed the independent sector and the major Hollywood studios. Independent production company Chartoff-Winkler made the *Rocky* films, which were distributed by United Artists or MGM/UA. Anabasis/Carolco made the *Rambo* trilogy, with *First Blood* distributed by the independent Orion and the latter two episodes handled by TriStar, a co-venture between Columbia Pictures, Home Box Office and CBS. Until the late 1980s, Stallone had worked only very occasionally for the Hollywood majors, on *Nighthawks* (1981) for Universal and *Rhinestone* for Twentieth Century Fox. After doing *Tango & Cash* for Warner Bros., Stallone increasingly turned towards working for the majors, and as the 1990s progressed he starred in films for Disney (*Oscar*), Universal (*Stop! Or My Mom Will Shoot* and *Daylight*) and Warner Bros. (*Demolition Man* [1993] and *Assassins*). Whether hired by independents or the majors, Stallone was positioned in the sector of film production aimed at the mass popular market. His voice and body therefore became marked as signs of economic value.

However, even when Stallone's star status was on the rise during the 1980s, his box-office power was variable. *Rocky III* (1982), *Rambo: First Blood Part II* and *Rocky IV* respectively grossed $119.4 million, $150.4 million and $125.4 million at the North American box office, but these highs were balanced against the lows of *Rhinestone* ($21.4 million), *Over the Top* (1987) ($16.1 million) and *Lock Up* ($22.1 million). As his career continued into the 1990s, Stallone remained only a modest attraction at the North American box office. Only *Cliffhanger* did reasonably well. His real power lay overseas, as the gross international box office for his films outstripped their takings in the domestic market. For example, *Cliffhanger* grossed $84 million domestically but $171 million internationally.

It was Stallone's international value which meant that in the 1990s, although he was much less of an attraction at the North American domestic box office than he had been in the previous decade, he was still able

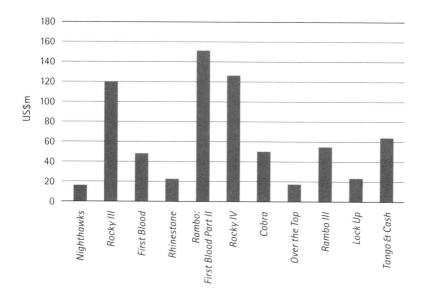

Figure 1 - Stallone at the Box Office: North American Grosses in the 1980s
Note: *Victory* (a.k.a. *Escape to Victory*) (John Huston, 1981) is not included as Stallone formed part of an ensemble cast and so cannot be regarded as the outright star of the film. **Source:** compiled from data at Box Office Mojo (www.boxofficemojo.com).

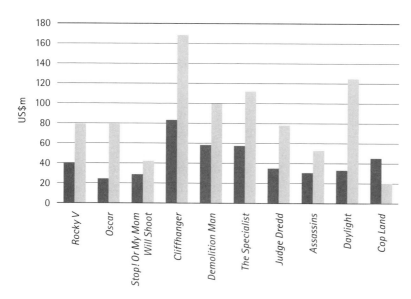

Figure 2 - Stallone at the Box Office: North American (in dark grey) and Overseas Gross Box Office in the 1990s. **Note:** Stallone's supporting roles in *The Good Life* (Alan Mehrez, 1997) and *An Alan Smithee Film: Burn Hollywood Burn* (Arthur Hiller, 1997), along with his voice work for *Antz* (Eric Darnell and Tim Johnson, 1998), are not included. **Sources:** compiled from data at Box Office Guru (www.boxofficeguru.com), Box Office Mojo (www.boxofficemojo.com), and Internet Movie Database (www.imdb.com).

to command high salaries. For *The Specialist* he reportedly received $12 million. He earned $15 million for *Assassins*. In December 1994, Ron Meyer, Stallone's agent at Creative Artists Agency, secured a deal with Savoy Pictures, committing the star to an unspecified action film scheduled for 1996 in return for $20 million against 20% of the gross (see Eller 1994: E8). Ultimately, however, no film appeared, as Savoy folded in the same year the deal was struck. Just a few months later, in March 1995, Meyer landed a further valuable deal with Universal for Stallone to appear in *Daylight*, which paid $17.5 million in upfront salary (see Fleming 1995: 1). Shortly afterwards, Meyer became president of MCA, the parent company of Universal, and in August 1995, Casey Silver (then president of Universal Pictures) agreed to a non-exclusive deal worth $60 million together with perks and backend guarantees for Stallone to star in three films for the studio (see Laski 1995: 5). This multi-picture deal took a long time to bear fruit, resulting only in *Eye See You* (eventually released in 2002) before the deal was terminated in February 2000 (see McNary 2000: 5). While largely unproductive, these deals nevertheless confirmed Stallone's voice and body held considerable economic value in the mid-1990s.

When considered in this context, Stallone's choice to work on *Cop Land* explicitly demonstrated a disavowal of his economic status. *Cop Land* was made by producer-distributor Miramax on an estimated budget of $15 million. To take the role, Stallone was paid 'scale', the minimum wage set by the Screen Actors Guild, earning around $50,000, but in return for what was reported as participation in a 'significant' share of backend revenues. When accepting the role, Stallone was dismissive of his previous action roles, saying they felt 'very hollow, like you are just part of an erector set', and in a direct gesture of economic disavowal, explained his choice to work on *Cop Land* for modest wages by stating 'I'm financially secure [...] now it's about doing things that make one happy' (in Evans 1996: 7, 27). That gesture also extended to how the role positioned Stallone in conditions of Hollywood film production. After building its reputation in the late 1980s and early 1990s as an independent distributor of foreign-language imports and American independent productions, Miramax was acquired by Disney in 1993. Subsequently, Miramax moved into producing and distributing for more commercial sectors of the market, although throughout the 1990s Disney always preserved the company as a subsidiary, granting a fair degree of operational autonomy so that it was never completely absorbed into the full studio system alongside the majors. By keeping footholds in both the independent and the studio sectors of production and distribution, Miramax came to represent the rise of 'Indiewood' in the 1990s. Working for Miramax moved Stallone outside the commercial core of the Hollywood studio system which serves the mass popular market, while taking a salary cut demonstrated his distance from the A-list aristocracy. *Cop Land* therefore repositioned Stallone in the film market and represented an act of economic disinterest.

3) VOCAL AND PHYSICAL TRANSFORMATION

Looking at genre, the industry and the market explains the contexts in which Stallone's performance in *Cop Land* appeared. But I now want to explore how the process of negotiation was enacted actually through that performance, and in order to do so it is necessary to focus on the voice and body.

Stallone's early roles established acting characteristics which have stayed with him throughout his career. For example, the opening to *First Blood* introduces the John Rambo character and exemplifies many of these characteristics. At the start of the film, Rambo arrives at the home of his former army buddy Delmar Barry only to be told by Barry's mother that he has died from exposure to Agent Orange while serving in Vietnam. Here body and voice work together to convey a sense of power but also gentleness. He walks very upright, suggesting both confidence and the past of his military training. As he approaches the Barry homestead he sees children playing and stops to give a faint benign smile in their direction. When he meets Delmar's mother he innocently asks 'Excuse me. ... Can you tell me, is this ... where Delmar Barry lives?' He speaks to the mother from a distance, looking directly at her, and accompanies his question with a large gesture of the arm towards the house, so that vocally and physically he confidently occupies space. When the mother curtly responds 'He ain't here', a sense of tension is introduced into the meeting. Stallone/Rambo does not respond defensively but rather manages the situation by using the voice and body to diminish any potential intrusion or threat which he may present. He breaks eye contact, lowering his head, and to prove his relationship to Delmar, reaches in his pocket to retrieve a notebook in which Delmar had written his address. Searching in the pocket again, he pulls out a chaotic handful of papers which he has to fumble through before he finds a photograph of him with Delmar. Over these actions, he speaks with a low volume to explain who is in the picture, fragmenting his sentences with short pauses, and once offering a small laugh as he fondly describes Delmar's physical stature. Together these features contribute towards his voice seeming soft and light. With these physical and vocal actions, Stallone/Rambo manages the challenge from the mother by using the body and voice to present a state of being deliberately passive. When he is told of Delmar's death, however, the news greets him as a shock. At this moment the sequence snaps to a close-up of Stallone/Rambo's face and in a state of disbelief he utters in a low tone 'What?' and his top lip flinches. When he is told Delmar died the previous year, Stallone/Rambo appears too shocked to actually speak until he asks 'Died how?' As the mother relates the circumstances of her son's passing, Stallone listens silently, and in close-up he is seen to swallow hard, his eyelids flickering to mark the character's recognition of the pain and injustice of the death. Realising there is nothing he could say or do to ease the situation, he leaves, passing the photograph to the mother and uttering a virtually inaudible 'very sorry ... very sorry' before walking away slowly and slightly stooped. Over the four minutes of the sequence, Stallone's voice and body therefore serve to represent the character's passage through three stages, from open assurance, to patient tameness, and finally contained grief.

As the film progresses, however, Stallone's acting settles into another manner. Once he breaks out of the police station after his arrest for vagrancy his actions take on a greater sense of purpose and intent. He hides in the woods, where he is hunted by the National Guard, and then comes down to wreak vengeance on the town. Now his performance is directed towards achieving specific goals. Speech is almost entirely missing, while gesture is direct and functional. This can therefore be understood as Stallone adopting a mode of action performance directed towards pure doing – the achievement of spectacular feats. Across the trajectory of *First Blood*, Stallone's acting moves from character portrayal to action instrument. And as the *Rambo* series progressed, so the action mode of performance came to predominate and define Stallone's acting. By *Rambo III*, the character's speech was reduced to the bare minimum and instead he 'spoke' through gestures, as actions displaced words, so that Stallone turned into a complete doing machine.

With *Cop Land*, Stallone appears to be acting in ways to reject the sheer functionality of action performance. *Cop Land* doesn't really see Stallone doing something new with his acting but rather attempting to return to and reclaim the manner of performance seen in *Rocky* and parts of *First Blood*. For example, to take a brief sequence of three

Figure 3 - Conveying unease. *Cop Land*. Producers Cary Woods, Cathy Konrad and Ezra Swerdlow; director James Mangold; DVD distributed by Miramax Home Entertainment.

scenes from approximately halfway through the film, when Tilden, the Internal Affairs investigator, questions Heflin about Donlan, Stallone sits silent, breaks eye contact and fiddles with objects on his desk to convey his unease with the situation. In the next scene, Donlan is hosting a party at his house. This comes the night after Murray (Michael Rapaport), a fellow police officer and nephew of Donlan's wife, supposedly jumped from the George Washington Bridge. Donlan staged the jump to cover up for Murray's shooting of two unarmed black males, and as Heflin knows Murray is alive, he visits the party to try to explain to Donlan how this may look to Internal Affairs, who already have suspicions about the episode. Talking to Donlan/Keitel, Heflin/Stallone is all awkwardness. He can't hold eye contact and his voice lacks authority as he speaks softly and his uncompleted sentences hang in the air. Rather than a figure of the law, Heflin/Stallone comes over more like a naughty boy trying to offer excuses to a punishing father. When Liz comes to his house that night he struggles to vocalise his feelings for her. Again he cannot maintain eye contact and frequently looks to the ground. Where the action mode of performance was all premised on directness and confrontation, here Stallone uses his voice and body to avoid contact with others. Acting in the action mode worked to perform assertiveness, function and purpose, while in *Cop Land* Stallone enacts gentleness and passivity. The significance of Stallone's use of the voice and body in *Cop Land* can therefore be understood in two ways. In terms of the narrative, it conveys the weaknesses of Heflin, but at the same time it also has a reference and a meaning beyond the film, as it

Figures 4–IMDB - Boyish awkwardness; avoiding contact; gentleness and passivity. *Cop Land*. Producers Cary Woods, Cathy Konrad and Ezra Swerdlow; director James Mangold; DVD distributed by Miramax Home Entertainment.

works to set this acting apart from most of his action past.

Action cinema identified Stallone not only with a certain mode of performance but also with a particular styling of the body. Stallone's body became a key sign of what Yvonne Tasker (1993) dubbed 'musculinity' in 1980s action film. Repeated outings for Rocky Balboa and John Rambo, together with performances in *Cobra* (1986), *Over the Top* and *Lock Up*, provided plenty of opportunities to show Stallone's pumped and ripped physique. Stallone therefore confirmed action as a genre of the body. Apart from the built shoulders and arms, a crucial element of that bodily display was Stallone's tightly muscled stomach. In the boxing ring scenes of the Rocky films or combat sequences of the Rambo series, narrative circumstances gave full justification to nakedly displaying Stallone's stomach. Even when Stallone kept his shirt on, as in *Judge Dredd*, the leanness of his stomach was still evident. Stallone's stomach therefore operated as a key physical sign of his potency as an action hero.

To play Heflin, Stallone physically marked his departure from the world of action. By ceasing to exercise and following a diet rich in whipped cream, peanut butter, pancakes, lasagne and cheesecake, he gained 39 pounds, expanding his waistline from 31 to almost 40 inches. It was the decision of director James Mangold to have Stallone gain the poundage: 'I wanted to feel the weight in Sly's face, in his cheeks. I didn't want that kind of amazing heroic gaunt look when he's at his chiselled perfection' (in Stein 1997: 36). This physical transformation carried meaning and significance in three ways. Repeatedly Stallone is framed so as to foreground the bulk of his stomach, and Heflin's flabbiness becomes a somatic index of the character's moral condition. The weight gain therefore carried narrative meaning, with Heflin's physical and spiritual inability to act symptomatically displaced onto the flaccidity of his body. Next, Heflin's flabby body contrasts with Rambo's hard body, which by the time of the second and third films in that series had become a sign of Reaganite jingoism (see Jeffords 1994). Heflin's body does not have any actual political significance but in the trajectory of Stallone's career represents a marked departure from the ideological legacy of Rambo.

Finally, Stallone's flabby stomach represented a negotiation of artistic legitimacy. Both the taut stomach of the action films and the flabby stomach of *Cop Land* were works of physical transformation. But the significance of those transformations differently positioned the star amongst the hierarchies of economic and cultural power which define relations in cultural production. As a key marker of his action roles, Stallone's muscled stomach was tainted with the markings of big-salary, high-grossing filmmaking for the popular market, what in Bourdieu's terms stands for 'the field of large-scale production, which is *symbolically* excluded and discredited' (1993: 39; emphasis in original). Stallone's taut stomach was therefore a sign not only of physical power but of economic power. Gaining weight for *Cop Land* demonstrated not only Stallone's commitment to the challenges of believably and plausibly representing character, but also a rejection of the sphere of commercial cultural production which had defined his career for two decades.

This bodily transformation can be understood within the dichotomy which Barry King has drawn between personification and impersonation in film acting. With personification, the actor as a known and familiar figure is foregrounded over and above the individual character. Impersonation, however, is achieved through transforming the voice and body with the aim of convincingly playing the particularities of character (1985: 30). King is using the term 'impersonation' in a different way to how Canby applied the term in his criticisms of Stallone. While both regard impersonation as requiring visible signs of transformation, for Canby impersonation meant representing the superficial externalities of characters, whereas King sees impersonation as a statement of actorly craft. Although King does not directly make this connection, personification appears to be a necessary component of star acting, as it is tied to the commercial objectives of preserving the continuities of the voice and body to foreground the performer as a recognisable and therefore marketable screen presence. In contrast, impersonation follows an artistic principle connected to the aims of realistic aesthetics, submerging the performer's identity in the narrative world with the intention of creating a believable characterisation.

Physical transformation in acting may create a new visible exterior for the actor, but its significance reaches beyond the surface of the body. As Kevin Esch notes, when actors transform their bodies it has the purpose of achieving 'greater fidelity of performance' (2006: 96). Weight can be simulated with fat suits, but by actually putting on the pounds, the actor does two things. The truth of the transformation is unquestionably confirmed in all its fleshy reality – look, see, it's true, I'm really fat – immersing the actor in the narrative circumstances of the character's drama, while at the same time the actor demonstrates commitment to, and sacrifice for, his or her artistic craft. By transforming the body, the actor changes external appearances but also gives impersonation lived depth and corporeal substance. It may be unsurprising then to find that the impersonatory task of bodily transformation has been recognised as a work of artistic merit in film acting. When Robert De Niro visibly gained weight to play the ageing boxer Jake La Motta in *Raging Bull* (1980), the actor won his second Academy Award. By the time *Cop Land* was made, De Niro's performance as La Motta was firmly canonised in film history as one of the greatest performances of American cinema. For male actors, on-screen weight gain combines physical impotency with artistic credibility. It was this same combination which helped George Clooney win the Academy Award for Best Supporting Actor with his performance in *Syriana* (2005). Likewise, Charlize Theron explicitly departed from her ballet and modelling past and gained artistic legitimacy when she put on weight for her Academy Award-winning performance as serial killer Aileen Wuornos in *Monster* (2003). What these examples suggest is that while bodily transformation may not be the measure of praiseworthy acting, it certainly helps. Stallone did not pick up any award nominations for his performance as Heflin, but when he put on the pounds he aligned himself with a celebrated tradition of artistic dedication.

Stallone's stomach therefore gave physical form to the other strategies of disavowal. Not only did it serve the purposes of the narrative and the renunciation of his action past, but it also worked as a strategy of artistic legitimisation, distancing him from the mass popular market while also 'embodying' his commitment to actorly craft.

'YOU CAN'T GO BACK AGAIN'

While recognising the process of negotiation at work, questions must be raised about how far commercially successful stars can gain legitimacy in cultural production. Critics are central to the process of artistic legitimisation. They are professional audience members with a gatekeeping role regulating what will be recognised as legitimate forms of artistic expression. As cultural arbitrators and opinion formers, critics guide audience responses, differentiating the good from the bad, and in the process imposing definitions of actorly credibility.

Generally, *Cop Land* received lukewarm to poor reviews. The most familiar criticism was that the film made a simple division between good guys and bad guys, eliminating any moral complexity. A mixed critical response greeted Stallone's performance. In many cases, critics judged Stallone to be representative of the film's general weaknesses: 'Cop Land is a lightweight movie with an overweight star and a paper-thin plot' (Alexander 1997: 18). His acting came in for particular scrutiny:

> The kindest description of Stallone's acting would be to say that he's out of practice. He seems to find a life-sized human being more alien than the time travellers and androids with which he's made his millions. ... The damp-eyed Stallone plays the hero as a cross between Baby Huey and Forrest Gump. He underlines Freddy's thought processes by grimacing painfully, indicates uncertainty by toddling about like a 2-year-old and suggests moral perplexity by reading his lines in a drowning man's gurgle. We get the picture, Sly. In his duets with the cold and forceful De Niro, the star suggests a plump, juicy rabbit transfixed by a cobra. (Campbell 1997: 4)

Writing in the *Village Voice*, Amy Taubin dismissively commented, 'A more skilled director than Mangold might have found a tactful way to tell Stallone that it's redundant for him to expend so much energy acting like a doofus since he already is a doofus. (Stallone is a more resourceful performer than he appears to be here)' (1997: 81). Others regarded the film more sympathetically. 'it's almost eerie to see a self-effacing Stallone acting with co-stars of dramatic weight delivering a performance of feeling ... the redemption extends to Stallone – 40 pounds heavier and in all ways less lightweight than he has been for years' (Clark 1997: D1). For *Variety*, Todd McCarthy considered Stallone as making up for some of the film's weaknesses, describing his performance as 'an agreeable one that gives the film a sympathetic centre, even if the role, as written, could have cut a bit deeper' (1997: 56).

Difficulties with accepting Stallone's performance were not confined to the critics. When *Cop Land* was first shown in test screenings, a scene in which Heflin wakes up and rolls over to briefly reveal his bare distended stomach had audience members groaning. As Stallone remarked, 'it caused such a distraction – it took them right out of the movie' (in Stein 1997). As test audiences could not be reconciled with the vision of a flabby Stallone, the scene was eventually excised from the film. Given the difficulties critics and test audiences alike had with Stallone's performance, what this may suggest is that despite the best efforts of the star to transform himself – into Heflin but also into a legitimate actor – the legacy of Rocky and Rambo continually shadowed and thwarted that ambition. The weight which the star carried as Heflin was not only

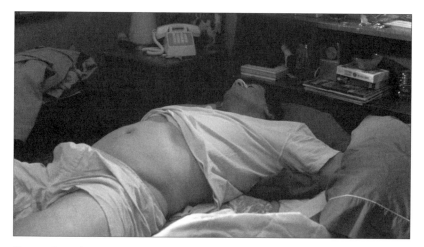

Figure 5 - Stomach spectacular. *Cop Land.* Producers Cary Woods, Cathy Konrad and Ezra Swerdlow; director James Mangold; DVD distributed by Miramax Home Entertainment.

corporeal but also symbolic: it was not just his stomach but his familiar image as an action star which was his burden to carry. Although making the actorly commitment to physical transformation, Stallone could not be fully recognised or believed in as a legitimate actor. As one critic commented:

> Stripped of his macho Rambo armour, Stallone's acting limitations are painfully exposed. He fails to elicit much in the way of sympathy or compassion for his doughy simpleton character. Clearly, he's trying to mine the same vein he did 20 years ago with the loveably dim Rocky Balboa ('Yo, Adrian'). But he just proves you can't go back again. (Alexander 1997: 18)

Cop Land did not win Stallone the artistic acceptance which he desired, and subsequently with his next films he therefore returned to more familiar ground, with action roles in *Get Carter* (2000), *Driven* (2001), *Eye See You* and *Avenging Angelo* (2002), well paid but also slimmer. The fact that none of these films performed well at the box office (*Eye See You* only received a very limited release in the US and *Avenging Angelo* did not open at all in North America but instead went straight to DVD) indicated that, with age, Stallone had even lost his credibility as a marketable action star. But when Stallone returned to his most notable roles, starring in and directing *Rocky Balboa* (2006) and *Rambo* (2008), he once again enjoyed modest hits, particularly at the overseas box office. This achievement required him not only to reprise his most famous characters but also to rebuild himself physically so that once again he had a body which could be sold.

CONCLUSION

Although film actors can actively and intentionally work to renegotiate their artistic status, the relations that structure the field of cultural production constantly constrain what positions performers may legitimately occupy. Cultural production inverts the logic of economic value found in the field of business, as commercial success frequently acts as a black mark discrediting the artistic status or credibility of actors and other creative practitioners. It is for this reason that Bourdieu describes cultural production as an 'anti-economy' (1993: 40). In Stallone's case, Rocky and Rambo made him a hit at the global box office, and that success was largely dependent on his construction of a hard body which could be deployed as a sign of commercial value. Yet according to the logics of cultural production, this success de-legitimatised Stallone as an actor.

Cop Land was his attempt to change all that. He intentionally aimed to renegotiate his place in the field, shifting genres and distancing himself from the taint of commerce by demonstrating economic disinterest through taking a drop in salary and moving into the Indiewood sector of production. But because Stallone's stardom was so defined in physical terms, ultimately any serious bid for actorly legitimisation had to come down to the body. Stallone's place in the field was fixed corporeally, for his 'musculinity' embodied the popular market, and so above all else, renegotiating his position in the field of cultural production had to be mediated through the body. As Rocky and Rambo he had achieved a marketable body but not an artistic body. Against that background, while Stallone's weight gain for Cop Land can be understood in terms internal to that particular film, for the heavy stomach represents Heflin's incapacity to act, its greater significance was formed through external points of reference, as it signified difference from Stallone's hard body heroes and his dedication to the actorly craft of impersonation. Even so, critics and audiences alike were unprepared to let Stallone leave his familiar associations with action performance. Stallone gained the pounds but could not shed the burden of his taut stomach and all the associations with action cinema which this carried. Taking up Holmlund's point that societies only tolerate certain kinds of bodies (2002: 18), the example of Stallone demonstrates that cultural production, as a field of social practice, is only accepting of certain corporeal categories. Working in this context, despite physical change, Stallone simply had the wrong body to be seriously considered as an actor.

In the field of cultural production Stallone is no ordinary actor, for his box-office success has given him considerable power. However, that power is limited by the field. Stallone has enjoyed commercial power but has been unable, despite his best efforts, and most likely due to his popular success, to acquire the symbolic power necessary to legitimise himself as a respected actor. Bourdieu regards cultural production as a dynamic field, a structured set of relations in which relative degrees of commercial success or artistic legitimacy define available positions of power, within which practitioners struggle to achieve different 'position takings' (1993: 30). As Stallone's example indicates, however, the taking of positions is never under the control of the individual, and unlike for writers or painters who stake their position in the field by their production of artefacts, for film actors the struggle for artistic legitimacy is always enacted through the body.

BIBLIOGRAPHY

Alexander, Al (1997) 'Flatfooted *Cop* Guilty of Wasting an All-Star Cast', *Patriot Ledger*, 15 August, 18.
Bourdieu, Pierre (1993 [1983]) 'The Field of Cultural Production or: The Economic World Reversed', in Pierre Bourdieu, *The Field of Cultural Production: Essays on Art and Literature*, Randal Johnson (ed.). Cambridge: Polity, 29–73.
Box Office Guru. Online. Available HTTP: http://www.boxofficeguru.com (5 June 2011).
Box Office Mojo. Online. Available HTTP: http://www.boxofficemojo.com (5 June 2011).
Campbell, Bob (1997) 'Big-Gun Actors Do Little to Bolster Weak *Cop Land*', *Star-Ledger*, 15 August, 4.
Canby, Vincent (1976a) 'In Films, Acting Is Behavior', *New York Times*, sec. II, 12 December, 1.
____ (1976b) 'Ringside Story', *New York Times*, sec. C, 22 November, 19.
Carr, Jay (1997) 'Stallone Succeeds in a Fat Role', *Boston Globe*, 15 August, D1.
Clark, Mike (1997) 'Pacing Trips Up Drama's Heavyweight Cast', *USA Today*, 15 August, D1.
Drake, Philip (2006) 'Reconceptualizing Screen Performance', *Journal of Film and Video*, 58.1–2, 84–94.
Eller, Claudia (1994) 'Stallone Cuts $20 Million Movie Deal', *Oregonian*, 21 December, E8.
English, James F. (2005) *The Economy of Prestige: Prizes, Awards, and the Circulation of Cultural Value*. Cambridge, MA: Harvard University Press.
Erstein, Hap (1997) 'Critics' Choice', *Palm Beach Post*, 22 August, 3.
Esch, Kevin (2006) '"I don't see any method at all": The Problem of Actorly Transformation',

Journal of Film and Video, 58.1–2, 95–107.

Evans, Greg (1996) 'Stallone Scales Back Payday', Daily Variety, 14 March, 7, 27.

Fleming, Michael (1995) 'Sly Sees Daylight', Daily Variety, 3 April, 1.

Golden Raspberry Award Foundation. Available HTTP: http://www.razzies.com (5 June 2011).

Guthmann, Edward (1991) 'Sly Punches Out Farcical Oscar', San Francisco Chronicle, 26 April, E1.

Hagen, Bill (1989) 'Rambo Does Hard Time: Stallone Should Be Arrested for Lock Up', San Diego Union-Tribune, 4 August, C1.

Holmlund, Chris (2002) Impossible Bodies: Femininity and Masculinity at the Movies. London: Routledge.

Internet Movie Database (IMDb). Online. Available HTTP: http://www.imdb.com (5 June 2011).

Jeffords, Susan (1994) Hard Bodies: Hollywood Masculinity in the Reagan Era. New Brunswick, NJ: Rutgers University Press.

Kelly, Christopher (2002) 'Stallone's Eye Fails Vision Test', Fort Worth Star-Telegram, 21 September, 21.

King, Barry (1985) 'Articulating Stardom', Screen, 26.5, 27–50.

Laski, Beth (1995) 'Meyer Makes Noise with $60 Mil Stallone Pact', Variety, 14 August, 5, 12.

McCarthy, Todd (1997) 'Cop Land', Variety, 11 August, 56.

McNary, Dave (2000) 'Sly, U Go Their Separate Ways', Daily Variety, 22 February, 5.

Rinaldi, Ray Mark (1995) 'Formulaic Stallone: Well, It Works', St. Louis Post-Dispatch, 2 July, D12.

Rodriguez, Rene (1997) 'Stallone Gets Serious', Miami Herald, 10 August, 1l.

Stein, Ruthe (1997) 'Stallone Plumps Up His Career', San Francisco Chronicle, 10 August, 36.

Tasker, Yvonne (1993) Spectacular Bodies: Gender, Genre, and the Action Cinema. London: Routledge.

Taubin, Amy (1997) 'Odd Men Out', Village Voice, 19 August, 81.

Yungbluth, Jason (1995) 'Comics Come of Age', Buffalo News, 13 October, 18G.

THE ROCKY EFFECT: SYLVESTER STALLONE AS SPORT HERO

ALEXANDRA KELLER & FRAZER WARD

> *People accept Rocky Balboa as authentic. I can't tell you how many people have come up to me and asked about my boxing career. It's like they really want to believe that Rocky exists. ... At one time I thought people would get over their fascination with the character. ... Didn't happen. After thirty years, Rocky has taken hold to a degree I never could have imagined.*
>
> – Sylvester Stallone (in Fernandez 2011)

INTRODUCTION: THE 'ROCKY EFFECT'

Sylvester Stallone's career is bound to heroes defined by sport. More than any other action star, Stallone has articulated his persona by embodying athletes. His sport roles include manager of a wrestling brother (*Paradise Alley*, 1978), soccer goalkeeper (*Victory*, 1981), arm-wrestler (*Over the Top*, 1986), mountain climber (*Cliffhanger*, 1993) and racecar driver (*Driven*, 2001). Stallone's investment is clear: these are among the movies that Stallone has not only starred in, but also (except *Victory*) written, and often directed. All inevitably funnel through his performance as boxer Rocky Balboa. Only John Rambo is as vital to Stallone's career and identity.

Audiences' attachment to Stallone has much to do with his athletic performance, at three levels. First, he performs a sport, which involves his training in and execution of a range of skills he is understood to have mastered, and about which he speaks volubly in interviews and other paratexts (for example, DVD extras, his website). Second, whatever sport Stallone performs, the audience cannot see it *qua* sport until it's been conventionalised in a cinematically specific way. Third, especially in the case of the *Rocky* series (1976–2006), the necessary conventionalising is conveyed to the audience in ways that point symptomatically to cinema's converging relation to other media. Because sport is consumed far more often as moving image than as live event (especially boxing, the primary sport through which Stallone's persona is organised), the consumption of Stallone's athletes, especially Rocky, in turn achieves a kind of meta-representational status.[1] As a representation, Rocky becomes increasingly mediatised over the series. Together with Stallone's authorship, this produces an unusual degree of conflation between star and role that feeds back into the narratives of some instalments. These connections coalesce into a 'Rocky Effect', producing ways of comprehending the 'real' world of boxing.

While the sport action film is not without casualties (Rocky's opponent-cum-friend, Apollo Creed, played by Carl Weathers, dies in the ring in *Rocky IV*), these narratives offer up different expressions of the active, masculine body than other hard-bodied genres. Stallone's athletes invest in rules of sport which prescribe Stallone's interest in the hero's self-regulation (hence the inevitable, often monastic training sequences). These films code Stallone's masculinity and agency via the protocols of specific sports and generalised notions that sport involves skills, training, competition and an audience. The films' audiences witness a doubled performance: Stallone as actor performs the sport for audiences both inside and outside the diegesis. The *Rocky* films develop an increasingly complex relation to contemporaneous screen cultures. In *Rocky* (1976) screen technologies have a negligible presence; by *Rocky Balboa* (2006), boxing is on ESPN on TV in a bar, with combatants produced with video game technology as CGI representations.

RINGS AND ROUNDS: SPORT AS CONTAINMENT

Stallone's other sport films would not be so meaningful without the *Rocky* films. Each was released in proximity to a *Rocky* film, offering ways to relate Stallone's performance of another sport to his performance of boxing. All involve sports that, like boxing, are contained by time and space – soccer fields and 'halves', wrestling rings and the time each round takes, arm wrestling tables and the time it takes for one combatant to get 'over the top', the various tracks on which the drivers race. In such containment, Stallone's athletes thrive. The exception is *Cliffhanger*, whose audience is restricted to one outside the film. This is the lone sport film in which the action is taken out of a contained space, and this is related to its rare representation of armed crime.

Paradise Alley is the sole sport film in which Stallone is not an athlete. Still, the opening credits roll over a rooftop race, in which Cosmo Carbone (Stallone) jumps ten roofs for a five-dollar prize. He, too, competes. The slow-motion sequence cuts between the competitors until Cosmo makes it to the last roof and his rival falls almost to his death. The victory is Pyrrhic – Cosmo's money is nailed to the wall of the last building such that he must remove it in shreds. Unlike our immediate introduction to boxing in *Rocky*, we don't see the wrestling central to the film for forty minutes, and it's preceded by youngest Carbone brother Victor's (Lee Canalito) arm wrestling victory over enormous Frankie the Thumper (Terry Funk).[2] Otherwise it hews to elements of the *Rocky* template: fraught familial relationships interlace with sport; training sequences use old school methods; the action ends on a freeze-frame of the victorious brothers in the ring.

The vital notion *Paradise Alley* transfers from *Rocky* to *Rocky II* (1979): fighting inevitably produces damage. Fighting makes money, but spends bodies to do so. While Victor never loses, he sustains an enormous amount of damage in the Rocky mode. To enable maximum damage, the climactic wrestling match between Victor and Frankie has no time limit, no rules, and exceeds twenty rounds – a reverberation of the 15-round final bout in *Rocky*.[3]

Between *Rocky II* and *Rocky III* (1982) came *Victory* (directed by John Huston), a rare Stallone period piece, set during World War II in a Nazi POW camp (it also stars Michael Caine, Max von Sydow, Pelé and other professional soccer players). An exhibition match between the German national team and Allied POWs becomes an escape opportunity for the POWs. The tension between sport (allegedly apolitical) and war (overtly political) is matched by a tension between Stallone's star body and his role as Hatch, an American POW. The other prisoners are neither cut nor buff. Even Stallone's clothing is tailored differently: his trousers and shirts tighter, his boots higher-heeled.

Before the match, Hatch makes a solo escape (articulating another tension: individual vs. collective survival). Briefly, he becomes a traditional action hero, before returning to play, but in the climactic series of match-deciding penalty kicks, as goalie he mobilises Rocky's underdog status. Kicked in the head, Hatch looks at the field out of focus, as

Rocky often does, yet single-handedly secures the victory. As the crowd rushes the field, Hatch's love interest (Carole Laure) finds him, much as Adrian (Talia Shire) does in *Rocky*.

The representation of any sport in cinema functions through conventions. This is challenging with arm wrestling. As spectacle, it has a tight focus. In *Over the Top*, our first glimpse of trucker Lincoln Hawk (Stallone) as an arm-wrestler is when Smasher (Magic Schwarz) challenges him at a truck stop. Son Michael (David Mendenhall) watches from the edge of the room, a privileged spectator, grudgingly admiring his father. Michael's reactions give the viewer someplace to breathe and break up the claustrophobic, mural-like shallowness of the crowded shots. This bout takes only eighty seconds, though there is no time limit in arm wrestling. Hawk, on the verge of losing, alters his grip and wins. This near-loss fits the *Rocky* template.

Instead of a training montage there is a roadside workout: a collage of toe touches, push-ups and 'shadow' arm wrestling using the front of the truck as gym equipment. Later, Hawk teaches Michael how to train while driving, using a pull-down machine. Michael learns to arm-wrestle using Hawk's signature grip shift, starting his salvation from spoiled brat status and Hawk's redemption from absentee dad status. Hawk's entrance into the Las Vegas Hilton Casino Hotel for the International Arm Wrestling Championship is crosscut with Michael's discovery of his father's letters sent over the years and kept from him by his mother. The tension between the familial realm and the spectacle of sport is consistent with other Stallone sport films.

In arm wrestling, unlike boxing or wrestling, there may be several bouts going at once. *Over the Top* educates its audience quickly. We see competitors lifting weights, chalking hands, even strapping on platform shoes to be level with their adversaries at competition tables. The announcer (actual sports announcer Bob Beattie) tells the audience in the hall that the contestants come from all over the world, that they are the best in their weight classes, that they must lose twice to be eliminated, and that there is a women's competition. Elimination rounds are compressed; anything involving Hawk and his ultimate adversary, Bob 'Bull' Hurley (Rick Zumwalt) has priority. We learn that Hawk, new to the competition, is someone to watch. The last rounds take on new intensity, as five hundred fighters are reduced to eight. In interview footage wrestlers offer their insights. Some are actual arm wrestlers, others former NFL players, others stuntmen. Hurley is introduced as a five-time world arm wrestling champion (this is true of Zumwalt).

Figure 1 - Underdog triumphant. *Over the Top.* Producers Yoram Globus and Menahem Golan; directed by Menahem Golan; DVD distributed by Warner Home Video.

Hawk's loss to Grizzly (Bruce Way) is shown in extreme slow-motion. A trainer suggests Hawk has sustained damage he'll have to fight through (again, familiar from the *Rocky* model). The final fight between Hawk and Hurley is orchestrated like a boxing match. The wrestlers' arms come apart, necessitating a strap to keep them together. The strap in place, Hurley punches Hawk in the nose, fighting dirty like some of Rocky's opponents. Because there are no rounds in arm wrestling, the contest is structured by the number of times each competitor verges on victory, on going 'over the top'. In slow-motion, witnessed by Michael (in the Adrian and, later, the Rocky Jr. position), the win looks like a Rocky victory: Hawk raises Michael in his arms, the crowd chanting behind them.

The *Rocky* model informs Stallone's script for *Driven*. Research and training, the casting of actual athletes and sportscasters, the underdog story, masculine codes passing from one generation to another, conflicts between romantic/familial and professional lives, and the funnelling of a sport through its media representation are recognisable. *Driven* treats drivers as athletes whose expertise is contained inside a vehicle *and* by the track. Of all Stallone's sport films, *Driven* relies most on blurring lines between a sport's technology and the physical and mental prowess of the athlete. Joe Tanto, Stallone's Indy car driver, articulates the underdog credo as 'will over skill'. The ageing Stallone remained preoccupied by this in *Rocky Balboa*, where the climactic fight is called 'Will vs. Skill'. In *Driven*, as in the *Rocky* series (*Rocky IV* and *Rocky Balboa* especially), there is tension between technology and the athlete, and the body *qua* body always wins out over the body aided by technology.

Stallone had wanted to do a Formula One film, and spent two years observing the global racing circuit, courting drivers and managers.

Rebuffed by Bernie Ecclestone (CEO of Formula One Management and Formula One Administration), Stallone turned to another open-wheel racing format, the American Championship Auto Racing Teams (CART) Champ Car series. Stallone suggested that CART was 'more open... It is extremely important to me that we create a film that accurately depicts the true sense of CART – [its] emotion, excitement, speed, technology, and glamour' (in Anon. 2012). Less glamorous than F1, CART's allure and globalism remain key to the film's logic (NASCAR, more popular in North America, resists glamming up, and made little sense for the global audience that was by 2001 increasingly responsible for Stallone's profitability. CART, like F1, runs on tracks around the world).

Manager Carl Henry (Burt Reynolds) calls the over-the-hill Joe Tanto (Stallone) back to help rookie sensation Jimmy Bly (Kip Pardue) win the season. Tanto stands apart from the sport's excesses (represented with more F1 style than actual CART culture). We meet him in the garage of his rural house, building a car. That he functions as his own mechanic belies the strong division between star (driver) and (pit) crew in CART and speaks to the kind of do-it-all masculinity he represents.

Stallone and director Renny Harlin reconfigure CART for cinematic legibility. The first image is dramatically matted, rendering it the size of a TV screen within the film screen. Racecars speed around a track in a blur while text relays CART statistics: '900 million spectators ... 250 miles an hour ... 20 races ... one championship.' This would be unnecessary were the sport as familiar as boxing – those 900 million spectators are not primarily American. The rest of the opening montage pictures CART's geographical spread: Long Beach, Miami, Mexico, Brazil, Canada, Australia, France. Voiceover explaining the rivalry between the two lead drivers is delivered with hyperbolic sportscaster affect. Like the *Rocky* films, *Driven* casts popular racecar drivers and owners (Juan Pablo Montoya, Chip Ganassi, Michael Andretti, Christian Fittipaldi, Jacques Villeneuve and Dario Franchitti). Throughout, commentary from TV anchors describes what's happening so that uneducated viewers can make sense of it. For these same viewers, the film takes liberties with the realities of racing: in spite of its velocity and drama, the sport isn't easily made a film narrative. As the *Rocky* series re-imagines boxing to make it coherent to a movie audience, *Driven* recasts racing, offering practice-like passing during races, in-race chatter between drivers and crews, and the marked alteration of pit-stop protocols. In a particularly pointed departure from the real, *Driven*'s set piece is a black-tie prototype show in the middle of race season (its formality and timing imaginary) where Jimmy, cracking under pressure, jumps into one of the prototypes and guns it out of the hall, Tanto in hot pursuit in the other, the pair racing through Chicago at 195 mph (as captured by a cop's speed gun). No matter that open-wheel cars don't start like street vehicles, or that it's hard to press the clutch in cowboy boots like Tanto does. Like much of the film, this sequence is a distillation of masculinity and athletic prowess, and its cinematic revision allows for dialogue and dramatic flow that fit mainstream narrative conventions in ways that open-wheel racing simply doesn't. As in the *Rocky* movies, the cinematic conventionalisation of sport may shape our experience of actual racing.

SLUGGERS AND BOXERS: RACE AND REAL LIFE IN ROCKY

The foundation of Stallone's star persona is, of course, Rocky Balboa and the six-film *Rocky* series.[4] More than his other sport films, *Rocky* lays the ground for a complex reading of race and sport. Boxing in the US has been riven by race since the call went out for a 'Great White Hope' to defeat Jack Johnson, the first African American heavyweight champion, who beat Canadian Tommy Burns in 1908. In 1982 versions of this racist rhetoric surfaced around white challenger Gerry Cooney prior to his fight with black champion Larry Holmes. Boxing fans have tended to associate styles and values with race, nowhere more so than

Figure 2 - Bloodied but unbowed. *Rocky.* Producers Robert Chartoff and Irwin Winkler; directed by John G. Avildsen; DVD distributed by 20th Century Fox Home Entertainment.

in the boxer vs. slugger distinction. The slugger is less athletically talented but punches hard, relying on his ability to withstand punishment in order to dish it out. He is typically white and often seems lacking in artifice. The only undefeated heavyweight champion, Balboa's namesake, Rocky Marciano, is the ideal type of the slugger. Balboa is based on a lesser slugger, white heavyweight Chuck Wepner, known as the 'Bayonne Bleeder' for his tendency to be cut.[5]

Creed, contra Rocky, is a boxer, clearly referencing Muhammad Ali, who knocked Wepner out in the last round of a 15-round fight in 1975. Creed is depicted as smart, loquacious and entrepreneurial.[6] He operates according to the boxer's principle of hit and don't be hit, using a long-lead left hand, or jab, to control the distance between combatants, avoiding exchanges of short blows at close quarters, using footwork to move in, out and laterally, controlling the movement and upsetting the rhythm of his opponent. Weathers mimes Ali's unorthodox stance, hands carried low: Ali, until the mid-1970s, typically relied on quick footwork and head movement to avoid blows. Save for the second fight against Clubber Lang (Mr. T) in *Rocky III*, Rocky remains a slugger, and Stallone accentuates Rocky's awkwardness by making him left-handed, a southpaw, meaning that he leads (insofar as Rocky leads at all) with his right hand. Stallone's mobilisation of the boxer/slugger distinction puts in play the question of relations between African American and white masculinity, though this is not systematically worked through.

There are two fights in *Rocky*, in the first and last scenes. In the first we know nothing about Rocky, and we take in as much about the ambience of boxing as we do about him. Held in the basement of a church, this fight is cartoonish: Rocky, depicted as a fighter whose violence is primal and without technique or style, absorbs blow after impossible blow. The slugger's masculine heroism is sado-masochistic: he must absorb damage before inflicting it. So, inevitably, as a slugger, Rocky rallies, able to land enough of his own blows to win.

The second fight is the heroic loss to Creed. Absent any defensive technique except to cross his arms in front of himself, Rocky plods forward trying to find his opponent, occasionally throwing wide, swinging punches. Rather than engaging one another in mobile exchanges – a punch necessarily entailing the risk of being hit, as in a real boxing match, Rocky and Creed take turns hitting one another – a pattern repeated throughout the series. Clearly, we are supposed to understand that, unlike Creed, Rocky is all need, desire and heart. This fight, too, is cartoonish. The famous scene in which Rocky beats up frozen sides of meat isn't about developing skill, it's about his inherent toughness.

The fights' exaggerated aspects are prompted by the fact that Stallone was making a movie for a larger audience than boxing fans. Television in the 1950s broadened boxing's audience, but this expanded audience likely shifted the appreciation of boxing in favour of the spectacular knockout over less immediately visible skills. Because boxing is not immediately legible in detail, and is not always spectacular, to reach a non-specialist audience Stallone grafted Rocky's fights onto existing cinematic conventions. Typically in Hollywood movies, people don't talk at the same time, as fighters do, in their exchanges. The simplified boxing in which Creed hits Rocky, then Rocky hits Creed, derives from the necessity of visual legibility. Scripting the fights becomes no different from scripting dialogue.

BOXING, FILM AND TELEVISION SPECTATORSHIP IN *ROCKY II*

Rocky II repeats the formula. A climactic fight ends the film, complete with freeze-frame. The big differences are television and Rocky's victory, and they are not entirely separable. The audience inside the diegesis sees the fight live and in person. The film spectator shares this perspective, but *also* sees the event organised through television and rearticulated through cinema. Linked most often to the perspective of Adrian, now Rocky's wife, we witness the fight in new ways because she's not there. The first film ended in a freeze-frame of Rocky and Adrian declaring their love without an apparent point of mediation. In *Rocky II*, when Rocky beats Creed to become world champion, the fight is televised. Adrian, now mother of an infant, watches from her living room. Rocky's victory speech initially addresses the immediate crowd. But after thanking God, he addresses his wife through the network, famously ending his speech with 'Adrian! I did it!'

The final fight is unimaginative and, for a serious boxing fan, unappealing, although it is the series' most direct expression of Rocky as slugger. As a realistic representation, it is ludicrous: for 13 rounds of a 15-round fight, Creed hits a defenceless, staggering Rocky with so many clean blows that in reality he'd be dead. Real boxing matches, especially heavyweight fights, feature relatively few completely clean blows – it doesn't take that many to knock someone out. Here, however, having absorbed more punishment than humanly possible, Rocky nonetheless

Figure 3 - Two trees falling. *Rocky II*. Producers Robert Chartoff and Irwin Winkler; directed by Sylvester Stallone; DVD distributed by 20th Century Fox Home Entertainment.

delivers a few massive blows of his own. Suddenly, Creed is reduced to the same staggering status as Rocky. They swing at one another, both fall, both try to haul themselves upright on the ring ropes. Creed falls down again. Rocky wins.

Looking for fidelity and accuracy misses the point. The fight makes more sense in simpler cinematic terms. To casual boxing fans and movie viewers what needs to be expressed isn't that one fighter is better than the other, but that Rocky can, at last, go the distance. That his boxing technique falls short is compensated for in other ways. *Rocky II* promotes its ties to reality by casting boxers like Roberto Duran, referee Lou Fillipo and sportscaster Brent Musburger as themselves. With the explicit production of a television broadcast inside *Rocky II*, the film viewer also watches the fight as a television spectator. Likely even less of a boxing aficionado than Adrian, the film viewer nevertheless watches with similar affection and emotional investment.

BOXING, PERFORMANCE AND AUTHENTICITY IN *ROCKY III*

Rocky III concerns itself with questions of performance and authenticity, and the restoration of order and rule(s), more than the first two films. It starts with the end of *Rocky II*, again unedited. Rocky's career is thriving. A montage sees Rocky defending his title, from Philadelphia to New York to Las Vegas to Europe. Lang watches Rocky's progress, witnessing one fight outside a store on a screen-wide bank of TVs. The montage is full of Rocky's magazine covers and endorsements. Stallone is pictured with Bob Hope, Gerald Ford, Jimmy Carter and Ronald Reagan: Stallone's real celebrity is mobilised to prove Rocky's fame. This conflation of real and representation is intensified with the unveiling of the Rocky statue in front of the Philadelphia Museum of Art, complete with a high school band playing the theme song, 'Gonna Fly Now', never before heard as diegetic music.

Early on, Rocky participates in a charity exhibition match against professional wrestler Thunderlips (Hulk Hogan), announced with the typical statistical imbalance – Rocky, 202 pounds, is far outweighed by the 390-pound Thunderlips. After Rocky's awkward but lucrative forays into acting in his endorsements, this hybrid match reasserts the 'authenticity' of boxing against the hyper-performativity (and hyper-masculinity) of pro-wrestling. Crucially the scene also confirms that boxing has *rules*, which pro-wrestling doesn't. Ultimately, the match is called a draw, because Rocky has in a single round learned to perform as well as Thunderlips. Having been thrown out of the ring, Rocky returns to hurl Thunderlips out of it. His training for his first fight with Lang is equally stagey, complete with audience, autographs, Rocky paraphernalia for sale and a band playing music as Rocky jumps rope. Crosscut scenes see Lang training for the fight alone, old style, as Rocky once did.

The Rocky–Lang match is broadcast live on radio and television. Rocky is interviewed, TV cameras present, beforehand. Lang shuns the crowd of reporters and cameras. 'Parasites, leeches, get out of here', he shouts, smashing all the cameras he can reach. Rocky is knocked out in

Figure 4 - Real celebrity as reel celebrity. *Rocky III.* Producers Robert Chartoff and Irwin Winkler; directed by Sylvester Stallone; DVD distributed by 20th Century Fox Home Entertainment.

the second round. Stylistically, like meets like: both are southpaws, and both walk in to one another trading crude, roundhouse bombs. Mickey (Burgess Meredith) has a heart attack after a pre-fight mêlée with Lang. Rocky, undertrained and under stress, can't muster his signature ability to absorb punishment.

After his loss, and the post-fight loss of Mickey, Rocky asks Creed to train him for a rematch. Recalling their even score as fighters, we know they can 'converse' with each other so that Creed can pick up where Mickey left off, with a difference. It's clear from their warm relationship that Stallone is proposing a vision of American masculinity tested by competition: hardly colour-blind, this pretends to solve at a personal level systemic American racial problems.

Creed brings Rocky to the Los Angeles ghetto he grew up in, revealing roots just as working class as Rocky's. Their training routine turns Rocky from a slugger to a boxer – something unheard of: styles develop and become habitual during years of hard training. Boxers learn new moves, but don't change their fundamental orientation towards their work. Arguably, given boxing's own mythologies, as Creed teaches Rocky to dance, he teaches him to be a black boxer. The requisite training montage shows Rocky and Creed all but doing the Hustle in an effort to teach Rocky better footwork.

The media intensity surrounding the rematch increases. At Madison Square Garden, a storied site for major fights, sportscaster Stu Nahan, ringside, says: 'We now switch to our remote cameras inside the dressing room.' TV cameras are prominent during the bout. Occasionally there is a low-angle shot, as if through the ropes, a TV fight coverage trademark. Like every fight in the series, this one makes much of its David-and-Goliath nature. Rocky was 201 pounds when he first fought the 235-pound Lang. Now the commentators describe him as 'looking twenty pounds lighter ... trim ... like a middleweight'. Rocky has dropped to 191 pounds (inside the cruiserweight limit of 195).

Lang and the commentators expect to see a slugger, but instead Rocky comes out fast, throwing long jabs in something like the classic manner of the boxer, from the 'outside' (using his jab to maintain distance between himself and Lang). Rocky does not 'counter and move' as Creed exhorts him to do, but leads and moves, setting the terms, not reacting to them. Perhaps because the problem of how to avoid the damage Lang is capable of inflicting has been solved in the transformation of Rocky's style ('style makes fights', says one boxing adage), this is the shortest of the culminating fights in the series: Rocky knocks

Lang out in the third. Still, Rocky reverts to his role as human punching bag in the second round, taunting Lang that his punches 'ain't so bad'. This suggests a condensed meditation on the career of Muhammad Ali, who, when young, embodied another boxing adage, 'speed beats power'. Cassius Clay/Ali was extraordinarily mobile for a heavyweight, and this is essentially what Creed teaches Rocky. Yet Ali's greatest triumph (against George Foreman in Zaire in 1974) saw Ali rely on the famous 'rope a dope' strategy: he leaned against the ring ropes, blocking many of Foreman's powerful punches with his gloves and arms, letting Foreman punch himself into exhaustion, before coming off the ropes in the eighth round to knock Foreman out. Rocky performs a version of this in the second round before returning to movement and the jab to set up his coup in the third.

SCREENING THE BODY IN *ROCKY IV*

Rocky III, with its improbable shift in Rocky's fighting style, subtly intensifies mass media's importance to the diegesis. *Rocky IV* uses media overtly in the service of national chauvinism. More than any other film in the series, this one has had the greatest impact on the actual sport of boxing. Again a tightly edited opening; we barely see *Rocky III*'s final fight. What's more important is the scene in which Apollo and Rocky spar privately, seemingly soon after the end of *Rocky III*. The light tone reminds us that the former adversaries are close friends. The scene ends in the same kind of freeze-frame that the series used to close previous bouts and films, this time just as the two make first punch contact. Next, Rocky, late for Paulie's (Burt Young) birthday party, gets out of his car at his mansion, his young son (Rocky Krakoff) coming at him with a home video camera. We see Rocky in black and white, the camera's viewing screen data on the side. His gift to his brother-in-law is a robot that serves the birthday cake, expresses itself with running text on an LED screen, and eventually serves as a telephone. Rocky takes the call from Creed that sets in motion the events leading to Creed's death from the robot phone, the two friends communicating through this mechanical body.

Our first view of Drago (Dolph Lundgren) is Creed's, as he watches television by his pool. The first six scenes of the film swing between the intimacy of Creed's private ring, Adrian and Rocky's bedroom, and four other scenes marked by representational technology: a video camera, news television, and screen measurements of Drago training. Drago is aestheticised *as information*, a technological compendium of images and read-outs. That scene ends with Drago, pasted-on heart monitor discs visible above the hammer and sickle on his tank top, smashing his gloves into a padded computer sensor. These details encapsulate *Rocky IV*'s intensification of the mediatisation begun in previous films.

Creed wants an exhibition match with Drago. He and Rocky begin to prepare by watching their old fights on tape (clips from *Rocky* films). After a press conference the action moves to Las Vegas. The silent Drago can't believe what he's seeing. We are treated to a James Brown floorshow, from the middle of which a boxing ring rises through the floor. Real-life boxing commentators Warner Wolf and Barry Tompkins look at the camera, as if broadcasting live, welcoming viewers to what Tompkins calls 'a most unusual event'. As the introductions drag on, we hear Wolf and Tompkins in voiceover, naturalising the collapse of our actual cinematic reception of the fight with the TV protocols embedded within it. After Creed's funeral, the narrative turns not to Rocky's revenge, but to the press conference in which it is announced under a montage of print media trumpeting Rocky's abdication of the title in order to fight Drago and avenge Creed.

The extreme training for each *Rocky* film peaked with *Rocky IV* (Lundgren's punches bruised Stallone's heart; he had to have surgery).[7] It's also the film that makes most of training sequences. Rocky trains in the Russian hinterland, where, to reinforce his old school-ness, he arrives in cap and leather jacket reminiscent of Cosmo Carbone. The montage that follows is crosscut with a crudeness symptomatic of the film's late Cold War politics. Drago's capacities are showcased through data and read-outs. Rocky 'does' things: he chops wood, moves rocks, pulls a sledge. Drago is always inside, wearing white spandex, attached to machines that go ping. He is always performing, and *always* observed. Drago runs on an inclined treadmill after being injected with steroids; Rocky runs up a mountain. The sun setting in front of him, he is reconstituted as brute nature.

The Soviet Fight Night spectacle is broadcast internationally. Again, American commentators speak straight into the camera (Tompkins now joined by Al Bandiero, a more generic media personality). Both are commenting for the USA television network. Founded as the Madison Square Garden channel, predominantly broadcasting sports events, USA's name and logo here echo the Us vs. Them ideology of the film. Reporters and broadcasters from around the world are present. As Rocky enters the ring with Adrian and his crew, his son and two friends watch at home. Paulie's female robot watches, too, dressed as Santa (it's Christmas Day) *and* wearing boxing gloves – one communications medium watching another. We don't see the three boys again until Rocky hurts Drago for the first time. The robot cheers, one boxing-gloved arm in the air. After winning, Rocky speaks through global television to his son, just as he did to Adrian in *Rocky II*.

In *Rocky III*, Rocky transformed himself into a different style of fighter. In *Rocky IV*, to fight the unhappy human robot, Drago, he reverts to his nature as slugger. The fight sequence is the most amped-up in the series, notably in terms of Stallone's and Lundgren's pumped and ripped bodies. Such a body is of little use to an actual boxer: while many are impressively muscled, they are better served by speed and fluidity. Drago's punches are stiff and formulaic, which contributes to the absurdity of the boxing. Repeatedly he cocks his right hand, signalling his punch (there are no feints in Rocky's fights), throwing it straight from the shoulder. Against an opponent who is doing anything to protect himself, this 'overhand right', so-called because it is thrown over the opponent's arms and gloves, would need an arc, but because Rocky marches forward, not so.

Rocky and Drago take turns unloading on one another. For much of the fight Rocky absorbs a superhuman amount of punishment. In the first round, sensibly, against a much taller opponent, he attacks Drago's mid-section ('chop down the body and the head will fall'). But Drago mocks him. In the second, Rocky characteristically draws strength from his beating, swarms Drago, and cuts him near the eye. His ability to keep coming back begins to earn Drago's respect: he growls that Rocky isn't human. Much of the rest of the fight is shown in a speedy montage. Rocky hurts Drago in round two, then until round six returns to absorbing punishment. After round six the montage turns into a split-screen in which Rocky sits on his corner stool, screen left, as if watching the action. Beating on Rocky, Drago finds his own humanity – and individualism – in Rocky's suffering and drive. Before the fifteenth round (by 1986 a 15-round unsanctioned non-title bout was unheard of), Drago picks up the politburo apparatchik who's just commanded him to win and throws him off the ring apron, yelling that he fights to win 'for me!' With that recognition in place (its importance emphasised by a cut-away to a Gorbachev lookalike), Drago loses: no human can resist Rocky's body attack.

BARE KNUCKLE BRUISING IN *ROCKY V*

As with *Rocky IV*, the opening fight in *Rocky V* (1990), again the last fight of the previous film, is re-edited for brevity. Then, for the first time in a *Rocky* film, we see Rocky naked. In long shot he stands, hands against the wall under a shower, presumably after the bout with Drago. Coming closer, he's as physically and mentally damaged as he's ever been.

Stallone's preoccupation with the media representation of sport returns in full force as Rocky speaks at a press conference back in the States. A stand-in for notorious promoter Don King, George Washington Duke (Richard Gant), tries to gin up a boxing spectacle in Japan against a black fighter, Union Cane (former heavyweight boxer Michael Anthony Williams). Shortly afterwards Rocky is told he's broke, and sees a doctor to approve his re-entry into the ring. Like Drago in *Rocky IV*, he is scanned by medical technology: MRIs, CT scans, infrared, and so on.[8] Told he has permanent brain damage and that no boxing association will license him, he paces the doctor's office, scanned images in the background. At scene's end, he turns away from Adrian and his doctors, only to be confronted with pictures of his damaged brain.[9]

Unable to fight, Rocky displaces that energy onto Tommy Gunn, played by then up-and-coming heavyweight Tommy Morrison, training him to be, as the newspapers say, 'Rocky's clone'. Morrison was an appropriate casting choice, a powerful puncher with some ability to withstand punishment who would go on to win a portion of the heavyweight title (the proliferation of sanctioning bodies – World Boxing Association, World Boxing Council, International Boxing Federation, etc – means there is no longer a single, linear champion, the man who beat the man who beat...). Gunn's success is confirmed, for Rocky, when he can see the latest fight rebroadcast on TV. The same holds true for Duke, watching Gunn on TV while doing business. At Duke's urging, Gunn abandons Rocky. Rocky watches Gunn fight Cane on TV. Where once Rocky used TV to speak to Adrian, his son and America, now it marks his expulsion from Gunn's inner circle, and from boxing. This Rocky cannot accept: he cannot merely watch the fight. He hits the heavy bag in his basement as Gunn punches Cane, the two events crosscut.

Cane defeated, Gunn has himself driven down to Rocky's local bar to call him out, Duke, reporters and a cameraman in tow. Gunn knocks Paulie down. Rocky accepts the challenge, saying: 'My ring is outside.' For the first time in the series, there's a fight without gloves, without ropes. The cartoonish aspect of *this* fight is that, while a blow from a bare fist may be more damaging to its recipient than that from a gloved hand, there's every chance that the bare fist will be damaged: boxing gloves protect a fighter's hands first of all. The prolonged street brawl, with kicks, elbows and repeated punches to Rocky's and Gunn's bony heads, is entirely fiction. Rocky Jr. (Sage Stallone) watches on TV and informs Adrian. The definition of a title fight temporarily becomes one that is broadcast live and unsanctioned. At the inevitable moment of underdog-near-defeat, Rocky calls on his ghosts (Drago, Creed, Mickey), who appear in artfully scratched, bleached clips from past *Rocky* films. He rises to fanfare from the *Rocky* theme. A news camera follows every move, as does the crowd. Rocky re-establishes elements of boxing's containment, saying: 'I didn't hear no bell ... one more round.' Predictably, Rocky Jr. and Adrian arrive in time for Rocky's final pummelling of Gunn, whom he plasters against the front of a bus. Mass media meets mass transit.

Intended to be the last *Rocky* film, *Rocky V* ends not with a fight but with Rocky and his son mounting the Philadelphia Art Museum steps, pausing briefly at Rocky's statue, and finally going in to look at the art. This film walks nostalgically back through the franchise. It has black-and-white stills from the first four films running under the end credits, as if they were 'real' artefacts from Rocky's life. The last image, of the Rocky statue, gradually changes from black and white to colour, suggesting a permanent present.

DIGITAL DEPLOYMENT IN *ROCKY BALBOA*

One way to see Stallone's nostalgia for the first *Rocky* film in the last of the series is by measuring the gap between the 1970s American realist cinema that he affects in *Rocky Balboa* as director and the 'new media' technologies he deploys within the story as screenwriter. The title, *Rocky Balboa*, suggests Rocky is no longer a professional fighter. When we meet him he has embraced 'civilian' life, seemingly content with the small-scale celebrity of a private citizen and has-been. The statue has been removed from the Museum steps (as actually happened), and Paulie has softened into an old man who paints pictures while working at the meatpacking plant.

The film opens differently from all previous instalments. There's a boxing match, but Rocky is not involved. We see two black fighters, neither with any relation to the saga so far. The fight is shown in black and white, with live voiceover HBO commentary. It is constructed as something not happening at that moment, with shots dissolving over shots, slow-motion, and high-contrast cinematography. Mason 'The Line' Dixon (Antonio Tarver), the undefeated world heavyweight champion (really a former light-heavyweight champion), is pelted with ice as he leaves the ring after another too-easy knockout. By the end, the shots have colour bled back into them, the slow-motion has returned to regular speed, the contrast is more realistic, and the voiceover describes the decline of heavyweight boxing.

Stallone's attention to the representation of the athletic body and of boxing in a media-driven culture is most pronounced in *Rocky Balboa*. After visiting Adrian's grave, Rocky goes to visit Rocky Jr. (Milo Ventimiglia), now working in finance, at his office. Rocky Jr.'s boss wants a picture with 'The Champ', and the son takes a picture of them with the boss's cell phone. Rocky poses for the digital image, a relic pantomiming boxing.

Rocky runs an Italian restaurant named after Adrian, telling well-worn ring stories that his customers fill in as he goes.[10] The warm tones of the candlelit restaurant cede to a shot of a glass high-rise from which a diamond-draped Dixon exits into his expensive car. He inserts a DVD into the dashboard and watches his own last fight. The spectator sees the opening fight again, now in extreme close-up, digital video pixels indicating it's a replay. The smallness of the frame is always apparent – we never cut into it as in previous matches in the series, even when these were broadcast on TV.

When we see ESPN's computer-simulated 'fight' between Dixon and Rocky to determine who is the greatest of all time, it's initially from Rocky Jr.'s point of view sitting in a pub with his buddies.[11] The perspective shifts to Dixon, whose friends call him inside to watch the fight on a mega-screen. At first we see the virtual fight between the two motion-capture/CGI-generated figures of Rocky and Dixon framed by the edges of television screens. Shortly after, the action becomes 'real'. Across the country, Rocky Jr. also observes the fight, but without the frame confining the action to the hypothetical computer match. 'Rocky' knocks 'Dixon' out cold.

The actual exhibition match between Balboa and Dixon, named 'Skill vs. Will', starts with the most scripted press conference of the series. Logos and endorsement signs blanket everything, an event so canned that the reporters' questions seem disembodied. There is the obligatory

Figure 5 - Mediatised culture. *Rocky Balboa.* Producers William Chartoff, Kevin King Templeton, Charles Winkler and David Winkler; directed by Sylvester Stallone; DVD distributed by Sony Pictures Home Entertainment.

training montage, complete with *Rocky* fanfare to start it off. But trainer Duke Evers (Tony Burton) has already ruled out most boxing training: Rocky is so old, his body so destroyed, that traditional training would only make things worse. All that remains is power ('blunt force trauma', says Evers). The subsequent montage sees Rocky running with his dog, weightlifting, doing minimal work on the heavy bag, before hitting sides of beef in the meatpacking plant. Boxers, as noted, don't lift weights to build muscle. They run to develop endurance, shadowbox, work the heavy bag to develop specific combinations of punches, and work on pads held by trainers to develop form, speed and power. They then put all of this together in sparring sessions. Highly ranked professionals hire good quality boxers to work with them. Rocky just builds physical strength; his training routines signal a 'brokenness' to be overcome. The clear point of reference – a comparison made by the ringside commentators – is George Foreman. Foreman was heavyweight champion in the 1970s, retired in 1977, came back in 1987, aged 38 (significantly younger than Rocky in *Rocky Balboa*), and won a version of the heavyweight title again, in 1994, before finally retiring in 1997, aged 48. In Act Two of his career, Foreman, never fast but always a fearsome puncher, maintained that power (boxing wisdom says power is the last thing a boxer loses), therefore keeping the puncher's chance. Rocky is again defined as someone who sustains an enormous amount of damage only to triumph by brute force; now, too, he must overcome ageing.

We go from Philly to Vegas in a dissolve. The weigh-in is done before a capacity crowd. If someone looks like an actual boxing commentator or referee, that's because more than any other *Rocky* film, this one collapses the division between performance and the real. Lou DiBella is a manager; Bert Sugar is a boxing journalist; Larry Merchant, whom we see doing HBO colour commentary with Jim Lampley and Max Kellerman, bloviates for HBO. Mike Tyson appears as himself. Dixon has been training, but he doesn't look like he has (Tarver had to gain weight for *Rocky Balboa*; clearly it wasn't muscle). Rocky doesn't take off his robe, nor do we ever see his exposed body during training. When Rocky does strip down to his trunks in the ring, we see an older but more muscled and ripped body than Dixon's. Before the fight, an HBO mini-feature splices Rocky's fictional fights with actual Tarver fights. The event is shown on HBO pay-per-view (like many of Tarver's real fights).

The film's real people are embedded in precise recreations of boxing mises-en-scène and cable protocols. *Rocky Balboa* thus distinguishes itself by being the single film in the series to be set firmly in the Age of New Media. Lampley, Merchant and Kellerman all stand where they would and say what they would for a real fight. Michael Buffer introduces the fight as he has any number of title bouts. Joe Cortez, a prominent referee, appears as himself. The protocols of a specific kind of televisuality gradually override cinematic conventions, transforming the spectator of *Rocky Balboa* into a spectator of HBO pay-per-view.

During the fight the high-definition camera sequencing corresponds to what the spectator sees on HBO, until Rocky starts to establish he's got a chance. From round three on, Stallone mobilises everything from the black-and-white cinematography and multiple speeds of *Raging Bull* to MTV cutting to 1970s New Hollywood zooms. We see rapid cut-ins of Adrian's headstone, shots where all colour has been drained except Rocky's red blood and Dixon's blue trunks, black-and-white freeze-frames dotted like traditional news photos. When, near the fight's end, Rocky's life flashes before his eyes, it is in clips from previous *Rocky* films, scratched and otherwise treated as something between an experimental film and a Nine Inch Nails video, with no stable aesthetic. Though the sequence briefly recalls *Rocky V*'s street brawl, it's unlike any other fight in the series.

But the fight's narrative arc is familiar. Rocky as underdog earns the respect of his opponent and everyone else – most importantly, his son – by the exchange of force. He is repeatedly beaten around the ring, only to recover. Yet for the first time in the series, Stallone and Tarver replicate something like the back and forth of real boxing. Tarver's skill perhaps contributed to this – unlike Morrison, Tarver is relatively quick. The HBO-style camerawork certainly helps. More and faster-moving cameras, closer to the ring, with more complex cutting and cropping of the frame, allow for a more realistic sense of physical conversation.

The result is a split decision for Dixon. Rocky is already on his way out of the arena when it comes. Rocky's point-of-view is now indivisible from Stallone's. In shooting, Stallone piggybacked his fight entrances and exits onto an HBO middleweight championship fight between Bernard Hopkins and Jermaine Taylor at Mandalay Bay. When Rocky/Stallone leaves to the roar of the crowd shouting, 'Rocky! Rocky!' not only are the crowds authentic, but their chants are unsolicited.

BACK TO REALITY: DRAGO VS. KLITSCHKO, INC.

The collapse between Rocky and Stallone preoccupied Stallone as screen-writer in *Rocky III*. After *Rocky IV* boxing itself responded. If the *Rocky* series increasingly mobilised boxing personages and state-of-the-art media to confirm its veracity, the Sweet Science has increasingly been understood in terms of Stallone-authored codes, not only by laypeople but by professionals. One of the challenges for Stallone's reality series, *The Contender* (2005–2007), was that, like the *Rocky* films, it had to navigate between boxing aficionados and casual fans whose under-standing of boxing came (more or less) from those films. It's one thing to reduce training to a montage (plus confessional, in the TV version), another to reduce the bout itself via editing. For its third season, the series went from NBC to ESPN, signalling a willingness to court the 'true' boxing fan with less editing, to restore the uninterrupted tempo-rality of an HBO fight.

The Contender never reached the centre of sports consciousness, but a 'Rocky Effect' has remained. Since *Rocky IV*, boxing writers have understood the generally robotic nature of Eastern European fight-ers via Drago. That focus sharpened considerably when Wladimir and Vitali Klitschko appeared. The Ukrainian brothers were introduced to global boxing consciousness in 1996, when Wladimir won the super heavyweight Olympic gold medal in Atlanta. Drago was also an Olympic champion, if a fictive one; Lundgren and both Klitschkos are well over six feet tall. The Klitschkos were immediately understood and described as living embodiments of Drago. That Wladimir, particularly, could be imagined to fight like Drago is largely happenstance. Earlier in his career, Wladimir demonstrated tendencies left over from the Soviet bloc amateur style, deploying an extended, pawing jab, but he's become the more technically correct boxer, and the more calculating, while Vitali is looser and more aggressive. Until the 1990s, heavyweight boxers over six feet tall and weighing more than 250 pounds were typically unexceptional except in size, but the Klitschkos (and British former champion Lennox Lewis) have changed that: they're not only huge, they're fit and mobile.

Klitschko/Drago comparisons are widespread. The references came from boxing fans on discussion forums with thread titles like, 'Better chin? Vitali Klitschko or Ivan Drago?' (Anon. 2005). Before Vitali's fight with Lewis, he resisted being represented in those terms, if ironically. In a Q&A in *Sports Illustrated* Klitschko was asked: 'You are 6-foot-8 and from the Ukraine. How many times have people called you Ivan Drago from *Rocky IV*?' His response: 'I don't want people to describe me as Ivan Drago. We are completely different. Ivan Drago did not have a brother, but I do' (Anon. 2003). *New York Times* sports writer Harvey Araton (2008) wrote about the resurgence of former Soviet boxers, in 'In All Corners, the Sons of Drago', which profiled Wladimir. Both Klitschkos have pointed out that they were not forced automatons like Drago, but they are occasionally happy to go with the moniker – on their own terms. 'Like Russian champ in *Rocky IV*', Vitali deadpans, 'We Ivan Drago One, Two' (in Lidz 2002). Both brothers have been world champion, sharing the available titles. Other boxers see the Klitschkos through *Rocky IV*, with interesting consequences in terms of race. Just as the *Rocky* films sometimes want race not to matter, so do boxers themselves. After tangling with Vitali outside the ring at a restaurant in Germany, black British fighter David Haye painted Vitali as Drago and himself as Rocky: 'He's watched *Rocky IV* way too many times. He thinks he's Ivan Drago. He stands there stiff as a board and it's not going to be Apollo Creed vs. Drago, it's going to be Rocky vs. Ivan Drago' (in Vester 2008) (contracted to fight Vitali, Haye ultimately fought Wladimir).

The blogosphere continues to speculate about how the Klitschkos would do against each of Rocky's opponents (Klitschko vs. Drago is deemed uninteresting as it pits like against like) (see Crofut 2011). Accounts by boxing historians also describe the Klitschkos as Drago (see, for example, Saunders 2011).

CONCLUSION: *ROCKY* AND THE RHETORIC OF BOXING

In summer 2011, the first image on Stallone's website was of Stallone and Mike Tyson. The headline read: 'Stallone inducted into the International Boxing Hall of Fame.' Stallone gave a speech, slowed by chants of 'Rocky! Rocky! Rocky!' from a crowd who, presumably, knew what actual boxing entailed. Stallone responded, 'Music to my ears!' He continued by distinguishing himself from real boxers, saying he'd never had those skills. He concluded, 'Yo Adrian! I did it!' The induction confirmed that Rocky and the *Rocky* series have had a disproportionate effect on the actual sport. In July 2012, Wladimir Klitschko presented Muhammad Ali with a humanitarian award, calling him the 'Rocky of Life', closing the representational circle. As if to corroborate this, one could access tickets to the new *Rocky* musical through the official Klitschko website.

Still, despite his improbable fistic triumphs, Rocky the character is fundamentally hurt. Rocky's authenticity remains grounded in his underdog, slugger's work ethic: always overmatched, he prepares well enough to give himself a puncher's chance if he can just withstand enough punishment. Hence the importance of the training montage. But it *is* montage: Rocky's body is mediatised from the outset, and increasingly so throughout the series. His body's authenticity is also fictional, however hard Stallone works in the gym, as is the masculinity it stands for.[12] Nonetheless this body and masculinity are not without significant rhetorical effects on the 'real' world of boxing and on media coverage of the sport.

NOTES

1   Mark S. Driscoll notes that one fight scene in *Rocky Balboa* 'uses backgrounds from an earlier fight that Sylvester Stallone actually attended prior to filming ... [I]t should be possible to see Stallone (as himself) in the audience while Stallone (as Rocky) is in the ring' (Anon. 2011).

2   Frank McRae, a former NFL player for the Chicago Bears, plays the undefeated champion, Big Glory. Terry Funk held the National Wrestling Alliance Heavyweight title from 1975 to 1977. He returns in *Over the Top*. These are early illustrations of Stallone's fondness for casting real sports figures as themselves or as athletes.

3   Championship boxing matches were reduced from fifteen rounds to twelve after the Ray Mancini–Duk Koo Kim fight that resulted in Kim's death in 1982.

4   For an earlier history of boxing and cinema, see Streible (2008). Valuable accounts of more recent films include Baker (2003) and Grindon (2011).

5   Wepner's propensity for bleeding is referenced in *Rocky* when, right eye bloody and closed, Rocky demands his cutman cut his eyelid so he can see for the final round. The cutman tends to the fighter between rounds, the trainer instructing and motivating. Al Silvani, a storied trainer, plays Rocky's cutman.

6   As Aaron Baker suggests, it's possible to see Creed more problematically: 'By showing Creed as less political than self-serving, the film indirectly attacks Ali's skepticism about a lack of black access to opportunity and therefore rejects the necessity for the society to redress racial injustice' (2003: 132).

7   See Corsello (2006) for Stallone's excessive approach to training and his resulting injuries.

8   The emphasis on medical technology suggests a largely sublimated response to the HIV/AIDS crisis. Back in his old neighborhood, Rocky encounters Tommy Gunn (Tommy Morrison). In 1996 Morrison disclosed he was HIV positive. Prior to his death in 2013, as Merrill (2013) indicates, the apparently confused and desperate Morrison would deny the existence of AIDS.

9   Stallone has given an account of why the brain damage in *Rocky V* had dissipated by *Rocky Balboa*: 'When Rocky was diagnosed with brain damage [he] never went for a second opinion and yielded to his wife's wishes to stop. So with the advent of new research techniques into brain damage, Rocky's was found to be normal among fighters and he was suffering the results of a severe concussion. By today's standards Rocky Balboa would be given a clean bill of health for fighters. In the film, Rocky is told that he has to train differently because he has lost a great deal of flexibility and mobility so hence the heavy weight training and power lifting that built Rocky into the shape that makes him a worthy opponent. P.S. he's still not in the same shape as he was in *Rocky IV*, he's just stronger' (in Knowles 2006).

10 This echoes the fate of Joe Louis, who later in life became a casino greeter and had his picture taken with customers before they settled down at the card tables.

11 The fight is based on the 1970 'Super Fight' between Ali and Marciano, which required the boxers to be filmed 'sparring' to conform to a computer's statistical construction. To many fans' disbelief, Marciano knocked out Ali in the thirteenth round. Ali commented that the computer was made in Alabama.

12 Stallone's support for the use of testosterone and human growth hormone (he was arrested in 2007 for importing into Australia) seems ironic. See Stein (2008) and Weise (2008).

BIBLIOGRAPHY

Anon. (2003) 'Q&A with Vitali Klitschko'. Online. Available HTTP: http://sportsillustrated.cnn.com/si_online/QandA/2003/0623/ (2 August 2012).

_____ (2005) 'Better Chin? Vitali Klitschko or Ivan Drago?' Online. Available HTTP: http://www.boxingscene.com/forums/showthread.php?t=7321 (2 August 2012).

_____ (2011) '*Rocky Balboa* (2006): Did You Know?' Online. Available HTTP: http://www.imdb.com/title/tt0479143/trivia (20 July 2011).

_____ (2012) 'Sylvester Stallone Drops Plans for F1 Movie'. Online. Available HTTP: http://en.espnf1.com/onthisday/motorsport/story/2269.html (10 August 2012).

Araton, Harvey (2008) 'In All Corners, the Sons of Drago', *New York Times*, 21 February. Online. Available   HTTP: http://www.nytimes.com/2008/02/21/sports/othersports/21araton.

html?_r=1&ref=wladimir_klitschko&pagewanted=print (2 June 2012).

Baker, Aaron (2003) *Contesting Identities: Sports in American Film*. Champaign: University of Illinois Press.

Box Office Mojo (n. d.) *'Driven'*. Online. Available HTTP: http://boxofficemojo.com/movies/?id=driven.htm (14 August 2011).

Corsello, Andrew (2006) 'Requiem for a Heavyweight', *Philadelphia Magazine*, December. Online. Available HTTP: http://www.phillymag.com/articles/requiem_for_a_heavyweight/ (15 August 2011).

Crofut, Lakota (2011) 'Vitali & Vladimir Klitschko vs. the Villains of Rocky'. Online. Available HTTP: http://www.rudetudesports.com/2011/10/13/opponents-vitali-klitschko/ (10 July 2012).

Fernandez, Bernard (2011) *'Rocky* Alter-Ego Stallone to Join Immortals on Boxing Hall of Fame'. Online. Available HTTP: http://articles.philly.com/2011-06-11/sports/29647341_1_john-rambo-character-rocky-balboa-international-boxing-hall/2 (9 June 2012).

Grindon, Leger (2011) *Knockout: The Boxer and Boxing in American Cinema*. Jackson: University Press of Mississippi.

Knowles, Harry (2006) 'Round One: Q & A with Sylvester Stallone'. Online. Available HTTP: http://www.aintitcool.com/node/30861 (12 June 2012).

Lidz, Franz (2002) 'The Bruise Brothers: A Pair of Brawny, Brainy Ukrainian Ph.D.'s, Vitali and Wladimir Klitschko, Hope to Soon Divide and Conquer the Heavyweight Division', *Sports Illustrated*, 18 November. Online. Available HTTP: http://quicktime.cnnsi.com/vault/article/magazine/MAG1027473/index.htm (15 August 2011).

Merrill, Elizabeth (2013) 'Tommy Morrison's latest big fight'. Online. Available HTTP: http://espn.go.com/espn/otl/story/_/id/9588582/tommy-morrison-latest-big-fight (6 October 2013).

Saunders, Charles R. (2011) 'Ivan Drago's Legacy'. Online. Available HTTP: http://boxscorenews.com/ivan-dragos-legacy-p11412-69.htm (10 July 2012).

'Stallone's Goalkeeper Preparations' (1998) *Victory* DVD extras. Burbank: Warner Home Video.

Stein, Joel (2008) 'Stallone on a Mission', *Time*, 24 January. Online. Available HTTP: http://www.time.com/time/magazine/article/0,9171,1706759-1,00.html (15 July 2012).

Streible, Dan (2008) *Fight Pictures: The History of Boxing and Early Cinema*. Berkeley: University of California Press.

Vester, Mark (2008) 'David Haye Gives His Side of the Klitschko Altercation'. Online. Available HTTP: http://www.boxingscene.com/?m=show&tid=17507 (9 June 2012).

Weise, Elizabeth (2008) 'Stallone Puts Muscle Behind HGH; Raises Alarms'. Online. Available HTTP: http://www.usatoday.com/news/health/2008-02-05-human-growth-hormone_N.htm (15 July 2012).

'WHO WOULDN'T WANT A BODY LIKE THAT?': MASCULINITY, MUSCULARITY AND MALE AUDIENCES FOR THE FILMS OF SYLVESTER STALLONE

IAN HUFFER

This essay examines the ways in which male audiences view Sylvester Stallone's body in relation to masculinity and how this is intersected by other aspects of identity, such as social class, sexuality and age. Stallone's muscles have been central to analysis of the social/cultural construction of masculinity in the star's films, symbolising 'the triumphal assertion of a traditional masculinity, defined through strength' and/or a 'hysterical image … of the male body (and masculine identity) in crisis' (Tasker 1993: 109).[1] However, this relationship between masculinity and the star's physique has been under-explored in *audience*-led approaches to the star, with neither Valerie Walkerdine (1986) nor Martin Barker and Kate Brooks (1998) questioning their participants on this subject.

My own research into British audience responses to Stallone has explored their engagement with the star's physique. To date I have examined how Stallone's weight gain in *Cop Land* affected male audiences' categorisation of the star and how heterosexual female audiences have eroticised a model of masculinity that combines physical strength with sensitivity (see Huffer 2003, 2007). Yet I have not addressed questions of masculinity in depth when writing about male responses. The exclusive focus on men in the analysis that follows is not to suggest that men's and women's relationships to the star are completely different, but rather to recognise that being gendered as male or female often produces materially different experiences of life.

More specifically, this essay maps the range of ways male audiences interpret Stallone's body. Some have emulated the star's physique through weight-training. Others identify with *and* erotically desire the star's body. Yet others view the star's physique as hysterical or unreal and/or value the star's sensitivity over his physical strength. This essay also considers how attitudes to the star's physique may change across time, asks how these differing responses might be connected to the men's understanding of masculinity (as intersected by other formations of identity), and explores some of the ways that these interpretations may be prompted by the film texts themselves. By considering such questions we can gain an insight into the models of masculinity circulating through Stallone's films and society, and learn how and why men are invested in them.

THE SURVEY

The following comments are taken from a qualitative questionnaire. It was distributed in 2001 to participants who responded to a letter I had placed in regional newspapers and national magazines in the UK.[2] At this moment Stallone's career was in jeopardy, commercially and critically, thanks to the failure of *Get Carter* (2000) and *Driven* (2001). What credibility or relevance could the star's representation of masculinity have at such a point in time? Through the respondents' comments we can see how Stallone retained significance for audiences, pointing us towards the star's potential relevance to this day.

A total of 51 people participated in the study (32 men – three of them gay – and 19 women; all white). The questionnaire consisted of forty open-ended questions. It included questions on how and when the respondents were introduced to Stallone's films, the contexts in which they viewed them, what their favourite Stallone films are, why they enjoy them, and whether their enjoyment has changed over time. It also asked for their opinion on Stallone's physique, whether they had attempted to emulate it, and how they understood his masculinity. The more specific focus of these latter questions formed part of a commitment 'to critically analysing culture as well as describing it' (Moores 1993: 4), directly addressing those debates raised above. These were balanced with more general questions, however, in a bid to submit myself to 'the possibility of ... "being surprised", of reaching knowledge not prefigured in one's starting paradigm' (Ang 1989: 110).

In addition, specific identificatory questions were asked covering name, location, age, gender, sexuality and ethnicity, while another question asked for a brief biography, incorporating jobs, education and family status. Respondents varied in the amount of detail they provided in this biography of their lives. Particular individuals are consequently emphasised in the following analysis due to the depth of the contextual information that they provided.

The men's comments cited here are taken from answers to the full range of questions. These comments have been selected and interpreted in relation to the starting paradigm outlined earlier, chosen for the relevance of their explicit statements and implicit assumptions (as revealed through the discourses that they employ).[3] The detail of the respondents' observations in turn helps to shape the structure and argument employed in this essay, including the interpretation of Stallone's films. Such an emphasis on the films alongside audience responses acknowledges that while 'film viewers are productive agents in the creation of meaning', film texts are still 'in some ways determinate, such that their internal properties inflect ... the uses to which they are put' (Austin 2002: 2).

EMULATION

Stallone's body held or still holds a potent allure for a number of the respondents, inspiring them to transform their body through 'extra-cinematic identificatory practices' (Stacey 1994: 159) in order to resemble him. When asked if they had attempted to emulate the star's physique, the following respondents replied:

Indeed I have. I have even had a fairly successful amateur boxing career all due to watching Rocky *at 11.* (Q12 – Jimmy)[4]

I think any young lad who had seen the training sequences in Rocky *would like to emulate Stallone physically. He inspired me to partake in a twelve-year obsession with body-building – increasing my body size from a small 11 stone to a powerful 16 stone. My appearance gave me confidence in most aspects of life.* (Q12 – Richard)

The Rocky *series of films inspired me to push myself into weightlifting and losing weight. ... I used to get bullied and teased about my size, and these films gave me inspiration.* (Q12 – Pete)

We do not have, but we all want, a physique like his and so that is why we want to watch his films (Q11). … Stallone, and even more so Schwarzenegger, have certainly introduced me to what can be achieved by body-building/ weight-training and they inspired me to take up the sport. After all, who wouldn't want a body like that? (Q12 – Paul)

I started down the gym at about 14. I was inspired after watching Rocky *and admiring the physique of Sly.* (Q12 – David)

Looking at the respondents' comments in more detail underlines how the star's physique symbolises strength and confidence through his films, clarifies why these men have found this so inspirational, and reveals how this strength is coded as male. Jimmy is a heterosexual 31-year-old[5] from Birkenhead, married for ten years with three children. Elsewhere in the questionnaire he writes of his enjoyment of 'the training montage from *Rocky*' because it 'proves that if you set your mind to something you can do it. He had trouble getting out of bed to start with, finally making it up those famous steps hardly out of breath (… it gives me goose bumps)' (Q7). Within this context, Stallone's physical transformation becomes symbolic of the star's determination to overcome adversity. This has special resonance for Jimmy due to the negative effects of his intermittent, class-bound employment history. He writes that he has had 'many jobs including builder, barman, electrician, warehouseman, shop assistant, truck driver and machine operator' (Q19). He adds, when asked if he felt a connection between Stallone's films and his own life, that 'I know what it feels like to fall on hard times, have no money, no home, but things always work out in the end' (Q23). Through locating success in the transformation of the body, specifically through the training sequences of *Rocky*, Stallone's films offer Jimmy a model of masculinity to emulate that provides him with the strength necessary to overcome these challenges. In addition, the *Rocky* films' representation of boxing as a 'counterpoint to the experience of oppression and powerlessness' (Walkerdine 1986: 172) proved appealing enough to lead Jimmy to take up the sport.

When asked to consider the brand of masculinity embodied by Stallone, Jimmy consequently describes the star as 'a man's man' due to this emphasis on physical strength. He adds that Stallone 'embodies a simple ruggedness, i.e. he is not politically correct. He isn't one of those "caring-sharing-new-age-men"' (Q37). Within the context outlined above, caring and sharing arguably signify a degree of weakness that undermines the strength Jimmy views as necessary to endure life's challenges. An appreciation of Jimmy's life thus provides us with a better understanding of why he may de-emphasise the sensitivity that others prize in Stallone's characters.

For Richard, a heterosexual 31-year-old from Bristol, the attraction of Stallone's physique is also connected to its ability to convey strength and power. Elsewhere in the questionnaire Richard writes that 'Stallone looked like he could kick ass – you never doubted who was the hero!' (Q11). His comment that 'any young lad … would want to emulate Stallone' also underlines the implicit maleness of this appeal. Through transforming his own body into a 'powerful 16 stone', Richard was thus able to acquire 'confidence in most aspects of life'. The fact that Richard lacked confidence while a 'small 11 stone', and that Pete was bullied and teased for being overweight, underlines the pressure to live up to an ideal of masculinity based on muscular strength. For Richard, this pressure may have been made more acute by being an adolescent at the time he first saw the star's films. He specifies that he was interested in Stallone's physique during his 'middle to late teens' (Q23), a period in which there are fewer ways to display power beyond the physical, such as the work-related 'management masculinities' (Beynon 2002: 22) available later in life. In addition, Richard writes that he 'left school at 16 to start an apprenticeship in reprographics print' (Q19), indicating his working-class status and thus the potentially greater difficulty of attaining alternative forms of power.

Richard's comment elsewhere that 'without the inspiration of *Rocky* I probably would not have looked at a weight' also reminds us of the central role Stallone's films played in creating pressure to meet an ideal of masculinity reliant upon bodily strength. Just like Jimmy, Richard picks out the training sequences from the *Rocky* films as most important, and adds that '*Rocky III* was the first film that I remember inspiring me to physically look after myself' (Q13). Looking at the training sequence from *Rocky III* (1982), we can see how costume, cinematography and editing are used to hide Stallone's physique when Rocky is expressing weakness, and emphasise it when the character is displaying strength. The sequence is preceded by Rocky's lowest point in the narrative, when, dejected after the death of his manager and the loss of his title, he rides around Philadelphia on his motorbike, dressed in jeans, a leather jacket and sweater. Moving to Los Angeles to commence training under the tutelage of Apollo Creed (Carl Weathers), Rocky is lethargic and preoccupied at first, lacking coordination as he and Creed practice footwork in front of the mirror. Significantly, Rocky is covered up in a sweat-top while Creed wears a vest. When Rocky's wife Adrian (Talia Shire) persuades him to put the demons behind him, the music kicks in ('Gonna Fly Now') and the clothes fall away. When we return to Rocky and Creed practising footwork, they now move in unison, both only wearing shorts. The two race each other in a beach sprint, with the viewer offered crosscut close-ups of the two characters' thighs in slow-motion. The montage ends with Rocky out-sprinting Creed and the two men embracing in the water. A final freeze-frame shows Rocky hugging Creed with one arm while raising the other in jubilation, allowing us to pause for a moment and contemplate Rocky's incredibly built-up biceps and forearm. While the climactic fights of the *Rocky* films may consolidate the character's strength and test it, then, it is these training sequences that most clearly illustrate the transformative power of the body, constructing the star, and a particular brand of masculinity, as a potent point of identification for Jimmy and Richard.

EROTICISM

The celebration of Stallone's and Creed's physiques and their climactic clinch in the training sequence from *Rocky III* also renders homoeroticism palpable. It is notable that the sequence places a kiss between Rocky and Adrian at its centre in a bid to allay homophobic fears among heterosexual male audiences. For one of the homosexual respondents, though, the desire to *be* and *have* Stallone is at the heart of his enjoyment of the star's films. His responses consequently draw further attention to the homoeroticism present in Stallone's films while deepening our understanding of how this intersects with the star's representation of masculinity.

Matt, a gay 19-year-old from London, writes that 'what I really like about Stallone is the way he looks first' (Q1), elaborating that

> I first really became a fan when I watched Demolition Man *for the first time. I was at school at that period in my life and since then I have just never really thought more about it, just that I fancied him like fuck.* (Q19)

When asked to elaborate on why he likes *Demolition Man* (1993), Matt singles out the particular moment of 'Stallone naked in the cryo-thingy. Lovely' (Q7). He also praises *Judge Dredd* (1995) for 'the blue contacts that Stallone wears in it and the surplus shots of him in tight shirts' (Q7). Such a desire *for* Stallone, however, does not negate Matt's simultaneous identification *with* the star, which he articulates in essentialist terms:

> *Sylvester Stallone is a REAL man. He represents men at their most basic and raw. He is a true embodiment of Macho Man. Sure, I believe that his acting is not the greatest ever but that's not why people want to see him in a film, they want to see him kill lots of people, blow stuff up, and generally come out of the movie the hero. Even gay men want that sort of respect. I know I would love it.* (Q37)

Matt's identification of macho masculinity as evidence of men 'at their most basic and raw' echoes the 'simple ruggedness' that Jimmy finds in Stallone, and helps to naturalise male power and authority. His stress that *even* gay men desire power and authority also points towards the way gays have been perceived as 'not men' or 'lesser men'. Matt's comments thus help to illustrate the attraction of macho culture as a 'response to oppression ... attempt[ing] to assert a power which has precisely been denied' (Tasker 1993: 120). While the politics and history of gay men's engagement with macho culture are more complex than this (see DeAngelis 2001: 132–7), Matt's 'cinematic identificatory fantasies' (Stacey 1994: 138) clearly pivot upon this promise of the respect acquired through macho masculinity.

Despite these fantasies, other comments in the questionnaire indicate that this model of masculinity is inaccessible to Matt. Asked about the star's physique, he replies, 'I would love to look like that' (Q11). When asked whether he has ever tried to emulate this physique, though, Matt replies, 'No. It would only depress me because I can't do it' (Q12). Moreover, Matt recognises that as the 'true embodiment of Macho Man' Stallone is heterosexual. Indeed, elsewhere in the questionnaire Matt writes, 'Why pick on him for sticking to what he does best – killing baddies, saving people and kissing women (bitches)' (Q40). Matt's positioning of the macho ideal embodied by Stallone as evidence of men 'at their most basic and raw' not only supports a hierarchical and binary gender system, then, but may also contribute to the reproduction of such a system within gay culture, in a way that could undermine gay men who are not macho. In addition, it reinforces the perception of gay men as lesser men due to their lack of heterosexuality.

Matt's essentialist reading of gender, and his eulogising of a model of masculinity that undermines his own identity, may be connected to his introduction to the star through his father. He comments that 'I was first introduced at such a young age that I can't actually remember what it was that first made me like him' (Q2) and that 'My father is a fan of those types of genre films more than I am, so I would watch them with him' (Q19). Such an introduction to the star was shared by a number of the respondents. When asked to recall their early viewing of Stallone's films the following men replied:

With my father at the time as he enjoys his films as well – Rockys, Rambos, Escape to Victory *etc.* (Q29 – John)

I used to watch them with my father. (Q29 – Garth)

With my twin brother and my Dad, enjoyed certain films of Stallone's – First Blood, Rocky, *and* Nighthawks – *my brother is a huge fan also so we've seen most of Stallone's films together.* (Q29 – Richard)

I used to watch Stallone's films with my step-father. We loved to watch action movies when my mother was out at work on nights. (Q29 – Mike)

I watched the Rocky *films,* Rambo I, II, III, Cobra, Lock Up, *and others with my dad and younger brother.* (Q29 – David)

I used to watch Stallone films with my dad and brother. Basically, because we hired videos as a family, the three males wanted action and mum hated Stallone, so we tended to watch films like Rocky, Cobra, *and* Tango & Cash *as a kind of testosterone bonding thing.* (Q29 – Chris)

These comments underline the role of Stallone's films in facilitating the bonding of fathers, sons and brothers through the establishment of an exclusively male, homosocial space. Some female respondents remembered a more inclusive family viewing (see Huffer 2007). Nevertheless, for these respondents, Stallone's films and, by implication, the representations within were essentially male. For Matt, such an introduction may have shaped the terms of his later engagement with the star, intersected by his sexuality, leading to his desire to possess this 'raw' masculinity in both senses.

What role, though, might the texts of Stallone's films play in this process? To what extent do these films facilitate Matt's homoerotic gaze and/or attempt to disavow it, and how might this intersect with the construction of a muscular, macho masculinity as an object of desire and/or identification? The most obvious starting point for such questions is *Demolition Man*, the film that prompted Matt to fancy Stallone 'like fuck'. Here Stallone appears as Detective Sergeant John Spartan, nicknamed the 'Demolition Man' for the havoc he leaves in his wake. Cryogenically frozen in the year 1996 after being framed by a criminal he captured for killing hostages, Spartan is de-thawed in the year 2032 to re-capture the same criminal, now on a rampage after early parole.

Matt's favourite moment, of Stallone 'naked in the cryo-thingy', occurs early in the film. The sequence finds Spartan, dressed in a hospital gown, placed in front of a prison warden. The warden reads Spartan his list of charges 'with some regret', to which the star replies 'skip it'. Guards remove Spartan's gown, revealing his sculpted torso in a mid-shot, then lower him into the cryogenic chamber, with the warden telling him, 'I'm sorry'. We see Spartan from the warden's point of view from above, but as Spartan returns his gaze the film cuts to the warden looking away. The chamber fills with a thick liquid and we are shown various naked parts of Spartan's body pressed against the glass as he squirms – his thigh, his calf, his bottom, his back and his shoulders. The scene is played out slowly to an accompaniment of haunting music, and it culminates in Spartan vainly slamming his hands against the glass, watched again from the point of view of the warden. When he is finally frozen, the camera swirls in close-up around Stallone's perfectly still muscles until a clock shows us that forty years have passed. The last image is of Spartan from above, completely naked, a bright light shining down on him, picking out his chest and biceps (but carefully hiding his penis in darkness).

The fact that this objectification of Stallone's physique is presented through a scene of punishment connects with those arguments that have stressed the need to disavow the homoerotic charge of images of the male body in action cinema, westerns and epics. Summarising Paul Willemen, Steve Neale notes that 'in a heterosexual and patriarchal

Figures 1 and 2 - John Spartan (Sylvester Stallone) 'naked in the cryo-thingy', as watched somewhat guiltily by the prison warden. *Demolition Man*. Producers Howard G. Kazanijian, Michael Levy and Joel Silver; director Marco Brambilla; DVD distributed by Warner Home Video.

society, the male body cannot be marked explicitly as the erotic object of another male look', leading to its mutilation in order to disqualify it 'as an object of erotic contemplation and desire' (1993: 14). What is interesting about the sequence from *Demolition Man* is that, unlike in the films where Rambo undergoes punishment in the 1980s, in this early 1990s film his flesh is not brutalised but rather left unmarked. The character is certainly punished – drowned, in part, by the fluid that envelops him – but the 'spectacle of pain' (Savran 1998: 203) is minimal, giving the audience nothing to wince at. When our look at the star is mediated by the look of other characters, such as the warden, it is not one of 'fear ... hatred or aggression' (Neale 1993: 18) but instead a mixture of admiration, pity and guilt. Of course, Stallone's own look back at the warden signifies some resistance to the empowered gaze of this character (and, by implication, the audience), but the star's face at this moment appears to express anxiety rather than anger. The sequence in itself does little to disavow its homoerotic component and potentially encourages Matt's, and other gay men's, engagement.

Homoerotic spectacle within the rest of the film is more conventionally located through action, and more closely aligned with a macho, violent masculinity. For example, the sequence that precedes Spartan's freezing, and indeed begins the film, features the character bungee jumping out of a helicopter on to the roof of a building, where he shoots a criminal upon landing. He then overpowers or eludes further bad guys as he makes his way through the building. The sequence culminates in a fist-fight with arch criminal Simon Phoenix (Wesley Snipes). Finally, Spartan drags Phoenix into custody as the building explodes. Throughout the sequence, Spartan is dressed in a tight-fitting and carefully coordinated outfit of black beret, T-shirt, combat vest, combat trousers and boots, forming parallels with the tight clothing Matt enjoys in *Judge Dredd*. Phoenix too is presented as spectacle, dressed in a white roll-neck sweater, black and yellow chequered leather jacket, and black and white striped trousers. He also sports bleached blond hair.[6]

The homoeroticism of *Demolition Man* is undercut by the homophobic representation of the rulers of the future world of 2032, described by GLAAD (Gay and Lesbian Alliance Against Defamation) in a press release at the time as 'a homophobe's wet dream. They are sneaky, underhanded, disloyal, cowardly, and interested in nothing but pursuing their own, greedy agenda' (1993). In addition, Spartan's presence fulfils the wishes of police officer Lenina Huxley (Sandra Bullock) for 'some action'. Their relationship is cemented at the end of the film when she is rendered unconscious by Spartan with a stun baton in order to protect her from the climactic fight with Phoenix. Confronting Spartan after his victory over the villain, Huxley protests, 'I thought we were supposed to be a team', prompting Spartan to sweep her back and kiss her, replying, 'We are'.

Thanks to Huxley's presence, the demonisation of stereotypically 'gay' characters, and the emphasis on Stallone's body in action, *Demolition Man* can reduce any threats it may pose to heterosexual male audience members. Indeed, Paul, the heterosexual respondent who in his comments above asks 'who wouldn't want a body like that?', also rates the film as one of his favourites, praising the action performances of its stars and their respective characters: 'Wesley Snipes is an accomplished martial artist and makes a great villain. ... Also the role he plays fits Stallone well, as he can fight first and asks questions later' (Q7).[7]

In this context, Stallone 'naked in the cryo-thingy' could be seen as 'an unresolved or uncontained representation of the body of the male [that] exceeds the narrative processes' (Smith 1993: 167). The pronounced eroticism of this scene, however, suggests that this is a conscious strategy in order to maximise the range of audience pleasures. Also, Matt's responses as a whole suggest that, despite its portrayal of the character in a moment of vulnerability, the homoeroticism of this moment gains its power for him precisely because of its contextualisation within the narrative, symbolising a brand of macho, muscular (and ultimately heterosexual) masculinity. Such a moment may exceed the narrative, but it does not necessarily challenge or undermine it.

HYSTERICAL/UNREAL

In contrast to the previous respondents' identificatory and/or erotic desire for Stallone's muscular physique, Simon, a gay 33-year-old man from Sheffield, adopts a critical position towards Stallone and the model of masculinity he finds to be represented by the star. He states that, with regard to Stallone, 'I find his body unrealistic, laughably unattractive' (Q11), and describes the star as 'overly macho' (Q37). He is the only one of my male respondents to critique the star's physique in this way. Rather than prevent pleasure, though, such a representation actually produces enjoyment for Simon, due to the camp appeal Stallone's films hold for him. His favourite Stallone film is *Rhinestone* (1984), as 'it's such a bad film it's fantastic' and because he enjoys 'the sense of campness of [Stallone] working with Dolly Parton' (Q7). He also enjoys *Rambo III*, as it was 'so bad it was achingly funny' (Q14). Simon's comments here both mobilise and embody the concept of camp as a reading strategy, praising that which is considered to be vulgar, excessive or artificial within culture (see Klinger 1994: 134). The use of Dolly Parton as an exemplar of camp also arguably calls upon gay mobilisations of this concept, picking out a star who highlights the artificiality and constructedness of gender through her 'impossible body' (Holmlund 2002: 159).[8] It is within this context that we can better understand the role that Stallone's equally 'unrealistic' physique may play in Simon's enjoyment, undermining the authority of the macho masculinity embodied by the star. *Rhinestone* may also be favoured due to the way it deliberately undermines this model of masculinity as a source of humour. Starring as an inept taxi driver training to be a singer under the tutelage of country star Jake (Dolly Parton), Stallone's body is frequently the site of comedy. Most memorably, the star contorts his face and body into a series of unruly positions through a deliberately terrible rendition of 'Tutti Frutti'. The naming of Parton's character also points to the film's playful approach to gender. This is furthered when Jake prevents Stallone's character, Nick, from retaliating after he is punched by her ex-fiancé, saving the punching for herself. Nick consequently complains to her that 'you're wrecking my masculinity'.

The politics underpinning Simon's engagement with the star become clearer in his response to a question asking him for his opinion of America:

Figures 3 and 4 - Nick (Sylvester Stallone) is rendered redundant when Jake (Dolly Parton) does the punching. *Rhinestone*. Producers Howard Smith and Marvin Worth: director Bob Clark; DVD distributed by Anchor Bay Entertainment.

Right wing, religious nutcases, bigots, a policeman of the world stamping on anybody they disagree with. ... Part of the enjoyment I get from Stallone films is that he reinforces this – so it's a bit of a love/hate relationship. (Q38)

Such an understanding echoes liberal middle-class journalistic and academic discourses circulating through the 1980s that equated Stallone via Rambo with a 'thuggishly violent nationalistic macho' (Tasker 1993: 93). Simon was at university during this time (1985–88), returning to complete an MA in the 1990s. He now works as a social researcher. Simon's background thus points to the relevance of, and his likely exposure to, such discourses. Of course, we need to be wary of simplistically equating the character of Rambo with an all-American nationalism (see Tasker 1993: 99). Indeed, in *Rambo III* (mentioned by Simon) the character refuses to join his friend Colonel Trautman (Richard Crenna) on a mission for the government. The film also finds Rambo living in a Buddhist monastery in Thailand, and befriending an Afghan boy, problematising his symbolism of bigotry and religious extremism. Nevertheless, Rambo's relentless slaying of Soviet soldiers still clearly encourages Cold War jingoism, prompting another respondent to write that 'by the third film it had just become America versus whoever, just an excuse for a bit of patriotic flag-waving rather than trying to tell a story' (Q14 – Paul). Importantly, Simon still gains enjoyment from these films *because* of his dislike of their politics, returning us to his ironic mode of engagement. Within this context, *Rambo III* may be 'achingly funny' because Stallone's heightened representation of macho masculinity calls into question the authority of America and its reactionary and imperialistic attitudes, as perceived by Simon.

The exaggerated nature of the character's strength in this film is highlighted by the comments of another respondent:

> Rambo III – *Getting a little silly now with Rambo taking on the whole Russian Army. There's only so much one man can do and Rambo did it ten times in this film.* (Q14 – Mark)

Indeed, while none of the other respondents adopt such a critical and/or ironic reading of Stallone as Simon, they do position Stallone's sculpted body, along with his characters' feats, as unrealistic. For example, when asked if they have attempted to emulate Stallone's physique the following respondents replied:

> *Used to be able to do one-handed Rocky press-ups when I was a kid but then I discovered beer. I think that as you grow up you realise that it's not a realistic physique, although it would be nice for a day.* (Q12 – Nick)

> *I enjoy beer too much to be able to emulate his physique but I wouldn't mind looking like that. I'm happy the way I am and don't think I'll be facing Dolph Lundgren any time soon.* (Q12 – Mark)

Nick is a heterosexual 23-year-old from Gloucestershire and Mark is a heterosexual 23-year-old from Glamorgan. Both position Stallone's physique within the realms of fantasy. This distancing from Stallone's physique is perhaps born out of the fact that its status conflicts with other, more accessible, ways of achieving status as a man, namely drinking beer. R. W. Connell offers a case study of a male Australian athlete whose pursuit of status through sport meant that 'much of what was defined in his peer culture as masculine was forbidden him', including drinking and sex (2005: 63). Nick and Mark seem aware of these tensions. However, while they may choose not to emulate Stallone's physique, they still admire it – 'it would be nice for a day', 'I wouldn't mind looking like that' – underlining the enduring appeal of the built body as a male status symbol (even in the light of the apparent contradictions they touch upon).

In contrast to Jimmy and Richard, who both left school at 16, Nick and Mark have both gone on to higher education, though not as far as Simon did. Nick writes that he was 'fairly successful at school', gaining '10 GCSE's and three A levels', and that he has 'recently graduated from Business School' (Q19). Mark also has '9 GCSEs, two A Levels' and an 'HND in computing'[9] and now 'manages a cheque cashing company' (Q19). For Nick and Mark, then, the pressure to develop their body appears less acute, given their greater access to alternative forms of power and success. The fact that they were both 23 when filling out the questionnaire, as opposed to Jimmy and Richard, who were both 31, also places them as teenagers during the growth in 'lad culture' that occurred in Britain during the 1990s (see Beynon 2002: 108–14). Such laddism, centred around hedonistic male camaraderie and exemplified by the men's magazine *Loaded* (launched in 1994), may have made them more comfortable aspiring to a model of masculinity privileging beer over body.

The laddishness of their engagement with Stallone is underlined by their preferred viewing partners. When asked who they watch Stallone's films with, if anyone, they replied:

Stallone films can be watched under any circumstances, apart from with the bird. Actually think the Rocky films are best when watched with mates. (Q28 – Nick)

With my mates as we all love his films. They make for great viewing partners as they have seen most of his films and know most of his classic lines. We always have a laugh watching them in a group. (Q14 – Mark)

Having a laugh with mates when watching the films repeats the friendly, homosocial contexts in which the films were first watched while indicating a new degree of critical distance. Again the act of viewing also may work to inscribe essentialist notions of gender. Given the strong associations between a muscular physique and essentialist conceptions of masculinity, it is thus not surprising that Stallone's body continues to have an appeal for Nick and Mark, however qualified.

SENSITIVITY

In mapping the respondents' engagement with Stallone's physique we also need to acknowledge how this may have changed over time. This is most marked in Richard's responses. As we saw earlier, Richard had an intense investment in the star's physique in his 'middle to late teens' (Q23), taking up weight-training in his bid to emulate the star. However, Richard writes that today 'his physique from my perspective bears less significance' (Q11) and that 'following injury and a change in temperament I no longer weight train' (Q12). Elsewhere in the questionnaire, he elaborates on this shift in temperament, connecting it to an increasing interest in Tai Chi and the introduction of family life:

Obviously things have changed somewhat since having a family! My main hobby/interest is the martial art of Tai Chi Chun, which I have been studying for the last two years. I was always interested in the Martial Arts but because of my commitment to weight training I only toyed with Aikido. But the whole practice of Tai Chi is very life-changing, very spiritual and the history of Chinese arts and philosophies appeals at a time in my life when I look for something deeper and more spiritual! (Q22)

This search for something deeper and more spiritual in life is mirrored by a greater interest in the emotional vulnerability and sensitivity displayed by Stallone's characters:

My favourite Stallone film is Rocky – *it was his big break and in fact was very now in its approach – it was a film of many layers – but, basically a love story with boxing thrown in – it also shows a sensitivity to Stallone, which although entertaining the likes of* Rambo III *or* Judge Dredd *did not show. It is his classic.* (Q7 – Richard)

We can thus see how Richard's definition of desirable masculinity has shifted, incorporating aspects of sensitivity and spirituality that are equated with a maturity produced, in part, through a transformation in life brought about by 'having a family'. His description of *Rocky* as 'very now in its approach', moreover, points towards the relevance of wider changes within cinema and society to his revised understanding of this film.[10] Elsewhere in the questionnaire he elaborates on what these shifts might be when he explains that 'I think that times have changed politically, so a huge part of the über-hero's attraction has died' (Q3). Such an observation implies his awareness of those discourses touched upon by Simon, equating the height of Stallone/Rocky/Rambo with Reagan-era America, and the negative implications of this. Indeed, when asked for his response to the representation of America in Stallone's films he writes that 'the whole USA vs. USSR thing was very naive if not juvenile – and that side of America, the flag waving, "we are best" mentality is a little nauseating if not patronising!' (Q38). His mobilisation of such a discourse reminds us that such an understanding of America and Stallone's films is not the sole preserve of the university-educated middle classes within Britain. Richard's positioning of the present as a post-'über-hero' era also suggests an awareness of the partial movement in post-1980s Hollywood away from 'hard-bodied male action heroes' towards a '"kinder, gentler" US manhood ... sensitive, generous, caring, and ... capable of change' (Jeffords 1993: 197).

Richard thus values *Rocky* precisely because of its relevance to his perception of the current era and his own life-stage. This is most clearly embodied by the love story in *Rocky*, providing a space for the articulation of male sensitivity that is highly engaging. Through his scenes with Adrian we are able to observe Rocky's insecurities and vulnerabilities, such as his upset at losing his locker to another fighter, his hurt at disparaging comments made about him by Apollo Creed, and his fears on the eve of the climactic fight. His encounters with Adrian are also marked by a tenderness and affection that appears to be born out of an awareness of his own insecurities, forming a marked contrast to the bullying ways of her insulting, alcoholic brother Paulie (Burt Young). Rocky is consequently able to win her love, providing him with the mental strength necessary to challenge for the world heavyweight title.

Rocky's emotional sensitivity is therefore positioned as an element of both vulnerability *and* strength. While his insecurities and anxieties must be overcome in order for him to succeed, seemingly playing

out a drama of power and powerlessness that echoes his physical
transformation, the sensitivity to
others that stems from them is one
of his defining qualities. In addition,
Rocky's willingness to express his
feelings *openly* facilitates the resolution of his insecurities. Elsewhere,
I have shown how a combination
of physical strength and emotional
sensitivity draws upon a rich his-

Figure 5 - A tender moment between Rocky (Sylvester
Stallone) and Adrian (Talia Shire). *Rocky.* Producers Robert
Chartoff and Irwin Winkler; director John G. Avildsen;
DVD distributed by MGM Home Entertainment.

tory of protective romantic heroes, forming a potent appeal to female
audiences for the star's films (see Huffer 2007). However, whereas many
romantic heroes are initially marked by 'an imperious, distant manner'
(Radway 1984: 139), only later revealing their inner sensitivity, Rocky
is marked by the externalisation of his sensitivity from the outset. The
importance of this externalisation, and of the love story as a whole, is
underlined by another respondent's account of the film's ending:

> *My favourite Stallone moment would have to be from the very end of the
> first* Rocky, *where he's screaming out for his girlfriend Adrian. He's just gone
> the distance with the world's number one boxer. He's just earned a ton of
> money and has achieved what any boxer in the world would give their right
> arm for (not literally!), yet his first and only concern is to hold her and reas-
> sure her that he's okay.* (Q7 – Craig)

Significantly, however, while *Rocky* stresses the value of male sensitivity, the film still positions physical strength as central to the definition
of masculinity that it offers. Also, the sensitive/spiritual transformation Richard has undergone leads not to a repudiation or critique of the
importance of a hard-bodied masculinity, but rather represents a *further* stage in his development as a man. He thus still values the role that
weight-training has played in his life, even if he is not engaged in it
now, appreciating the power and confidence it gave him in his youth.

CONCLUSION

The respondents' comments point us towards the complexity of
Stallone's representation of masculinity and the diversity of possible

interpretations, while also highlighting important continuities. In addition, they reveal some of the textual and contextual forces that produce such difference and similarity. We are able to gain an understanding of how the star's body may convey a traditional masculinity defined through strength to male audiences, and why they are invested in this. For example, Jimmy's and Matt's experience of being working class and gay, respectively, makes representations of Stallone's strength acutely appealing to them. The homoerotic display of the star's physique also works to reinforce macho masculinity as attractive to *be* and *have*. In contrast, Simon finds Stallone's body to be a hysterical image of masculinity. This is rooted in the intersection of his class, sexual identity and political beliefs, which produce a critical distance from the star. However, this critical distance is also encouraged, in part, via the self-reflexive humour of one of the films that he discusses. Tensions surrounding the unreal nature of the star's body and/or its political associations are also evident in the responses of Nick, Mark and Richard. These are produced by a range of contextual factors, but most specifically through the men's adoption of modes of masculinity in their everyday lives that privilege beer or sensitivity over the built body. Nick and Mark are able to negotiate these tensions due to the ongoing appeal of Stallone's physique as fantasy, however, and Richard is able to negotiate these tensions by focusing on Stallone's roles marked by strength and sensitivity.

Together, these men's responses to the representation of Stallone underline masculinity's status as a social/cultural construction that is 'diverse, mobile, even unstable' (Beynon 2002: 2). This might produce some potential tension for the respondents, but such mobility and instability also *enables* the men to find continuing relevance in Stallone as a representation of masculinity despite developments and/or divergences in their own identities. If Stallone's physique may retain significance for these men, though, this does not mean that this is always as a symbol of strength that subordinates and/or subsumes other ways of being a man. Masculinity as strength *is* clearly privileged by Jimmy and Matt, and Richard's emphasis on the symbiosis of strength and sensitivity is arguably hierarchical, as the former precedes and frames the latter for him. However, Nick's and Mark's investment in the star's physique as fantasy does not outrank or undermine their everyday commitment to alternative models of masculinity. Most strikingly, Simon's engagement pivots upon his rejection of masculinity as strength. Nevertheless, if a model of masculinity as strength is not always privileged in these encounters, all except Simon still validate it as *an* important way of being a man, warning us from underestimating the role of Stallone's films (and his body) in perpetuating associations between maleness and power.

NOTES

1   See Chris Holmlund (1993) for further discussion of the way that Stallone reveals masculinity to be a masquerade in his films.
2   See Huffer (2007) for the full questionnaire.
3   See Ien Ang for the need to interrogate 'what is behind the explicitly written, for the presuppositions and accepted attitudes concealed within' respondents' comments (1985: 11).
4   Participants' names have been changed. All comments have been transposed verbatim.
5   Ages given are for the year in which the questionnaire was distributed: 2001.
6   This coding of Stallone through the terms of order and of Snipes through the terms of excess invites consideration of the stars' bodies as raced. However, there is not the space to do justice to this discussion here.
7   For a detailed discussion of Paul's engagement with the star see Huffer (2003).
8   See Andy Medhurst (1997) for further discussion of the distinctions and debates surrounding the relationship between gay and straight uses of camp.
9   GCSEs (General Certificate of Secondary Education) are studied for in particular subjects between the ages of 14 and 16 in the UK (barring Scotland). A Levels (Advanced Level) are typically studied for between the ages of 16 and 18 in the same territories as the GCSE, forming the entry qualification for university. HNDs (Higher National Diploma) are vocationally oriented higher education qualifications which last two years full time and may act as qualifications for entry onto the second or third year of a university degree.
10   See Jackie Stacey for the importance of considering the intersection of 'private narratives' with 'public discourses' in audience memories (1994: 63, 70). The full role of memory in shaping the respondents' recollections as transformative and often nostalgic is not interrogated here, and is an area worthy of further investigation.

BIBLIOGRAPHY

Ang, Ien (1985) *Watching 'Dallas': Soap Opera and the Melodramatic Imagination.* London: Methuen.
_____ (1989) 'Wanted: Audiences. On the Politics of Empirical Audience Studies', in Ellen Seiter, Hans Borchers, Gabriele Kreutzner, and Eva-Maria Warth (eds) *Remote Control: Television, Audiences, and Cultural Power.* London: Routledge, 96–115.
Austin, Thomas (2002) *Hollywood, Hype, and Audiences: Selling and Watching Popular Film in the 1990s.* Manchester: Manchester University Press.
Barker, Martin and Kate Brooks (1998) *Knowing Audiences: 'Judge Dredd' – Its Friends, Fans, and Foes.* London: University of Luton Press.
Beynon, John (2002) *Masculinities and Culture.* Buckingham: Open University Press.
Connell, R. W. (2005) *Masculinities.* Second edition. Berkeley: University of California Press.
DeAngelis, Michael (2001) *Gay Fandom and Crossover Stardom.* Durham: Duke University Press.

GLAAD Media Briefs (1993), 3 December. Online. Available HTTP: http://www.qrd.org/qrd/orgs/GLAAD/old/sfba/1993/media.news.briefs-12.03.93 (23 June 2009).

Holmlund, Chris (1993) 'Masculinity as Multiple Masquerade: The "Mature" Stallone and the Stallone Clone', in Steven Cohan and Ina Rae Hark (eds) *Screening the Male: Exploring Masculinities in Hollywood Cinema*. London and New York: Routledge, 213–29.

_____ (2002) *Impossible Bodies: Femininity and Masculinity at the Movies*. London and New York: Routledge.

Huffer, Ian (2003) '"What interest does a fat Stallone have for an action fan?": Male Film Audiences and the Structuring of Stardom', in Thomas Austin and Martin Barker (eds) *Contemporary Hollywood Stardom*. London: Arnold, 155–66.

_____ (2007) '"I wanted to be Rocky, but I also wanted to be his wife!": Heterosexuality and the (Re)Construction of Gender in Female Film Audiences' Consumption of Sylvester Stallone', *Participations: Journal of Audience and Reception Studies*, 4.2. Online. Available HTTP: http://www.participations.org/Volume%204/Issue%202/4_02_huffer.htm (20 June 2010).

Jeffords, Susan (1993) 'The Big Switch: Hollywood Masculinity in the Nineties', in Jim Collins, Hilary Radner, and Ava Preacher Collins (eds) *Film Theory Goes to the Movies*. London and New York: Routledge, 196–208.

Klinger, Barbara (1994) *Melodrama and Meaning: History, Culture, and the Films of Douglas Sirk*. Bloomington: Indiana University Press.

Medhurst, Andy (1997) 'Camp', in Andy Medhurst and Sally Rowena Munt (eds) *Lesbian and Gay Studies: A Critical Introduction*. London: Cassell, 274–93.

Moores, Shaun (1993) *Interpreting Audiences: The Ethnography of Media Consumption*. London: Sage.

Neale, Steve (1993) 'Masculinity as Spectacle: Reflections on Men and Mainstream Cinema', in Steven Cohan and Ina Rae Hark (eds) *Screening the Male: Exploring Masculinities in Hollywood Cinema*. London and New York: Routledge, 9–20.

Radway, Janice A. (1984) *Reading the Romance: Women, Patriarchy, and Popular Literature*. Chapel Hill: University of North Carolina Press.

Savran, David (1998) *Taking It Like a Man: White Masculinity, Masochism, and Contemporary Culture*. Princeton: Princeton University Press.

Smith, Paul (1993) *Clint Eastwood: A Cultural Production*. London: University College London Press.

Stacey, Jackie (1994) *Star Gazing: Hollywood Cinema and Female Spectatorship*. London: Routledge.

Tasker, Yvonne (1993) *Spectacular Bodies: Gender, Genre, and the Action Cinema*. London: Routledge.

Walkerdine, Valerie (1986) 'Video Replay: Families, Films, and Fantasy', in Victor Burgin, James Donald and Cora C. Kaplan (eds) *Formations of Fantasy*. London: Methuen, 167–99.

Willemen, Paul (1981) 'Anthony Mann: Looking at the Male', *Framework*, 15–17 (summer), 16–20.

SYLVESTER STALLONE AND JOHN RAMBO'S TREK ACROSS ASIA: POLITICS, PERFORMANCE AND AMERICAN EMPIRE

GINA MARCHETTI

I really am a manifestation of my own fantasy.
    – Sylvester Stallone (IMDb, 'Biography for Sylvester Stallone')

Stallone's John J. Rambo emerged out of Ronald Reagan's America with an axe to grind in Asia in the aftermath of America's war in Vietnam. Both Stallone the star and Rambo the character are contradictory manifestations of fantasies that chronicle nearly thirty years of American imperial ambitions in Asia. Although Edward Said was speaking of 'European culture', the American character Rambo, too, 'gained in strength and identity by setting itself off against the Orient as a sort of surrogate or even underground self' (1978: 3). As with all manifestations of Orientalism, 'none of this Orient is merely imaginative' (1978: 2), and Rambo has taken on a discursive life of his own as a popular icon with a global reach.

The opening of *Rambo III* (1988) makes this crystal clear. The sequence is unique in the four *Rambo* features, alluding to and providing a contrast with Stallone's other screen icon, Rocky, by placing the Vietnam-vet expatriate in the Thai boxing arena as a prizefighter. As in the *Rocky* films, this gives Stallone the opportunity to put his body on display and show what he can do physically on screen. Rambo, the guerrilla fighter known for his stealth and use of unconventional weapons, seldom has the opportunity to face off against an equally matched opponent, so this scene places him in a situation that literally exhibits what Asia has 'made' of him. Before Rambo turns to look at the camera

Figure 1 - Fragmented shots of Rambo's (Sylvester Stallone) hair tied out of the way against his muscular back. *Rambo III.* Producer Buzz Feitshans; director Peter McDonald; DVD (Hong Kong) distributed by Canal+ Distribution and Panorama Distributions Co. Ltd.

in close-up, fragmented shots of hands wrapped for combat, hair tied out of the way, muscular back to the camera, provide a sense of mystery. Three Buddhist monks (two boys and one older man) accompany him, and the film shows them gazing at Rambo, before Rambo looks back. With the exception of Rambo's mentor Colonel Trautman (Richard Crenna), who arrives during the fight, all the spectators surrounding the makeshift ring appear to be Asian.

While Stallone the director creates his Orient to be looked at, Rambo serves as the cynosure of that spectacle as a non-Asian who has come to embody the 'mysterious' East. His opponent, played by martial artist Harold Diamond (originally Harold Roth), mirrors him with a similarly muscular physique, wavy long dark hair, and naked torso. The doubling of the sculpted flesh conjures up the type of narcissism or exhibitionism associated with women (and the 'Orient') in Western iconography. The point of the match, within the diegesis, may be for the local Thais to see two 'exotic' Westerners fight. The men pick up sticks associated with the Philippine arts of escrima, kali and arnis, use kicks characteristic of a variety of Asian martial arts (Muay Thai, karate, tae kwon do) and include liberal portions of throws reminiscent of the World Wrestling Federation (fo example, Rambo uses one of the sticks to pick up and throw his opponent by hooking him by his groin cup). The competition, then, celebrates the Westerners' ability to absorb the Asian arts, hybridise them, and, presumably, surpass the local competition.

Beyond this, Rambo clearly displays moral as well as physical superiority. With his opponent down, he pauses, breathing heavily, his face distorted by what appears to be an angry grimace. His arm is raised with his stick poised to skewer the other man. Slow-motion shots of the cheering crowd, cash in hand, distorted cheers on the soundtrack, indicate the Asian spectators' bloodlust. However, Rambo holds back and politely offers his stick to the loser to get to his feet. Rambo takes his winnings from a cigar-chomping Asian man, returns to the boat that brought him, and hands his earnings over to the monks. Calm, surrounded by his Buddhist escorts, he taps one of the boy monks on the leg in a gesture that seems to offer assurance that he fights to help out, not for the thrill of the kill. Just as the other stick fighter mirrors Rambo on screen, the spectators (Trautman as well as the Asian fight fans) mirror the presumed audience – titillated by naked flesh and blood, while resting assured that it has some sort of higher moral purpose. The spectacle and the spectators split, so that the tensions between the two positions do not easily divide into East and West, but, rather, provide positions that Rambo can mediate through the power of Stallone's body.

Credited with co-writing the script for all four films featuring Rambo, and with directing the last one, Stallone has had a role in crafting this character that goes beyond his on-screen performance. The relationship between Stallone and Rambo, however, is complicated. Stallone, through Rambo, manifests taboo wishes, unspoken desires, violent and socially unacceptable thoughts – the 'underground self' of the Orientalist imagination. However, Stallone also seems to be at odds with Rambo, a character who sometimes appears to take on a life of his own, defying his creator and offering a potentially deviant view of his maker's handiwork. Stallone, too, may be at odds with himself as director, actor and writer, since Rambo manifests his fantasies in ways that pit what the character does against the few things he says as well as against what 'Rambo' signifies for the public via the mass media. As Yvonne Tasker points out:

> reference to 'Rambo' is usually characterised by an assumption of the very
> obviousness of what is meant ... Of course the meaning of 'Rambo' is in some
> senses clear, precisely because it has been used so often to signify a slug-
> gishly violent nationalistic macho. That is to say, that the term has acquired a
> meaning through its repeated use in a variety of journalistic and political as

well as cinematic contexts. It isn't possible to look at the film or think about the term without reference to the complex history of signification in which it has been involved. (1993: 97)

Rambo is, clearly, a product of changing times and contradictory sentiments. Because of the drawn-out hostage crisis in Iran (1979–80) and its media coverage, captives were clearly on America's mind when *First Blood* had its premiere. The controversy surrounding the case of Robert (Bobby) Garwood, who had been a POW, finally leaving Vietnam in 1979 and claiming, on his return, that others were still held captive years after the end of the war also made the issue of lingering POWs in post-war Vietnam a concern. Labelled a collaborator and deserter rather than a prisoner, Garwood brought down the wrath of the US military establishment on himself, and Senator John McCain became his official nemesis. In fact, Garwood managed to bring all the ambivalence about American involvement in Vietnam to the surface – the thin line between victim and traitor, between murderous monster and casualty of war. McCain himself had written a 'confession' in the Hanoi Hilton, and, perhaps, his anger came from those mixed feelings the character of John Rambo represents so well – rage at those who appear to give in to Vietnamese demands while knowing how easy it can be to cross that line.

Coming in the wake of the Garwood controversy, *Rambo: First Blood Part II*'s (1985) Marshal Murdock (Charles Napier) appears to voice McCain's vitriolic insistence that Garwood's assertion that he had seen POWs after the end of the war is a lie. Murdock's words reverberate with the way in which McCain's remarks were perceived at the time:

> *What if some burn-out POW shows up on the six o-clock news? What do you want to do ... start the war all over again? You wanna bomb Hanoi? You want everybody screaming for armed invasion? Do you honestly think somebody's gonna get up on the floor of the United States Senate, and ask for billions of dollars for a couple of forgotten ghosts?* (IMDb, 'Rambo: First Blood Part II (1985): Quotes')

In contrast to fellow Republican McCain's interpretation of events, Reagan clearly admired the renegade POW hunter and reportedly said, during a 1985 hostage crisis, 'After seeing *Rambo* last night, I know what to do the next time this happens' (in Lane 2008).[1] However, Stallone, indirectly dismissing Reagan's enthusiasm, claims, 'I never saw Rambo as a Republican' (in Stein 2008).

Embodying the contradictions of the times, the *Rambo* series moves from stories involving a rebellious questioning of the US government, the war and American cultural values (*First Blood*, 1982), to a rewriting of the American war in Vietnam (*Rambo: First Blood Part II*, 1985), to fighting the Cold War in Afghanistan (*Rambo III*, 1988), to helping Christianity thrive in Burma (*Rambo*, 2008). The first three instalments intersect with Reagan's two terms as president and provide an ideological chart of the unsteady foundation for the right-wing agenda associated with his time in office. Opposition to 'big government' was wedded to increased military expenditures. Celebration of Christian 'family values' met up with a domestic agenda that devastated the working-class family by breaking unions, eroding social services and shifting wealth to a shrinking percentage of the population. Reagan's policies thus offered only a fantasy of peace and prosperity for the general population. Loner, outsider, expatriate, Rambo may be the ideal 'cowboy' hero representing American individualism, but the character only spends time in jail in Reagan's America – a land he may 'love' but cannot seem to inhabit, except in prison or on the lam.

In 2008, Stallone chose to revive Rambo, twenty years after the character had last appeared on screen. That same year he became one of the first major Hollywood stars to endorse John McCain (the 'anti-Rambo' of the POW/MIA controversy) as the Republican candidate for president of the United States. In the two decades between *Rambo III* and *Rambo*, much had changed in the American imagination of war, imprisonment and torture. Guantanamo Bay and Abu Ghraib brought the debate surrounding torture of prisoners to a new level, and America did a complete about-face on its policy in Afghanistan and Iraq after the break-up of the Soviet Union. Just as the American government went from supporting the Mujahideen, as Rambo does in *Rambo III*, to going to war against the Taliban/Al-Qaeda in Afghanistan, Stallone took Rambo back to Southeast Asia, rather than the Middle East, for a Christian crusade against the junta in Myanmar/Burma to highlight the religious dimension of America's international posturing in Asia.[2]

As *Rambo* resonates with these events, a closer examination of that particular performance of the character may help to shed some light on how Stallone manages to keep Rambo alive on screen. Stallone's approach to writing, directing and performing the character in 2008 opens up a way of examining Stallone contemplating what 'Rambo' means as a manifestation of his authorial fantasies as well as the popular Orientalist imagination.

THE RAMBO ACT

Rambo has always been an 'act'. As William Warner notes: 'If to pose as ultra male comes to be understood as "acting like Rambo", then it cannot any longer be what it might have seemed at one time – "being a (real) man"' (1992: 686). Most Orientalist fantasies take on a gendered dimension, with Asia seen as 'feminine', often embodied by an exotic, alluring, passive woman associated with the mysterious and dangerous 'East', and the Occident portrayed as white, male, active and aggressive. However, the white male, in these yarns, often becomes 'tainted' by his contact with Asia – emasculated and enervated in a process that sees him 'go native'.

Even before the novel *First Blood* was written, John Rambo was a cliché. When Stallone brought him to the screen as a performer and writer, he embroidered on a type that all knew well. Rooted in the American reluctant hero of films such as *Casablanca* (1942) and the flawed Westerner of captivity stories such as *The Searchers* (1956), 'Rambo' had been part of Hollywood.[3] His Asian adventurism linked him to silent film fantasies, World War II war stories and post-war romantic fiction.

The unpopularity of the war in Vietnam highlighted the darker aspects of these tales. Long before *First Blood* had its screen debut, newspapers, television and pulp fiction overflowed with depictions of the 'crazed', out-of-control 'Rambo'. Far from returning as heroes, Vietnam-era veterans were portrayed as suffering from the after-effects of the war, prone to explode into violence or dissolve into tears at any moment, unable to readjust to civilian life, guilty of war crimes and angry over the outcome of the conflict and public disregard of their military service.[4] The decorated vet who returns to go on a violent killing spree, rendered psychotic by his war experiences, may be a fixture of war in general, but the specific version of the type that belonged to Vietnam still haunts the popular imagination.

Stallone took the cliché of the psychotic veteran and reworked it through his body. Stallone's Rambo was famously muscular, with flawed speech and brooding good looks. As others have pointed out, Stallone allowed Rambo to 'win' the war in his own way, creating a hero in the aftermath of one of the most divisive moments in American history (see Jeffords 1989). Rambo has added certain elements to the cliché of the vet – some in keeping with Stallone's star image and others at odds with the star's public persona. The cliché speaks through Stallone, and Stallone performs Rambo in a particular way, through his physical movements and vocalisations, which take up and transcend the cliché.

Born in 1947, the character Rambo, created by novelist David Morrell (*First Blood*, 1972), did not choose to go to war; he was drafted and sent to Vietnam. He is so conflicted about his involvement there that he is reduced to tears when called a 'baby killer', likely as much because he knows he participated in atrocities as because he is hurt by America's 'rejection' of the returning Vietnam veterans. None of the films in the series deals directly with Rambo's actual military career; however, the flashback glimpses of his past indicate that his training and war experiences created a Frankenstein-like killing machine (vividly described by his 'mad creator', Colonel Trautman, who boasts, 'God didn't make Rambo. I made him'). The films remain ambivalent about Rambo's violence – justifying it by references to 'blood' and absolving him of guilt by blaming the US military. There are allusions, for example, to his Native American/German ancestry, which gives him the ethnic/genetic mystique of the perpetrators and victims of genocide, and he claims to go into fighting mode only after his opponents have drawn 'first blood'. The films appear to condemn the US government for creating a killing machine only fit for war and discarding it when the political tides turn. Drafted, brutalised as a prisoner of war, jailed as an out-of-control Vietnam veteran in small-town America, Rambo embodies the classic 'reluctant' hero of American fiction, and he snaps into action only out of some sense of loyalty to his commander/father figure Trautman in *Rambo: First Blood Part II* and *Rambo III*.

Stallone the performer, writer and, more recently, director uses Rambo in much the same way Trautman does, as a foot soldier in a wider battlefield. Stallone's box-office ambitions, desire for the limelight and political sensibilities vie with Rambo's desires to live in obscurity and pursue a 'warrior's path' to spirituality – allowing for moments of violence to be vindicated by a 'just cause' – as cathartic for the character as for his fans. However, as with the classic western hero, Rambo's violence keeps him out of polite society. The Rambo films, as Richard Dyer points out, 'have qualms' (1997: 161), and Yvonne Tasker labels their national politics 'strangely oppositional' (1993: 99).

Rambo acts against the machinations of small government (the police in *First Blood*) and big government (Marshal Murdock, played by Charles Napier, in *Rambo: First Blood Part II*) – operating out of his own individual interest. He stubbornly refuses to leave town in *First Blood*, for example. He goes rogue to rescue POWs in *Rambo: First Blood*

Part II. He has no desire to go to Afghanistan until Trautman becomes captive in *Rambo III.* Although he lives on the Burmese border, he takes no interest in the plight of the Karen people until he encounters a good-looking missionary in *Rambo.* He is an ambiguous figure – off the grid, a loner, a Native American, unassimilated, perpetually angry, and not easily placed within America's political party structure. Bloodied by the American police as well as his Communist torturers, it is hard to pin down his beliefs.

THE ICONIC RAMBO

Words, values and ideas, however, fail to adequately define Rambo. Shirtless, glistening with perspiration, ripping apart the chains that bind him, emerging out of the mud or from exploding ordinance, gun, knife or bow and arrow in hand, Rambo commands a larger-than-life position as a spectacular image that belies the other qualities of his character. Violent, inarticulate, sado-masochistic, antisocial, suffering: Rambo, in fact, does not seem to have much to recommend him. However, he concretises the dream and the nightmare of the 'typical' American man. Rambo desperately wants to mind his own business, but he ends up at the service of corrupt imperialists. He symbolises all those things that may be the 'best' as well as the 'worst' in the working-class male. He is strong, good with his hands, able to live independently, and can certainly take care of himself without any social support, but his individualism and free spirit also make him a lonely outsider, unable to find a mate, and unfit for civilisation. He embodies the half-native 'noble savage', more at home in the wilderness than in society, and he serves as a juvenile dream of playing 'Indian', handling snakes, living in the open, fishing with a bow and arrow, never needing to take a bath, his greasy hair held in place with a headband. He represents the ideal labourer – able to fix any motor, build any contraption out of next to nothing. He acts a 'man's man', keeping women at a remove, on a pedestal, and befriending men according to his own standards of 'manliness' – generally based on an ability to deliver as well as endure pain.

These dreams of being 'Native American', 'working class' and 'male' work together to become simply 'American' – defined from the right rather than left – so that indigenous claims, minority rights, the labour movement, unions, the peace movement, veteran groups against the war, and post-feminist, post-Stonewall redefinitions of 'man' recede.

'America' becomes synonymous with jingoism, imperialism and interventionism. Given Rambo does not articulate any of this verbally,
Stallone must play Rambo in a way that makes this crystal clear.
Stallone's interpretation, then, tends to close down other readings of
Rambo as an anti-government rebel, a Buddhist, a Frankenstein born
of the machinations of American military training during the Vietnam
war, a downtrodden Native American still suffering from the near
genocide of his people, and/or an expatriate who despises American
international policy and would rather live in the Thai jungle than have
anything to do with the States.

To do this, Stallone works against several aspects of Rambo's character. In *First Blood*, for example, Sheriff Teasle (Brian Dennehy) pegs
Rambo as a 'dirty hippie' the minute he sees him, and, in his own way,
he hits the nail on the head. Although 'ram bow' may point to Rambo's
Native American ethnicity, David Morrell had the arch-bohemian
French poet Arthur Rimbaud in mind when he conceived the character,
and Rambo maintains a countercultural veneer on screen (see Morrow
2008). Long hair and jeans, an unkempt look, a drifter on the road,
Rambo's look brings him closer to the counterculture than to any notion
of clean-cut, Reagan-era conservative Republicans. Rambo also seems
to have other tendencies associated with hippies, including an interest
in what could be termed 'New Age spirituality' – spending time with
Buddhist monks, for example.[5]

Rambo appears to be plagued by remorse, and his spirituality may
be an outgrowth of that guilt. Every time he uses his martial skills to
save a captive, in fact, he works through this guilt and turns to religion
(Buddhism, Islam and Christianity) to reconcile his spiritual ambitions
with his violence. This is part of the reason why Stallone must deliver
Rambo as a tortured figure. Although the Christian references to salvation through suffering are quite clear, Rambo also suffers for America's
ostensible 'sins' – imperial ambitions and excessive violence to further
its foreign policy objectives.

If Rambo has an uncanny ability to rescue others from captivity,
Stallone also has a gift for saving Rambo from his own poor judgement and turning him into a hero. When 'Rambo' appears in print as
shorthand for virility and patriotic pride, few consider the fact that
the character is riddled with guilt and damaged by American foreign
policy, and that, although he may win battles, he has always been on
the losing side of every war he has fought. That Stallone manages to
perform Rambo against the facts of the narrative, and, indeed, play up

his own interpretation of the character to attempt to resolve ideological contradictions, merits further attention.

THE RAMBO RELIGION

Religion provides a case in point. In recent years, Stallone has renewed his Catholic faith, and he claims *Rambo* is a 'Christian' movie (see Anon. 2007a). However, Rambo's own belief system seems squarely outside any Judeo-Christian worldview. Although Stallone calls Rambo 'a borderline atheist', for luck the character wears a jadeite Buddha that he got from the dying Co Bao (Julia Nickson) in *Rambo: First Blood Part II*. He lives in Thailand helping Buddhist monks in *Rambo III* and *Rambo*. In *Rambo III*, he is working on rebuilding a Buddhist monastery when Trautman tries to recruit him for a clandestine trip to help the Taliban in Afghanistan. Once there, he gives this good luck Buddha to a boy soldier.[6] In *Rambo*, the missionary Sarah (Julie Benz) gives Rambo her cross as she persuades him to help her cause. Moving from Buddhism through Islam to embrace Christianity, Rambo seems to float above all inconsistencies, celebrating 'religion' over 'godless Communism' or 'heathen' authoritarianism.

The choice of Burma in 2008 is astute. The military junta there has few friends internationally, and the fact that the leader of the opposition, Aung San Suu Kyi, has won the Nobel Prize helps to justify the cause. The plight of the Burmese people has been in the news for decades and, periodically, makes headlines. Two films in particular serve as touchstones for *Rambo*. *Beyond Rangoon* (John Boorman, 1995) follows the

Figure 2 - The missionary Sarah (Julie Benz) gives Rambo (Sylvester Stallone) her cross. *Rambo*. Producers Avi Lerner, Kevin King Templeton and John Thompson; director Sylvester Stallone; DVD distributed by Lionsgate.

plight of a young woman who goes grudgingly to Burma as a tourist and finds her calling helping the resistance to the junta. Released before the 1962 coup, several World War II stories also take place within the China-Burma theatre. Set in Thailand on the Burma Road, *Bridge on the River Kwai* (1957) features blood, guts and explosions in a Japanese POW camp during World War II. *Rambo* pays tribute to the David Lean war epic by providing Rambo with some unexploded British ordinance to use against the Burmese military. The roots of the conflict in British colonialism, however, remain out of the picture.[7]

As Hannah Beech of *Time Magazine* puts it:

There's something about Burma. Zimbabwe, Laos, North Korea, Sudan, Uzbekistan – all these countries are plagued by repressive rulers. But none of these places grips the popular imagination like this isolated nation in the heartland of Asia. With its thuggish ruling junta and defiant, beautiful opposition leader, Burma inspires unparalleled international sympathy and the passions of do-gooders. (2009)

From the points of view of the left (human rights violations, martial law) as well as from the right (crackdown on Christian minorities, closed to the Western 'free' market), Burma offers a cause that Rambo can embrace without the taint of Vietnam, Afghanistan or Iraq. The line between the 'good guys' and the 'bad guys' cannot be challenged, and the question of when intervention becomes appropriate structures the narrative.

Rambo takes up the conflict less as a political war (Aung San Suu Kyi's calls for democratic reform) and more as a religious struggle (the plight of the Christian Karen minority). Although many Karen remain Buddhist, Karen Christianity dates back to the British colonial period, and the minority's disputes with the Burmese predate the Myanmar junta's seizure of power in 1962. Voiceover commentary at the beginning of *Rambo* calls it a 'sixty-year civil war – longest running in the world'. Conveniently, too, the Karen cause enables Rambo to become involved in a Christian mission without directly engaging Islam (Burma also has Muslim minority insurgents, but *Rambo* avoids them). He takes up arms in a just struggle, and he continues to redress wrongs in Southeast Asia, still trying to 'win' the war in Asia somehow. As American conservatives move from anti-Communist posturing against the Soviet 'evil empire' to the 'axis of evil' dominated by a ragtag band of Muslim fundamentalists and military strongmen, Burma suits the new rhetoric quite well. Evangelical Christian zeal replaces anti-Communism, the East remains a threat, and Rambo can be recruited to save the day.

On a crusade without Muslims, being tortured by the Burmese rather than torturing alleged Al-Qaeda fighters in Guantanamo, supporting insurgents while preaching non-violence, *Rambo*'s missionaries seem to be the answer to an ideological prayer. The missionaries may condemn violence, but the group's pastor willingly hires a motley assortment of mercenaries (including an Asian American to dispel any racist overtones to the mission) to extract the captive preachers, and, in the end, even the diehard pacifist Michael Burnett (Paul Schulze) grits his teeth and stones the enemy. Stallone can redeem American violence in the Middle East and Rambo's own support of the Taliban/Al-Qaeda in *Rambo III* by fighting with the Christian Karen in Burma in *Rambo*. Like the US government, Rambo seamlessly switches sides – moving from Muslim to Christian fundamentalism.

Yet, as usual, Rambo seems more at odds with his fellow Americans and mercenary allies than with the Burmese – however bloodthirsty and cruel they may be. His Burmese nemesis, Major Pa Tee Tint (Maung Maung Khin), proves to be a rather distant opponent, and Rambo butts heads much more frequently with Burnett and the mercenary leader Lewis (Graham McTavish). Typically, Rambo struggles with the people who should be on his side more than with his actual enemies, and Rambo's ability to take abuse from his own comrades vies with his gift for withstanding physical punishment. This follows a pattern in the series. Rambo's sadistic foreign opponents give him more respect than most of his so-called allies and fellow compatriots. In *Rambo: First Blood Part II*, the Soviet commander observes: 'To me, you are a comrade, similar to myself, just opposed by an act of fate.' In this regard, too, Rambo stays close to the generic western hero. He remains more at home among the savages than with the civilised, and he has a talent for appreciating and appropriating the enemy's weaponry and tactics.

RAMBO'S SEXUAL MYSTIQUE

While Rambo is beneath contempt in the eyes of Burnett and mercilessly ridiculed by the mercenaries, the major – silent and impassive behind his dark glasses – seems to recognise a worthy adversary in Rambo, who is also deadly, unrelenting, quiet, cruel and cool under pressure. The queer spark at the heart of this dynamic gets expressed directly in the film. In this case, the Burmese major takes a page out of *Lawrence of Arabia* (1962) and sodomises his young male captives. This is certainly not the first time that a 'queer' eye has been on Rambo and/or his comrades. Although Stallone keeps his shirt on in *Rambo*, the male body still provides the cynosure of most compositions. As a creature of the screen environment, Rambo's association with the sensuality of the exotic Asian jungle, a space intimately connected with the 'feminine', puts masculinity on display as well as making it open to doubt. In earlier films, Rambo's sexuality came into question on several occasions.[8] His long hair, his pectoral muscles that look like female 'breasts', the feminised to-be-looked-at-ness of his spectacular sculpted body, his Yukio Mishima-like/St. Sebastian torture poses, and his clear delight in sado-masochism 'queer' him on screen.

Beyond this, Rambo does not seem fond of women trespassing into his homosocial environment. In *Rambo: First Blood Part II*, the appearance of anti-Communist holdout Co Bao irritates him at first, although he warms up to her. Her death cuts short their budding romance. The Taliban women are off limits in *Rambo III*, but the Christian missionary Sarah appears in *Rambo* to add a smidgen of romance. Like resistance fighter Co, she appears to be a bit of a fanatic – putting herself in danger in order to deliver humanitarian supplies to a remote Karen village. Rambo, at first, as with Co, wants nothing to do with putting a woman in harm's way, but, eventually, he comes to admire her commitment to the cause.

Sarah also highlights the centrality of bondage to the depiction of Rambo on screen. The character's existence revolves around stories of his imprisonment (in Vietnam as well as in the United States), the jailing of his comrades (in Vietnam, Afghanistan and Myanmar), and his deliverance along with the release of his friends. As well as being analogous to the story of Christ's capture, crucifixion and resurrection, these bondage fantasies have a potent sexual dimension – associated with sado-masochistic rituals, rape fantasies and illicit gratification. Captivity tales titillate as well as contain desire, predating the advent of the cinema, serving as narratives that legitimate American expansionism, male protectionism and the exercise of violence. Echoing Hollywood westerns and adventure epics, *Rambo* offers Sarah as the white woman who goes into the wilderness as a beacon of Christian civilisation but becomes a captive of the native forces of darkness. Paralleling the journey of his own soul from the captivity of sin to redemption, the hero saves himself by rescuing the woman from the 'fate worse than death', that is, rape by the foreign, non-white male. The closing scene of Rambo's return to the American West hints at the redemptive power of Sarah's faith. He loses the girl, but he manages to return 'home'.

The hero's own desire for the pure white woman muddies the waters. But Rambo struggles less with his obvious desire for Sarah than with his real animosity towards Burnett and Lewis, and the story remains largely a male-defined drama. Burnett and Lewis represent polar opposites, and Rambo serves as a moderating middle ground – as unlikely as that may seem – between these two models of masculinity. Burnett, the evangelical Christian leader of the missionary group, condemns Rambo's use of force against pirates as they go into Burma, and the two men seem delighted to go their separate ways when Burnett tells Rambo that he does not need to wait with the boat. The hardened mercenary Lewis represents the other end of the spectrum. Foulmouthed and hot tempered, he takes an immediate dislike to the 'boatman' Rambo as well.

The plot, as may be expected, shows the inadequacy of Burnett and Lewis under the circumstances. Both men are clearly out of their element; as Lewis puts it, 'Only a fucking ape would live here. What the fuck am I doing here?' Rambo, however, feels at 'home' in the 'hell' of the Southeast Asian jungle and rice paddies – as Trautman made clear in *Rambo: First Blood Part II*: 'What you choose to call hell, he calls home.' After seeing his fellow missionaries fed to the pigs in the prison camp, the anti-violent Burnett, in the heat of combat, bashes the brains out of one of the Burmese soldiers. The film dishes out the opposite punishment to Lewis, who steps on a mine and must crawl around during the penultimate scene to engage with the enemy at all. The rest of the men – missionaries, mercenaries, Karen insurgents and Myanmar's State Peace and Development Council (SPDC) forces – provide further background colour. While the Karen appear as noble fighters, the SPDC as sadistic killers and rapists, and the missionaries all as saintly pacifists, the mercenaries provide a broader range of races, accents, nationalities and attitudes. School Boy (Matthew Marsden), for example, defends the missionaries as 'noble' when Lewis expresses his distain, and becomes a natural ally for Rambo, who places Sarah in his care.[9]

Ultimately, all of these characters serve only one purpose, and that is to justify Rambo's actions, to support him as the 'natural' leader under all circumstances – whether the goal involves humanitarian relief, anti-government insurgency or a mercenary operation. Rambo manages the contradictions voiced within the narrative, reconciling the native and the foreign, the western hero and the Asian continent, the white and the non-white, the sadist and the masochist, the Christian and the non-Christian, the interventionist and the isolationist, the pacifist and the warrior. Reluctant, but ready, Rambo is the man of action in the post-Vietnam era: he keeps his serrated knife sharpened and his bow and arrow at hand. However, twenty years after *Rambo III*'s foray into Afghanistan, the appearance of the younger and more thoughtful School Boy raises the question of Stallone's ability to keep Rambo in play and relevant.

STALLONE PERFORMS RAMBO

The question remains, then, as to how the ageing Stallone manages to perform Rambo so that the character can conform to the ideological myth he has come to represent. The fact that Stallone can accomplish this attests to his performance skills. Given the character's corporeality, it also highlights Stallone's considerable abilities as a physical performer that goes beyond the self-discipline (and HGH drugs) shaping his physique.

While many stars create characters in keeping with their racial, ethnic and/or class backgrounds, Stallone has managed to 'become' Rambo, a character diametrically opposed to the actor: Native American and German rather than of Italian and Jewish extraction; a rural Westerner rather than an East Coast urbanite; a draftee rather than a dodger; educated through the military rather than at an elite Swiss college; skilled in carpentry, popular mechanics, hunting and fishing rather than acting; on the edges of the working classes rather than a member of the Hollywood elite. Still, Stallone proves not only to be convincing, but to be inspirational. Hovering somewhere between truth and fiction, Stallone/Rambo manages to be where the action is – from Vietnam to Afghanistan and Burma. Stallone makes the world root for Rambo rather than being appalled by his violent meddling or pitying his masochistic attachment to the US military, which considers him 'expendable'.

Indeed, the most important war fought in the Rambo series does not involve the US government, the Soviet military or Southeast Asian forces; rather, it involves the battle between the story of Rambo as a character and the sight of Rambo as a spectacular screen presence. Although Stallone helped to craft the character (as screenwriter and,

more recently, director), it is his performance of Rambo – his owner-
ship of the character through physical embodiment – that seems to tilt
the ideological scales from left (anti-war, New Age, Buddhist, hippie) to
right (pro-military, imperialist, interventionist) in the popular understanding of the character.

In his book *Stars* (1979), Richard Dyer, following on the work of
Orrin E. Klapp, analyses star images as ideology – as 'conservative',
'seductive' (involving non-threatening rule breaking) or 'transcendent'
(moving beyond the status quo). Of course, stars drift across these
categories throughout their careers and fans always exercise their pre-
rogative to 'misread' the image. In the case of Sylvester Stallone and
John Rambo, however, there appears to be considerable dissonance
between the way in which the character can be interpreted, Stallone's
performance of the character, and the ways in which the character has
been taken up in the popular imagination.

Stallone portrays Rambo as a conservative icon rather than as a critique of US military adventurism. In *Rambo*, this becomes clear with the
first appearance of the character on screen. As director and co-writer
as well as star, Stallone has had the most control over this iteration of
the character, so it seems safe to say that this particular embodiment
of Rambo represents Stallone's understanding of the character. Against
the backdrop of the Southeast Asian jungle, with *Rambo*'s plangent
theme music on the soundtrack, John Rambo appears in his element
as a hunter, working with a group of Asian men to capture cobras.
Although his sweaty clothes and worn headband indicate his relative
impoverishment, Rambo, larger and more muscular than the other men
in the scene, literally takes up more space within the frame. Using gestures, he controls the cobra's capture, and the others literally look to
him for their cues. Director Stallone merges seamlessly into the character Rambo through the act of directing these characters.

The opening scene, then, inserts Rambo into Asia as an American
still in charge, a 'natural' part of the landscape, willing to face danger and lead the natives effortlessly within a 'homeland' that Rambo
implicitly claims as his own. Stallone's physique, deft movements in
bagging the cobra, control of the gaze, and manner of strutting at the
head of the group transform Rambo from an expatriate drifter down
on his luck to a dominant part of the fabric of the Asian landscape and
society. In the next scene, Rambo's physical skill and spiritual superiority surface as well: he uses a bow and arrow to fish and then gives the
fish as an offering to a Buddhist monk passing on another boat.

Figure 3 - Rambo (Sylvester Stallone) uses a bow and arrow to fish. *Rambo*. Producers Avi Lerner, Kevin King Templeton and John Thompson; director Sylvester Stallone; DVD distributed by Lionsgate.

Unlike the Rambo of *First Blood*, who makes his initial impression as a victim of the war, mourning the loss to Agent Orange of an African American war buddy, this Rambo claims a place on screen as a superior individual – outstanding because of his courage, leadership, martial skills and generosity, as well as his musculature. His cultivation of these virtues eclipses these qualities in others. He stands out not only as a 'natural' man but as a 'natural' leader – affirming America's 'right to rule' in Asia. Wordlessly, Stallone manages to do quite a lot of ideological work in a couple of scenes, and this colours the way in which the character's words, actions and thoughts (as shown in flashback and through voiceovers) are interpreted subsequently.

Of course, Rambo forges his own destiny. Similar to shots showing him sharpening his serrated knife in *Rambo: First Blood Part II*, the scenes featuring Rambo doing metalwork allow Stallone to show him pounding out his own fate as well as utilising the tools of his trade. The chiaroscuro lighting from the flames shows off Stallone's musculature to best advantage. He performs the role of the working man in classic fashion – striking steel, using his body to shape his environment, affirming the physical mastery of even the most despised and downtrodden labourer.

The film shows viewers Rambo in a way that other characters miss. Rambo moves between the elegance of action – stepping on the hand of the pirate leader and shooting him point-blank in the head in one motion – and his characteristic scowl and faraway stare. The mercenary Lewis is dismissive of the stare, and he confronts Rambo about it: 'You can drop that thousand-yard stare – I've seen it all before and I'm not impressed.' The stare, for Lewis, indicates that Rambo is putting on an act – one that Stallone has perfected. As a performer, Stallone alternates between being completely aloof and being thoroughly physically engaged, so that Rambo's actions say more – in less time – than either his facial expressions or his mumbled lines of dialogue.

Stallone the director/writer/performer enjoys the action, loves to blow things up, and expresses a wellspring of emotion through physical violence. Rambo may experience moral agony and psychological trauma as he sweats through a nightmare featuring a flashback from the earlier instalments in the series, but Stallone clearly is having fun reprising the role – showing an old man still has some fight left in him. Stallone, the scriptwriter, even allows Rambo to admit this in a voice-over interior monologue while forging his weapons:

> *War is in your blood. Don't fight it. You didn't kill for your country, you killed for yourself. God is never going to make that go away. When you're pushed, killing is as easy as breathing.*

The dialogue seems to raise the question of whether Rambo must go through this soul searching in order to get beyond the sin of killing or whether Stallone asks the audience to accept that war is in America's 'blood' and to equate a country that kills with killing out of self-interest. The ideological operation of the film may enable working-class Americans to relate to the US wars in Asia as killing 'for yourself' not just to profit the American military-industrial corporate establishment. Imperialism is in the 'blood'. Rambo may be reluctant, but he is easy to convince. Two highlights of the series formula feature Rambo coming out of nowhere to devastate his enemy (for example, his emergence from the mud in *Rambo: First Blood Part II*) and his pulling his weapon on his boss (shooting up Murdock's office in the same film). These are also on display in *Rambo*. When Lewis and his party of mercenaries find themselves under siege, Rambo appears suddenly and kills all the Myanmar soldiers with his bow and arrow. He then draws his bow, threatening Lewis to convince him to continue the rescue mission. In a Mexican standoff worthy of John Woo, Rambo convinces the others, who all have guns drawn threatening him, by saying: 'There isn't one of us that doesn't want to be someplace else, but this is what we do, who we are. Live for nothing, or die for something.' The shot/reverse-shot of the standoff emphasises Stallone's performance. Rambo may be crazy, but he does not 'look' crazy: the commanding gaze and sincerity of the expression on Stallone's face make Rambo persuasive. Following School

Boy's lead, they all fall in behind Rambo, who now becomes their puta-tive leader. Again, the dialogue can be read as ideological. America wants to be 'someplace else' (not in Iraq or Afghanistan), but this is what 'we' (Americans) 'do' (militarily intervene in foreign lands). It may be ugly, but, as Stallone the writer articulates it, it is 'who we are'.[10]

Rambo alone kills most of the bad guys and rips the larynx out of the neck of Sarah's assailant. So that his brutality does not seem as shock-ing, *Rambo* carefully documents the excessive cruelty of the SPDC. The SPDC sows minefields and makes a sport out of betting which prisoner will trip the first mine. They napalm villages and kill infants. They rape and brutalise women. They feed crucified prisoners to the pigs. During the climactic battle, Rambo comes up behind an SPDC gunner, beheads him, and goes on a shooting frenzy, mowing the Burmese soldiers down with the big gun. As is typical of the series, wounded, he fights with even greater ferocity: it is, after all, drawing 'first blood' that really gets him going. He has enough energy left to ambush the fleeing Major Tint, impale him on his iconic serrated knife and disembowel him for good measure.

After the fight, Rambo surveys the field from a hillside. He watches Sarah's search for Burnett and Burnett's absorption in tending to one of the wounded. Although Sarah and Rambo exchange glances, Sarah stays to help Burnett. Rambo turns his back on them. Stallone's perfor-mance in this scene is telling. He cradles his arm in a way reminiscent of John Wayne as Ethan Edwards in John Ford's *The Searchers*.[11] Both Rambo and Ethan are flawed heroes who remain outside of the 'civilised' world and appear to caress and comfort themselves with this gesture.

Wayne as Ethan Edwards stays in the wilderness at the end of the film – unacceptable within a multiracial, multicultural society of the new frontier.[12] Rambo is in a similar situation. Caressing his arm and referencing the Duke, the ageing Stallone seems like a nostalgic evoca-tion of the action past, quoting other films, including the earlier Rambo movies, rather than offering any original action models. Stallone, the actor, may feel a particular kinship with the type of character Wayne played in his later years: that is, out of touch, out of date, vanishing with the wilderness, heroic but a creature of past history.

In this respect, Stallone may lose and Rambo, the guilt-ridden, hippie Buddhist, win. Rambo goes back West, in search of his Native American father, and the film ends on an elegiac note in a strikingly green valley that stands in stark contrast to the arid desert of Arizona – or the locations of the US's current engagements in the Middle East. No matter how far right Stallone pushes Rambo, the character manages to bounce back, keeping his countercultural mystique intact as he wrestles with his violent, vengeful explosions of xenophobic rage. Stallone, following Hollywood formula, may consciously write, direct and perform Rambo to keep contradictions in play. What is certain is that Rambo, the non-conformist, remains elusive and outside the procrustean mould in which Stallone and others have tried to constrain him.

THE AFTERLIFE OF RAMBO

Beyond Stallone's interpretation of the character and Rambo's appearance on screen and in fiction, Rambo lives as a cartoon character, action toy and video game avatar, and as a brand name attached to a variety of other tie-ins. Of course, these other iterations of the character feed back into Stallone's performance of the character. Given the way the character has been marketed to young boys, the appearance of young men as more prominent in the plots in *Rambo III* and *Rambo* may make the films additionally attractive to younger audiences.[13] In *Rambo III*, Rambo takes a young Taliban boy under his wing as a boy soldier. This is counter to the Taliban's own rules of not taking beardless boys into battle. The boy helps Rambo but he remains on the sidelines throughout most of the action. Though older, *Rambo*'s School Boy similarly plays a surrogate son and provides a point of identification for adolescents, if not children.

Meanwhile older wannabe Rambos populate the news media. The press, over the years, has labelled many figures, such as Oliver North after the Iran/Contra scandal, 'Rambo'. While many shun the moniker, journalists come up with a likely new 'Rambo' quite regularly. In June 2010, Pakistani police arrested Gary Brooks Faulkner, on his one-man hunt for Osama bin Laden, and the international media immediately dubbed him 'Rambo', following on a comment from Faulkner's brother.[14] Armed with a Bible as well as more lethal weapons when apprehended, Faulkner has been described as an ex-con hungry for the bounty on his enemy's head, a patriot infuriated by the 9/11 attacks, a lunatic vigilante and as sane as 'you or me'.

Vietnam-era vet John William Yettaw, another 'Rambo', performs a version of the character eerily close to the plot of *Rambo*. According to internet reports, Yettaw, disabled because of post-traumatic stress disorder, left his occasional work in construction to bring a Bible and/

or the Book of Mormon to Aung San Suu Kyi, under house arrest at the time. Yettaw swam to her estate twice – once in 2008 and again in 2009, when he was caught, arrested and, eventually, released. Unable to leave Southeast Asia behind, Yettaw and Rambo return to that part of the world – starting in Thailand and moving across the border to Burma. Captives attract both, and Yettaw as well as Rambo seem unable to resist being in the presence of saintly women held against their wills.

Stallone, of course, leads the wannabe Rambo pack. Although far from a 'real-life' Rambo, Stallone has developed a screen persona that takes in Rambo as part of the mix. This can clearly be seen in his portrayal of Barney Ross in *The Expendables* (2010), which Stallone also co-wrote and directed. The film serves as a tribute to/send-up of Stallone as an action star, with much of its tongue-in-cheek pastiche of his earlier work revolving around the figure of Rambo. The title of the film, of course, refers to *Rambo: First Blood Part II* and Co Bao's questioning of Rambo's remark that he's 'expendable'. As Stallone ages, he may, indeed, feel even more 'expendable' than Rambo, and in *The Expendables*, he seems determined to take his action buddies – from Arnold Schwarzenegger to Bruce Willis – with him. Although not on his team, the cameo appearances of Schwarzenegger and Willis contribute to the idea that *The Expendables*, taken as a whole, serves as a summation of the action fantasies Rambo defined.

In fact, the mercenary team, as a whole, more than the sum of its parts, adds up to 'Rambo'. The team, as a group, contains the military knowledge and skills that Rambo has as an individual. Its members exhibit their expertise in demolitions, weapons manufacture, sharp shooting, knife fighting, aviation, guerrilla warfare and Asian martial arts. However, the team most properly mirrors Rambo not in their skills but in their contradictions. The bloodiest confrontation among the confederates, in fact, involves the Asian member (Yin Yang, played by Jet Li) and the Nordic member (Gunnar Jensen, played by Dolph Lundgren). Ross saves Yin Yang from Gunnar twice in the film, and although the traitorous, drug-addicted giant appears to die, he is resurrected in order to keep the unit intact and imaginatively reconcile the contradictions he represents. Ross mediates, and, even though the smaller Yin Yang appears to be at a disadvantage, he is, in many respects, less sympathetic than the broken Gunnar.

In effect, Yin Yang performs the Orientalism that Rambo perpetually conjures and holds in check. As the character's name implies, Yin Yang cannot be pinned down to a specific identity: he represents duality. He functions more like Co Bao – loyal to a point, but pragmatic, dependable to a degree, but small, comparatively weak, and in need of the protection of a more virile male. As the 'feminine/masculine' dyad in Taoism, the 'yin' and the 'yang' of Jet Li's character keep the members of the Expendables team guessing: he serves as the 'forever foreign' Asian element in the American melting pot. Yin Yang demands more money because he is 'smaller' and must work harder to support his 'family' – but this family is non-existent. Yin Yang's masculinity is therefore perpetually in doubt, not only because size does 'matter', but also because his comments recall the US military's 'don't ask, don't tell' policy on homosexuality. Confronted with the fact that he has no family to worry about, he counters: 'You don't ask, I don't tell.'

In Stallone's trek across Asia, Yin Yang/Jet Li becomes a sore point. He alludes to an entire constellation of issues involving the remnants of Rambo's Asian encounters that remain unresolved, including issues surrounding masculinity, sexual orientation, family relations, professionalism, the value of labour and the ability to fit into a multicultural mix dominated by white America. Ross, as the leader, supported by another older veteran, Tool (Mickey Rourke, who has played his share of Rambo-like, Vietnam-era veterans), keeps both Yin Yang and Gunnar, his nemesis, on track, in action and at the service of the 'mission', which, in this case, means action entertainment. Gunnar and Yin Yang's cage fight, in fact, may be the highlight of *The Expendables*. Stallone may, indeed, as he ages, need help to continue to be Rambo. Or, perhaps, with all Rambo's iterations and permutations, no single performer can adequately enact this contested icon of American posturing in Asia.

NOTES

My gratitude goes to Chris Holmlund for her perceptive and detailed comments on an earlier version of this chapter. Special thanks to Fanny Chan and Natalie Wong for their work on the citations.

1   For more on the ideological ramifications of *Rambo: First Blood Part II* in relation to Stallone's star image, see Waller (1990).
2   There is some irony to the fact that one of the scandals of McCain's bid for president involved the resignation of two lobbyists involved with his campaign, Douglas Goodyear and Doug Davenport, because of their ties to the military junta in Myanmar. In fact, McCain seems to play both sides off against the middle, since he had a highly publicised meeting with opposition leader Aung San Suu Kyi in June 2011.
3   For more on Rambo and the Western hero, see Sweeney (1999).

4   For more on national guilt, victimisation and Rambo, see Studlar and Desser (1988).
5   Some of this aspect of Rambo's character may come from Tom Laughlin's Billy Jack in the 1971 film of the same name – also a half-Indian, half-white ex-Green Beret who has strong connections to the hippie counterculture. For more on Rambo and the counterculture, see Kellner (1991).
6   Given the Taliban destroyed Afghanistan's monumental Buddhist sculptures in 2001 (before 9/11 turned the country into a war zone again), it seems ironic in retrospect that Rambo should show his support for Islamic insurgency by giving this particular token.
7   For more on Burma on screen, see Selth (2009).
8   For more on this, see Tasker (1993).
9   A popular singer and television personality from the UK, Marsden has action credentials that include *Black Hawk Down* (2001).
10   Carl Boggs and Tom Pollard comment: 'No fewer than 236 human beings were brutally killed in this *Rambo* (or 2.59 per minute of footage), compared with measly totals of 69 and 132 for episodes two and three. In one of the great movie celebrations of militarised violence ever, human beings are bombed, blasted, stabbed, shot, blown up by grenades, incinerated by fire or flamethrowers, bludgeoned, stomped, beaten, beheaded, and tossed out of aircraft. ... Some cynical observers have commented that Rambo might well have returned in the nick of time, calculating that he is the one warrior persona able to deliver victory out of defeat in the latest catastrophic American imperial venture, Iraq' (2008).
11   Stallone clearly had Wayne and *The Searchers* in mind when making the film, as can be seen in interview; see Anon. (2007b: online). For more on Rambo and *The Searchers*, see Studlar and Desser (1988).
12   Ford's story deals with a racist Confederate vet who returns from the war to hunt for his niece, taken captive by Native Americans. By exploring the psychology of its anti-hero, the film attempts to reconcile America's deep-rooted racism with changing attitudes towards black/white relations during the civil rights era; see Henderson (1985).
13   The image of the native orphan befriended by the US military is deeply entrenched in the genre's makeup (for example, Short Round in Sam Fuller's *Steel Helmet* [1951] and a Chinese orphan given the same name in *Indiana Jones and the Temple of Doom* [1984]).
14   Given that Rambo fought with the Mujahideen against the Soviets in *Rambo III*, it seems ironic that Faulkner should be called 'Rambo' in his battle against Mujahideen leader Osama bin Laden.

BIBLIOGRAPHY

Anon. (2007a) '"*Rambo IV* is also a Christian film," Sylvester Stallone Confirms', *Catholic News Agency*, 1 March. Online. Available HTTP: http://www.catholicnewsagency.com/news/rambo_iv_is_also_a_christian_film_sylvester_stallone_confirms/ (3 August 2010).
_____ (2007b) 'Whoa Whoa Whoa.... Who Says It Ain't Gonna Be Called JOHN RAMBO?', *Ain't It Cool News*, 12 October. Online. Available HTTP: http://www.aintitcool.com/node/34423 (3 August 2010).
Arnold, Gordon (2006) *The Afterlife of America's War in Vietnam: Changing Visions in Politics and on Screen*. Jefferson, NC: McFarland.
Beech, Hannah (2009) 'Viewpoint: Why Foreigners Can Make Things Worse for Burma by Tuesday', *Time Magazine*, 19 May. Online. Available HTTP: http://www.time.com/time/world/article/0,8599,1899595,00.html (3 August 2010).
Boggs, Carl and Tom Pollard (2008) 'The Imperial Warrior in Hollywood: Rambo and Beyond',

New Political Science, 30.4. Online. Available HTTP: http://pdfserve.informaworld. com/850929_751315072_906043187.pdf (3 August 2010).

Dyer, Richard (1979) *Stars*. London: British Film Institute.

_____ (1997) *White: Essays on Race and Culture*. London: Routledge.

Henderson, Brian (1985) '*The Searchers*: An American Dilemma', in Bill Nichols (ed.) *Movies and Methods*, volume II. Berkeley: California University Press, 429–50.

Internet Movie Database (IMDb). 'Biography for Sylvester Stallone'. Online. Available HTTP: http://www.imdb.com/name/nm0000230/bio (3 August 2010).

_____ '*Rambo: First Blood Part II* (1985): Quotes'. Online. Available HTTP: http://www.imdb.com/ title/tt0089880/quotes (3 August 2010).

Jeffords, Susan (1989) *The Remasculinization of America: Gender and the Vietnam War*. Bloomington: Indiana University Press.

Kellner, Douglas (1991) 'Film, Politics, and Ideology: Reflections on Hollywood Film in the Age of Reagan', *Velvet Light Trap*, 27, 9–24.

Lane, Megan (2008) 'Which *Wuthering Heights* Character Are You?', *BBC NEWS*, 10 July. Online. Available HTTP: http://news.bbc.co.uk/2/hi/uk_news/magazine/7499421.stm (16 June 2011).

Morrow, Martin (2008) 'Soul Brothers Rambo and Rimbaud: Two Complicated Dudes', *CBCNews. ca*, 25 January. Online. Available HTTP: http://www.cbc.ca/arts/film/rambo.html (3 August 2010).

Said, Edward W. (1978) Orientalism. New York: Pantheon Books.

Selth, Andrew (2009) 'Burma, Hollywood, and the Politics of Entertainment', *Continuum*, 23.3, 321–34.

Stein, Joel (2008) 'Stallone on a Mission', *Time*, 24 January. Online. Available HTTP: http://www. time.com/time/magazine/article/0,9171,1706759,00.html (16 June 2011).

Studlar, Gaylyn and David Desser (1988) 'Never Having to Say You're Sorry: Rambo's Rewriting of the Vietnam War', *Film Quarterly*, 42.1, 9–16.

Sweeney, Frank (1999) '"What Means Expendable?": Myth, Ideology, and Meaning in *First Blood* and *Rambo*', *Journal of American Culture*, 22.3, 63–9.

Tasker, Yvonne (1993) *Spectacular Bodies: Gender, Genre, and the Action Cinema*. London and New York: Routledge.

Waller, Gregory A. (1990) '*Rambo*: Getting to Win This Time', in Linda Dittmar and Gene Michaud (eds) *From Hanoi to Hollywood: The Vietnam War in American Film*. New Brunswick, NJ: Rutgers, 113–28.

Warner, William (1992) 'Spectacular Action: Rambo and the Popular Pleasures of Pain', in Lawrence Grossberg, Cary Nelson and Paula Treichler (eds) *Cultural Studies*. New York: Routledge, 672–88.

STALLONE, AGEING AND ACTION AUTHENTICITY

YVONNE TASKER

The underdog, violence, and the body as both a site of subjection and a possible locus of resistance are all tropes central to Stallone's movie roles. These elements are played out most obviously in Stallone's status as an action star, rather than in his comedic or dramatic roles. And it is particularly with action, and the ageing body in action, that I am concerned here, responding amongst other things to the late career revival of the characters of Rocky in *Rocky Balboa* (2006) and John Rambo in *Rambo* (2008).

Reviews and promotional interviews for both films emphasised the star body in a revised frame, one bounded by ideas about age. In *Rocky Balboa* Stallone offered a nuanced nostalgia, acknowledging the physical changes and personal loss of ageing alongside a celebration of the defining determination of the iconic boxer. *Rambo* serves as the inverse or counterpoint to that more reflective mode, a re-presentation as much as a re-working of one of the two film heroes that have defined Stallone's career. *Rocky Balboa* is explicitly a film about ageing and loss; in *Rambo* Stallone's age is barely alluded to, although it arguably haunts the text.

The vital statistics that have circulated in late 2000s media coverage relate to Stallone's body, referencing both his age and his size. A brief quote from a profile in *Time* magazine is indicative: 'Playing a guy who acts with only his eyes and his biceps is harder than playing a fast-talking, earnest boxer, especially on a 61-year-old body. Which is one of the reasons Stallone wanted to do it. He pumped up to a freakish 209 lbs. (95 kg); in *Rambo II* he weighed only 168 (76 kg)' (Stein 2008).

The maintenance – indeed the enhancement – of a muscular physique by the contemporary sixtyish actor Stallone clearly means something different than it did in earlier phases of his stardom. Stein's use of the adjective 'freakish' in what is largely a positive profile of the star suggests an ambivalence underlying the admiration. The story of ageing stars, and of squeamish cultural responses to that ageing, is hardly new; yet there is perhaps a particular resonance to these discourses for the kind of physical actor that Stallone has long embodied. In what follows, I suggest that the different value accorded to Stallone's body in the 2000s has to do not only with ageing, though this is undoubtedly central, but with changes in celebrity culture and in action cinema as a Hollywood genre.

Media coverage of Stallone's star body in the 2000s turns on tropes of health and authenticity versus artifice and spectacle, an opposition in which diet and exercise stand as the *natural* against the use of steroids and surgery as unnatural, inauthentic. As I will develop further below, such mediated preoccupations with health, physical fitness and the natural are complexly bound up with ideas about ageing. Culturally, the natural processes of physical change associated with ageing also function as signs of abjection, in that they underline human mortality. And, as Sadie Wearing notes, cultural constructions of age operate 'primarily in terms of decline and disintegration rather than accumulation and growth' (2007: 280).

Stardom, whether in the world of sports or movies, is a fascinating site via which ideas about ageing and the natural yet high-performing body are mediated within our culture. For athletes, whose careers are defined by distinct age spans (though that span varies depending on the sports in which they are involved), ageing typically means decline. Movie stars and sportspeople alike are admired when they achieve atypical longevity in career terms. At the same time, sustained high-level performance in the world of sports is often met with a degree of cynicism as to how that performance has been achieved. Scrutiny of actors' ageing bodies and faces for signs of 'work' are equally sceptical, with age itself increasingly becoming the tacit subject of profiles.

For Stallone, a flashpoint for these issues of ageing and authenticity came in the form of media coverage of the star's 'steroid' use.[1] In February 2007, while on a promotional tour for the commercial and critical hit *Rocky Balboa*, Stallone fell foul of Australian customs regulations and was subsequently charged with bringing into the country quantities of a Human Growth Hormone and testosterone. In early 2008, following an interview in *Time* magazine (the interview cited above), the story developed as Stallone insisted that his use of prescription testosterone and HGH did *not* equate to steroid use. The star specifically linked his use of these substances to ageing, remarking that 'Testosterone to me is so important for a sense of well-being when you get older' (see Stein 2008).

The same month lurid headlines resulted from ex-fiancée Janice Dickinson's comments that she had seen Stallone injecting steroids during their early 1990s relationship. Her claim that he had even injected *her* with steroids (as opposed to HGH) – guaranteed to garner maximum attention – was immediately and strongly disputed. Dickinson's remarks set off a series of salacious stories in news media and gossip blogs, with her own age and surgically altered body functioning as signs of excess. In the process Stallone's association with HGH and his advocacy of artificial testosterone were repositioned from the star's preferred discourse of health and well-being to the very different context of celebrity culture, addressed by scholars such as Su Holmes and Sean Redmond (2006).

With respect to ageing, the characteristic double discourse of celebrity culture oscillates between prurient fascination with puncturing vanity on the one hand, while on the other admonishing those celebrities (in particular women) perceived as allowing the effects of ageing to go unchecked. As a performer whose stardom is fundamentally bound up with the built body, these cultural preoccupations are particularly resonant for Stallone.

The title of this essay foregrounds a notion of 'action authenticity' which frames my interrogation of Stallone's contemporary stardom. Authenticity is a term most often found in scare quotes in academic writing; unsurprising since the word has so often been used to perpetuate assumptions about supposedly natural (but actually acutely specific in historical and cultural terms) values or to argue for the preservation of an essentialist idea of the inherent qualities of a thing or practice. I use it here since a concept of authenticity (and, consequently, of the inauthentic) seems so pertinent to the questions of performance, appearance and the body.

I tackle three aspects of Stallone's star persona, in the process drawing out how a notion of masculine authenticity has been central to that persona, and how this has shifted in the 2000s. In the first section, 'Sports, Steroids, Struggle', I explore the ways in which discourses about fitness and scandals regarding doping within professional sports inform Stallone as a star who has been strongly associated with the worked-on body and who was himself caught up in controversy regarding the use of HGH. I take note of the importance of ideas of naturalness and authenticity to Stallone's star persona, drawing out the significance of ethnicity in these discourses. In section two, 'Constructed Celebrity Bodies', I explore the impact on notions of authentic performance of a contemporary media culture which emphasises celebrity bodies as routinely enhanced and/or constructed through surgery and cosmetic manipulation. I consider how the emphasis on the natural in Stallone's persona makes sense in this context, positioning his stardom in relation to a mainstreaming of the built body as an expectation for Hollywood's male stars.

An intense fetishisation of youth, and the vigour for which it stands as a sign, are central to the celebrity culture explored in section two. Consequently in the final section, 'Ageing and Action Authenticity', I turn to the sorts of physical performance required of star bodies within action as a genre. In the process I talk about the ways in which the broad generic label 'action' encompasses a number of subgenres involving different sorts of star bodies and concepts of (action) authenticity. In an era of digital action/spectacle, in which our sense of belief in what actual star bodies can accomplish is provisional and to some degree beside the point, what significance can a performer's age really have? As a genre, action allows and even depends upon staging the impossible. Yet it seems that audiences and critics may be more able to make allowances in relation to some subgenres than others. Cultural anxieties over ageing – and the humour attendant on those anxieties – seem to be particularly acute.

SPORTS, STEROIDS, STRUGGLE

Stallone's association with cinematic sports and with action cinema bridges ideas about authentic and fictional performance in fascinating ways. As a built movie body and a movie boxer/fighter/footballer/ climber/arm wrestler, Stallone has long been linked to quite contradictory ideas about physical performance. He repeatedly plays an authentic fighter (with authenticity clearly figured in ethnic and class terms) who wins against the odds, deploying low-tech skills against better-funded, high-tech opponents (or alternatively large numbers of unskilled opponents, as in *Rambo III* [1988]). Yet Stallone is strongly associated with body-building, a sport whose very raison d'être is the body as spectacle and in which steroid use is routine. These contradictions are at work *within* body-building too, to the extent that it is a competitive sport centred on staged routines: body-builders develop muscle for display and are judged on their ability to strike poses. The muscular or built body may be worked on for display rather than utility, but work is necessary for its generation. Indeed, the advent of the built body in 1980s action cinema provided an appropriately excessive narrative context within which such bodies could both perform (pose) and demonstrate conventional masculine attributes of strength and authority. Movies such as *First Blood* (1982), that is, made the built male body meaningful as well as decorative.

Unlike his 1980s box-office competitor Arnold Schwarzenegger, Stallone did not emerge from professional body-building, instead coming to prominence as writer and star of the Academy Award-winning boxing movie *Rocky* (1976). Just as significantly, his screen persona as spectacular everyman – exemplified by the underdog Rocky role – contrasts with the highly worked bodies seen posing in competition in the documentary *Pumping Iron* (1977). Nonetheless, Stallone's built body was – and remains – crucial to his film roles and his star persona. The *Rocky* films' training montage sequences, for example, emphasise the effort required to develop the boxer's strength, to achieve the sort of body needed to succeed in contact sports. Rocky's efforts are insistently framed as simple – based in either natural or community settings – and as authentic.

This framing remains very much in evidence in *Rocky Balboa*, with Rocky's training reprising familiar scenes such as the meat processing plant. More than that, the film evokes a media context in which the reigning world champion, Mason Dixon (Antonio Tarver), is perceived as inauthentic, lacking the 'heart' that characterises Rocky. Dixon's dissatisfaction with his career and his handlers is evident in his decision to return to his old gym; the exhibition bout with Rocky is presented as a necessary affirmation, one made explicit when Balboa tells him afterwards: 'You're a great champion – you've got heart.'

In enforcer (rather than sporting) roles in films such as *Cobra* (1986), *Demolition Man* (1993) and *Judge Dredd* (1995), Stallone's body works differently, suggesting implacable strength. In *Rocky Balboa* the former champ's trainer advises him that his ageing body can no longer deliver on speed or sparring; instead their regime must concentrate on developing enough 'horse power' to make any hits Balboa is able to land count. Rocky himself extends his ability to take punishment into a moral code, advising his son that life is about 'how hard you can get hit and keep moving forward'. As veteran John Rambo, Stallone's body once again signifies athletic strength but also struggle and suffering (the ability to keep going). Central themes of struggle, of sporting roles, and of physical performance all work to put Stallone's 2000s star persona in dialogue with contemporary debates regarding the legitimacy of an artificially enhanced body.

Enhancement means very different, and in many ways contradictory, things in the worlds of sports and cinema; Stallone's association with movie sports and with spectacular cinema make his a particularly interesting persona in this context. The initial story of Stallone's encounter with Australian customs over the importing of testosterone generated only minor media coverage; there was relatively little surprise and certainly nothing approaching scandal. Indeed much British and US coverage was playful in tone, as with journalist Marina Hyde's *Guardian* op-ed 'Rocky Joins Cast of Fallen Sporting Heroes'. Here Hyde archly recalls the lengthy training montage featured in *Rocky IV* (1985) in which Stallone/Rocky's natural training techniques are contrasted to the use of steroids by his Russian opponent (Dolph Lundgren), pondering in the process the future of 'fake sport'; 'Like all sports doping allegations', Hyde remarks, 'the story is essentially one of lost innocence' (2007). This juxtaposition came in the wake of ongoing high-profile scandals relating to the use of performance-enhancing drugs in the world of sports including baseball and cycling.[2] Here the fake sport of the movie world stands for inauthentic achievements in the world of sports.

Perhaps the key question posed in debates about doping and sports has been whether or not sporting achievements can be truly valued if they are produced 'artificially'. In his book *Genetically Modified Athletes*, Andy Miah, like Marina Hyde, references Stallone's *Rocky IV*, noting its replication of the standard 'drug cheat story' featured in news media, a story whereby 'the naturally gifted and strong-willed athlete overcomes the evil, drug-enhanced, techno-athlete' (2004: 15). As Miah and others make clear, our culture typically displaces questions about doping into debates about character (as in *Rocky IV*). Thus doping as cheating is understood as 'attributable to a flaw in the athlete's character' (2004: 14). For Miah this results in the evasion of full, complex ethical debates regarding enhancement. Defining what is artificial enhancement and distinguishing this from the natural is far from straightforward.

In a sport bedevilled by accusations of drug (ab)use such as cycling, technological innovations in bike and suit design are also crucial to enhancing performance. In the late 2000s intense debates have been conducted with respect to professional swimming, a sport in which highly specialised swimsuits – and the corporations both responsible for their development and heavily involved in sponsoring the sport – have allowed world records to be broken in a seemingly unprecedented manner. Such dramatic shifts in performance possibility pose fundamental challenges to ideals of equality between national teams and individual competitors, raising as yet unresolved questions for the sport's ruling body.

Drawing attention to the nuances of such questions, Miah writes: 'It is hard to rationalise the ethical difference between an altitude chamber and blood doping, or an aluminium baseball bat and a neoprene swimming costume' (2004: 15). That is, in the highly commercial world of professional sports, it is impossible to set aside the enhancements to performance that money can (legally) buy. Indeed, arguments in favour of legalising various performance-enhancing substances and technologies frequently centre on equality, suggesting the desirability of a level playing field. Critics argue that such an outcome would result in all sport becoming like professional wrestling, an enjoyable movie-style spectacle in which the result of contests between colourful sporting characters is predetermined.

Of course those issues of inequality – such as access to training facilities, equipment and time to train, for instance – are already endemic to professional sports in a globalised, celebrity-fuelled economy. Nonetheless the idea of equality and the possibility of finding 'raw talent' underpin professional sports. The sports world shares this particular Cinderella story with the world of entertainment, including Hollywood. It is precisely this theme – the underdog makes good – that Stallone has so successfully exploited and even embodied over the course of his film career.

In both sports and movies, cultural perspectives on what is 'natural' repeatedly collide with our conception of the unnatural or inauthentic, what is constructed. The built body exemplifies this conundrum; deemed alternately desirable and grotesque, it makes plain that the natural is inaccessible to us, though we may firmly believe that we know it when we see it. While Hollywood and sports media equally revel in Cinderella stories of talent and ambition realised, cheating in movies is not really an issue in the same way as is cheating in sports. Indeed, both movie stars themselves and the cinema as a medium are self-conscious constructions (even, or perhaps especially, when they trade in ideas of the natural or simplicity); designed to produce pleasure through illusion, movies deal in fantasy and spectacle. Thus, within Stallone's films, despite both scandals over HGH and the physical impact of ageing, the credibility of the star's body as a sign of authentic struggle remains undiminished.

Crucial to Stallone's mid-career roles is not the body as machine (famously embodied by Schwarzenegger in the title role of *The Terminator* [1984]) or even primarily the body as weapon, though this trope does feature in Stallone's films. Most often the body is portrayed in Stallone's 1980s films as a site of violence and resistance, and of course as spectacle. *Lock Up* (1989) exemplifies these themes with the Stallone character subject to intense mental and physical trials; the built body signifies not only his character's physical toughness but also virtues of openness and endeavour. Stallone's Frank Leone is an affable convict, a model prisoner who becomes subject to an unjust regime of violence and harassment. The extraordinary regular-guy persona deployed here allows Leone's violence to be framed as a legitimate response to oppressive treatment, rather than as an inherent quality of the built/machine body.

Stallone's action films, whether sporting or not, typically dramatise struggle against an unjust or illegitimate authority. Leone's battle of wills against deranged warden Drumgoole (Donald Sutherland) enacts an intensely melodramatic example. In *First Blood*, John Rambo's confrontation with Sheriff Teasle (Brian Dennehy) initiates this formula of struggle as a key theme of the series; in *Rambo: First Blood Part II*, Rambo battles the Russian-backed Vietnamese forces but is (melo)dramatically in conflict primarily with his US handler Murdock (Charles Napier). Imagery suggestive of the body's physical potential, and its physical limits, supports these movies' central themes of conflict. Like the comeback story favoured in sports coverage, physical vulnerability or distress of some kind is a necessary component of those movies in which Stallone plays the underdog who comes good or proves himself (images of defeat and torture – ultimately to be overcome – are routine). Thus *Lock Up* makes a spectacle of its star body only when it/he becomes the site of cruelty.

Physical vulnerability and themes of struggle serve at least two purposes in terms of hard-bodied action's narrative logic. First, they allow a delay to the ultimate resolution, much as obstacles are placed between the lovers in tales of romance. Second, they enhance motivation such that the hero acts to secure revenge; his violence is thus retributive and effectively justified. Within hard-bodied action, violence is also redemptive, serving to regenerate the hero. Figures who are on the periphery of society or are lowly within the organisations in which they operate move centre stage in this mode of action (as when Stallone plays fighter, arm wrestler, truck driver, veteran, cop). Stallone has played elite operatives too, as in *Cobra*, *Demolition Man* (though the film jokes at his expense) and *Tango & Cash* (1989), but his most successful action roles construct his character as socially marginal, even expendable.

The title of Stallone's *The Expendables* (2010) nods to the significance of the term in the action movie lexicon. The idea of expendability is central to the Rambo character, encompassing a degree of rage and resentment quite absent from, say, John Wayne's elegiac Bataan movie *They Were Expendable* (John Ford, 1945), in which patriotic self-sacrifice is celebrated. In the *Rambo* films expendability encompasses self-sacrifice but in a manner that emphasises the character's isolation and exclusion from America. The films thus signal Rambo as both emblematic of the US soldier and outside the military; he is simultaneously an everyman figure (a populist presentation of class resentment) and an exceptional hero. Stallone's highly-worked star body visually signifies his exceptional status, as does the insistence that this body is able to withstand repeated physical assaults.

Rocky Balboa manages these themes of marginality in fascinating and fruitful ways. Rocky is a former champion defined by personal loss and the physical and emotional experience of ageing; a genial host at his restaurant, he regales customers with tales of his fighting days. Though he is clearly respected and has a place within the community, Rocky is repeatedly seen in the cemetery mourning his beloved wife Adrian (Talia Shire). This visual association with death and loss contextualises the film's familiar training sequences. Though the film's climactic exhibition fight in Vegas suggests a defiance of ageing (and the social exclusion or marginality it imposes), Rocky acknowledges the crowds' appreciation from the sidelines, already on his way out of the auditorium. The movie's final scene takes us away from the ring and back to Adrian's grave. Here Rocky's figure fades away in a poignant image which puts an effective end to the cycle.

Ethnicity is a crucial element to the presentation of Rocky as a marginal yet socially located figure within *Rocky Balboa*. His restaurant serves as a focal point, drawing on strong associations between food, community and ethnic identity. As Diane Negra notes, numerous US films, TV shows, advertisements and theme restaurants engage in a nostalgic process of 'fetishising ethnic food' as a marker for a simple or authentic mode of life that is deemed to be lost; 'food becomes not only a channel for sincerity and emotional expressivity but a sign of nonindustrialized production that bespeaks the values and customs of an earlier era' (2002: 63). While *Rocky Balboa* does not show the ex-boxer preparing food, a montage depicts him buying goods for his restaurant from a

number of market stalls (where he is evidently a familiar figure). Rocky's involvement with food is a marker of his ethnicity, generosity and authenticity.

Indeed, throughout the *Rocky* films Stallone's Italian American ethnicity is foregrounded in ways that are bound up with ideas about authenticity and the body, representing a significant point of contrast with the Rambo films. Notions of exclusion and

Figure 1 - Food as sign of ethnic authenticity. *Rocky Balboa.* Producers William Chartoff, Kevin King Templeton, Charles Winkler and David Winkler; director Sylvester Stallone; DVD (non-US) distributed by Twentieth Century Fox Home Entertainment.

physical struggle take on a distinct set of meanings with respect to ethnicity, suggesting tropes of self-invention in the context of American mythology. Discussing female stars, Negra outlines how ethnicity has long been used to signal authenticity within Hollywood cinema. She cites Allen L. Woll and Randall M. Miller's observation that 'Whatever their occupation, sex, or locale, Italian characters seemingly dealt with the world in a primitive way' (2001: 147). For Negra this ethnic authenticity is fundamentally nostalgic, connected to traditional ideas about family and gender.

Such associations frame the commitment to family and to community insisted on in the *Rocky* films and also in *Lock Up*. Rocky's relationship with love interest Adrian offers a sentimental anchor for the character, allowing the expression of emotion. The role of Melissa (Darlanne Fleugel) in *Lock Up*, the love interest that Leone seeks to protect, secures not only the heterosexuality of the film's male lead (this is a prison movie after all) but also his ties to an outside world of intimacy and connection. The way in which ethnicity seals the deal is made explicit in an early embrace between the couple in which a kiss is followed by Leone's assertion: 'Now, *that's* Italian.' In both *Rocky* and *Lock Up* (as well as earlier films like *Paradise Alley* [1978]) ethnicity, and the immigrant experience of physical labour and self-fashioning to which it refers, amplifies the theme of the underdog as well as foregrounding connotations of an unaffected, supposedly 'natural' mode of being.

As with the theme of ageing, the contrasts between the *Rocky* and *Rambo* films are as telling as the continuities. In the *Rambo* films this aspect of Stallone's persona works differently since Italianness has never been emphasised. However, as various critics have noted, the character instead exploits discourses of primitivism via costuming which draws on Native American iconography. Thus Gaylyn Studlar and David Desser identify the 'Indianness' of the character's 'costume signifiers – long hair, bare chest, headband and necklace/pendant', suggesting that the film works symbolically via an 'appropriation of the iconography of the noble savage'. Drawing out the way in which ethnicity is used to suggest a proximity to nature, Studlar and Desser stress the film's visual discourse of primitivism: 'Emerging from the mud of the jungle, from the trees, rivers and waterfalls, Rambo displays a privileged, magical relationship with the Third World wilderness not evidenced by even the Vietnamese' (1990: 108).

In the 2008 *Rambo*, once again the central figure is introduced as a primitive figure, even a man of nature – he hunts snakes, fishes and forges his own knife. Such imagery works to connect a moral imperative to the natural, as opposed to the artificial. In this way Rambo's alignment with nature performs similar work to Rocky's presentation in terms of ethnic authenticity, albeit in very different terms. Both discourses of natural primitivism and appeals to an authenticity bound up in a nostalgically imagined ethnic identity foreground qualities of directness and simplicity. The built body and the foregrounding of

Figure 2 - Rambo (Sylvester Stallone) aligned with nature. *Rambo.* Producers Avi Lerner, Kevin King Templeton and John Thompson; director Sylvester Stallone; DVD distributed by Sony Pictures Home Entertainment.

ethnicity (however indeterminate) each emphasise natural, authentic (primitive) qualities. Yet in the *Rambo* films these qualities signify violence and instability.

Surely the most crucial difference between the thematic resonances of the body in these cycles of films is the extent to which the work of producing it is foregrounded or elided. The energetic training montage is a staple of the *Rocky* films, following and celebrating the work it takes for the hero to get into shape. Rambo by contrast is presented as a body always ready for action/violence. The theme of an outsider's struggle in the *Rocky* series allows the ethnic Italian fighter to ultimately represent the nation. In *Rocky Balboa* the undefeated champion Dixon seems to require the former champion's endorsement. In contrast, the themes of exclusion and struggle tell a different story of Rambo's characteristic inability (until the most recent film, that is) to find a place for himself in America. Rambo's potential for violence is naturalised through the worked body, but it signals instability as well as authenticity.

CONSTRUCTED CELEBRITY BODIES (IN ACTION)

As Kirsty Fairclough writes, 'the gossip blog has become a key component of contemporary celebrity culture' (2008). Facilitated by the internet and the rapid circulation of images and commentary it allows, celebrity culture has intensified and is more pervasive in the 2000s than in earlier decades. Since Stallone's mid-career success in the 1980s, the emergence of the blogosphere and websites such as TMZ allow the rapid dissemination of tabloid stories, scandal and gossip. For Fairclough, 'Blogs encourage a cynical awareness of the production of celebrity culture and encourage us to question the mechanisms through which we are positioned as consumers' (ibid.). Contemporary media culture takes as its default position the view that celebrity bodies are routinely enhanced and/or constructed through surgery and cosmetic manipulation. Indeed, cosmetic surgery is no longer in itself necessarily a media-worthy story (although failed surgery may well attract attention). In the context of the pervasive makeover culture analysed by scholars such as Dana Heller (2007) and Brenda Weber (2009) attempts to preserve authenticity as a component of stardom or celebrity are both necessary and doomed to fail.

The cynicism Fairclough describes is of course at odds with the emphasis on the natural/primitive in Stallone's star image, manifest in differing ways in the *Rocky* and *Rambo* films. Stallone the star endorses exercise and regulated diet as the route to a healthy, built body, as the title of his 2005 book – *Sly Moves: My Proven Program to Lose Weight, Build Strength, Gain Will Power and Live Your Dream* – makes clear. The discourses of discipline and structured endeavour that form the focus of this book come up squarely against gossip culture's interest in surgery and steroids. Gossip blogs fix on signs of seeming inauthenticity linked to ageing and appearance. An image of the smiling star posted on TMZ on 6 December 2006 under the generic heading 'you might want to rethink' is tagged 'Sylvester Stallone: Rambotox?' Another pair of images contrasts a younger Stallone with his 2006 image. The only text for this posting is 'Are words even necessary?' The comments that follow supply the words, bemoaning, defending and gloating over signs of age and surgery.

Within a cultural context in which the built male body is positioned as natural *and* constructed, age, like fat, is construed as an enemy to be held at bay. Fat is often allied with ageing, the two mutually informing each other in an imagery of middle-age comfort. Gossip blogs and tabloid media focus on the enhanced or altered celebrity body, taking cruel delight in scrutinising images for signs of failure (too big/too skinny, not trying enough/trying too hard). Again, the terms of nature and culture are set in problematic opposition to each other in these forums: problematic since enhancement and augmentation, whether cosmetic or surgical, are suppressed norms within Hollywood. A cheeky tabloid heading, 'RambOAP' (alluding to an acronym for those of retirement age: old age pensioner), in the British paper the *Daily Mirror* featured a shot of Stallone on the *Rambo* set with an inset image of the star as seen in *First Blood* some 25 years earlier.

An August 2008 feature in *The Mail Online* scrutinised paparazzi shots of a holidaying Stallone and family for signs of what it terms the 'ravages of time'. Framing the story around what it terms the 'actor's never-ending quest to retain his youthful looks', the feature offers a close-up of the veins on Stallone's muscular arms as evidence of both the work put into the body and the failure to eradicate the signs of age. Though her focus is largely on female celebrity, Fairclough's observation that 'celebrities are also regularly deemed as having "gone too far" in their quest for youth and beauty and as such, are publicly condemned in the gossip blog' (2008) is pertinent here. Fairclough adds that 'older female celebrities such as Cher, Farah Fawcett and Melanie Griffith are regularly vilified for not "growing old gracefully" and for having too much surgery so that the extensive labor involved in maintaining this "ideal self" is revealed' (ibid.). Thus the same *Mail* feature that mocks Stallone for attempting to hold onto lost youth praises his (younger) wife for keeping in shape. Such contrasts make clear that male and female ageing are framed by very different and highly gendered expectations and limits.

As these examples attest, ageing within celebrity culture is frequently a source of humour, a comedy of the seemingly inappropriate. This masculine version of 'mutton dressed as lamb', a derogatory phrase usually directed at women, suggests that the attempt to retain youthful appearance/experience potentially opens the performer up to ridicule. Such ridicule is in some ways the corollary of a culture featuring explicitly commoditised male bodies, as I will develop further below. It also has to do with the type of hard-bodied action that Stallone embodies, a subgenre associated with the 1980s. The on-screen ageing of action stars of the 1980s – an era in which the genre was defined in large part by muscular male bodies on display – has attracted caustic media attention and mixed box-office results. Yet this is not simply reducible to age: Stallone had experienced fallow periods before entering his sixties or even his fifties; nor have his commercial successes been confined to the films he made during his thirties. Readers' comments online, meanwhile, offer a familiar mix of admiration and disgust, suggesting that while celebrity culture may deride a muscular body deemed age-inappropriate, fans do not share that view. Instead they repeatedly express their admiration for the star's longevity and their desire to emulate him.[3]

Stallone's hyperbolic masculinity, already bound up in oppositions of authenticity and artifice, thus plays out differently in the 2000s. It is not only cosmetic surgery or performance enhancing drugs that are at issue here, however. Since Stallone's mid-career 1980s hits, the built body has been aggressively mainstreamed, shifting from the periphery of popular culture to become a staple of advertising. Thus while Stallone represented a physical ideal of the built body for the 1980s, a younger star like Brad Pitt suggests how during the 1990s a buff body effectively became a requirement for male Hollywood stars. The male sports/movie star as pin-up has been seen to disavow the implicitly passive position in which he is placed through physical endeavour, violence and an iconography of active masculinity. Two rather different configurations of this scenario are at work in Pitt's roles in *Fight Club* (1999) and *Troy* (2004), both films showcasing the star's worked-on body (in the first via the theme of fighting and Tyler Durden's function as ego ideal, in the second via the conventions of the historical epic). In each case the film frames the display of the body through narrative and generic context: it is effectively *explained* to us while it is being presented as spectacle.

Male athletes pursue lucrative ancillary/parallel careers in modelling, endorsements and clothing lines. For sportsmen, in contrast to movie stars, the professional endeavours for which they are primarily known are to some degree separate from their work in advertising and endorsements. Nonetheless, male athletes and performers are increasingly drawn together in a visual economy that values male muscle and physical achievements. In this context critics have argued that conventional understandings of masculinity and the worked-on body as a sign of masculine strength have become even further denaturalised. Leslie Heywood and Shari L. Dworkin argue for the profound significance of a development by which 'the male body is now a similarly commoditized object, valued for its approximation of cultural ideals of male beauty', a development which means that 'men, like women, have their own "body projects"' (2003: 100). Stallone's persona and advocacy of health and fitness via working out articulates precisely such a body project. Yet as Heywood and Dworkin make clear, ideas of the natural built body are equally problematic. For them Brad Pitt served as 'the voice of bad faith' when, in promoting the film *Fight Club*, he claimed not to have really trained for the role and that 'the look of his body is natural' (ibid.). If Pitt seems to be attempting to deflect attention from the work put into his body (or alternatively acknowledging that this is simply the work of being a star rather than restricted to any particular role), Stallone increasingly embraces his definition as a physical actor, a performer whose bodily presence is in many ways more significant in his roles than facial expressions or verbal inflection.

The male pin-up can't but draw attention to the very qualities of spectacle (the male body as object/thing to be consumed) that suggestions of action, strength and labour seem to disavow. Similarly, Stallone's still-muscular physique points up the ways that muscle, while it may be associated with youthful strength, is not in itself a sign of youth. The more youthful muscular body of earlier films guarantees a sort of physical strength coupled, as discussed above, to recurrent images of nature and the primitive, but Stallone's older muscular body underlines in

Figure 3 - Star body: bigger and yet less visible. Rambo. Producers Avi Lerner, Kevin King Templeton and John Thompson; director Sylvester Stallone; DVD distributed by Sony Pictures Home Entertainment.

new ways the work undertaken to inhabit/perform it. Stallone's comments on his use of testosterone – and indeed his advocacy for its use as affirmative, despite the damaging side effects – specifically respond to the experience of male ageing. Presumably in partial recognition of these tensions, Stallone's Rambo is both bigger and less visible in *Rambo*, the first film of the series in which he keeps his upper body covered.

AGEING AND ACTION AUTHENTICITY

Action cinema has long been coupled with the staging of seemingly impossible or at the least improbable stunts and forms of spectacle. The built male body has also long been a factor in the staging of that spectacle, seen in the 1930s and 1940s in swimmer (and sometime model) Johnny Weissmuller's series of Tarzan movies, or the bare-chested acrobatics of Burt Lancaster in films such as *The Crimson Pirate* (1952). Authenticity is an issue of a particular kind for action cinema as a genre which has continued to experience box-office success but which has changed significantly from the period of Stallone's box-office dominance during the 1980s.

Indeed, from a contemporary vantage point the action subgenre through which Stallone came to prominence – one centred on a tormented yet triumphant male veteran hero, which Susan Jeffords (1994) terms hard-bodied – has been supplanted several times over: first by films which followed in the wake of the immense commercial success of *Die Hard* (1988), with its resourceful but far from pumped everyman hero; then by effects-driven disaster movies in the 1990s such as *Independence Day* (1996); and subsequently by other high-profile subgenres or action types. These subgenres include spectacular martial arts epics (*Crouching Tiger, Hidden Dragon* [2000], *Hero* [2002]), reinvigorated espionage fantasies/franchises such as the James Bond, *Bourne* (2002, 2004, 2007, 2012) and *Mission Impossible* films (1996, 2000, 2006), video game adaptations such as *Lara Croft: Tombraider* (2001) and *Resident Evil* (2002, 2004, 2007) and high-style, special-effects-led superhero movies such as *Spider-Man* (2002, 2004, 2007), *X-Men* (2000, 2003, 2006, 2009) and *The Matrix* (1999, 2003, 2003) (see Lichtenfeld 2007).

The immense commercial success of fantasy and adventure scenarios which prominently feature action sequences, most notably *The Lord of the Rings* (2001, 2002, 2003), is indicative of how far Hollywood action has moved from 1980s hard-bodied action, even while its traces are more evident in the spectacular bodies of films like *Troy, Gladiator*

(2000) and *300* (2006), which exploit digital effects to the full. The recent reworkings of the Rocky and Rambo characters are thus framed by a significantly changed generic context in which new forms of spectacle – and new technologies for producing that spectacle – are foregrounded.

In this context, successfully reviving both the Rocky and Rambo characters has involved the management of ideas about ageing. Unlike *Rocky Balboa*, *Rambo* does not explicitly reflect on the star/character's ageing, whether humorously, sentimentally or even tragically; ageing is simply not mentioned. The highly physical scenarios of the 1980s Hollywood action cinema were heavily invested in male strength. While hardly youthful – indeed it was in many ways crucial to the genre in this period to centre on heroes who had lived and struggled, expressed typically by their veteran status – star bodies such as Stallone's required an image of physical fitness to function. Actors and action stars age in ways that lead audiences and media commentators to speculate on the very physicality that brought them celebrity.

Perhaps it is this focus on the body that differentiates Stallone from the late-career roles played by John Wayne or, rather more recently, Clint Eastwood. Physical stature – standing/walking tall – was/has been fundamental for both Wayne and Eastwood as action stars. The shorter Stallone signified strength differently – through muscle – in his signature roles, frequently battling larger opponents (or large numbers of opponents in some instances). Tensions and conflict with the younger mercenaries in *Rambo*, while clearly present, are not conducted on the basis of age. Thus in contrast to Wayne or Eastwood, Stallone's Rambo remains an outsider rather than an old-timer whose experience and knowledge younger men must learn to respect (although the mercenaries do indeed follow Rambo's lead once he takes action). Age, then, is ignored rather than assigned the positive value of experience.

Key to the genre's changing 1990s/2000s aesthetic is its presentation of action as a spectacular special effect which does not require, or at least does not depend so exclusively on, an idea of the action body as an authentic (muscular) site and sign of action. Nonetheless, reviewers and arguably fans take a keen interest in drawing distinctions between performers whose bodies seem to authenticate their character's identities and abilities, and those whose bodies do not. These themes manifest in critical discourse in a range of ways, from praise for actors who perform their own stunts,[4] to a delight in the spectacular inauthenticity evoked by *The Matrix*'s bullet time, to a concern that CGI is used inappropriately or excessively. Lisa Purse explores the latter specifically in relation to 'the very nature of the spectator's engagement with the action body' (2007: 9). She argues convincingly that action movies have modified their use of CGI in 'an implicit acknowledgment of the importance of the pro-filmic body' (2007: 22).

This emphasis on authentic action coupled with constructed/ enhanced bodies framed the release of *Rambo* in quite particular ways. Following the headlines suggesting his use of steroids, Stallone's muscular body was understood as simultaneously a site of labour and a sign of artifice, a tension or contradiction only amplified by ageing. The special effects exploited in the film's gruesome evocation of bodies torn apart, and in the mega-explosion that features in the climactic showdown, further move *Rambo*'s visual style away from the authenticating body as the site of action. The fact that the Stallone of 2008's *Rambo* is significantly bulkier than the Stallone of earlier films is of course highly suggestive, as is the fact that the star keeps his body covered. Coupled with the extraordinary ferocity of the film's violence, the latest *Rambo* seems to revise the terms of Stallone's earlier stardom, in the process tacitly acknowledging the ageing that *Rocky Balboa* takes as its explicit subject.

In *Rambo: First Blood Part II*, Rambo, in Studlar and Desser's words, 'rejects computer-age technology to obliterate truckloads of the enemy with bow and arrow', albeit an enhanced version (1990: 108). That film also sees him wield an M60 – on one arm, an image widely used in the film's promotion. In *Rambo* he relies on bigger guns, improvising an explosion from a bomb left over from World War II (the blast flattens the area) and decimating bodies with a machine gun so enormous it seemingly cannot be lifted.[5] Only at the end of the climactic battle with the soldiers does Rambo return to the knife we have seen him craft, dispatching a sadistic officer with seeming relish.

Effects are also extensively used in *Rambo*'s depiction of bodily disintegration: Rambo throttles and then rips out a man's throat with his bare hands; others are beheaded and blown apart by machine gun fire. Thus the physical integrity of Stallone's star body is set against the instability of his enemies. What is most striking in terms of the previous films is the departure from the formula in the characterisation of the hero. Rambo himself may be reviled and disregarded by both missionaries and mercenaries (at least initially), but he is neither captured nor tortured; the physical suffering endured and responded to with violence in the earlier films is replaced by the violence enacted against the people of Burma and the American missionaries. Interior monologue repositions Rambo's violence not as a response to oppression but as an inherent and natural feature of his character: 'You know who you are, what you're made of, war is in your blood.' These words are spoken over a montage sequence in which Rambo works to forge a weapon, self-consciously preparing for battle (a weapon which evokes the earlier Rambo films: he is seen sharpening the blade of his knife before being dropped into Vietnam in *Rambo: First Blood Part II*, for instance).

A nostalgia for and the loss of a younger self are here compensated for by an amplification of Rambo as killing machine, a trait that is progressively emphasised over the series. He is thus ironically reinscribed as a natural-born rather than a reluctant, government-issue killer, in line with the film's narrative of unsponsored military action. Moreover, the film's closing shots suggest a return to the US and to a family home not mentioned in the preceding three movies. In both *First Blood* and *Rambo III*, Rambo repairs his own wounded arm (with needle and thread rendered in close-up in the former, by cauterising the wound with gun powder – again seen in close-up – in the latter). *Rambo* by contrast has the bulked-up hero viewing the carnage at the film's end, as he stands removed from the scene. Rambo clasps his wounded arm in an echo of the earlier films, yet the emphasis on self-regeneration cannot be visualised in the same way.

Writing elsewhere on the emergence of female action heroes in the Hollywood cinema since the late 1990s, I argue that tropes of physical authenticity and the fantastic are routinely juxtaposed (see Tasker 2006). The presentation of martial arts skills as downloadable and spectacular in *The Matrix* was indicative of the digitally enhanced action that would come to predominate in Hollywood cinema. As Leon Hunt writes, Hollywood performers in films such as *Mission Impossible 2* (2000), *X-Men* (2000) and *Charlie's Angels* (2000) 'came to "know" kung fu through Hong Kong choreographers like Yuen Wo-ping, "wirework" and CGI effects' (2003: 184). For Hunt the question here is the place of martial artists in a cinema of simulation. For my purposes the emphasis falls on a related question of how in contemporary Hollywood cinema the muscular body – no longer plausible as a straightforward sign of authenticity or masculine endeavour – signifies a different relationship to violence, action, power.

Given the extent of his stardom's investment in notions of health and the natural on the one hand, enhancement and excess on the other, the ways in which Stallone responded to the steroid stories in the news media (health and well-being) are particularly telling. The terms and images through which Hollywood action and ageing are discussed and enacted – authenticity; regenerative suffering; the spectacularly constructed, playful action performance – are intensely value-laden. Indeed, the moral discourses of authentic physicality and achievement played out in the context of sports are also central to the kind of action with which Stallone is associated, even as many of the star's films showcase and celebrate an excess very far from the realist: an accelerating excess with respect to the number of antagonists slain in the Rambo films; consistent excess in the ability to endure pain and defeat opponents who are younger, faster and more obviously enhanced. And, as I have suggested in this essay, this seems hyperbolic not only because Stallone's latest Rambo is so much bigger and more deathly – in contrast to the more modest ambition and achievement of his boxing hero in *Rocky Balboa* – but also because Hollywood action genres have shifted in significant ways in the period between the 1980s Rambo and that of the 2000s, and because celebrity culture is so cynical with respect to the natural, so insistent on the constructedness of stars and stardom.

NOTES

1 While HGH is not a steroid, as Stallone insists in his *Time* interview, media coverage surrounding Stallone's use of HGH frequently uses the terms in an interchangeable manner (see Stein 2008).

2 Professional cycling has been the site of persistent scandals about doping in recent years. In terms of the US media, attention has been long focused on seven-times Tour de France winner Lance Armstrong. Armstrong's admission of doping and his use of banned substances via an interview with Oprah Winfrey in January 2013 dramatically underlined not only the extent of such practices in cycling but the intense relationship between sports and celebrity culture. In a piece entitled 'Doctors Slam *Rambo* for Drug Comments', David Templeton (2008) cites medics who compare the place of sports and Hollywood celebrities in terms of their potential influence.

3 One comment on a *Daily Mail* piece on *The Expendables* read, 'love the guy, great that he does his own stunts. Puts men half his age to shame' (Ellwell-Sutton 2009). In a vitriolic piece from the same paper, another reader commented, 'Stallone looks great. I hope I age half as well', and another adds, 'My god he looks amazing for his age' (see Anon. 2009).

4 *Guardian* critic John Patterson is not alone in bemoaning 'airless, suspense-free CGI action sequences obviously rigged up with wires and bluescreen' (2007). For Patterson, action star Jackie Chan exemplifies the authenticating action body; yet the ageing Chan faces challenges of his own. Promotional interviews for Steven Spielberg's *Indiana Jones and the Kingdom of the Crystal Skull* (2008) included an emphasis on 'real' stunts (with the director bemoaning lazy digital effects) alongside a focus on the fitness and performance of 65-year-old star Harrison Ford.

5   Chris Holmlund writes of Clint Eastwood's ageing in movies that 'following trends estab-
     lished by action films ... Clint's big guns get ever bigger as he ages' (2002: 146). Such a
     trend is also apparent in the Rambo series.

BIBLIOGRAPHY

Anon. (2009) 'Rocky Star Stallone Looks Punch Drunk', Daily Mail. Online. Available HTTP:
    http://www.dailymail.co.uk/tvshowbiz/article-453927/Rockystar-Stallone-looks-punch-
    drunk.html (14 July 2010).
Ellwell-Sutton, Chris (2009) 'Sly Stallone Shows Off Ripped Physique and Performs His Own
    Stunts to Prove He's Still an Action Man at 62', Daily Mail, 7 April. Online. Available HTTP:
    http://www.dailymail.co.uk/tvshowbiz/article-1168203/Sly-Stallone-shows-ripped-
    physique-performs-stunts-prove-hes-action-man-62.html. (14 July 2010).
Fairclough, Kirsty (2008) 'Fame Is a Losing Game: Celebrity Gossip Blogging, Bitch Culture,
    and Postfeminism', Genders, 48. Online. Available HTTP: http://www.genders.org/g48/
    g48_fairclough.html.
Heller, Dana (ed.) (2007) Makeover Television: Realities Remodelled. London: IB Tauris.
Heywood, Leslie and Shari L. Dworkin (2003) Built to Win: The Female Athlete as Cultural Icon.
    Minneapolis: University of Minnesota Press.
Holmes, Su and Sean Redmond (eds) (2006) Framing Celebrity: New Directions in Celebrity
    Culture. London: Routledge.
Holmlund, Chris (2002) Impossible Bodies: Femininity and Masculinity at the Movies. New York:
    Routledge.
Hunt, Leon (2003) Kung Fu Cult Masters: From Bruce Lee to Crouching Tiger. London: Wallflower
    Press.
Hyde, Marina (2007) 'Rocky Joins Cast of Fallen Sporting Heroes', Guardian, 22 February.
Jeffords, Susan (1994) Hard Bodies: Hollywood Masculinity in the Reagan Era. New Brunswick:
    Rutgers University Press.
Lichtenfeld, Eric (2007 [2004]) Action Speaks Louder: Violence, Spectacle, and the American
    Action Movie. Second edition. Middletown, CT: Wesleyan University Press.
Miah, Andy (2004) Genetically Modified Athletes: Biomedical Ethics, Gene Doping, and Sport.
    London: Routledge.
Negra, Diane (2001) Off-White Hollywood: American Culture and Ethnic Female Stardom. New
    York: Routledge.
____ (2002) 'Ethnic Food Fetishism, Whiteness, and Nostalgia in Recent Film and Television',
    Velvet Light Trap, 50, 62–76.
Patterson, John (2007) 'If only ... we had a way of keeping middle-aged action heroes off
    the screen', Guardian, 30 June. Online. Available HTTP: http://www.theguardian.com/
    film/2007/jun/30/culture.news.
Purse, Lisa (2007) 'Digital Heroes in Contemporary Hollywood: Exertion, Identification, and the
    Virtual Action Body', Film Criticism, 32.1, 5–25.
Stallone, Sylvester (2005) Sly Moves: My Proven Program to Lose Weight, Build Strength, Gain
    Will Power, and Live Your Dream. New York: Harper Collins.
Stein, Joel (2008) 'Stallone on a Mission', Time, 24 January. Online. Available to subscribers
    HTTP://http://content.time.com/time/magazine/article/0,9171,1706759,00.html.
Studlar, Gaylyn and David Desser (1990) 'Never Having to Say You're Sorry: Rambo's Rewriting
    the Vietnam War', in Linda Dittmar and Gene Michaud (eds) From Hanoi to Hollywood:
    The Vietnam War in American Film. New Brunswick and London: Rutgers University Press,

101–12.

Tasker, Yvonne (2006) 'Fantasizing Gender and Race: Women in Contemporary US Action Cinema', in Linda Ruth Williams and Michael Hammond (eds) *Contemporary American Cinema*. London: McGraw Hill, 410–28.

Templeton, David (2008) 'Doctors Slam Rambo for Drug Comments', *Pittsburgh Post-Gazette*, 31 January. Online. Available HTTP: http://www.postgazette.com/pg/08031/853623-114.stm. (14 July 2010).

Wearing, Sadie (2007) 'Subjects of Rejuvenation: Ageing in Postfeminist Culture', in Yvonne Tasker and Diane Negra (eds) *Interrogating Postfeminism: Gender and the Politics of Popular Culture*. Durham: Duke University Press, 277–310.

Weber, Brenda R. (2009) *Makeover TV: Selfhood, Citizenship, and Celebrity*. Durham: Duke University Press.

FILMOGRAPHY
SYLVESTER STALLONE
(minor and uncredited film roles not included)

The Party at Kitty and Stud's (1970)

Director: Morton Lewis
Production: Milton Lewis for Stallion Releasing Inc.
Writer: Milton Lewis
Cinematography: Rolph Laube
Editing: Ron Kalish, Ralph Rosenblum
Production Design: Martin Stewart
Music: Kay Leodel
Cast: Sylvester Stallone (Stud), Henrietta Holm (Kitty), Jodi Van Prang (Jodi), Nicholas Warren (Nick), Frank Micelli (Frank), Barbara Strom (Barb)
Running Time: 71 min.

No Place to Hide (1970)

Director: Robert Allen Schnitzer
Production: David Appleton and Robert Allen Schnitzer for Galaxy Films
Writers: Larry Beinhart, Louis Pastore (additional dialogue), Robert Allen Schnitzer
Cinematography: Marty Knopf
Editing: LaReine Johnston
Music: Joseph Delacorte
Sound: Bill Meredith and others
Cast: Sylvester Stallone (Jerry Savage), Tony Page (Tommy Trafler), Rebecca Grimes (Laurie Fisher), Vickie Lancaster (Estelle Ferguson), Dennis Tate (Ray Brown), Barbara Lee Govan (Marlena St. James), Roy White (William Decker), Henry G. Sanders (James Henderson), Jed Mills (Chuck Bradley), David Orange (Richard Scott), Joe Kottler (Warehouse Attendant), Linda Adana (Dance Teacher), Laura Giammarco (Dance

Student), Lillian Baley (Dance Student), Susan Glassman (Dance Student)
Running Time: 80 min.

The Lord's of Flatbush (1974)

Director: Martin Davidson, Stephen Verona
Production: Stephen Verona for Ebbets Field
Writers: Stephen Verona, Gayle Gleckler, Martin Davidson, Sylvester Stallone (additional dialogue)
Cinematography: Edward Lachman, Joseph Mangine
Editing: Muffie Meyer, Stan Siegel
Art Direction: Glenda Ganis
Music: Joseph Brooks
Sound: Vincent Deleo (sound recordist), Nigel Nobel (sound recordist) and others
Cast: Perry King (David 'Chico' Tyrell), Sylvester Stallone (Stanley Rosiello), Henry Winkler (Butchey Weinstein), Paul Mace (Wimpy Murgalo), Susan Blakely (Jane Bradshaw), Maria Smith (Frannie Mallincanico), Renee Paris (Annie Yuckamanelli), Paul Jabara (Crazy Cohen), Bruce Reed (Mike Mambo), Frank Stiefel (Arnie Levine), Martin Davidson (Mr. Birnbaum), Joe Stern (Eddie), Ruth Klinger (Mrs. Tyrell), Joan Neuman (Miss Molina), Dolph Sweet (Mr. Rosiello)
Running Time: 86 min.

Capone (1975)

Director: Steve Carver
Production: Roger Corman for Santa Fe Productions
Writer: Howard Browne

Cinematography: Villis Lapenieks
Editing: Richard C. Meyer
Art Direction: Ward Preston
Sound: Robert Gravenor (sound mixer) and others
Cast: Ben Gazzara (Al Capone), Harry Guardino (Johnny Torrio), Susan Blakely (Iris Crawford), Sylvester Stallone (Frank Nitti), John Cassavetes (Frankie Yale), Frank Campanella (Big Jim Colosimo), John Orchard (Dion O'Banion), Carmen Argenziano (Jack McGurn), George Chandler (Robert E. Crowe), John Davis Chandler (Hymie Weiss), Royal Dano (Anton J. Cermak), Joe De Nicola (Charles Fischetti), Angelo Grisanti (Angelo Genna), Peter Maloney (Jake Guzik), Dick Miller (Joe Pryor)
Running Time: 101 min.

Death Race 2000 (1975)

Director: Paul Bartel
Production: Roger Corman for New World Pictures and Columbia Associates
Writers: Robert Thom (screenplay), Charles B. Griffith (screenplay), Ib Melchior (story)
Cinematography: Tak Fujimoto
Editing: Tina Hirsch
Art Direction: Beala Neel, Robin Royce
Sound: Lee Alexander (sound mixer) and others
Cast: David Carradine (Frankenstein), Simone Griffeth (Annie Smith), Sylvester Stallone (Machine Gun Joe Viterbo), Mary Woronov (Calamity Jane), Roberta Collins (Matilda the Hun), Martin Kove (Nero the Hero), Louisa Moritz (Myra), Don Steele (Junior Bruce), Joyce Jameson (Grace Pander), Carle Bensen (Harold), Sandy McCallum (Mr. President), Paul L. Ehrmann (Special Agent), Harriet Medin (Thomasina Paine), Vince Trankina (Lt. Fury), Bill Morey (Deacon)
Running Time: 80 min.

Farewell, My Lovely (1975)

Director: Dick Richards
Production: Jerry Bruckheimer, George Pappas for EK and ITC Entertainment
Writers: David Zelag Goodman (screenplay), Raymond Chandler (novel)
Cinematography: John A. Alonzo
Editing: Joel Cox, Walter Thompson
Production Design: Dean Tavoularis

Music: David Shire
Sound: Tom Overton (sound mixer) and others
Cast: Robert Mitchum (Phillip Marlowe), Charlotte Rampling (Helen Grayle), John Ireland (Det. Lt. Nulty), Sylvia Miles (Jessie Halstead Florian), Anthony Zerbe (Laird Brunette), Harry Dean Stanton (Det. Billy Rolfe), Jack O'Halloran (Moose Malloy), Joe Spinell (Nick), Sylvester Stallone (Jonnie), Kate Murtagh (Frances Amthor), John O'Leary (Lindsay Marriott), Walter McGinn (Tommy Ray), Burton Gilliam (Cowboy), Jim Thompson (Judge Baxter Wilson Grayle), Jimmy Archer (Georgie)
Running Time: 95 min.

Rocky (1976)

Director: John G. Avildsen
Production: Robert Chartoff, Irwin Winkler for Chartoff-Winkler Productions and United Artists
Writer: Sylvester Stallone
Cinematography: James Crabe
Editing: Scott Conrad, Richard Halsey
Production Design: William J. Cassidy
Art Direction: James H. Spencer
Music: Bill Conti
Sound: Harry W. Tetrick (sound), Gene Ashbrook (sound mixer) and others
Cast: Sylvester Stallone (Rocky Balboa), Talia Shire (Adrian Pennino), Burt Young (Paulie Pennino), Carl Weathers (Apollo Creed), Burgess Meredith (Mickey Goldmill), Thayer David (George Jergens), Joe Spinell (Tony Gazzo), Jimmy Gambina (Mike), Bill Baldwin (Fight Announcer), Al Silvani (Cut Man), George Memmoli (Ice Rink Attendant), Jodi Letizia (Marie), Diana Lewis (TV Commentator), George O'Hanlon (TV Commentator), Larry Carroll (TV Interviewer)
Running Time: 119 min.

F.I.S.T. (1978)

Director: Norman Jewison
Production: Norman Jewison for Chateau Productions
Writers: Joe Eszterhas (story), Sylvester Stallone (screenplay), Joe Eszterhas (screenplay)
Cinematography: László Kovács
Editing: Graeme Clifford
Production Design: Richard Macdonald
Art Direction: Angelo P. Graham

Music: Bill Conti
Sound: Charles M. Wilborn (sound mixer) and others
Cast: Sylvester Stallone (Johnny Kovak), Rod Steiger (Senator Madison), Peter Boyle (Max Graham), Melinda Dillon (Anna Zarinkas), David Huffman (Abe Belkin), Kevin Conway (Vince Doyle), Tony Lo Bianco (Babe Milano), Cassie Yates (Molly), Peter Donat (Arthur St. Clair), John Lehne (Mr. Gant), Henry Wilcoxon (Win Talbot), Richard Herd (Mike Monahan), Tony Mockus Jr. (Tom Higgins), Ken Kercheval (Bernie Marr), Elena Karam (Mrs. Zerinkas)
Running Time: 145 min.

Paradise Alley (1978)

Director: Sylvester Stallone
Production: John F. Roach, Ronald A. Suppa, Jeff Wald for Image Ten
Writer: Sylvester Stallone
Cinematography: László Kovács
Editing: Eve Newman
Production Design: John W. Corso
Art Direction: Deborah Beaudet
Music: Bill Conti
Sound: Charles M. Wilborn and others
Cast: Sylvester Stallone (Cosmo Carboni), Lee Canalito (Victor Carboni), Armand Assante (Lenny Carboni), Frank McRae (Big Glory), Anne Archer (Annie), Kevin Conway (Stitch), Terry Funk (Frankie the Thumper), Joyce Ingalls (Bunchie), Joe Spinell (Burp), Aimée Eccles (Susan Chow), Tom Waits (Mumbles), Chick Casey (Doorman), James J. Casino (Paradise Bartender), Fredi O. Gordon (Paradise Alley Hooker), Lydia Goya (Bar Room Hooker #1)
Running Time: 107 min.

Rocky II (1979)

Director: Sylvester Stallone
Production: Robert Chartoff, Irwin Winkler for Chartoff-Winkler Productions
Writer: Sylvester Stallone
Cinematography: Bill Butler
Editing: Stanford C. Allen, Janice Hampton
Art Direction: Richard Berger
Music: Bill Conti
Sound: Charles M. Wilborn (sound mixer) and others

Cast: Sylvester Stallone (Rocky Balboa), Talia Shire (Adrian), Burt Young (Paulie), Carl Weathers (Apollo Creed), Burgess Meredith (Mickey Goldmill), Tony Burton (Duke), Joe Spinell (Tony Gazzo), Leonard Gaines (Agent), Sylvia Meals (Mary Anne Creed), Frank McRae (Meat Foreman), Al Silvani (Cutter), John Pleshette (Director), Stu Nahan (Announcer), Bill Baldwin (Commentator), Jerry Ziesmer (Salesman)
Running Time: 119 min.

Nighthawks (1981)

Director: Bruce Malmuth, Gary Nelson
Production: Herb Nanas, Martin Poll for Universal Pictures, Herb Nanas Productions, Layton Productions, Martin Poll Productions and The Production Company
Writers: David Shaber (screenplay), David Shaber (story), Paul Sylbert (story)
Cinematography: James A. Contner
Editing: Stanford C. Allen, Christopher Holmes
Production Design: Peter S. Larkin
Music: Keith Emerson
Sound: Les Lazarowitz (sound mixer) and others
Cast: Sylvester Stallone (Deke DaSilva), Billy Dee Williams (Sgt. Matthew Fox), Lindsay Wagner (Irene), Persis Khambatta (Shakka Holland), Nigel Davenport (Peter Hartman), Rutger Hauer (Heymar 'Wulfgar' Reinhardt), Hilary Thompson (Pam), Joe Spinell (Lt. Munafo), Walter Mathews (Commissioner), E. Brian Dean (Sergeant), Caesar Cordova (Puerto Rican Proprietor), Charles Duval (Dr. Ghiselin), Tony Munafo (Big Mike), Howard Stein (Disco Manager), Tawn Christian (Disco Hostess)
Running Time: 99 min.

Victory (Escape to Victory, UK title) (1981)

Director: John Huston
Production: Freddie Fields for Lorimar Film Entertainment and Victory Company
Writers: Yabo Yablonsky (story), Djordje Milicevic (story), Jeff Maguire (story), Evan Jones (screenplay), Yabo Yablonsky (screenplay)
Cinematography: Gerry Fisher
Editing: Roberto Silvi
Production Design: J. Dennis Washington

Music: Bill Conti
Sound: Colin Charles (sound mixer), Leslie
Hodgson (supervising sound editor) and others
Cast: Sylvester Stallone (Captain Robert Hatch),
Michael Caine (Capt. John Colby), Pelé (Cpl. Luis
Fernandez), Bobby Moore (Terry Brady), Osvaldo
Ardiles (Carlos Rey), Paul Van Himst (Michel
Fileu), Kazimierz Deyna (Paul Wolchek), Hallvar
Thoresen (Gunnar Hilsson), Mike Summerbee
(Sid Harmor), Co Prins (Pieter Van Beck), Russell
Osman (Doug Clure), John Wark (Arthur Hayes),
Søren Lindsted (Erik Ball), Kevin O'Callaghan
(Tony Lewis), Max Von Sydow (Major Karl Von
Steiner)
Running Time: 116 min.

Rocky III (1982)

Director: Sylvester Stallone
Production: Robert Chartoff, Irwin Winkler for
United Artists
Writer: Sylvester Stallone
Cinematography: Bill Butler
Editing: Mark Warner, Don Zimmerman
Production Design: William J. Cassidy
Art Direction: Ron Foreman, J. Dennis
Washington
Music: Bill Conti
Sound: Frank E. Warner (supervising sound
editor), Charles M. Wilborn (sound mixer) and
others
Cast: Sylvester Stallone (Rocky Balboa),
Talia Shire (Adrian), Burt Young (Paulie), Carl
Weathers (Apollo Creed), Burgess Meredith
(Mickey Goldmill), Tony Burton (Duke), Mr. T
(Clubber Lang), Hulk Hogan (Thunderlips), Ian
Fried (Rocky Jr.), Al Silvani (Al), Wally Taylor
(Clubber's Manager), Jim Hill (Sportscaster),
Don Sherman (Andy), Dennis James (Wrestling
Commentator), Jim Healy (Wrestling
Commentator)
Running Time: 99 min.

First Blood (1982)

Director: Ted Kotcheff
Production: Buzz Feitshans for Anabasis N.V.
and Elcajo Productions
Writers: David Morrell (novel), Michael Kozoll
(writer), William Sackheim (writer), Sylvester
Stallone (writer)

Cinematography: Andrew Laszlo
Editing: Joan E. Chapman
Production Design: Wolf Kroeger
Music: Jerry Goldsmith
Sound: Fred J. Brown (supervising sound
editor), Rob Young (sound mixer) and others
Cast: Sylvester Stallone (Rambo), Richard
Crenna (Trautman), Brian Dennehy (Teasle), Bill
McKinney (Kern), Jack Starrett (Galt), Michael
Talbott (Balford), Chris Mulkey (Ward), John
McLiam (Orval), Alf Humphreys (Lester), David
Caruso (Mitch), David L. Crowley (Shingleton),
Don MacKay (Preston), Charles A. Tamburro
(Pilot), David Petersen (Trooper), Craig Huston
(Radio Operator)
Running Time: 93 min.

Staying Alive (1983)

Director: Sylvester Stallone
Production: Sylvester Stallone, Robert Stigwood
for Paramount Pictures and Cinema Group
Ventures
Writers: Nik Cohn (characters), Sylvester
Stallone (written by), Norman Wexler (written
by)
Cinematography: Nick McLean
Editing: Peter E. Berger, Mark Warner, Don
Zimmerman
Production Design: Robert F. Boyle
Art Direction: Norman Newberry
Sound: Don Hall (supervising sound editor) and
others
Cast: John Travolta (Tony Manero), Cynthia
Rhodes (Jackie), Finola Hughes (Laura), Steve
Inwood (Jesse), Julie Bovasso (Mrs. Manero),
Charles Ward (Butler), Steve Bickford (Sound
Technician), Patrick Brady (Derelict), Norma
Donaldson (Fatima), Jesse Doran (Mark), Joyce
Hyser (Linda), Deborah Jenssen (Margaret),
Robert Martini (Fred), Sarah M. Miles (Joy)
Running Time: 93 min.

Rhinestone (1984)

Director: Bob Clark
Production: Howard Smith, Marvin Worth for
Twentieth Century Fox Film Corporation
Writers: Phil Alden Robinson (story), Sylvester
Stallone (screenplay), Phil Alden Robinson
(screenplay)

Cinematography: Timothy Galfas
Editing: Stan Cole, John W. Wheeler
Production Design: Robert F. Boyle
Art Direction: Frank Richwood
Music: Dolly Parton
Sound: Michael Evje (sound mixer) and others
Cast: Sylvester Stallone (Nick), Dolly Parton (Jake), Richard Farnsworth (Noah), Ron Leibman (Freddie), Tim Thomerson (Barnett), Steve Peck (Father), Penny Santon (Mother), Russell Buchanan (Elgart), Ritch Brinkley (Luke), Jerry Potter (Wait), Jesse Welles (Billie Joe), Phil Rubenstein (Maurie), Thomas Ikeda (Japanese Father), Christal Kim (Japanese Grandmother), Arline Miyazaki (Japanese Mother)
Running Time: 111 min.

Rambo: First Blood Part II (1985)

Director: George P. Cosmatos
Production: Buzz Feitshans for Anabasis N.V.
Writers: David Morrell (characters), Kevin Jarre (story), Sylvester Stallone (screenplay), James Cameron (screenplay)
Cinematography: Jack Cardiff
Editing: Larry Bock, Mark Goldblatt, Mark Helfrich, Gib Jaffe, Frank E. Jimenez
Production Design: Bill Kenney
Sound: Fred J. Brown (supervising sound editor), Rob Young (sound mixer) and others
Cast: Sylvester Stallone (Rambo), Richard Crenna (Col. Samuel Trautman), Charles Napier (Marshall Murdock), Steven Berkoff (Lt. Col. Podovsky), Julia Nickson (Co), Martin Kove (Ericson), George Cheung (Tay), Andy Wood (Banks), William Ghent (Captain Vinh), Voyo Goric (Sergeant Yushin), Dana Lee (Captain Kinh), Baoan Coleman (Gunboat Captain), Steve Williams (Lifer), Don Collins (P.O.W. #1), Christopher Grant (P.O.W. #2)
Running Time: 86 min.

Rocky IV (1985)

Director: Sylvester Stallone
Production: Robert Chartoff, Irwin Winkler for United Artists and Metro-Goldwyn-Mayer (MGM)
Writer: Sylvester Stallone
Cinematography: Bill Butler
Editing: John W. Wheeler, Don Zimmerman
Production Design: Bill Kenney

Art Direction: William Ladd Skinner
Music: Vince DiCola
Sound: Frank E. Warner (supervising sound editor), Charles M. Wilborn (sound mixer) and others
Cast: Sylvester Stallone (Rocky Balboa), Talia Shire (Adrian), Burt Young (Paulie), Carl Weathers (Apollo Creed), Brigitte Nielsen (Ludmilla), Tony Burton (Duke), Michael Pataki (Nicoli Koloff), Dolph Lundgren (Drago), Stu Nahan (Commentator #1), R. J. Adams (Sports Announcer), Al Bandiero (American Commentator #2), Dominic Barto (Russian Government Official, Rocky Krakoff (Rocky Jr.), Danial Brown (Rocky Jr.'s Friend), James Brown (The Godfather of Soul), Rose Mary Campos (Maid)
Running Time: 91 min.

Cobra (1986)

Director: George P. Cosmatos
Production: Yoram Globus, Menahem Golan for Cannon Group, Golan-Globus Productions and Warner Bros.
Writers: Paula Gosling (novel), Sylvester Stallone (screenplay)
Cinematography: Ric Waite
Editing: James R. Symons, Don Zimmerman
Production Design: Bill Kenney
Art Direction: Robert Gould
Music: Sylvester Levay
Sound: Fred J. Brown (supervising sound editor), Michael Evje (sound mixer) and others
Cast: Sylvester Stallone (Lieutenant Marion 'Cobra' Cobretti), Brigitte Nielsen (Ingrid), Reni Santoni (Sergeant Gonzales), Andrew Robinson (Detective Monte), Brian Thompson (Night Slasher), John Herzfeld (Cho), Lee Garlington (Nancy Stalk), Art LaFleur (Captain Sears), Marco Rodriguez (Supermarket Killer), Ross St. Phillip (Security Guard), Val Avery (Chief Halliwell), David Rasche (Dan), John Hauk (Low Rider), Nick Angotti (Prodski), Nina Axelrod (Waitress)
Running Time: 87 min.

Over the Top (1987)

Director: Menahem Golan
Production: Yoram Globus, Menahem Golan for Cannon Group, Golan-Globus Productions and

Warner Bros.

Writers: Gary Conway (story), David Engelbach (story), Stirling Silliphant (screenplay), Sylvester Stallone (screenplay)
Cinematography: David Gurfinkel
Editing: James R. Symons, Don Zimmerman
Production Design: James L. Schoppe
Art Direction: William Ladd Skinner
Music: Giorgio Moroder
Sound: Frank E. Warner (supervising sound editor), Charles M. Wilborn (sound mixer) and others
Cast: Sylvester Stallone (Lincoln Hawk), Robert Loggia (Jason Cutler), Susan Blakely (Christina Hawk), Rick Zumwalt (Bob 'Bull' Hurley), David Mendenhall (Michael Cutler), Chris McCarty (Tim Salanger), Terry Funk (Ruker), Bob Beattie (Announcer), Allan Graf (Collins), Magic Schwarz (Smasher), Bruce Way (Grizzly), Jimmy Keagan (Big Boy-Richie), John Braden (Colonel Davis), Tony Munafo (Tony), Randy Raney (Mad Dog Madison)
Running Time: 93 min.

Rambo III (1988)

Director: Peter MacDonald
Production: Buzz Feitshans for Carolco Pictures
Writers: David Morell (characters), Sylvester Stallone (written by), Sheldon Lettich (written by)
Cinematography: John Stanier
Editing: O. Nicholas Brown, Andrew London, James R. Symons, Edward Warschilka
Production Design: Bill Kenney
Music: Jerry Goldsmith
Sound: Fred J. Brown (supervising sound editor), Eli Yarkoni (sound mixer) and others
Cast: Sylvester Stallone (Rambo), Richard Crenna (Col. Samuel Trautman), Marc de Jonge (Colonel Zaysen), Kurtwood Smith (Griggs), Spiros Focás (Masoud), Sasson Gabai (Mousa), Doudi Shoua (Hamid), Randy Raney (Kourov), Marcus Gilbert (Tomask), Alon Aboutboul (Niseem), Mahmoud Assadollahi (Rahim), Joseph Shiloach (Khalid), Harold Diamond (Stick Fighter), Matti Seri (Gun Dealer), Hany Said El Deen (Gun Dealer)
Running Time: 102 min.

Lock Up (1989)

Director: John Flynn
Production: Charles Gordon, Lawrence Gordon for White Eagle, Carolco Pictures and Gordon Company
Writers: Richard Smith (written by), Jeb Stuart (written by), Henry Rosenbaum (written by)
Cinematography: Donald E. Thorin
Editing: Don Brochu, Robert A. Ferretti, Michael N. Knue, Barry B. Leirer
Production Design: Bill Kenney
Art Direction: Bill Groom (New York), William Ladd Skinner (Los Angeles)
Music: Bill Conti
Sound: Davd B. Cohn (supervising sound editor) and others
Cast: Sylvester Stallone (Frank Leone), Donald Sutherland (Warden Drumgoole), John Amos (Captain Miessner), Sonny Landham (Chink Weber), Tom Sizemore (Dallas), Frank McRae (Eclipse), Darlanne Fluegel (Melissa), William Allen Young (Braden), Larry Romano (First Base), Jordan Lund (Manly), John Lilla (Wiley), Dean Rader-Duval (Ernie), Jerry Strivelli (Louie Munafo), David Anthny Marshall (Mastrone), Kurek Ashley (Chink's Gang Member)
Running Time: 109 min.

Tango & Cash (1989)

Director: Andrei Konchalovskiy, Albert Magnoli
Production: Peter Guber, Jon Peters for Warner Bros. and The Guber-Peters Company
Writer: Randy Feldman
Cinematography: Donald E. Thorin
Editing: Hubert de La Bouillerie, Robert A. Ferretti
Production Design: J. Michael Riva
Art Direction: Richard Berger, David F. Klassen
Music: Harold Faltermeyer
Sound: Robert R. Rutledge (supervising sound editor), Charles M. Wilborn (sound mixer) and others
Cast: Sylvester Stallone (Lt. Raymond Tango), Kurt Russell (Lt. Gabriel Cash), Teri Hatcher (Katherine 'Kiki' Tango), Jack Palance (Yves Perret), Brion James (Requin), James Hong (Quan), Marc Alaimo (Lopez), Philip Tan (Chinese Gunman), Michael J. Pollard (Owen), Robert Z'Dar (Face), Lewis Arquette (Wyler), Edward

Bunker (Capt. Holmes), Leslie Morris (Hendricks), Roy Brocksmith (Fed. Agent Davis), Susan Krebs (Prosecutor)
Running Time: 104 min.

Rocky V (1990)
Director: John G. Avildsen
Production: Robert Chartoff, Irwin Winkler for Star Partners III Ltd., United Artists
Writer: Sylvester Stallone
Cinematography: Steven Poster
Editing: John G. Avildsen, Robert A. Ferretti, Michael N. Knue
Production Design: William J. Cassidy
Art Direction: William J. Durrell Jr.
Music: Bill Conti
Sound: David B. Cohn (supervising sound editor) and others
Cast: Sylvester Stallone (Rocky Balboa), Talia Shire (Adrian), Burt Young (Paulie), Sage Stallone (Rocky Balboa Jr.), Burgess Meredith (Mickey Goldmill), Tommy Morrison (Tommy 'Machine' Gunn), Richard Gant (George Washington Duke), Tony Burton (Duke), Jimmy Gambina (Jimmy), Delia Sheppard (Karen), Mike Girard Sheehan (Merlin Sheets), Michael Anthony Williams (Union Cane), Kevin Connolly (Chickie), Hayes Swope (Chickie's Pal)
Running Time: 104 min.

Oscar (1991)
Director: John Landis
Production: Leslie Belzberg for Silver Screen Partners IV and Touchstone Pictures
Writers: Claude Magnier (play), Michael Barrie (screenplay), Jim Mullholland (screenplay)
Cinematography: Mac Ahlberg
Editing: Dale Beldin
Production Design: Bill Kenney
Art Direction: William Ladd Skinner
Music: Elmer Bernstein
Sound: Richard C. Franklin (supervising sound editor), William B. Kaplan (sound mixer) and others
Cast: Sylvester Stallone (Angelo 'Snaps' Provolone), Ornella Muti (Sofia Provolone), Don Ameche (Father Clemente), Peter Riegert (Aldo), Tim Curry (Dr. Thornton Poole), Vincent Spano (Anthony Rossano), Marisa Tomei (Lisa

Provolone), Eddie Bracken (Five Spot Charlie), Linda Gray (Roxanne), Chazz Palminteri (Connie), Kurtwood Smith (Lt. Tommey), Yvonne De Carlo (Aunt Rosa), Ken Howard (Kirkwood), William Atheton (Overton), Martin Ferrero (Luigi Finucci), Harry Shearer (Guido Finucci)
Running Time: 109 min.

Stop! Or My Mom Will Shoot (1992)
Director: Roger Spottiswoode
Production: Michael C. Gross, Joe Medjuck, Ivan Reitman for Northern Lights Entertainment and Universal Pictures
Writers: Blake Snyder, William Osborne
Cinematography: Frank Tidy
Editing: Mark Conte, Lois Freeman-Fox
Production Design: Charles Rosen
Art Direction: Diane Yates
Music: Alan Silvestri
Sound: Lon Bender (supervising sound editor) and others
Cast: Sylvester Stallone (Sgt. Joe Bomowski), Estelle Getty (Tutti Bomowski), JoBeth Williams (Lt. Gwen Harper), Roger Rees (Parnell), Martin Ferrero (Paulie), Gailard Sartain (Munroe), John Wesley (Tony), Al Fann (Lou), Ella Joyce (McCabe), J. Kenneth Campbell (Det. Ross), Nicholas Sadler (Suicide), Dennis Burkley (Mitchell), Ving Rhames (Mr. Stereo), Jana Arnold (Mitchell's Girl), Chris Latta (Gang Member)
Running Time: 87 min.

Cliffhanger (1993)
Director: Renny Harlin
Production: Renny Harlin, Alan Marshall for Carolco Pictures, Canal+, Pioneer, RCS Video and Cliffhanger Productions
Writers: John Long (premise), Michael France (screen story), Michael France (screenplay), Sylvester Stallone (screenplay)
Cinematography: Alex Thomson
Editing: Frank J. Urioste
Production Design: John Vallone
Art Direction: Maria-Teresa Barbasso, Aurelio Crugnola, Christiaan Wagener
Music: Trevor Jones
Sound: Gregg Baxter (sound designer/sound supervisor) and others

Cast: Sylvester Stallone (Gabe Walker), John Lithgow (Eric Qualen), Michael Rooker (Hal Tucker), Janine Turner (Jessie Deighan), Rex Linn (Richard Travers), Caroline Goodall (Kristel), Leon (Kynette), Craig Fairbrass (Delmar), Gregory Scott Cummins (Ryan), Denis Forest (Heldon), Michelle Joyner (Sarah), Max Perlich (Evan), Paul Winfield (Walter Wright), Ralph Waite (Frank), Trey Brownell (Brett)
Running Time: 112 min.

Demolition Man (1993)

Director: Marco Brambilla
Production: Howard G. Kaznjian, Michael Levy, Joel Silver for Warner Bros. and Silver Pictures
Writers: Peter M. Lenkov (story), Robert Reneau (story), Daniel Waters (screenplay), Robert Reneau (screenplay), Peter M. Lenkov (screenplay)
Cinematography: Alex Thomson
Editing: Stuart Baird
Production Design: David L. Snyder
Art Direction: Walter P. Martishius
Music: Elliot Goldenthal
Sound: Tim Cooney (sound mixer), Michael Geisler (sound designer), William Griggs (sound designer), Robert G. Henderson (supervising sound editor), Kevin Spears (sound designer) and others
Cast: Sylvester Stallone (John Spartan), Wesley Snipes (Simon Phoenix), Sandra Bullock (Lenina Huxley), Nigel Hawthorne (Dr. Raymond Cocteau), Benjamin Bratt (Alfredo Garcia), Bob Gunton (Chief George Earle), Glenn Shadix (Associate Bob), Denis Leary (Edgar Friendly), Grand L. Bush (Zachary Lamb – Young), Pat Skipper (Helicopter Pilot), Steve Kahan (Captain Healy), Paul Bollen (T.F.R. Officer), Mark Colson (Warden William Smithers – Young), Andre Gregoy (Warden William Smithers – Aged), John Enos III (Prisoner)
Running Time: 115 min.

The Specialist (1994)

Director: Luis Llosa
Production: Jerry Weintraub for Warner Bros., Jerry Weintraub Productions, Iguana Producciones
Writers: John Shirley (novels), Alexandra Seros
Cinematography: Jeffrey L. Kimball

Editing: Jack Hofstra
Production Design: Walter P. Martishius
Art Direction: Alan E. Muraoka
Music: John Barry
Sound: Mark P. Stoeckinger (supervising sound editor) and others
Cast: Sylvester Stallone (Ray Quick), Sharon Stone (May Munro), James Woods (Ned Trent), Rod Steiger (Joe Leon), Eric Roberts (Tomas Leon), Mario Ernesto Sánchez (Charlie), Sergio Doré Jr. (Strongarm), Chase Randolph (Stan Munro), Jeana Bell (Alice Munro), Brittany Paige Bouck (Young May), Emilio Estefan Jr. (Piano Player), LaGaylia Frazier (Singer #1), Ramón González Cuevas (Priest at Cemetery), Tony Munafo (Tony), Cheito Quinonez (Singer at Party)
Running Time: 110 min.

Judge Dredd (1995)

Director: Danny Cannon
Production: Charles Lippincott, Beau Marks for Hollywood Pictures and Cinergi Pictures Entertainment
Writers: John Wagner (characters), Carlos Ezquerra (characters), Michael De Luca (story), William Wisher Jr. (story), William Wisher Jr. (screenplay), Steven E. de Souza (screenplay)
Cinematography: Adrian Biddle
Editing: Harry Keramidas, Alex Mackie
Production Design: Nigel Phelps
Art Direction: Don Dossett
Music: Alan Silvestri
Sound: Leslie Shatz (sound designer/sound re-recording sound mixer); Chris Munro (sound mixer) and others
Cast: Sylvester Stallone (Judge Joseph Dredd), Armand Assante (Rico), Rob Schneider (Herman 'Fergee' Ferguson, Jürgen Prochnow (Judge Griffin), Max von Sydow (Chief Justice Fargo), Diane Lane (Judge Hershey), Joanna Miles (Judge Evelyn McGruder), Joan Chen (Dr. Ilsa Hayden), Balthazar Getty (Cadet Nathan Olmeyer), Maurice Roëves (Warden Miller), Ian Dury (Geiger), Christopher Adamson (Mean Machine), Ewen Bremner (Junior Angel), Peter Marinker (Judge Carlos Esplosito), Angus MacInnes (Judge Gerald Silver)
Running Time: 96 min.

Assassins (1995)

Director: Richard Donner
Production: Richard Donner, Bruce A. Evans, Raynold Gideon, Andrew Lazar, Joel Silver, Jim Van Wyck for Canal+, Donner/Shuler-Donner Productions, Evansgideon/Lazar, Silver Pictures and Warner Bros.
Writers: Andy Wachowski (story), Lana Wachowski (story), Andy Wachowski (screenplay), Lana Wachowski (screenplay), Brian Helgeland (screenplay)
Cinematography: Vilmos Zsigmond
Editing: Lawrence Jordan, Richard Marks
Production Design: Thomas E. Sanders
Art Direction: Daniel T. Dorrance (supervising art director), Steve Arnold, Nathan Crowley, Leticia Stella
Sound: Robert G. Henderson (supervising sound editor) and others
Cast: Sylvester Stallone (Robert Rath), Antonio Banderas (Miguel Bain), Julianne Moore (Electra), Anatoli Davydov (Nicolai Tashlinkov), Muse Watson (Ketcham), Steve Kahan (Alan Branch), Kelly Rowan (Jennifer), Reed Diamond (Bob), Kai Wulff (Remy), Kierry Skalsky (Buyer with Remy), James Douglas Haskins (Buyer with Remy), Stephen Liska (Cop), John Harms (Cop), Edward J. Rosen (Cemetery Caretaker), Christina Orchid (Dowager)
Running Time: 132 min.

Daylight (1996)

Director: Rob Cohen
Production: John Davis, David T. Friendly, Joseph Singer for Davis Entertainment and Universal Pictures
Writer: Leslie Bohem
Cinematography: David Eggby
Editing: Peter Amundson
Production Design: Benjamín Fernández
Art Direction: Pier Luigi Basile (supervising art director), Marco Trentini (supervising art director), Maria-Teresa Barbasso, Mark Zuelzke
Music: Randy Edelman
Sound: Richard L. Anderson (supervising sound editor) and others
Cast: Sylvester Stallone (Kit Latura), Amy Brenneman (Madelyne Thompson), Viggo Mortensen (Roy Nord), Dan Hedaya (Frank

Kraft), Jay O. Sanders (Steven Crighton), Karen Young (Sarah Crighton), Claire Bloom (Eleanor Trilling), Vanessa Bell Calloway (Grace Calloway), Renoly Santiago (Mikey), Colin Fox (Roger Trilling), Danielle Harris (Ashley Crighton), Trina McGee (La Tonya), Marcello Thedford (Kadeem), Sage Stallone (Vincent), Jo Anderson (Bloom)
Running Time: 114 min.

Cop Land (1997)

Director: James Mangold
Production: Cathy Konrad, Ezra Swerdlow, Cary Woods for Miramax Films, Woods Entertainment and Across the River Productions
Writers: James Mangold
Cinematography: Eric Alan Edwards
Editing: Craig McKay
Production Design: Lester Cohen
Art Direction: Wing Lee
Music: Howard Shore
Sound: Allan Byer (sound mixer), Philip Stockton (supervising sound editor), Steven Ticknor (sound mixer) and others
Cast: Sylvester Stallone (Freddy Heflin), Harvey Keitel (Ray Donlan), Ray Liotta (Gary Figgis), Robert De Niro (Moe Tilden), Peter Berg (Joey Randone), Janeane Garofalo (Deputy Cindy Betts), Robert Patrick (Jack Rucker), Michael Rapaport (Murray Babitch), Annabella Sciorra (Liz Randone), Noah Emmerich (Deputy Bill Geisler), Cathy Moriarty (Rose Donlan), John Spencer (Leo Crasky), Frank Vincent (PDA President Lassaro), Malik Yoba (Detective Carson), Arthur J. Nascarella (Frank Lagonda)
Running Time: 104 min. (116 min. – director's cut; 120 min. – extended director's cut)

Antz (1998)

Director: Eric Darnell, Tim Johnson
Production: Brad Lewis, Aron Warner, Patty Wooton for DreamWorks SKG, Pacific Data Images (PDI) and DreamWorks Animation
Writers: Todd Alcott (screenplay), Chris Weitz (screenplay), Paul Weitz (screenplay)
Editing: Stan Webb
Production Design: John Bell
Art Direction: Kendal Cronkhite
Music: Harry Gregson-Williams, John Powell
Sound: Richard L. Anderson (supervising sound

editor), Gregg Landaker (sound mixer), Steve
Maslow (sound mixer) and others
Cast: Woody Allen (Z – voice), Dan Aykroyd
(Chip – voice), Anne Bancroft (Queen – voice),
Jane Curtin (Muffy – voice), Danny Glover
(Barbatus – voice), Gene Hackman (General
Mandible – voice), Jennifer Lopez (Azteca –
voice), John Mahoney (Grebs – voice), Paul
Mazursky (Psychologist – voice), Grant Shaud
(Foreman – voice), Sylvester Stallone (Weaver
– voice), Sharon Stone (Princess Bala – voice),
Christopher Walken (Colonel Cutter – voice), Jim
Cummings (additional voices), April Winchell
(additional voices)
Running Time: 83 min.

Get Carter (2000)

Director: Stephen Kay
Production: Mark Canton, Neil Canton,
Elie Samaha for Morgan Creek Productions,
Franchise Pictures and The Canton Company
Writers: Ted Lewis (novel), David McKenna
(screenplay)
Cinematography: Mauro Fiore
Editing: Gerald B. Greenberg
Production Design: Charles Wood
Art Direction: Helen Jarvis
Music: Tyler Bates
Sound: Richard King (sound designer / sound
supervisor), Eric Batut (sound mixer) and others
Cast: Sylvester Stallone (Jack Carter), Miranda
Richardson (Gloria), Rachael Leigh Cook
(Doreen), Rhona Mitra (Geraldine), Johnny
Strong (Eddie), John C. McGinley (Con McCarty),
Alan Cumming (Jeremy Kinnear), Michael Caine
(Cliff Brumby), John Cassini (Thorpey), Mickey
Rourke (Cyrus Paice), Mark Boone Junior (Jim
Davis), Garwin Sanford (Les Fletcher), Darryl
Scheelar (Security Guard), Crystal Lowe (Girl
#1), Lauren Lee Smith (Girl #2)
Running Time: 102 min.

Driven (2001)

Director: Renny Harlin
Production: Renny Harlin, Elie Samaha,
Sylvester Stallone for Franchise Pictures, Epsilon
Motion Pictures and Trackform Film Productions
Writers: Jan Skrentny (story), Neal Tabachnick
(story), Sylvester Stallone (screenplay)

Cinematography: Mauro Fiore
Editing: Steve Gilson, Stuart Levy
Production Design: Charles Wood
Art Direction: Nigel Churcher, Chris Cornwell
Music: BT
Sound: Christopher S. Aud (sound effects
recordist / supervising sound editor), J. Paul
Huntsman (supervising sound editor) and others
Cast: Sylvester Stallone (Joe Tanto), Burt
Reynolds (Carl Henry), Kip Pardue (Jimmy Bly),
Stacy Edwards (Lucretia Clan), Til Schweiger
(Beau Brandenburg), Gina Gershon (Cathy
Heguy), Estella Warren (Sophia Simone), Cristián
de la Fuente (Memo Heguy), Brent Briscoe
(Crusher), Robert Sean Leonard (Demille Bly),
Verona Pooth (Nina), Jasmin Wagner (Ingrid),
Chip Ganassi (Team Owner), John Della Penna
(Team Manager), Dan Duran (Commentator #1)
Running Time: 116 min.

Eye See You (US title; original German title *D-Tox*) (2002)

Director: Jim Gillespie
Production: Karen Kehela Sherwood, Ric Kidney
for Universal Pictures, KC Medien, Capella
International and Soul Simple Productions
Writers: Howard Swindle (book), Ron L.
Brinkerhoff (screen story), Ron L. Brinkerhoff
(screenplay)
Cinematography: Dean Semler
Editing: Timothy Alverson, Steve Mirkovich
Production Design: Gary Wissner
Art Direction: Gary Pembroke Allen, Nancy
Ford, Gershon Ginsburg (supervising art
director)
Music: John Powell
Sound: Lon Gender (supervising sound editor),
Barney Cabral (supervising sound editor) and
others
Cast: Sylvester Stallone (Jake Malloy), Charles
S. Dutton (Hendricks), Polly Walker (Jenny), Kris
Kristofferson (Doc), Mif (Brandon), Christopher
Fulford (Slater), Jeffrey Wright (Jaworski), Tom
Berenger (Hank), Stephen Lang (Jack Bennett),
Alan C. Peterson (Gilbert), Hrothgar Mathews
(Manny), Angela Alvarado (Lopez), Robert
Prosky (McKenzie), Robert Patrick (Noah),
Courtney B. Vance (Reverend Jones)
Running Time: 96 min.

Avenging Angelo (2002)

Director: Martyn Burke
Production: Tarak Ben Ammar, Elie Samaha, Stanley Wilson for Dante Entertainment, Epsilon Motion Pictures, Quinta Communications, Cinema Holdings, Lionweed, Franchise Pictures and Warner Bros.
Writers: Will Aldis (story), Will Aldis (screenplay), Steve Mackall (screenplay)
Cinematography: Ousama Rawi
Editing: Davod Codron
Production Design: Eric Fraser
Art Direction: Stefano Maria Ortolani, Evan Webber
Music: Bill Conti
Sound: Maurizio Argentieri (sound) and others
Cast: Sylvester Stallone (Frankie Delano), Madeleine Stowe (Jennifer Barrett Allieghieri), Anthony Quinn (Angelo Allieghieri), Raoul Bova (Marcello / Gianni Carboni), Harry Van Gorkum (Kip Barrett), Billy Gardell (Bruno), George Touliatos (Lucio Malatesta), Angelo Celeste (The Priest), Ezra Perlamn (Rawley Barrett), Carin Moffat (Ashley), John Gilbert (Whitney Towers), Dawn Greenhalgh (Peggy Towers), Angelo Tsarouchas (Thug), Nancy Beatty (Meter Maid), Lori Alter (Kay)
Running Time: 97 min.

Shade (2003)

Director: Damian Nieman
Production: Chris Hammond, Ted Hartley, David Schnepp for Cobalt Media Group, Hammond Entertainment, Judgement Pictures, Merv Griffin Entertainment, Omen Pictures and RKO Pictures
Writer: Damian Nieman
Cinematography: Anthony B. Richmond
Editing: Scott Conrad, Glenn Garland
Art Direction: Nicole Gorg
Sound: John Bires (sound engineer), Jeff Glueck (sound engineer), Glenn T. Morgan (supervising sound editor) and others
Cast: Joe Nicolo (Ritchie), Carl Mazzocone Sr. (Older Wiseguy), George Tovar (Paulie), Frank Medrano (Sal), Jason Cerbone (Young Dean Stevens), Mark De Alessandro (Hitman #1), Doc Duhame (Hitman #2), Shane T. Anderson (Hitman #3), Thandie Newton (Tiffany), Glenn Plummer (Gas Station Attendant), Gabriel Byrne

(Charlie Miller), Mick Rossi (Club Patron #1), Sean Stanek (Club Patron #2), Holly Catarncuic (Girl in Hallway, Carl Mazzocone (Doorman), Andrea C. Robinson (Club Girl), Stacie Randall (Dealer), Jamie Foxx (Larry Jennings), Talbert Morton (Card Player #1), Rodney Rowland (Jeff), Stuart Townsend (Vernon), Michael Harney (Micky Swift), Jenifer Neme (Blonde Turbo), Tom Reynolds (Casino Man), Shawn Frances Lee (Black Dress Bimbo), Greg Suddeth (Floorman), Ted Hartley (Teddy the Surgeon), Bo Hopkins (Lieutenant Scarne), Bret Anthony (Butler), Dina Merrill (Dina), Angela Fratto (Hot Girl), Shaun Jones (Ose), Mark Boone Junior (Leipzig), Tony Amendola (Daley), Roger Guenveur Smith (Marlo), B-Real (Nate), Adrianne Incarnate (Stripper), Sylvester Stallone (Dean 'The Dean' Stevens), Melanie Griffith (Eve, Chris Rommelmann (Bartender), Hal Holbrook (The Professor)
Running Time: 95 min.

Spy Kids 3-D: Game Over (2003)

Director: Robert Rodriguez
Production: Elizabeth Avellan, Robert Rodriguez for Dimension Films, Los Hooligans Productions and Troublemaker Studios
Writer: Robert Rodriguez (script)
Cinematography: Robert Rodriguez
Editing: Robert Rodriguez
Production Design: Robert Rodriguez
Art Direction: Jeanette Scott
Music: James Johnzen, Christopher Young
Music: Rebecca Rodriguez, Robert Rodriguez (score by)
Sound: Dean Beville (sound designer / supervising adr editor / supervising sound editor), Nerses Gezalyan (sound mixer), William Jacobs (sound designer), Carla Murray (sound designer / sound effects editor), Steven Ticknor (sound designer) and others
Cast: Antonio Banderas (Gregorio Cortez), Carla Gugino (Ingrid Cortez), Alexa Vega (Carmen Cortez), Daryl Sabara (Juni Cortez), Ricardo Montalban (Grandfather), Holland Taylor (Grandmother), Sylvester Stallone (Toymaker), Mike Judge (Donnagon Giggles), Salma Hayek (Cesca Giggles), Emily Osment (Gerti Giggles), Ryan Pinkston (Arnold), Robert Vito (Rez),

Bobby Edner (Francis), Courtney Jines (Demetra)
Running Time: 84 min.

Rocky Balboa (2006)

Director: Sylvester Stallone
Production: William Chartoff, David King
Templeton, Charles Winkler, David Winkler
for Metro-Goldwyn-Mayer (MGM), Columbia
Pictures, Revolution Studios and Rogue Marble
Writer: Sylvester Stallone
Cinematography: Clark Mathis
Editing: Sean Albertson
Production Design: Franco-Giacomo Carbone
Art Direction: Michael Atwell, Jesse Rosenthal
Music: Bill Conti
Sound: Anthony J. Ciccolini III (supervising
sound editor), Steve Maslow (supervising sound
mixer) and others
Cast: Sylvester Stallone (Rocky Balboa), Burt
Young (Paulie), Antonio Tarver (Mason 'The
Line' Dixon), Geraldine Hughes (Marie), Milo
Ventimiglia (Robert Balboa Jr.), Tony Burton
(Duke), A. J. Benz (L. C.), James Francis Kelly III
(Steps), Talia Shire (Adrian – archive footage),
Lou DiBella (Lou DiBella), Mike Tyson (Mike
Tyson), Henry G. Sanders (Martin), Pedro Lovell
(Spider Rico), Ana Gerena (Isabel), Angela Boyd
(Angie)
Running Time: 102 min.

Rambo (2008)

Director: Sylvester Stallone
Production: Avi Lerner, Kevin King Templeton,
John Thompson for Lionsgate, The Weinstein
Company, Millennium Films, Nu Images Films
and Equity Pictures Medienfonds GmbH & Co.
KG IV
Writers: Art Monterastelli, Sylvester Stallone,
David Morrell (characters)
Cinematography: Glen MacPherson
Editing: Sean Albertson
Production Design: Franco-Giacomo Carbone
Art Direction: Suchartanun 'Kai' Kuladee
Music: Brian Tyler
Sound: Barney Cabral (supervising sound
editor), Greg Chapman (sound mixer), Perry
Robertson (supervising sound editor), Scott
Sanders (sound designer / supervising sound
editor) and others

Cast: Sylvester Stallone (John Rambo), Julie
Benz (Sarah), Matthew Marsden (School Boy),
Graham McTavish (Lewis), Reynaldo Gallegos
(Diaz), Jake La Botz (Reese), Tim Kang (En-Joo),
Maung Maung Khin (Tint), Paul Schulze (Michael
Burnett), Cameron Pearson (Missionary #4
– Jeff), Thomas Peterson (Missionary #2
– Dentist), Tony Skarberg (Missionary #3 –
Videographer), James With (Missionary #5
– Preacher), Kasikorn Niyompattana (Snake
Hunter #2), Shaliew 'Lek' Bamrungbun (Snake
Hunter #1)
Running Time: 92 min. (99 min., extended)

The Expendables (2010)

Director: Sylvester Stallone
Production: Avi Lerner, John Thompson for
Millennium Films, Nu Image Films and Rogue
Marble
Writers: Dave Callaham (screenplay), Sylvester
Stallone (screenplay), Dave Callaham (story)
Cinematography: Jeffrey L. Kimball
Editing: Ken Blackwell, Paul Harb
Production Design: Franco-Giacomo Carbone
Art Direction: Drew Boughton, Daniel Flaksman
Music: Brian Tyler
Sound: Christopher Eakins (supervising sound
editor), David Esparza (supervising sound
effects editor), Toninho Muricy (sound mixer)
and others
Cast: Sylvester Stallone (Barney Ross), Jason
Statham (Lee Christmas), Jet Li (Yin Yang),
Dolph Lundgren (Gunnar Jensen), Eric Roberts
(James Munroe), Randy Couture (Toll Road),
Steve Austin (Paine), David Zayas (General
Garza), Giselle Itié (Sandra), Charisma Carpenter
(Lacy), Gary Daniels (The Brit), Terry Crews
(Hale Caesar), Mickey Rourke (Tool), Hank Amos
(Paul), Amin Joseph (Pirate Leader)
Running Time: 103 min.

The Expendables 2 (2012)

Director: Simon West
Production: Avi Lerner, Danny Lerner, Kevin
King Templeton, John Thompson, Les Weldon for
Millennium Films and Nu Image Films
Writers: Richard Wenk (screenplay), Sylvester
Stallone (screenplay), Ken Kaufman (story),
David Agosto (story), Richard Wenk (story),

Dave Callaham (characters)
Cinematography: Shelly Johnson
Editing: Todd E. Miller
Production Design: Paul Cross
Art Direction: Alexei Karagyaur, Adam A. Makin (supervising art director), Ivalio Nikolov, Keith Pain, Ivan Ranghelov, Sonya Savova
Music: Brian Tyler
Sound: Christopher Eakis (supervising dialogue & ADR editor / supervising sound editor), Vladimir Kaloyano (sound mixer), A. Josh Reinhardt (sound mixer) and others
Cast: Sylvester Stallone (Barney Ross), Jason Statham (Lee Christmas), Jet Li (Yin Yang), Dolph Lundgren (Gunnar Jensen), Chuck Norris (Booker), Jean-Claude Van Damme (Vilain), Bruce Willis (Church), Arnold Schwarzenegger (Trench), Terry Crews (Hale Caesar), Randy Couture (Toll Road), Liam Hemsworth (Billy the Kid), Scott Adkins (Hector), Nan Yu (Maggie), Amanda Ooms (Pilar), Charisma Carpenter (Lacy)
Running Time: 103 min.

Bullet to the Head (2012)

Director: Walter Hill
Production: Alfred Gough, Alexandra Milchan, Miles Millar, Kevin King Templeton for Dark Castle Entertainment, IM Global, After Dark Films, Automatik Entertainment, EMJAG Productions, Headshot Films, Millar Gough Ink and Silver Reel
Writers: Allesandro Camon (screenplay), Alexis Nolent (based on the graphic novel Du plomb dans la tête [Lead in the Head]), Colin Wilson (illustrator of the graphic novel Du plomb dans la tête)
Cinematography: Lloyd Ahern II
Editing: Timothy Alverson
Production Design: Toby Corbett
Music: Steve Mazzaro
Sound: Mark Larry (supervising sound editor), Lee Orloff (sound mixer) and others
Cast: Sylvester Stallone (James Bonomo), Sung Kang (Taylor Kwon), Sarah Shahi (Lisa), Adewale Akinnuoye-Agbaje (Robert Nkomo Morel), Jason Momoa (Keegan), Jon Seda (Louis Blanchard), Holt McCallany (Hank Greely), Brian Van Holt (Ronnie Earl), Weronika Rosati (Lola), Dane Rhodes (Lt. Lebreton), Marcus Lyle Brown

(Detective Towne), Andrew Austin-Peterson (Crawfish Hollow Band), Paul Etheredge (Crawfish Hollow Band), Robert Cavan Carruth (Crawfish Hollow Band)
Running Time: 92 min.

Escape Plan (2013)

Director: Mikael Håfström
Production: Robbie Brenner, Mark Canton, Remington Chase, Randall Emmett, Kevin King Templeton for Summit Entertainment, Emmett/Furla Films, Mark Canton Productions, Enivision Entertainment Corporation, Boles/Schiller Film Group and Atmosphere Entertainment MM
Writers: Miles Chapman (screenplay), Jason Keller (screenplay), Miles Chapman (story)
Cinematography: Brendan Galvin
Editing: Elliot Greenberg
Production Design: Barry Chusid
Art Direction: James A. Gelarden, David Lazan
Music: Alex Heffes
Sound: B. J. Len (sound mixer), Richard Schexnayder (sound mixer), Derek Vanderhorst (sound designer / supervising sound editor) and others
Cast: Sylvester Stallone (Ray Breslin), Arnold Schwarzenegger (Emil Rottmayer), Jim Caviezel (Hobbes), Faran Tahir (Javed), Amy Ryan (Abigail), Sam Neill (Dr. Kyrie), Vincent D'Onofrio (Lester Clark), Vinnie Jones (Drake), Matt Gerald (Roag), 50 Cent (Hush), Caitriona Balfe (Jessica Miller), David Joseph Martinez (Captain Newal Beradah), Alec Rayme (Pilot), Christian Stokes (Babcock), Graham Beckel (Brims)
Running Time: 115 min.

Homefront (2013)

Director: Gary Fleder
Production: Sylvester Stallone, Kevin King Templeton, John Thompson and Les Weldon for Homefront Productions, Millennium Films, Nu Image Films
Writers: Sylvester Stallone (screenplay), Chuck Logan (based on the novel by)
Cinematography: Theo van de Sande
Editing: Padraic McKinley
Production Design: Greg Berry
Art Direction: A. Todd Holland
Music: Mark Isham

Sound: Christopher Eakins (supervising dialogue editor), Jay Meagher (sound mixer), A. Josh Reinhardt (sound mixer), Martyn Zub (sound designer / supervising sound editor) and others
Cast: Jason Statham (Phil Broker), James Franco (Morgan 'Gator' Bodine), Izabela Vidovic (Maddy Broker), Kate Bosworth (Cassie Bodine Klum), Marcus Hester (Jimmy Klum), Clancy Brown (Sheriff Keith Rodrigue), Winona Ryder (Sheryl Marie Mott), Omar Benson Miller (Teedo), Rachelle Lefevre (Susan Hetch), Frank Grillo (Cyrus Hanks), Chuck Zito ('Danny T' Turrie), Pruit Taylor Vince (Werks), Linds Edwards (Jojo Turrie), Austin Craig (Teddy Klum), Owen Harn (Clay)
Running Time: 100 min.

Grudge Match (2013)

Director: Peter Segal
Production: Michael Ewing, Bill Gerber, Mark Steven Johnson, Ravi D. Mehta, Peter Segal for Callahan Filmworks, Gerber Pictures and Warner Bros.
Writers: Tim Kelleher (screenplay), Rodney Rothman (screenplay), Tim Kelleher (story)
Cinematography: Dean Semler
Editing: William Kerr
Production Design: Wynn Thomas
Art Direction: Alice Alward (art department coordinator)
Music: Trevor Rabin
Sound: Terry Rodman (sound re-recording sound mixer / supervising sound editor) and others
Cast: Robert De Niro (Billy 'The Kid' McDonnen), Sylvester Stallone (Henry 'Razor' Sharp), Jon Bernthal (B. J.), Kim Basinger (Sally Rose), Kevin Hart (Dante Slate, Jr.), Corrina Roshea (Beautiful Woman), Alan Arkin (Lightning), Steffie Grote (Beautiful Woman), Starlette Miariaunii (College Student), Paul Ben-Victor (Lou Camare), Nicole Andrews (Carla), Han Soto (Kenji), Judd Lormand (Car Salesman), Joey Diaz (Mike), Griff Furst (Dr. Morgan)
Running Time: 113 min.

Reach Me (2014)

Director: John Herzfeld
Production: Cassian Elwes, John Herzfeld, Buddy Patrick for Seraphim Films Inc., New

Redemption Pictures and Windy Hill Pictures
Writer: John Herzfeld
Cinematography: Vern Nobles
Editing: Steven Cohen
Art Direction: Tudor Boloni
Music: Tree Adams
Sound: Casey Genton (sound designer / supervising sound editor) and others
Cast: Lauren Cohan (Kate), Sylvester Stallone (Gerald), Elizabeth Henstridge (Eve), Cary Elwes (Kersey), Terry Crews (Wilson), Ryan Kwanten (Jack Burns), Thomas Jane (Wolfie), Kelsey Grammer (Angelo AldoBrandini), Tom Berenger (Teddy), Kevin Connolly (Roger), Kyra Sedgwick (Colette), Tom Sizemore (Frank), David O'Hara (Dominic), Nelly (E-Ruption), Danny Aiello (Father Paul)
Running Time: TBD

The Expendables 3 (2014)

Director: Patrick Hughes
Production: Avi Lerner, Danny Lerner, Kevin King Templeton, John Thompson and Les Weldon for Nu Image / Millennium Films, Millennium Films, Nu Image Films
Writers: Katrin Benedikt (screenplay), Dave Callaham (characters), Creighton Rothenberger (screenplay), Sylvester Stallone (screenplay) (story)
Cinematography: Peter Menzies Jr.
Editing: Sean Albertson and Paul Harb
Production Design: Daniel T. Dorrance
Art Direction: Tom Brown (supervising art director)
Sound: Emil Evtimov (sound mixer), Vladimir Kaloyanov (sound mixer) and others
Cast: Sylvester Stallone (Barney Ross), Jason Statham (Lee Christmas), Jet Li (Yin Yang), Antonio Banderas (Rapido), Wesley Snipes (Surgeon), Mel Gibson (Conrad Stonebanks), Dolph Lundgren (Gunnar Jensen), Harrison Ford (Max Drummer), Arnold Schwarzenegger (Trench), Kellan Lutz (Smilee), Terry Crews (Hale Caesar), Sarai Givaty (Camilla), Kelsey Grammer (Bonaparte), Robert Davi (Goran Vogner), Victor Ortiz (Mars)
Running Time: TBD

INDEX

Academy Awards ('Oscars'). See awards

action films 1, 20n15, 53, 72, 121, 129, 132, 134, 141, 143n.6, 156, 248; acting 8, 128–34, 142, 150–3, 159–65; authenticity 17, 171, 190–3, 241–60; contemporary 54–5, 62, 103, 134; digital effects 44, 46, 48, 187–91, 244, 257, 259, 260n.4; display and spectacle 6, 9, 19n.11, 32–42, 44, 46, 48, 50n.6, 55, 62, 65, 112–16, 127, 152–3, 163, 174, 194, 201, 206, 214, 217–19, 229, 234, 242, 244–5, 248, 254–7; martial arts 211, 218, 237, 256, 259; 1980s 'hard body' 2, 3, 163, 168. See also spectacle; violence; weapons

Adams, Rachel 21, 135

Afghanistan 10, 12, 221, 224, 226–7, 229, 231, 235

African Queen, The 100

ageing 4, 17, 42, 44, 123, 136, 165, 175, 189, 231, 235, 241–45, 249, 251, 253–60, 261n.5; decline (loss) 188, 242; fitness 2, 242–3, 255; in men 243, 255, 257, 260n.4; in women 243, 255. See also Botox; celebrity culture; human growth hormone (HGH); masculinity; plastic (cosmetic) surgery; testosterone

Ali, Muhammad (Cassius Clay) 183

Allen, Woody 27, 136–7

All the President's Men 14

Al-Qaeda 221, 228

American Film Institute 15

Anderson, Wes 28

Angel of the City (song) 67, 69

animation 7, 13, 17

Anton, Susan 14

Antz 17, 136–7, 142, 157; acting 17, 136–7, 142; critical response 137, 142

Armstrong, Lance 260n.2

arm wrestling 172–5

Assassins 11, n.19, 148, 155–8

audience 2, 3, 6, 9–11, 15–17, 19n.9, 62, 66, 69, 75, 78, 83, 91, 98, 100–105, 112, 114, 116, 121, 130, 132, 139–142, 143n.6, 165–168, 171–6, 179, 181, 193n.1, 197–9, 201–7, 209, 211, 213–15, 218, 234, 236, 244, 257; British 17, 98, 197; and class (social) 142, 197, 234; cult 6, 9; education 176, 199; female 197–8, 213; gay 17, 203, 198, 202, 206–7, 214; male (heterosexual) 130, 214, 202, 207; youth 114, 236

auteurs/auteurism 2, 3, 12, 16, 28, 42–50, 72, 102, 129

authenticity 17, 180–1, 193, 241–4, 250–2, 254, 256, 259–60. See action films

Avenging Angelo 10, 19n.9, 167

Avildsen, John G. 18, 34, 76, 81, 213

awards 15, 141, 143n.15, 149; Academy ('Oscars') 14, 76–7, 108, 125, 127, 134, 136, 147, 165, 245; acting 136, 141, 147, 165; critical response 127, 134, 141, 147–9; Golden Raspberry ('Razzies') 147–8; Jaeger–LeCoultre Glory to the Filmmaker 15, 141; Stockholm Film Festival 136

Bancroft, Anne 136

Banderas, Antonio 134

Barker, Jennifer 9

Barker, Martin 6, 9, 16, 20n.16, 197

Baron, Cynthia 139, 142

Bartel, Paul 8

Bean, Jennifer 53, 73n.1

Bend It Like Beckham 34
Bernstein, Abbie 131
Better Tomorrow, A 73
Beyond Rangoon 226
Billy Elliot 27, 34
bin Laden, Osama 236, 239n.14
Bionic Woman, The (TV series) 97, 101
blockbusters 6–11, 32
body 2, 3, 6, 9, 10, 13, 15, 17, 38, 40, 42,
    113–14, 116n.3, 121–2, 126, 129–33, 136,
    138–9, 142n.8, 150–6, 158–65, 168–9,
    172–5, 183–5, 188–190, 193, 197–202,
    205–11, 214–15, 217, 219–22, 229, 233,
    241–59, 260n.4. See also body-building;
    celebrity culture; human growth
    hormone (HGH); masculinity; muscles
    and muscularity; steroids; testosterone;
    weight-lifting (-training)
body-building 114, 122, 143n.2, 199–200,
    244–5. See also class (social); human
    growth hormone (HGH); muscles and
    muscularity; steroids; testosterone;
    weight-lifting (-training)
Bordwell, David 6, 16, 19n.2, 32, 39, 40, 51n.6,
    54–5, 59, 72
Borzage, Frank 55, 59
Botox 4, 121, 253. See also celebrity culture;
    plastic (cosmetic) surgery 4, 17, 113, 121,
    242, 244, 252–4
Bound for Glory 151
Bourdieu, Pierre 122, 125, 140–2, 143n.n.5–6,
    149–50, 164, 168–9
boxing 4–17, 38, 51n.8, 78, 85, 90, 92, 95n.5,
    171–193, 199–200, 211, 217, 245, 260;
    boxer–slugger distinction 178–9, 182,
    185, 193; and race 177–8, 192
Boxing Hall of Fame 17, 193,
box office 5, 6, 9–11, 19n.7, 20n.20, 27, 116n.1,
    118n.20, 128, 139, 149–50, 156–7, 167–8,
    169, 223, 245, 254, 256; domestic 11,
    116n.1, 118n.20, 156; world/global 5, 9,
    19n.7, 20n.20
Brando, Marlon 123
Brewster, Ben 54, 62
Bridge on the River Kwai 227
Brooks, Kate 6, 9, 16, 197
Brown, James 41, 86, 184,
Buddhism 225–6. See religion
Bukatman, Scott 50n.5
Bullet to the Head 11
Bullitt 134
Bullock, Sandra 134, 206

Burma (now Myanmar) 221, 226–8, 230–1,
    237, 239n.6, 259. See also Myanmar
Butler, Bill 39–40

Caine, Michael 97–8, 106–7, 109–10, 114–15,
    118n.19, 127, 173
camp films 6, 9, 10, 20n.21, 30, 81, 207–8,
    215n.8,
Canby, Vincent 150–2, 164
Cannon 12
Cannon, Dany 9
Capra, Frank 14, 126
Carnicke, Sharon 139, 142
Carolco Pictures 12, 156, 117n.17
Carradine, David 151
Casablanca 7, 222
CBS 156
celebrity culture 17, 105, 242–4, 252–4, 260
    See also ageing; Botox; human growth
    hormone (HGH); plastic (cosmetic)
    surgery; steroids; testosterone
Center Stage: Turn It Up 34
Chan, Jackie 260n4
Chaplin, Charlie 14, 18, 126–7
Chariots of Fire 34
Charlie's Angels 259
Charney, Leo 51n.7
Chartoff, Robert 18, 36–7, 46–7, 75, 81, 84, 87,
    89, 90, 95n.3, 156, 177, 180–1, 213, 250
Cher 253
Chinatown 100
Christianity 221, 225, 226–7. See religion.
class (social) 125, 139, 142, 197, 200, 208, 212,
    214, 231, 244, 249; and legitimacy 140–1,
    165, 168–9; professional 11, 38, 109, 113,
    114, 141, 154, 245; working–class 7, 33,
    101, 104, 111, 113, 122, 125, 130, 141, 182,
    201, 214, 234. See also body-building;
    weight-lifting (-training)
Cliffhanger 6, 17, 132–3, 141–2, 143n.3,
    155–7, 171, 173; acting 17, 132, 141–2;
    cinematography 133, 142; costume 128,
    133; critical response 17, 128, 141–2, 155;
    Stallone's diet and training 17, 132
Clooney, George 165
Cobra 16–7, 19n.3, 53–73, 74n.9, 112, 122, 132,
    140, 148, 157, 163, 166, 204, 245, 249;
    colour 63–64; editing (montage) 53,
    57, 63–7, 69–70; fight (action) sequences
    53, 57–8, 71; 81–3, 86, 71, 249;
    iconography 16, 54, 62, 64, 70; lighting
    60, 70–2, 140; as melodrama 16, 53–5,

Cobra cont.
  58–63, 66, 69–70, 73; and music video
  57, 66, 68–9; narrative structure 16,
  54–5, 59, 62, 67–8, 70, 73n.6, 163;
  violence 63–4; weapons 60, 63
Coen Brothers 28
Cold War 184, 209, 221
Collette, Toni 13
Columbia Pictures 125, 133, 138, 143, 156
comedy 17, 19n.1, 42, 109, 123, 126, 131, 137,
  142, 152–3, 155, 208, 268; acting in 17,
  123, 142, 152–3
Conan the Barbarian 108
Connell, R. W. 210
Contender, The (TV series) 191
Conti, Bill 19n.8 , 35, 44, 90, 107
cop/crime films 2, 11. *See also* thrillers
Cop Land 17, 121, 128, 134, 142, 149–50, 153,
  159–61, 163–7; acting 17, 121, 128, 134,
  142, 144n.16, 148–53, 159–61, 163–7;
  cinematography 134; costume 128,
  206; critical response 115, 147, 150, 165;
  and genres 128, 168; and independent
  film 115, 134, 156, 158–9; and
  legitimacy 17, 149–50, 163, 165, 169;
  Stallone's diet 121, 163; violence 153
Corman, Roger 8, 19n.13
Corrigan, Timothy 7, 50n.6
Cosmatos, George P. 2, 53, 65, 68, 70–2
Couture, Randy 1, 3
Crabbe, James 76
Creative Artists Agency (CAA) 98
Creative Management Associates 106
Crews, Terry 1, 3
Crimson Pirate, The 256
Crist, Judith 124
Crouching Tiger, Hidden Dragon 256
cult films 5, 6, 8, 9, 114
Czach, Sasha 14

Davenport, Nigel 102, 113
Daylight 11, 48, 155–8
Day of the Jackal, The 101
Death Race 2000 8, 9, 19n.9, 19n.13; costumes
  8; as cult film 8, 9; special effects 8, 9
Demolition Man 17, 20n.21, 15–7, 202,
  205–7, 245, 249; audience response
  17, 202, 207; and costume 202, 206;
  and heterosexuality 202, 205, 207;
  homoeroticism 202–3, 205–7; and
  homophobia 202
De Niro, Robert 121, 134, 148–154, 165–6

Desser, David 239n.4, 251, 258
DeVito, Danny 115
Dickinson, Janice 14, 243
Die Hard 104, 256
Die Hard franchise (series) 73, 256. *See also*
  Die Hard
direct cinema 29. *See also* documentary
Dirty Harry 9, 53, 60–1, 63, 69, 70–1, 73
Disney Studios 115, 117n.8, 156
documentary 29, 30, 39, 47–9, 245. *See also*
  direct cinema
doping 243, 246–7, 260n.2. *See also* steroids.
Drake, Philip 153,
drama 2, 17, 30, 33, 36, 38, 41, 89. *See also*
  melodrama
Dressed to Kill 107
Driven 17, 19n.9, 138, 148, 167, 171, 175–6,
  198; CART 176; Formula One 175–6;
  racing professionals in 175–7; *Rocky* as
  model 175–6
D-Tox (original German title) 138. See *Eye See*
  You (US title)
Dworkin, Shari L. 255
Dyer, Richard 143n.4, 223, 232

Eastwood, Clint 18, 27, 53, 60, 63, 257, 261n.5
Ebert, Roger 129,
Edwards, Eric Alan 135, 143n.13
Elvis 10,
Emigrants, The 108
Empire Strikes Back, The 101
English, James F. 145
epics 205, 229, 256
Escape to Victory (UK title) 107, 116n.3, 157,
  204. See *Victory* (US title)
Esch, Kevin 164
E.T. 111
ethnicity 113, 117n.4, 199, 225, 244, 249–51;
  and food 138, 249, 264; Italian 84, 123,
  130–1, 231, 250–1; Italian American 33,
  250; off-white 101, 117n5. *See also* race
Everhart, Angie 14
Exorcist, The 108
Expendables, The 1–5, 17, 19n.7, 50n1, 121,
  237–8, 249, 260n.3; cinematography 4;
  colour 4, 50; Stallone's diet 17, 121;
  violence 3–4
Expendables, The franchise (series) 1, 4, 6; and
  ageing 4, 249, 260; critical response 4,
  5, 19n.11, 121, 260n.4; and homoeroticism
  3; as melodrama 3, 16, 50. See also *The*
  Expendables; *The Expendables 2*

Expendables 2, The 1–5, 19n.7; Eye of the Tiger (song) 13, 19n.8, 35, 86
Eye See You (US Title) 19n.9, 138, 152, 158, 167; audience response 4, 19n.9, 138, 152, 167

Fairbanks, Douglas, Sr. 129
Fair Game: 1974/1978 novel 55, 58, 73n.2; 1995 film 59, 60, 73n.2
Faulkner, Gary Brooks 238
Fawcett, Farrah 253
Fight Club 254–5
film noir 30–2
First Blood 2–4, 10, 13, 16–7, 47, 97–9, 112, 116, 117n.17, 128–30, 135, 141, 147–8, 155–7, 159–60, 177, 204, 220–6, 228–30, 233–7, 238n.1, 245, 248, 253, 258–9; acting 17, 118, 128, 141, 147, 159–60, 222; cinematography 47, 190, 245; and comedy 17, 155; costume 98, 129, 130, 135, 228; critical response 116, 141, 147–8, 155; and ethnicity 112–13, 118, 130, 223, 225; as independent film 117n.17, 129, 143n.7, 156, 159; Stallone's diet 17, 88; violence 3, 4, 13, 64, 222, 225, 228–9, 234, 248, 258–9
F.I.S.T. 50n.n.3–4, 121–3, 140, 143n.1; acting 123, 140; costume 143; critical response 123; Stallone's diet 121, 143n.1
Flashdance 27, 34
Flash Gordon 108
Flavin, Jennifer 14, 135
football (soccer, in US) 19n12, 105–111, 114, 118n.n.18–19 127–8, 24. *See* soccer
Ford, Harrison 18, 260n.4
Foreman, George 183, 189
48 Hours 11
French Connection, The 29, 104, 117n.14, 134
Fresh Prince of Bel Air (TV series) 13
Fuchs, Cynthia 16

Gallagher, Mark 16, 34
gangster films 30
Garwood, Robert (Bobby) 220
genre 2, 3, 15, 28–34, 38–9, 50, 53–6, 59–61, 69, 72–3, 88–99, 104, 115, 128, 131, 134, 141, 143n.6, 155, 158, 163, 168, 172, 204, 239n.13, 242, 244, 254, 256–7, 260. *See* individual film genres/modes (action films; animation; comedy; cop/ crime films; documentary; drama; epics; *film noir*; gangster films; horror films; melodrama; musicals; sports films; thrillers; war films; Western films)

Geraghty, Christine 11, 141
Get Carter (2000) 19n.9, 138, 148, 167, 198
Gladiator 256
Glover, Danny 138
Godfather, The 29
Golan, Menahim 65, 68, 71–2, 140, 175
Golden Raspberry ('Razzie') Award. *See* awards
Gondry, Michel 103
Gonna Fly Now (song) 35–6, 39, 44–5, 90, 181, 202
Good Guys Wear Black 1
Gosling, Paula 54–6, 59, 60
Great Escape, The 106, 128
Griffith, Melanie 253
Guantanamo 221, 228
Guest, Cornelia 14
Guignols de l'info, Les ('the news puppets') (French TV series) 13, 20n.22
Guns of Navarone, The 110
Guthmann, Edward 152

Hackman, Gene 20n.25, 117, 136
Halloween 58
Halloween II 58
Hand, The 107
Harlin, Renny 133, 176,
Hauer, Rutger 97–8, 101–5, 111, 113–14
Heller, Dana 252
Hemsworth, Liam 1
Hero 256
heterosexuality 113, 130, 197, 200–3, 205, 207, 210, 250. *See also* homoeroticism; homosexuality; masculinity
Heywood, Leslie 255
Higgins, Scott 16, 33, 54–5
High Noon 155
Hill, Walter 11
Holmes, Su 243
Holmlund, Chris 3, 143n.4, 150, 168, 208, 215n.1, 238, 261n.5
Home Box Office 156
homoeroticism 3, 202, 204–8, 214. *See also* heterosexuality; homosexuality; masculinity
homosexuality 202, 238. *See also* heterosexuality; homoeroticism; masculinity
Honey, You Got Served 34
horror films 58
Houston, John 128
Huffer, Ian 6, 16, 17, 20n.21, 204, 213, 215n.2, 215n.7

human growth hormone (HGH) 121, 242, 194n.12. *See also* ageing; body-building; masculinity; muscles and muscularity; steroids; testosterone; weight-lifting (-training)

Hunt, Leon 259

Huston, John 89, 100, 106–7, 110, 115

imperialism 225, 234

Inconnus, Les ('the unknowns') (French TV comedy troupe) 13, 20n.22

Independence Day 256

independent film 5, 12, 115, 117n.9, 117n.17, 129, 134, 138, 143n7, 156, 158–9

Indiana Jones and the Kingdom of the Crystal Skull 260n4

Ingalls, Joyce 14, 31

In Her Shoes 13

Invincible 34

Island, The 107

Jacobs, Lea 54, 62

Jaeger-LeCoultre Glory to the Filmmaker Award. *See* awards

Jeffords, Susan 16, 143n.4, 163, 212, 222, 256

Jewison, Norman 50n.3

John, Elton 95n.8, 96

Jonze, Spike 103

Judge Dredd 9, 16–7, 20n.15, 148, 152, 157, 163, 202, 208, 211, 245; audience response 9, 17, 202, 208; costume 152, 202, 208; critical response 152, 211; as cult film 9; special effects 9, 16; violence 9

Kael, Pauline 126

Kamen, Stan 98, 118n.2

Karate Kid, The 34

Kassar, Mario 107, 117n.17

Katzenberg, Jeffrey 136

Keaton, Buster 18

Keitel, Harvey 121, 134–6, 148–9, 153–4, 161

Keller, Alexandra 17, 171

Khambatta, Persis 101–2

Kinder, Marsha 34

King, Barry 164

King, Geoff 44, 50n.6

Klitschko, Vitali 191–2

Klitschko, Wladimir 191–3

Kotcheff, Ted 47

Kóvacs, László 30–1, 50n.n.3–4, 140

Kyi, Aung San Suu 226–7, 237, 238n.2

Lachman, Ed 124

Lady Sings the Blues 101

Lancaster, Burt 256

Lara Croft: Tombraider 256

Last Tycoon, The 151

Lawrence of Arabia 229

Leibovitz, Annie 142

Lerner, Avi 5, 48–9, 226, 233, 251, 255

Lethal Weapon 73, 104

Lethal Weapon 4 144

Lethal Weapon franchise (series). *See also* *Lethal Weapon 4*

Lichtenfeld, Eric 16, 19n.3, 44, 54, 60–3, 70, 74n.9, 75, 95n.6, 117n.10, 118n.21, 143n.6, 256

Li, Jet 1, 5, 17, 237–8

Liotta, Ray 121, 134–5, 153–4

Lithgow, John 132, 143n.11

Living in America (song) 86

Lock Up 17, 19n.9, 148, 152, 156–7, 163, 204, 248, 250; critical response 152; and ethnicity 250; heterosexuality 250; spectacle 152, 248

Lopez, Jennifer 136–7

Lord of the Rings, The 256

Lord's of Flatbush, The 17, 123, 125, 128, 142; acting 17, 123, 142; costume 126, 124; critical response 126, 128; as independent film 123; Stallone's diet 17, 124

Lundgren, Dolph 1, 4, 19n.5, 36–7, 80, 112, 183–5, 191, 209, 237, 246,

Lyne, Adrian 103

MacDonald, Peter 47

MacPherson, Glen 48

Magnum Force 63

Mahogany 101

Malmuth, Bruce 102, 103, 105–6, 117n10

Maltby, Richard 127, 129, 143n.12

Maltese Falcon, The 100

Mangine, Joseph 124

Mangold, James 134–5, 143n.13, 161–3, 166–7

Manhunter 87

Mann, Michael 28, 66–7

Marciano, Rocky 19n.8, 178, 194n.11

Marty 125

masculinity 15–17, 34, 60, 97, 113, 116, 172, 176–8, 181–3, 197–215, 229–30, 238, 254–5. *See also* ageing; heterosexuality; homoeroticism; homosexuality; human growth hormone (HGH); muscles and muscularity; steroids; testosterone

M*A*S*H* 29
Maslin, Janet   113, 131, 133
Mathis, Clark   45-6
Matrix, The   256-7, 259
McCain, John   220-1, 238n.2
McCarthy, Todd   10, 20n.20, 133, 155, 166
McDonald, Paul   17, 98, 121, 147
Medhurst, Andy   215n.8
melodrama   3, 16, 27-29, 30-42, 50, 51n.8,
   53-63, 69-70, 73, 73n.1, 110, 127, 129,
   248; family melodrama   33, 53; male
   melodrama   33, 110; narrative structure
   28-30, 32, 34, 51n.8, 54-5, 59, 62, 127;
   spectacle   32-4, 42, 55, 62; weepies   53,
   74n.10; women's pictures   53
Meyer, Ron   98, 116n.2, 158-9
Miah, Andy   246-7
Miami Vice (TV series)   66, 73n.6
Miramax   115, 136, 158-9, 161-2, 167
Mission Impossible   256
Mission Impossible 2   259
Monster   165
Morrell, David   129, 223, 225
Morrison, Tommy   92, 186, 191, 194n.8,
Mortensen, Viggo   15, 134
mountain-climbing (mountaineering)   13, 132
Murphy, Eddie   13
muscles and muscularity   1, 17, 53, 88, 116,
   122, 129, 132-3, 137, 197, 205, 229. See
   also body; body-building; human growth
   hormone (HGH); masculinity; steroids;
   testosterone; weight-lifting (-training)
musicals   16, 27, 34-5
Myanmar (formerly Burma)   12, 44, 221, 227,
   229-30, 234, 238n.2. See also Burma

nationalism   86-8, 106, 209. See also
   patriotism
Neale, Steve   53, 73n.1, 205-6
Negra, Diane   117n.5, 249-50
Network   14
New Land, The   108
Newman, Paul   20n.25
Nickson, Julia   112, 226
Nielsen, Brigitte   14, 56, 68, 73n.7, 113
Nighthawks   16, 97-109, 111-16, 116.n.n.1-2
   ,117, 118n.23, 123, 156-7; casting   16,
   100-2, 105, 107, 109, 112-15; costume
   98, 106-7, 113; creative personnel
   100-2; critical response   99, 104-5, 113,
   115-16, 123; and ethnicity   100, 111-16;
   and genres   99, 104, 115; locations   16,

100, 104-7; marketing   16, 100-5
Norris, Chuck   1, 19n.n.5-6
North, Oliver   236
Nuls, Les ('the dummies') (French TV comedy
   troupe)   13, 20n.22
Nutty Professor, The   13

Obama, Barack   13
Omega Man, The   109
O'Neal, Ryan   20n.25
On the Waterfront   123, 125
Orientalism/the 'Orient'   217-19, 221, 237
Orion Pictures   156
Oscars (Academy Awards). See awards
Oscar   17, 19n.9, 128.130-1, 148, 152, 155-7;
   acting   17, 147, 152-3; critical response
   128, 131, 147
Over the Top   17, 19n.9, 140, 148, 156, 163, 171,
   174-5, 193n.2 ; cinematography   140;
   training sequences   140, 171, 174-5

Pacino, Al   20n.25, 148-9
Pakistan   12, 236
Paradise Alley   16-7, 19n.9, 27-32, 50, 50n.4,
   75, 140, 171, 173, 250; cinematography
   29-30, 140; colour   28-31, 50; editing
   (montage)   27-9, 32, 50; and ethnicity
   250; mise-en-scène   28-9; training
   sequences   140, 171, 173; wrestling   30,
   171, 173
Paramount Pictures   12, 41, 98, 127
Parton, Dolly   9, 10, 20n.17, 20n.19, 208
patriotism   76, 84-6. See also nationalism
Peary, Danny   9, 20n.14
Pelé   98, 106, 108-12, 127-8, 173
Persepolis   13
Personal Best   34
Philadelphia Museum of Art   7, 13, 35, 83, 94,
   181, 187. See also Rocky steps; Rocky
   statue
Pirates of the Caribbean   114
Pitt, Brad   254-5
plastic (cosmetic) surgery   4, 17, 113, 244,
   252-4. See also Botox; celebrity culture
Poe, Edgar Allen   11, 15
Pumping Iron   245
Purse, Lisa   258

race   94, 104, 177, 192, 230; African American
   85, 177-8, 233; Asian   218-9, 226, 232,
   237-8; Native American   85, 223-5, 231,
   235, 239n12. See also boxing; ethnicity

racing (car) 8, 59, 62, 68, 152, 173, 176-7, 202; American Championship Auto Racing Teams (CART) 176; Formula One 175-6; Nascar 176,

Raging Bull 41, 134, 165, 190

Raiders of the Lost Ark 125

Ramaeker, Paul 16, 19n.1, 20n.28, 27, 51n.9, 66

Rambo 3, 6, 12, 29, 42-50, 54, 115, 132, 147, 158, 160, 167, 217, 221, 224, 226-79, 232, 234-6, 241, 251-3, 259; acting (performance) 6, 16-7, 128, 132, 160, 167, 221, 232, 234, 236; ageing 4,17, 42, 44, 123, 138, 231, 235, 241, 244-5, 249, 251, 253-60; and Buddhism 209, 219, 225, 227, 232, 235, 239n.4; and Burma 221, 226-31, 237, 259; and Christianity 221, 225-7; cinematography and lighting 48, 141, 147, 233; colour 44, 46, 48-50; costume 10, 13; critical response 115, 123, 128-9, 141, 147-8, 155, 166-8, 244, 251, 255; and documentary 47-9; editing 3, 4, 11, 27, 29, 44, 49, 50; and ethnicity 111-15, 130, 223-5, 244, 249-52; homoeroticism 3, 204, 206; marketing 29; nostalgia 29, 241; sado-masochism 229; special effects 256-8; violence 3, 44, 48, 222, 225, 228-9, 234, 239n.10, 241, 248, 252, 258-9; weapons 2, 10, 224, 228, 231-37, 248, 251, 258-9

Rambo: First Blood Part II 2-4, 10, 13, 16-7, 47, 112, 128-30, 141, 147-8, 155-57, 160, 220-1, 223, 226, 228-30, 233-4, 237, 238n.1, 245, 248, 258-9; cinematography 41, 147, 233; and melodrama 2, 3, 16, 248; weapons 2, 10, 224, 228, 231-7, 248, 251, 258-9

Rambo franchise (series) 4, 6, 16-7, 54, 95n.6, 136, 160, 221; audience response 2, 3, 6, 10, 11, 15, 17 130-2, 168, 171-2, 206, 219, 234, 236, 244, 257; and ethnicity 111-15, 130, 223-25, 244, 249-52; and race 228, 230-1; weapons 3, 10, 224, 228, 23-7, 248, 251, 258-9. *See also First Blood*; *Rambo: First Blood Part II*; *Rambo III*; *Rambo*

Rambo Solo (play) 13, 2

Rambo III 3, 10, 12-3, 20n.22, 47, 147-8, 155, 160, 204, 208-9, 211, 217-8, 221-31, 236, 239n.14, 244; acting 3, 12, 27, 147, 160, 221, 223, 231, 236; and Afghanistan 10, 12, 221, 224, 226, 229, 231, 239n.6; audience response 10, 112, 244;

Rambo III cont. and Buddhism 226; as camp film 10, 207-8 ; cinematography 10, 47, 160; costume 10, 13; editing (montage) 3, 50; fighting in 156, 221, 223, 228 ; nationalism 209, 236

Reagan, Ronald 2, 16, 97, 111, 115, 117n.12, 181, 212, 217, 220, 221, 225

Redford, Robert 20n.25

Redmond, Sean 243

religion 225-6. *See* Buddhism; Christianity

Resident Evil 256

Revolution Studios 43, 138

Rhinestone 9, 10, 17, 19n.9, 20n.21, 115, 123, 128, 147-8, 156-7, 207-8; acting 17, 123, 147-8; audience response 10, 17, 19n.9, 115, 123, 128, 207; as camp film 9, 10, 20n.21, 207-8; costumes 10

Rimbaud, Arthur 225

Rocky 2, 8, 10, 14-5, 17, 75-81, 90-1, 113, 127, 140, 156, 172, 245; audience response 15, 17, 76, 199-201, 204, 209, 210-13, 250; acting 77, 91, 121, 123, 125-7, 132, 135, 140, 144n.16, 147, 150, 160, 179; cinematography 27, 76-9, 81, 82; and class (social) 77-9, 81, 125; critical response 14, 16, 42, 143n.14, 144n.16, 147, 150-1, 167; editing (montage) 40, 76-8; and ethnicity 177; fight sequences 90, 178; as independent film 75; as melodrama 3, 29, 32-4, 38, 40, 127; mise-en-scène 77, 78, 81-2, 90, 125; myth of origin 75; and race 177-8; Stallone's diet and training for 114, 121, 142n.1; training sequences 82, 89

Rocky Balboa 3, 8, 17, 20n.28, 27, 32, 42-50, 87-8, 92-4, 138-9, 142, 144n.16, 167, 187-91, 194n.9, 241-3, 245-6, 249, 250-2, 257-260; acting 49, 93-4; and ageing 43-4, 138-9, 187, 189, 241-3, 249, 256-60; cinematography 29, 45-6, 188; colour 45-6, 87-8; costume 251; critical response 42, 94, 138-9; editing (montage) 44, 94, 188-9, 250; and ethnicity 94, 249-52; fight sequences 45-6, 175, 188; marketing 94, 242; music 92; narrative structure 43-4, 92-5, 187, 190, 249; nostalgia 43, 92-4, 187; soundtrack 44, 93, 95n.8; Stallone's diet and training 138; television 46, 172, 188, 190-1, 245, 249; training sequences 88, 189, 245, 249

Rocky IV 2, 4, 7, 15, 27, 32, 36, 38, 80–2, 84, 85–7, 111, 147–8, 156–7, 172, 175, 183–5, 191, 246; cinematography 39, 41, 45, 85 colour 45; costume 85–6; editing (montage) 32, 36, 40, 89; fight sequences 195, 194n.5; marketing 88, 195; as melodrama 34, 50; mise-en-scène 36; music 35, 82, 86; nationalism 85–7; patriotism 85–7; television 195; training sequences 35–8, 40, 89, 194

Rocky V 90, 92, 157, 196–7; cinematography 92, 197; editing (montage) 92, 196; fight sequences 92, 196–7; music 19n.8, 197; religious imagery 92; television 196

Rocky franchise (series) 3, 6, 7, 13, 16–7, 27, 29, 30, 32–50, 51n.10, 54, 75–96, 98, 99, 100, 105, 107, 108, 111, 115, 155–6, 163, 171–95, 217, 245, 250, 252; audience response 6, 12, 29. 94, 116n.1, 168, 171–95, 193, 197–216; and family 33, 204, 212, 250; professional sportscasters 175, 180, 95n.5, 192; training sequences 34–5, 66, 89, 245, 251. *See also Rocky*; *Rocky II*; *Rocky III*; *Rocky IV*; *Rocky V*; *Rocky Balboa*

Rocky Horror Picture, The 7

Rocky statue 7, 35, 83–4, 95n.3, 181, 187. *See also* Philadelphia Museum of Art; *Rocky* steps

Rocky steps 7, 13, 19n.12 , 83–4, 89, 90, 92–4, 187, 200. *See also* Philadelphia Museum of Art; Rocky statue

Rocky III 2, 10, 13, 27, 32, 35, 79–80–4, 92, 111, 116, 116n.1, 156–7, 178, 190–3, 191, 201–2; audience response 13, 93, 156, 157, 201–2; cinematography 39, 79, 80, 83, 201–2; colour 83; costume 201; editing (montage) 40, 201; fight sequences 35, 180; imagery 83–4; as melodrama 34, 50; mise-en-scène 80, 82–3; and race 85, 112, 178, 192; real celebrities 181; training sequences 83, 202

Rocky II 3, 15, 27, 32, 35, 79, 80, 82–3, 88–90, 97, 103, 107, 116n.1; cinematography 40; editing (montage) 35, 39, 40, 83; fight sequences 34; as melodrama 34, 50, 89; mise-en-scène 83; professional athletes 175, 193n.2; television 179–80; training sequences 39

Rookie, The 34

Roth, Joe 43

Rourke, Mickey 1, 236

Rush Hour 114

Russell, Kurt 3

Said, Edward 217

Santoni, Reni 56, 60, 70, 112, 195; as melodrama 34, 50; mise-en-

Satrapi, Marjane 13

Saturday Night Fever 33, 38

Save the Last Dance 34

Savoy 158

Schatz, Thomas 50n.6, 117n.4

Schubart, Rikke 16, 19n.19, 51n.10, 88

Schwarzenegger, Arnold 1, 4, 5, 18, 19n.n .4–5, 56, 111, 115, 200, 237, 245, 248

Scott, Ridley 103

Scream 19n.9

Screen Actors Guild 158

Searchers, The 222

Serpico 104, 117n.13

Shade 19n.9, 138

Shining, The 58

Shire, Talia 35, 78, 91, 125, 174, 202, 213, 249

Silver, Casey 158,

Simpsons, The (TV series) 13

Singer, Ben 53–4, 73n.1

Smithsonian Museum 15

Snipes, Wesley 134, 206–7

soccer (US) 98, 106, 114, 127, 171–3. *See* football

Soldier of Orange 102

Son of Rambow 13

Specialist, The 10, 19n.9, 148, 155, 157–8

spectacle 6, 9, 16, 19n.11, 29, 32–6, 38–40, 42, 44, 46, 48, 50n.6, 55, 62–3, 65, 127, 152, 174, 184, 186, 206, 218–19, 242, 244, 247–8, 254–7; and body 9, 38, 40, 42, 152, 206, 219, 242, 244, 247–8, 254–7; visual 16, 29, 32–4, 38–9, 62, 255

Spider-Man 256

Spielberg, Steven 260n.4

sports 85, 99, 100, 108–10, 113, 143n.15, 153, 172, 184, 191–2, 193n.2, 206, 242–8, 260n.2; doping 243, 246–7, 260. *See also* arm wrestling; body–building; boxing; football; mountain–climbing (mountaineering); weight–lifting

sports films 2, 17, 27, 34–5, 50, 97, 115, 174–5; conventions 27–8, 53–4, 174, 177, 179; conventions on television 179–81

Stacey, Jackie 199, 203, 215n.10

Staiger, Janet 54–5

Stallone, Frank 38, 44

Stallone, Sage 14, 92, 187
Stanislavski, Konstantin 122
Star Is Born, A 89
Star Trek: The Motion Picture 102
Statham, Jason 1, 5, 19n.13, 28, 32,
Staying Alive 16, 27–9, 32–5, 38–42, 50,
    128; cinematography 39, 40;
    colour 28, 39, 41, 50; editing
    (montage) 27, 28, 32, 34–5, 38–41, 50;
    as melodrama 27–8, 32–4, 38, 40, 42,
    50; as musical 16, 27–8, 34–5, 38, 40,
    42, 50, 128
Step Up 34
Step Up 2: The Streets 34
Step Up 3D 34
steroids 121, 184, 243–6, 252, 258. See
    also body-building; human growth
    hormone (HGH); masculinity; muscles
    and muscularity; sports; testosterone;
    weight-lifting (-training)
Stone, Sharon 10, 136
Stone III, Charles 103
Stop! Or My Mom Will Shoot 11, 19n.9, 128,
    131, 147–8, 155–7
Streisand, Barbra 89
Studlar, Gaylyn 239n.4, 251, 258
Superman II 112
Symons, James 64, 87
Syriana 185

Taliban 12, 221, 226, 228–9, 236, 239n.6
Take You Back (song) 44
Tango & Cash 3, 19n.9, 148, 155–7, 204, 249;
    as comedy 155
Tarantino, Quentin 3
Tarver, Antonio 43, 87, 143n.15, 188, 190–1,
    245
Tarzan 256
Tasker, Yvonne 15, 17, 50n.6, 53, 73n.1, 111,
    143, 163, 197, 203, 208–9, 219, 223,
    239n.8, 241, 259
Taubin, Amy 155, 166
Taxi Driver 14
Ten Little Indians 19n.9
Terminator, The 54, 56, 71, 73n.3, 248
Terms of Endearment 54
testosterone 194n.12, 204, 242–3, 246, 255.
    See also ageing; body-building; human
    growth hormone (HGH); masculinity;
    muscles and muscularity; steroids;
    weight-lifting (-training)
Theron, Charlize 165

They Were Expendable 249
Thompson, Kristin 6, 50n.7, 54–5
Three Days of the Condor 101
300 257
thrillers 2, 56, 97–8, 101, 104, 155. See also
    cop/crime films
To Live and Die in L.A. 66
Touchstone Studios 130
Troy 254, 256
Turan, Kenneth 94, 132, 134
Turner, Janine 132,
Twentieth Century Fox 9, 10, 12, 156, 250,
Twins 115
2001: A Space Odyssey 109
Tyson, Mike 17, 190, 193

United Artists 20n.25, 75, 85, 98, 158
Universal Pictures 30, 156, 158

Vajna, Andrew 107, 117n.17
Van Damme, Jean-Claude 1, 4, 19n.5
Varda, Agnès 141
Verhoeven, Paul 102
Victory (US title) 16–7, 19n.9, 97–100,
    104–16, 116n.n.1–3, 117n.17, 118n.22,
    127–8, 157, 171, 173, 204; acting 17,
    116, 123, 127–8; cinematography 106;
    costume 106, 114, 128; creative
    personnel 100–5; critical response
    104–5, 115–16, 126–7; as cult film
    114–15; and genres 99, 104, 115;
    locations 16, 100, 104–7; marketing
    16, 97–100, 104–6; Stallone's diet and
    training 109, 114, 127–8, 171–3, 175.
    See Escape to Victory (UK title)
Vietnam war 55, 159, 217, 220–5, 227, 229,
    231, 259
violence 3, 9, 16, 34, 44, 48, 63–4, 85, 178,
    222, 225, 228–9, 234, 239n.10, 241, 248,
    252, 254, 258–9; hand to hand combat.
    See also weapons
von Sydow, Max 97–8, 107–8, 127, 173

Wagner, Lindsay 97, 101, 117n.6
Waite, Ric 64, 71
Walken, Christopher 136, 148, 149
Walkerdine, Valerie 6, 15, 197, 200
Ward, Frazer 171
war films 2, 110, 209, 223, 258, 259
Warner Bros. 12, 30, 141, 156
Warriors, The 11, 102
Wayne, John 235, 239n.11, 249, 257

weapons 1–3, 234, 236–7; bombs 1, 2, 6, 11,
101, 182; bow and arrow 224, 231–4,
258; guns 1, 5, 58, 60, 69,177, 234, 258,
261n.5; knives 58, 67–8, 224, 231, 233,
235, 237, 251, 258–9
Wearing, Sadie 242
Weathers, Carl 33, 78, 112, 172, 178, 201
Weber, Brenda 252
weight-lifting (-training) 122, 174, 189,
194n.9, 199. *See also* body-building;
class (social); masculinity; muscles and
muscularity; human growth hormone
(HGH); steroids; testosterone; weight-
lifting (-training)
Weissmuller, Johnny 256
Welles, Orson 14, 127
Wepner, Chuck 75, 178, 194n.5
Western films 121, 134, 155, 222–3, 229
Where Eagles Dare 110
White, Vanna 14
Willemen, Paul 205

William Morris Agency 98
Williams, Billy Dee 97, 101–2, 113
Williams, Linda 33–4, 53
Willis, Andy 100
Willis, Bruce 1, 4, 5, 18, 19n.5, 237
Winkler, Irwin
Wise Blood 106
Woods, James 134
Woo, John 72–3, 74n.10, 234
Wo-ping, Yuen 259
World War II 99, 100, 102, 105–6 , 123, 127,
173, 222, 227, 258
wrestling 171–5, 181, 193n.2, 218, 247

X-Men 256, 259

Yettaw, John William 236–7
Yu, Nan 1

Zimmerman, John 64, 67
Zsigmond, Vilmos 141